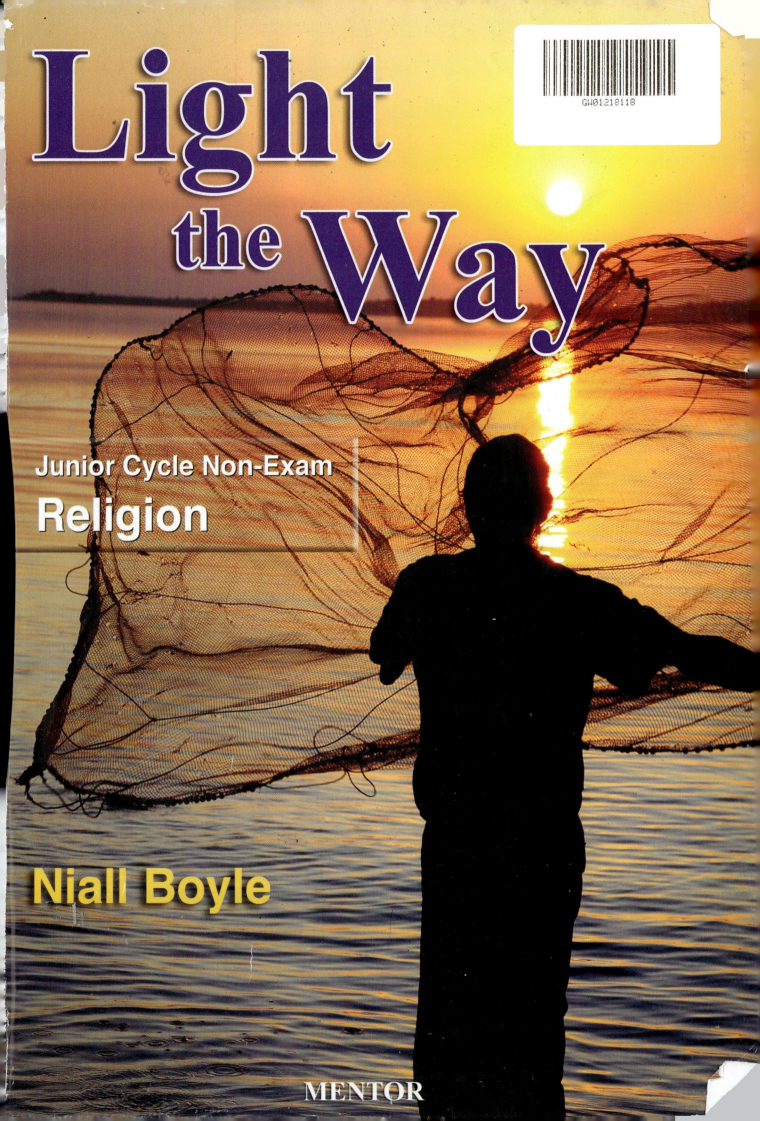

Light the Way

Junior Cycle Non-Exam Religion

Niall Boyle

Imprimatur: Most Reverend Michael Smith DCL, Bishop of Meath.

MENTOR BOOKS

Contents

Section A:
Communities of Faith 9

Chapter	1	Community	10
	2	Building Community	18
	3	Communities of Faith	31
	4	What is Revelation?	35
	5	The Founders	41
	6	What is a Sacred Text?	54
	7	Religious Identity	60
	8	Christianity Today	64
	9	Religious Commitment	86
	10	Vocation	91
	11	Sectarianism	98

Section B:
Foundations of Religion - Christianity . . . 113

Chapter	1	Daily Life in the Time of Jesus	114
	2	Under Roman Rule	122
	3	How We Know about Jesus	133
	4	The Early Life of Jesus	144
	5	The Public Ministry of Jesus	150
	6	The Teachings of Jesus	158
	7	The Miracles of Jesus	165
	8	Conflict with Authority	172
	9	The Passion and Death of Jesus	181
	10	The Resurrection of Jesus	189
	11	The Early Christians	196

Contents

Section C:
Foundations of Religion -
Major World Religions. 203

Chapter 1	**Being a Hindu**	. . . .	204
2	**Being a Jew**	. . . .	215
3	**Being a Buddhist**	. . . .	228
4	**Being a Muslim**	. . . .	242

Section D:
The Question of Faith 259

Chapter 1	**Religious Belief and Practice Today**	. . . .	260
2	**What is Religious Faith?**	. . . .	268
3	**Religious Faith in Action**	. . . .	279

Section E:
The Celebration of Faith. 289

Chapter 1	**Prayer**	. . . .	290
2	**Sign and Symbol**	. . . .	299
3	**The Sacraments**	. . . .	314
4	**The Liturgical Year**	. . . .	330
5	**Pilgrimage**	. . . .	340

Section F:
The Moral Challenge. 355

Chapter 1	**Introduction to Morality**	. . . .	356
2	**Making Moral Decisions**	. . . .	369
3	**Sin and Forgiveness**	. . . .	384
4	**Stewardship**	. . . .	394
5	**The Afterlife**	. . . .	404

Mentor Books Ltd
43 Furze Road
Sandyford Industrial Estate
Dublin 18
Republic of Ireland
Tel: +353 1 295 2112/3 Fax: +353 1 295 2114
e-mail: admin@mentorbooks.ie www.mentorbooks.ie
A catalogue record for this book is available from the British Library.

Copyright © Niall Boyle, 2015

The right of Niall Boyle to be identified as the author of this work has been asserted
by him in accordance with the Copright, Design and Patents Act 1988.
All rights reserved. No parts of this publication may be reproduced,
stored in a retrieval system, or transmitted in any form or by any means electronic, mechanical,
photocopying, recording, or otherwise, without prior written permission of the publisher.
The paper used in this book is made from the wood pulp of managed forests.
For every tree felled, at least one tree is planted, thereby renewing natural resources.

ISBN: 978-1-909417-32-8

Editor: Deirdre O'Neill
Cover design and layout: Kathryn O'Sullivan
Artwork: Brian Fitzgerald

Acknowledgements
The publishers would like to thank:
Thinkstock; Alamy; Bridgeman Art Library; Columba Press; Corbis Images; Getty
Images; www.hughoflaherty.com; The Church of Ireland Diocese of Armagh; Dublin
Archdiocese; the Church of Ireland Press Office; The Methodist Church in Ireland;
Focolare/Centro S. Chiara Audiovisi Soc. Corp. a.r.l.; The World Council of Churches;
Atelier et Presses de Taizé, *The Irish Examiner*; Defence Forces Press Office; Patrick
Comerford; the Islamic Cultural Centre of Ireland.

The publishers have made every effort to trace and acknowledge the holders of copyright
for material used in the book. In the event of a copyright holder having been omitted, the
publishers will come to a suitable arrangement at the first opportunity.

Section A

Communities of Faith

Chapter 1:	Community	10
Chapter 2:	Building Community	18
Chapter 3:	Communities of Faith	31
Chapter 4:	What is Revelation?	35
Chapter 5:	The Founders	41
Chapter 6:	What is a Sacred Text?	54
Chapter 7:	Religious Identity	60
Chapter 8:	Christianity Today	64
Chapter 9:	Religious Commitment	86
Chapter 10:	Vocation	91
Chapter 11:	Sectarianism	98

CHAPTER 1 COMMUNITY

The Meaning of Community

The Olympic Games is the world's foremost sporting competition. Athletes from nearly every nation on Earth compete with one another to decide who is the very best of the best in twenty-eight different sports.

The Olympic Games first began in ancient Greece about 3,000 years ago. They were held every four years at Olympia in honour of the god Zeus. These games featured mainly athletic sports such as running and jumping. However, they also included combat sports such as wrestling and chariot racing. The Olympic Games continued to be held until the Roman Emperor Theodosius I closed them down in 393 CE.

The Olympic Games were revived in modern times thanks chiefly to the tireless efforts of a French sportsman named Pierre de Coubertin. With the help of other enthusiastic men and women, he founded the International Olympic Committee (IOC) in 1894. This organisation has since served as the governing body of the modern Olympic Games.

It is the IOC that selects a particular city to stage the games. This city's authorities and its nation's National Olympic Committee then form a joint committee to plan, organise and supervise the games. Usually they are given seven years to get ready.

Since they were revived, the Olympic Games have continued the tradition of being held every four years. The only times the games have been called off was when the two world wars were being fought.

The official symbol of the modern games is five interlocking coloured rings. These five rings represent the five inhabited continents of Africa, Asia, Europe, North America and South America. The Olympic flag consists of these five rings – coloured blue, yellow, black, green and red – on a white background. These colours were chosen because every nation has at least one of these colours on its national flag.

In 1994, the IOC decided to hold separate summer and winter games. While each continues to be held every four years, they alternate every two years.

In modern times the games have expanded massively in scale. For example, when the first modern Olympic Games were held at Athens in 1896, some 241 participants representing forty nations took part. However, by the time of the Summer Olympics at London in 2012, the games had grown to involve more than 10,500 athletes, representing 204 nations.

All these athletes spend years in training for these games. They take to heart the Olympic motto: **Faster, Higher and Stronger** and make it their own. They dedicate their lives to sport in the hope that they will, one day, get an opportunity to stand on one of the three tiers of the winners' rostrum. The athlete who finishes first is awarded a gold medal, while those who come in second and third are awarded silver and bronze respectively. In 2012, some 2,484 medals were awarded.

The Olympic motto is 'Faster, Higher and Stronger'.

However, every athlete gets to take part in the opening ceremony. This is held in a massive purpose-built stadium. Like the games themselves, this event is broadcast live and watched by millions of people across the world. The ceremony begins with the raising of the host nation's flag and the playing of its national anthem. Then the worldwide audience is presented with a spectacular display that showcases all that is best in the host nation's performing arts – cinema, dance, music, singing, television and theatre – and in its history. This is followed by a grand parade of all the athletes into the stadium. They are grouped according to their nation and each national team enters in alphabetical order. Traditionally, Greece is given the honour of leading the parade as it was the birthplace of the Olympic Games. The host nation's athletes are the last to enter.

Next, speeches are given to formally open the games. Finally, the Olympic torch is brought into the stadium by the last members of a vast relay team. Its many members have passed the torch along a great chain of runners that stretches all the way back to Greece itself. Usually a successful athlete from the host nation is given the honour of being the final torch-bearer. He/she gets to light the Olympic flame in a huge cauldron that towers over the stadium.

Have you ever stopped to think about what an enormous challenge it must be for a city to successfully stage the Olympic Games?

During the London games of 2012, there were some 860 different types of job to be done across 80 different venues to make the games possible. In addition to a large, professional managerial staff, some 70,000 people volunteered their services and demonstrated great goodwill by working a total of 8 million hours for free. The city of London had to cater for the needs of 9 million visitors.

Communities of Faith — SECTION A

All these different parts do not come together by accident. They are not put together overnight. The Olympic Games are the final product of years of careful planning and hard work by a huge number of people.

Think of all the people who are involved, in some way, with staging the games:

- **The planners** who begin the whole process by listing all the things that must be done to make the games possible.

- **The fundraisers** who must raise the money needed to stage the games by: (a) selling broadcasting rights; (b) obtaining sponsorship from large corporations; and (c) selling stadium tickets and sporting merchandise.

- **The architects** who design the venues, especially the Olympic stadium and the Olympic village, where all the athletes will be housed.

- **The engineers** who must deliver a transport system that will get the huge influx of spectators safely and efficiently to and from the venues.

- **The accountants** who must oversee all spending on the games. For example, the London Olympics of 2012 cost just under £9 billion to stage.

- **The organisers** who decide when and where the different competitions will be held.

- **The lawyers** who draw up the rules which the athletes must follow.

- **The medical personnel** who must monitor the athletes to ensure they do not take banned substances, i.e. drugs that would give them an unfair advantage over other participants.

- **The police and armed forces** of the host nation who must ensure the security of all those who participate in and attend the games.

- **The athletes and their coaches** who dedicate years of their lives so that they can take part in this great sporting occasion.

For the Olympic Games to succeed, all these different people must cooperate.

REMEMBER!
To cooperate means to work together.

LIGHT THE WAY

Clearly cooperation is essential if an important event is to be a success. This does not only apply to a great international occasion such as the staging of the Olympic Games. It also applies to a very personal event, such as where a medical team is trying to save your life following a traffic accident. The paramedics, anaesthetists, surgeons and nurses who treat you must pool their experience and skills to work together if you are to survive and recover.

In any situation where we come together to do something, we form what is called **a community**.

REMEMBER!
A community is where people choose to come together to do something they think is good or worthwhile, such as:
- Live together
- Play together
- Travel together
- Work together
- Worship together.

12

Communities of Faith   SECTION A

ACTIVITIES

1. Wordsearch

Find the following words:

Olympic Games
Summer
Winter
Athlete
Pierre de Coubertin
Athens
Host nation
Stadium
Ceremony
Flame
Medal
Gold
Silver
Bronze
Cooperate
Community

P	Z	F	A	Z	D	W	A	I	H	F	Y	O	O	E	L	K
T	I	E	T	A	R	E	P	O	O	C	N	L	Q	C	J	B
C	Q	E	I	W	T	E	S	A	M	X	O	Y	W	C	E	R
H	T	K	R	E	P	T	T	L	E	V	M	M	M	U	Q	G
W	W	Y	L	R	N	H	A	Y	F	Z	E	P	J	R	K	O
K	J	H	Y	A	E	D	C	L	O	R	R	I	F	K	A	O
A	T	V	T	N	E	D	S	S	Y	Q	E	C	A	D	U	C
A	Y	I	S	M	V	O	E	N	U	J	C	G	O	L	D	B
W	O	T	R	S	U	O	G	C	H	M	L	A	U	A	V	M
N	Y	D	I	E	Y	Y	I	B	O	I	M	M	Q	E	B	S
H	J	H	U	N	Z	Q	L	U	P	U	W	E	J	M	K	W
P	G	A	H	Z	U	N	Q	S	U	Q	B	S	R	A	D	I
S	T	A	D	I	U	M	O	Y	G	D	H	E	Y	L	L	N
K	H	U	P	Y	R	S	M	R	S	G	D	N	R	F	W	T
R	E	V	L	I	S	I	O	O	B	L	Y	V	H	T	C	E
R	V	W	T	T	P	S	X	J	C	Z	I	Y	T	K	I	R
N	H	I	Z	Z	O	V	X	F	C	S	C	O	U	W	B	N

2. Fill in the missing words!

(a) The Olympic Games is the world's foremost _____ competition.

(b) The men and women who take part in the games are called _____.

(c) The Olympic Games first began in ancient _____ about 3,000 years ago. They were held every _____ years at Olympia.

(d) The Olympic Games were revived in modern times by a French sportsman named _____.

(e) The International Olympic Committee (IOC) serves as the _____ body of the modern Olympic Games.

(f) The official symbol of the modern games is the five interlocking coloured _____. These represent the five _____ continents.

(g) In 1994, the IOC decided to hold separate _____ and _____ games.

(h) The first modern Olympic Games were held at _____ in 1896.

(i) The Olympic motto is _____.

(j) The athlete who finishes first is awarded a _____ medal, while those who come in second and third are awarded _____ and _____ respectively.

(k) Every athlete gets to take part in the _____ ceremony. This is held in a massive purpose-built _____.

(l) The Olympic torch is brought into the stadium by the last members of a vast _____ team.

(m) Usually, a successful athlete from the _____ nation is given the honour of being the final torch-bearer. He/she gets to light the Olympic flame in a huge _____ that towers over the stadium.

13

LIGHT THE WAY

3. Say what it means!

(a) To cooperate means to _____.

(b) A community is where _____
_____.

4. Think about it!

Pierre de Coubertin said that the whole point of the Olympic Games is 'not about winning but about taking part'.

(a) Do you think many athletes share this idea today? Why do you think this?

(b) Do you agree with de Coubertin? Give a reason for your answer.

The Types of Community

The Earth is now home to more than 7 billion people. If you stop to think about it, you soon realise that we are all linked to one another by many different **kinds** of community. Look at this diagram:

Our world of connected communities

Read this diagram from the **centre outwards**.

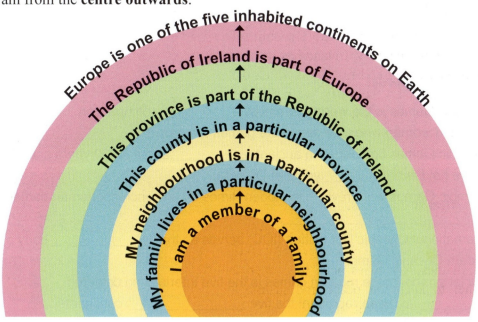

All these communities combine to form our human world.

As you grow from an infant into an adult, each of these different types of community affects your life in different ways. They help to make you the kind of person you are. Think about the impact they have on your life:

1. Your family

This is where you first learn what it means to be a member of a community:
- You figure out who you are and what you want out of life.
- You learn how you should behave towards others.

Your family should help you to grow and develop into a confident, open-minded person with a healthy respect for yourself and for other people.

14

Communities of Faith   SECTION A

2. Your neighbourhood

This is where you develop your understanding of community further. Here you have the opportunity to become a member of several different kinds of community. For example:

- In school you are a student. You are also a member of a **peer group** (i.e. one made up of people who are the same age as you).
- In a football club you can be either a player or a supporter.
- In a drama group you can be either a performer or a member of the production team.
- In a charity group you can be a fundraiser or work directly with people in need.

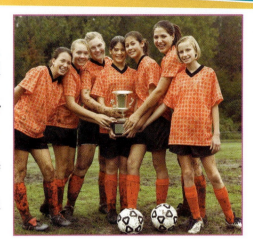

Joining any of these communities gives you an opportunity to discover and develop your own particular **talents**.

> **REMEMBER!**
> **A talent** is a gift for doing something well.

Developing your talents helps you to become a happier and more fulfilled person.

3. The national community

You live in a particular country – the Republic of Ireland. Like every other country, Ireland has its own distinctive **culture** (i.e. way of life). Think about the way we talk to one another, the music we make, the stories we tell, the sports we enjoy, the things we think are important. You share this way of life with all the other people who live here.

4. The international community

Although we live in a particular country, we know also that we share this planet with the people of many other countries too. All these countries need to cooperate with one another to keep the peace and sustain a healthy environment. Without this, life on Earth would be impossible.

Our Need for Community

Sometimes, you get angry or frustrated. It may be because someone has offended you. It can be tempting to think:

'I don't need anyone, I'm better off on my own.'

Deep down, however, you know that this is not really the case. Just think about the following questions:

- What would be the point of going away on a holiday if you had no one to share it with?

15

LIGHT THE WAY

- What would be the point of going to a concert if you had no one to share the experience with or to talk about it with afterwards?
- What would be the point of keeping your home tidy and well-maintained if no one was ever going to visit you there?

Clearly, many things in life only seem worthwhile when you **share** them with others. You are not meant to live alone. You must be a member of a community in order to satisfy your **needs**.

> REMEMBER!
> **Needs** are the things you must have to live a fully human life.

We can only find happiness and fulfilment by satisfying our needs. But what are our needs?

This was the question that **Abraham Maslow** wanted to answer. He was a psychologist who spent many years studying how people live, love, play, work and worship together. He identified what he called our **hierarchy of needs**.

> REMEMBER!
> **The Hierarchy of Needs** is a scale that shows the five different needs that are common to all.

Read the following chart from the **bottom upwards**.

Explanation of needs

5. Self-fulfilment	I need to develop my particular talents. I need to become the kind of person I am meant to be.
4. Esteem	I need to develop a healthy respect for myself. I need to know that I am respected by others too.
3. Social acceptance	I need to be loved and wanted. I need to feel that I belong somewhere. This gives me self-confidence, as I know who I am and where I fit in.
2. Safety	I need a stable, orderly and secure place in which I can live, love, learn, work and worship.
1. Physical care	I need clean water, nourishing food, clean clothing, adequate sleep and warm shelter. I must have them to enjoy good health.

Our physical needs are our most basic needs. They must be taken care of first.

Clearly, none of us can satisfy our needs on our own. We need other people to help us do so.

Communities of Faith SECTION A

ACTIVITIES

1. Fill in the missing words!

(a) The Republic of Ireland is part of _____.

(b) Europe is one of the five inhabited _____ on Earth.

(c) Your _____ group is made up of people who are the same age as you.

(d) Developing your _____ helps you to become a happier and more fulfilled person.

(e) Each country has its own distinctive _____, i.e. way of life.

(f) Abraham Maslow was a _____ who spent many years studying how people live, work and worship together.

2. Say what it means!

(a) A talent is a _____.

(b) Needs are _____.

3. Crossword

Across

1. You have to be a member of a community to satisfy them.

7. What I receive when I get nourishing food, clean clothing and warm shelter (2 words: 8, 4)

Down

2. What I want when I ask to be loved and wanted (2 words: 6,10).

3. What I get when I become the kind of person I am meant to be.

4. Where you first learn to be a member of a community.

5. Job where you study how people live, play, work and worship together.

6. What I find when I have a stable, orderly and secure place to live in.

8. What I get when I develop a healthy respect for myself.

17

LIGHT THE WAY

CHAPTER 2   BUILDING COMMUNITY

The Importance of Respect

A community can be either successful or unsuccessful. So what makes a community successful? The following story may help to answer this question.

Archbishop Desmond Tutu makes an impassioned speech in Washington D.C. in 1985.

The year was 1940. At that time, South Africa was controlled by a white minority regime that treated the majority black community very badly. Black people had had their lands stolen from them and were given no say in how the country was governed.

Desmond Tutu was a nine-year-old boy living in Klerksdorp in the Transvaal province.

One morning he and his mother were walking down a street when they saw a tall white man dressed in black coming towards them. In those days, when a black person and a white person met while walking on a footpath, the black person was expected to step off into the gutter to allow the white person to pass and nod their head as a gesture of respect. However, that day, Desmond Tutu witnessed something he would never have thought could happen. Before he and his mother could step off the footpath, the white man stepped off the footpath and, as he and his mother passed, tipped his hat in a gesture of respect to them!

Desmond was amazed by what he had just witnessed. He had never seen a white person behave in this way. He asked his mother who that white man was. She told him that he was Trevor Huddleston, an Anglican priest and a man of God. Huddleston was a leading figure in the campaign to get equal rights for South Africa's black population.

South African township.

Many years later, when Desmond Tutu was giving his acceptance speech upon receiving the Nobel Prize for Peace, he said that what Trevor Huddleston did that day long ago had changed the whole direction of his life. He was so struck by the example he gave that he too decided to become an Anglican priest and dedicate his life to serving God and his fellow human beings.

> **REMEMBER!**
> **Respect** means showing that you care in what you say and do.

> Why did Trevor Huddleston treat Desmond Tutu and his mother in this way? Because he believed that they were just as much members of the community as he was. As a Christian, he believed that all people are created by God and so are of equal value. The colour of their skin or their social status is of no importance.

Communities of Faith SECTION A

Huddleston stepped off the footpath to let Desmond Tutu and his mother walk by because he believed that it was the right thing to do. He realised that, in a community, we need to care for one another and look after one another's needs in practical ways. Above all, Huddleston knew that the most basic need we all have is to be treated with **respect**.

A community can only succeed when we respect one another. We can show our respect in two ways – through **communication** and **sharing**.

> REMEMBER!
> **Communication** happens when we listen to one another and are honest with one another.
> **Sharing** means dividing things fairly so that we all have what we need.

You cannot play a positive and worthwhile **role** in your community if you are not prepared to communicate and share with those around you.

The Roles We Play

Imagine you are a member of a famous soccer team. This team is made up of a number of players. Each player performs a particular **role**.

> REMEMBER!
> **A role** is a specific job you do or contribution you can make to your community.

Look at the following diagram. It illustrates the different roles played by the members of a soccer team.

The mid-fielders must pass the ball to the forwards / strikers.

The forwards / strikers are tasked with scoring goals.

One of these players acts as your **team captain.**

The goalkeeper is the last line of defence.

The defenders must block the opposing forwards.

The coach / manager on the sideline issues instructions to you and your teammates and makes substitutions when necessary.

19

LIGHT THE WAY

Now ask yourself: when is a soccer team most likely to win? When **all** the team members cooperate and play well.

Sometimes we can give too much attention to the role played by one particular player. We might say that a team's success is all due to one star player's performance on the field. However, this would be unfair. Every player on a winning side contributes, in some way, to its success. Perhaps this contribution is less noticeable than that of the star player. However, victory on the field depends on the goalkeeper just as much as the top goal-scorer.

Of course there is nothing wrong with recognising and praising one person's outstanding contribution. However, you also need to keep in mind that no one individual has all the talents necessary to make a community successful. Everyone has something to contribute. This is true of school too.

Your First Day

Think back to your first day at second-level school. First, you and your fellow students were probably gathered together in the school's assembly hall or gym. Then, the principal welcomed you and introduced you to your year head. After this, you were divided up into different class groups: each class with its own tutor or class teacher. You were then taken to a room where your class teacher read through the school rules and explained the timetable. After this, you were assigned a particular locker.

Later on, you were taken on a tour of the school buildings. You were shown the science laboratories, the computer room, the library and the practical rooms for art, home economics, music and so on. You hoped you would be able to find them on your own the next day.

As the days passed, you became more at ease in your new surroundings. You began to make new friends and felt you belonged in your new school community. You also became more aware of how your school community is made up of many different people – each one performing a particular role – but all making a contribution.

Think about the following diagram:

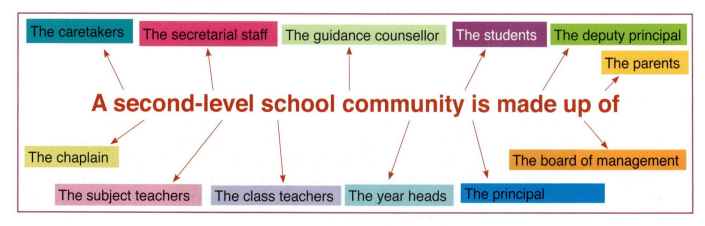

School Rules

The whole purpose of education is to help you develop your talents and become someone who makes a positive contribution to society. This can only happen when you have a safe place to learn. This is why every school has **rules**.

20

Communities of Faith **SECTION A**

> **REMEMBER!**
> **A rule** tells you how you should behave.

Rules are necessary. A school cannot succeed without them.

School rules exist for the good of **all**. They help to create a safe environment where you can learn and make new friends.

Generally speaking, schools do their best to meet the needs of their students. In turn, most students realise that it is in their own best interests to accept and follow their school's rules.

When Community Fails

We all know by now what a community should be: a place where you are helped to fulfil your needs. Sadly, this is not always the case.

Some people are forgotten, isolated or neglected. Think about the following story:

On the morning of Sunday, 18 March 2012, Gardaí were called to a house at Lower John Street in Wexford. When they gained entry, the Gardaí found the decomposed remains of a man in his sixties. He had been dead for three months. The only reason his body had been discovered was because a passer-by had grown concerned when he noticed a Christmas tree with lights still on inside the house.

No one had noticed this man's absence. This is not what community is about. Indeed, this is a tragic example of **community breakdown**.

> **REMEMBER!**
> **Community breakdown** is what happens when we fail to respect and care for one another.

Think about the following examples of community breakdown:

■ You disagree with what the majority in your community wants to do. You offer good reasons for the stand you are taking. However, they do not respect your right to disagree. They do not give you a fair hearing. First, they respond by ignoring you. Then they unfairly criticise you. Finally, they isolate you.
■ Due to old age, illness or disability you are not able to take an active part in community life. Because of this, some people only think of you as a nuisance. They dismiss you and do not respect your right to be heard like any other citizen. They ignore your needs.
■ You are a new arrival in a community – such as a migrant worker or a refugee. You might be treated with distrust and hostility. Some people might want to blame you for all the things that have gone wrong in their own lives. You might be denied access to jobs and services. You might be made to feel unwelcome and even persecuted.

LIGHT THE WAY

ACTIVITIES

1. Wordsearch

Find each of the following words:

South Africa
Equality
Sharing
Player
Staff
Illness
Desmond Tutu
Respect
Role
School
Students
Disability
Trevor Huddleston
Communication
Team
Rule
Age
Refugee

T	A	E	T	D	S	M	S	X	P	B	O	F	B	M	T
B	S	T	E	F	Q	H	T	M	P	Z	P	Q	R	R	U
A	K	S	H	G	A	Z	L	B	R	Y	Y	U	E	E	T
R	C	S	T	R	U	O	N	B	S	L	L	V	S	Y	U
T	A	I	I	U	O	F	W	V	Y	E	O	U	P	A	T
E	D	N	R	H	D	I	E	T	B	R	M	F	E	L	D
A	G	X	C	F	D	E	I	R	H	C	A	Q	C	P	N
M	B	S	K	Z	A	L	N	U	K	A	S	R	T	W	O
S	T	A	F	F	I	H	D	T	K	S	N	Z	C	N	M
S	O	C	Y	B	N	D	T	S	S	E	N	L	L	I	S
E	I	Z	A	O	L	E	Q	U	A	L	I	T	Y	H	E
U	M	S	O	E	U	U	J	N	O	G	N	T	P	L	D
R	I	A	S	N	U	S	C	B	M	S	C	Q	F	O	L
D	O	T	N	O	I	T	A	C	I	N	U	M	M	O	C
L	O	L	E	G	A	T	K	P	T	R	Q	J	L	A	N
N	B	K	E	A	C	Z	C	E	J	L	H	W	P	U	F

2. Say what it means!

(a) Respect means _____ .

(b) Communication means _____ .

(c) Sharing means _____ .

(d) A role is _____ .

(e) A rule tells you _____ .

(f) Community breakdown is what happens _____ .

3. Think about it!

(a) Why does every school have rules?

(b) What do you think is the most important rule to remember?

(c) Why did you choose that rule rather than another?

4. Look it up!

Search for an example of community breakdown in recent news stories. Write a brief report on it. Say why you think this breakdown happened.

Communities of Faith   SECTION A

The Meaning of Commitment

Think about the promises we make to one another:

> 'Don't worry! I'll be there in plenty of time.'
>
> 'No problem! You can depend on me.'
>
> 'Take it easy! I won't let you down. I'll get the job done.'

Whenever we say such things, we are making **a commitment**.

> **REMEMBER!**
> **A commitment** is a promise to give the time and energy needed to complete some task.

Friendships are built on commitment. If two of us want to be friends, we have to work at our relationship. We have to make time for one another and make the effort to do things together. If we don't do this, our friendship will not last. Just think about how important it is for friends to do the following:

- Really listen in a conversation.
- Give an honest answer to a question.
- Be patient.
- Be loyal.
- Be willing to forgive.
- Show kindness in practical ways.
- Offer support in difficult times.

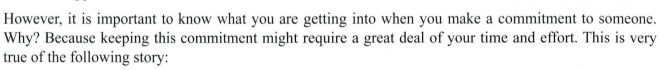

However, it is important to know what you are getting into when you make a commitment to someone. Why? Because keeping this commitment might require a great deal of your time and effort. This is very true of the following story:

The Story of Wilma Rudolph

Wilma Rudolph (1940–1994) was born in Clarksville, Tennessee in the USA. Her family was very poor but her parents were honest, loving and hardworking people. They struggled to do the best they could for their children.

When Wilma was four years old, her parents noticed that her left leg and foot were becoming weak and deformed. They brought her to the local doctor who told them that Wilma had contracted polio – a crippling disease that had no cure. Worse still, the doctor warned them that soon Wilma would no longer be able to walk at all.

Despite contracting Polio as a child, Wilma Rudolf went on to win 3 gold medals at The Olympics in 1960.

Wilma's mother refused to accept that nothing could be done. She promised Wilma that she would never give up on her. She would do whatever was necessary to help her walk.

Wilma's mother lived up to her **commitment**. However, it demanded an enormous amount of her time and effort. She found a doctor at a hospital in Nashville who would treat her daughter, but this was fifty miles from their home. They had to use public transport to get there. This didn't stop Wilma's mother taking the little girl to the hospital twice a week every week for the next two years. After this, Wilma was able to

23

LIGHT THE WAY

walk with the aid of a metal leg brace.

The doctor taught Wilma's mother how to give her physical therapy at home. Her brothers and sisters then joined their mother in helping Wilma do her leg-strengthening exercises each day. They also encouraged her to keep trying and not to lose hope.

Finally, by age twelve, Wilma no longer needed braces, crutches or corrective shoes. She could not only walk but now showed an extraordinary and unexpected speed when running. Eight years later, Wilma became the first American woman to win three gold medals for running at the Summer Olympics, held in Rome in 1960.

Clearly, Wilma Rudolph was most fortunate to be born into such a loving and caring family. Their love for her made all the difference. Their care helped her to recover her health. Their commitment made her sporting success possible. Her family were willing to make great sacrifices to offer her **the service** she needed to recover from polio.

> **REMEMBER!**
> **A service** is anything that helps you fulfil your needs.

Offering a Service

We all need to live in some kind of community. This is because only a community can provide us with the services we need. If you doubt this, think about the following:

- Who provides you with clothing, food, shelter and so on? **Your family**.
- Who provides you with medical care when you become ill or suffer an injury? **The health services**.
- Who provides you with opportunities to learn and form friendships? **The education system**.

We only have these services because, in each case, people – parents/guardians, doctors, nurses, teachers and students – combine their different talents and work together.

A community **thrives** (i.e. is successful) only when its members care about each other's welfare and happiness. For this to happen, we need to be willing **to give** as well as to receive. This means we must be ready to take practical steps to help one another.

One very worthwhile way of giving is called **voluntary** work.

> **REMEMBER!**
> **Voluntary work** is where you offer your free time to do unpaid work to help those in need.

This can be a difficult and demanding thing to do. However, it can also be very rewarding.

Communities of Faith **SECTION A**

The Challenges and Rewards of Voluntary Work

You may sometimes hear people say that it is a waste of time doing voluntary work. Why should you take on an unpaid job with a charitable organisation?

Certainly, you might find the work challenging. You might be helping to feed the homeless or care for people with a disability. It might take you out of your comfort zone. However, would that really be such a bad thing? Think about **the benefits** of doing voluntary work.

You could:

- Learn to get along better with other people.
- Come to see life from someone else's point of view.
- Learn more about life from the people you meet.
- Gain a better understanding of your own strengths and weaknesses.
- Develop lasting friendships with other, like-minded volunteers.
- Have the satisfaction of knowing that what you are doing is helping to improve the lives of others.

ACTIVITIES

1. Wordsearch

Find each of the following words:

Commitment
Honest
Service
Promise
Forgive
Thrive
Time
Kindness
Voluntary
Energy
Family
Benefits
~~Loyal~~
~~Support~~
~~Patient~~

S	K	F	N	T	D	R	F	V	I	X	H	N	C	S
O	S	O	O	V	S	T	S	U	C	E	C	O	I	U
G	E	E	D	R	B	E	Z	K	S	A	M	O	A	P
U	Y	P	N	T	G	T	N	I	Z	M	S	N	E	P
D	L	T	V	D	O	I	M	O	I	J	T	V	A	O
G	I	Q	H	F	N	O	V	T	H	F	I	L	Y	R
E	M	Y	X	B	R	I	M	E	U	R	F	M	K	T
P	A	E	K	P	R	E	K	U	H	V	E	Z	Q	D
I	F	F	S	T	N	E	P	T	C	H	N	T	R	S
R	M	U	E	T	L	O	Y	A	L	U	E	M	E	U
F	P	H	A	Y	K	F	T	M	C	L	B	R	W	I
P	A	T	I	E	N	T	E	I	U	L	V	H	R	N
U	Q	O	Y	G	R	E	N	E	M	I	I	J	G	A
Y	R	A	T	N	U	L	O	V	C	E	B	X	X	R
R	Q	V	M	Q	V	P	Q	E	C	C	E	A	T	P

2. Say what it means!

(a) A commitment is _____

_____ .

(b) A service is _____ .

(c) Voluntary work is where _____

_____ .

25

LIGHT THE WAY

3. Crossword

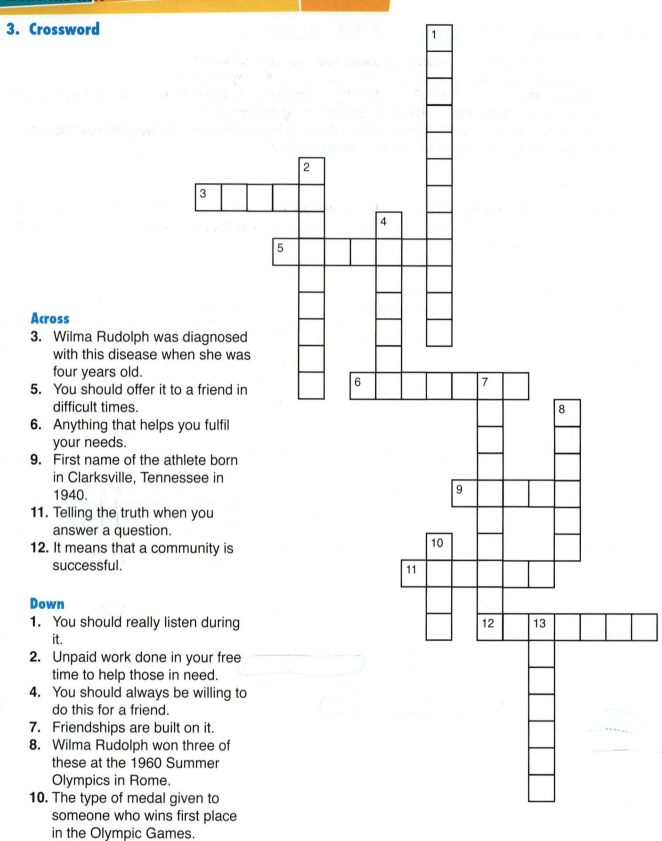

Across

3. Wilma Rudolph was diagnosed with this disease when she was four years old.
5. You should offer it to a friend in difficult times.
6. Anything that helps you fulfil your needs.
9. First name of the athlete born in Clarksville, Tennessee in 1940.
11. Telling the truth when you answer a question.
12. It means that a community is successful.

Down

1. You should really listen during it.
2. Unpaid work done in your free time to help those in need.
4. You should always be willing to do this for a friend.
7. Friendships are built on it.
8. Wilma Rudolph won three of these at the 1960 Summer Olympics in Rome.
10. The type of medal given to someone who wins first place in the Olympic Games.
13. Surname of the athlete born in Clarksville, Tennessee in 1940.

Communities of Faith   **SECTION A**

4. Think about it!

(a) What are the three most important qualities you look for in a friend?
Why do you think these qualities are more important than any others?

(b) Remember the story of Wilma Rudolph. Why is it important to know what you are getting yourself into **before** you make a commitment to do something for someone?

(c) What do you think are the two greatest benefits of doing voluntary work? Why did you choose these two rather than any of the others listed on p. 25?

5. Look it up!

Do a web search to find out about each of the voluntary organisations listed below. Then rearrange the explanations and match the service offered in column **B** with the organisation listed in column **A**. Fill in your answers in the spaces provided below.

A. ORGANISATION	B. SERVICE IT OFFERS
Alcoholics Anonymous	We support people suffering from depression.
Aware	We support people who have lost a loved one through suicide.
Bóthar	We care for terminally ill people.
Console	We give emergency medical aid to victims of man-made and/or natural disasters.
Focus Ireland	We offer high-quality mobility training and aftercare services to blind and visually impaired people.
Irish Guide Dogs for the Blind	We support people with an addiction to alcohol.
The Hospice Movement	We help families in the developing world overcome hunger and poverty and restore the environment in a sustainable way.
The Red Cross	We work to combat and prevent homelessness.

A. ORGANISATION	B. SERVICE IT OFFERS
Alcoholics Anonymous	
Aware	
Bóthar	
Console	
Focus Ireland	
Irish Guide Dogs for the Blind	
The Hospice Movement	
The Red Cross	

27

LIGHT THE WAY

The Simon Communities in Ireland

Being homeless

Imagine what it is like to be **homeless**. If you are a homeless person, you spend each day in the clothes you have slept in. You have no money and no mobile phone. You may not eat a hot meal for several days at a time. Often you will have to sleep rough (i.e. in doorways and alleyways). However, you may also be forced to live in emergency accommodation (e.g. a shelter) or in a place that is dilapidated (i.e. falling down and unsafe). Once night falls, you can never truly relax. You must be continually on your guard. You fear for your safety. You have neither privacy nor security.

The first thing you notice is that, as a homeless person, you become invisible to many people. Sure, you may sit on a park bench or at the side of a busy street, but you will be ignored by most people. Most will do everything they can to avoid eye contact. Some people will even walk on the far side of the street to avoid you. Others will give you a brief look of pity and then continue on their journey.

It is easy to forget that the homeless are people too. Indeed, it could very easily be any one of us in their place, if anything went wrong in our lives.

The homeless have needs just like everyone else, especially the need for respect. But where can they go for help?

Leadership

This was the question that **Anton Wallich-Clifford** wanted to answer. He worked as a probation officer in London in the 1960s. Part of his job was to help find accommodation for newly released or paroled prisoners. Many found it very difficult to find a decent place in which to live. So, through his work, Wallich-Clifford became very aware of the serious problems facing the homeless.

A committed Christian, Wallich-Clifford believed in leading by example. He set up the first **Simon Community** to help the homeless in London in 1963. Many others have since followed his example.

A homeless man on O'Connell Bridge in Dublin

Vision

Wallich-Clifford was inspired by the pioneering work of an American Catholic social reformer named Dorothy Day. He wanted the Simon Community to provide a new kind of service to the homeless. It would not offer them a hostel. Instead, it would offer them **a home** – a place where the homeless and the housed could live together in community.

In a Simon Community, the homeless are treated with respect:

- They are accepted for who they are.
- They are offered an opportunity to share in community life.
- They are provided with food, clothing and shelter.

In such a community, the homeless can find a sense of belonging. They can once more experience privacy and safety. This helps them to regain their self-respect.

Community

The first Simon Community was set up in Ireland by a group of university students. They were inspired by a talk given to them by Anton Wallich-Clifford himself. Their first project was to organise soup runs for those sleeping rough in the streets of Dublin.

Volunteers for the Dublin Simon Community carol-singing on Grafton Street in Dublin, 2013.

The first centre run by the Simon Community in Ireland was opened on Sarsfield Quay, Dublin in 1970. The next was in Belfast the following year. Others were later set up in Cork, Dundalk and Galway.

Today, there are eight such communities providing for the needs of the homeless in Ireland. Together, these form the national federation called the **Simon Communities in Ireland**.

Although each Simon Community is independent and self-financing, they all work together. Their efforts are coordinated by a national office in Dublin. This national office is governed by a board made up of representatives from each of the eight communities, as well as some experts in the fields of mental health and social services.

Service

Each of the Simon Communities in Ireland delivers a wide range of services to those who, for a variety of reasons, are homeless. These services include:

- **Street outreach** – offering food and clothing to the homeless.
- **Emergency accommodation** – providing a safe, warm place in which to sleep, nourishing food to eat and a warm, friendly environment.
- **Ongoing support** – helping those who are trying to set up a home on their own but finding the adjustment from homelessness difficult to make.

As there are thousands of people homeless in Ireland, there is a considerable demand for the services provided by these Simon Communities.

Roles

People can support the work of the Simon Communities in Ireland in any of the following ways:

- By volunteering to work with the homeless.
- By raising funds to support programmes to assist the homeless.
- By putting pressure on elected representatives to provide more affordable housing, as this helps people to escape from homelessness.

LIGHT THE WAY

ACTIVITIES

1. Fill in the missing words!

Imagine what it is like to be homeless. You spend each day in the _____ you have slept in. You have no _____ and no _____ _____. You may not eat a _____ for several days at a time. Often you will have to sleep _____. However, you may also be forced to live in a place that is _____. Once night falls, you can never truly _____. You must be continually on your _____. You fear for your _____. You have neither _____ nor security.

2. Tick the box!

In each of the following, say whether it is true or false.

	True	False
1. Anton Wallich-Clifford worked as a probation officer in Dublin in the 1960s.		
2. Anton Wallich-Clifford was a committed Buddhist.		
3. Many newly released prisoners found it easy to find a decent place to live in.		
4. Anton Wallich-Clifford was inspired by the example of Dorothy Day.		
5. The first Simon Community was set up in London in 1953.		
6. Anton Wallich-Clifford wanted the Simon Community to offer homeless people a new kind of service – not a hostel, but a home instead.		
7. In a Simon Community the homeless are treated with respect.		
8. The first Simon Community in Ireland was set up by a group of secondary school students.		
9. The first Simon Community in Ireland was opened in Sarsfield Quay in Cork, in 1970.		
10. The Simon Community organises soup runs to feed the homeless.		
11. Six local communities have come together to form the Simon Communities in Ireland.		
12. Street outreach means providing a safe, warm place in which to sleep, nourishing food to eat and a warm friendly environment.		
13. Ongoing support means offering food and shelter to the homeless.		
14. One way to tackle homelessness is for the state to make affordable housing more available.		

3. Think about it!

(a) Read the following statement:

'Anyone could become homeless if something went very wrong in their life.'

(i)   What kind of things might cause someone to become homeless?

(ii) What, do you think, might be the impact on your self-respect if you become homeless?

(iii) What kind of help would you hope to be offered if this were ever to happen to you?

(iv) How would you want to be treated?

(b) What is the importance of a voluntary organisation such as the Simon Community for our society?

CHAPTER 3   COMMUNITIES OF FAITH

The Meaning of Faith

Think about some of the things we all accept without question:

- The Earth orbits the sun.
- The sun will rise tomorrow morning at dawn.
- The sun will set tomorrow evening at dusk.
- What goes up must come down.

In each of these examples, we state **a belief**.

> **REMEMBER!**
> **A belief** is something you accept as true.

Sometimes you can have strong reasons for holding a belief. However, at other times, you cannot be completely sure if a belief is justified or not. In such a situation, you need to have faith.

> **REMEMBER!**
> **Faith** means putting your trust in someone or something.

Think about the essential role faith plays in your life:

- When you share a secret with a friend, you make **an act of faith**. You trust someone not to reveal this secret to anyone else, without first asking your permission to do so.
- When you study subjects such as geography, history and science, you make **an act of faith**. You must be willing to accept as facts things you have not personally experienced. Otherwise, you cannot make any progress in your education.

Making Sense of Life

Faith plays an important role too in helping us to make sense of our lives. Deep down, we all want to know the answers to four big questions:

- Who am I?
- Why am I here?
- How should I live?
- What happens when I die?

These questions ask us to think about the meaning and purpose of our lives. People seek answers to these questions in the teachings of a **community of faith**.

LIGHT THE WAY

> **REMEMBER!**
> **A community of faith** is where a group of people share a common set of beliefs about the meaning of life.

Many people say that being a member of a community of faith gives them the hope and strength they need to cope with the many stresses and strains of life. Further, knowing more about the meaning and purpose of your life can help you find inner peace.

The Different Communities of Faith

In this book, we will focus on those communities of faith we call **religions**.

> **REMEMBER!**
> **A religion** is a way of life that is centred on belief in and worship of God.

There are members of many different religions living in Ireland today.

These religions are listed here in the order in which they emerged in history.

The name of the religion	When it was founded	Where it was founded	What its followers are called	The number of followers it has today
Hinduism	c. 2000 BCE	India	Hindus	1 billion
Judaism	c. 1850 BCE	Israel	Jews	14.5 million
Buddhism	c. 563 BCE	Nepal	Buddhists	500 million
Christianity	c. 33 CE	Israel	Christians	2.25 billion
Islam	622 CE	Saudi Arabia	Muslims	1.6 billion
Sikhism	1499 CE	Pakistan	Sikhs	24 million

Communities of Faith SECTION A

The different kinds of religion

Generally speaking, a religion falls under one or other of the following headings:

(a) **monotheism**; or (b) **polytheism**.

> **REMEMBER!**
> **Monotheism** says that there is only one **God**.
> **God** is the Supreme Being who created and sustains the universe.

If you accept monotheism you are called **a monotheist**. Christians, Jews and Muslims are all monotheists.

> **REMEMBER!**
> **Polytheism** says that there is **more** than one **god**.

If you accept polytheism you are called **a polytheist**. Hindus are polytheists.

Did You Know?
Buddhists disagree among themselves about God. Some Buddhists are polytheists. Other Buddhists do not believe in a God or gods of any kind.

ACTIVITIES

1. Wordsearch

Find each of the following words:

- Belief
- Faith
- Religion
- God
- Monotheism
- Polytheism
- Hinduism
- Judaism
- Buddhism
- Christianity
- Islam
- Sikhism

R	H	N	Y	M	Z	Y	Y	U	I	N	S	A	M	I
C	H	R	I	S	T	I	A	N	I	T	Y	S	C	S
Z	C	T	M	I	G	K	U	S	U	R	I	F	G	L
M	X	Q	P	A	F	S	Z	J	E	H	U	J	V	A
Q	O	V	R	D	T	A	U	L	K	Z	Y	G	Q	M
Q	M	N	X	U	S	I	I	Y	G	Q	S	C	P	
N	M	C	O	J	Y	G	S	T	O	B	C	J	J	O
H	A	S	Z	T	I	S	T	D	H	J	C	X	V	L
R	Z	N	I	O	H	Q	J	N	Y	H	D	O	H	Y
I	X	Q	N	H	X	E	U	O	W	B	C	N	J	T
R	N	Z	G	N	D	P	I	Y	U	C	Y	O	H	
B	E	L	I	E	F	D	J	S	D	Q	P	E	G	E
Y	X	X	I	F	X	R	U	D	M	W	Z	M	O	I
M	S	I	U	D	N	I	H	B	A	I	I	Y	Q	S
R	B	N	Q	S	B	K	O	K	R	O	G	V	E	M

33

LIGHT THE WAY

2. Say what it means!

(a) A belief is _Something you believe in_.

(b) Faith means _Putting your trust in something_

(c) A community of faith is _something lots of people believe in._

(d) A religion is _a god or gods you beleive in_

(e) Monotheism says that _you beleve in one God_.

(f) God is _your creater_.

(g) Polytheism says that _you have more gods_.

3. Fill in the missing information!

The name of the religion	When it was founded	Where it was founded	What its followers are called	The number of followers it has today
Hinduism	c. 2000 bce			billion
Judaism				million
Buddhism				million
Christianity				billion
Islam				billion
Sikhism				million

4. Think about it!

(a) Here are four questions:

Who am I? Why am I here? How should I live? What happens when I die?

Why are these the most important questions you can ask about life?

(b) What are the benefits of being a member of a community of faith/religion?

Communities of Faith   SECTION A

CHAPTER 4   WHAT IS REVELATION?

A World Without Us

Think about what life on Earth would be like if, right now, every single human being were to disappear completely off the face of the planet:

- Within **seventy-five years** all of the six hundred million automobiles in the world would have rusted into barely recognisable heaps of metal.
- Within **three hundred years** all metal bridges and towers would have collapsed.
- Within **five hundred years** all residential neighbourhoods would have become rainforests.
- Within **ten thousand years** there would be hardly any trace left to show that human beings had ever existed. All our great cities and all their contents would have turned to dust and crumbled away.

However, life on Earth would continue without us. As there would no longer be any people around to prey upon them, some species of animal that are currently threatened with **extinction** (i.e. dying out altogether) would probably make a spectacular recovery in numbers in just a few centuries. This would be good news for elephants, tigers and whales.

Yet, while all these remarkable animals would continue to live and thrive upon the Earth, something very important would be missing. Without human beings, there would be no one to think about the Earth, to talk about it or to wonder about their own role upon it. There would be no one to appreciate the beauty of a rainbow and no one to ask why it rains at all. There would be no one to ask **questions**.

Asking questions is an essential part of being human. Without them we cannot learn and grow as individuals.

Just think of all the different kinds of questions you can ask: **Who? What? When? Where? How? Why?**

Often, we take our ability to ask such questions for granted. However, no other creature on Earth can do this. We are the only ones on this planet who can think about life and ask questions about it.

As we grow older, we look for answers to many different kinds of questions. Some of these questions are more important and difficult to answer than others. This is because some questions deal with **problems**, while other questions deal with **mysteries**.

35

LIGHT THE WAY

The Difference Between a Mystery and a Problem

In everyday conversation, the word 'mystery' is often confused with the word 'problem'. However, there are important **differences** between the two.

Think about the following questions:

- How are mountain ranges formed?
- What causes lightning to strike?
- How can a disease be cured?
- What caused the extinction of the dinosaurs?

Each of these questions refers to **a problem**.

> **REMEMBER!**
> **A problem** is something you can figure out and solve.

However, it may require a lot of thought, time, energy and resources to find a solution.

Yet, important and worthwhile as problems are, they are not the only kind of questions that we need to answer. There are other more profound questions we must face. These include:

- Where can I find true happiness?
- Why do bad things happen to good people?
- Is there life after death?

Each of these questions refers to **a mystery**.

> **REMEMBER!**
> **A mystery** is something so vast and so complex that it is beyond your capacity to ever completely figure out and solve.

The best you can hope for is to gain insights into a mystery. However, such insights do not come easily. They may require great effort and patience.

The Big Questions

Sometimes, people begin asking big questions about the meaning of life at quite an early age. Usually, this is due to some important, personal experience that prompts us to ask questions such as:

- **Why did someone I love have to die?**
- **Will we ever be reunited?**

Later, as we pass through adolescence and move on into adulthood, we become more aware of how complicated life can be. We experience love and hate, health and illness, gain and loss, birth and death. Usually, these experiences lead us to ask questions about the meaning of life.

Asking questions is an essential part of being human. Without questions you cannot learn and grow as an individual. Throughout history, people have turned to one or other of the world's major religions for answers to these questions.

A Religion as a Source of Answers

Sometimes you may hear someone say '**Oh, all religions are just the same.**' However, this is not true. Think about this:

- Every religion offers its **own** set of teachings to help us make sense out of life.
- Each religion provides us with different ways of celebrating and remembering important moments in our lives, such as birth, marriage and death.

Indeed, look at how the world's religions can be divided into two distinct groups:

(a) **The Prophetic Outlook** and (b) **The Wisdom Outlook**.

What do these mean?

The Prophetic Outlook – This applies to Judaism, Christianity, Islam and Sikhism

These religions say that, no matter how intelligent we may be, we will never be able to find the answers to life's great questions from any purely human source. We need God's help. God offers us this help through **revelation**.

This was how God communicated with Moses.

The Wisdom Outlook – This applies to Hinduism and Buddhism

These religions say that we should not look to God for the answers to life's great questions. Instead, we should ask a seer (i.e. a wise and holy person) to help us find the answers we seek.

The Buddha was a great seer.

The Meaning of Revelation

It is 3,000 years ago. The place is the Middle East. Your name is Moses and all you want now is a quiet life. After all, your life has had more than its fair share of excitement so far.

Shortly after you were born, **the pharaoh** (i.e. the king of Egypt) ordered his soldiers to kill every male Jewish infant. However, you escaped because your mother placed you in a wicker basket and hid you among the thick reeds along the banks of the river Nile. The pharaoh's soldiers never thought to look there.

Then, an Egyptian princess found you and adopted you as her own child. You grew up as a member of the royal family. For many years you led a very comfortable and carefree life.

Everything seemed fine until the day you learned that you were not an Egyptian but a Jew. This shocked you, because the Jews had been forced into slavery by the Egyptians.

Then, not long afterwards, you saw an Egyptian foreman cruelly beating an exhausted Jewish slave. This made you very angry, so you stepped in to stop him. However, things got completely out of hand and you accidentally killed the Egyptian.

When the pharaoh was told what you had done, he ordered your arrest. However, you escaped to the neighbouring land of Midian, where the pharaoh's men were unable to find you.

You settled down in Midian. You married and started a family. You earned a modest but honest living as a shepherd. You were happy. Your life seemed set. Until, one day, something totally unexpected happened; an event that pointed your life in a whole new direction.

LIGHT THE WAY

Your day started out just like any other day. You went out as usual that morning to check on your flock, to count them and move them on to fresh pastures.

Then you noticed smoke ahead. This worried you because it could mean a brush fire. A fire would panic your flock and scatter them. Every animal was precious to you and you could not afford to lose any.

So you moved closer to see if you could put out the fire with your cloak before it spread. It was then that you saw there was only one bush on fire. You were relieved at this. You realised that the fire could be put out easily.

However, as you got closer, you noticed two strange things:

- First, there was no heat from the fire.
- Second, the bush was on fire but it was not being burned up by it.

This did not make any sense. How could it be happening?

Then you heard a sound that changed your whole life. A deep, loud voice called out to you:

'Moses! Moses!'

This shocked and frightened you.

Then the voice identified itself as belonging to God. Suddenly, you could feel that you were in the presence of something greater than any words could ever express. So you fell down on your knees and replied:

'Yes Lord, I am listening.'

God told you that he had heard the cries for help from the Jewish slaves in Egypt. You were overjoyed when God told you that he would answer their prayers. However, your joy was short-lived. You were shocked when God said that he was sending you to lead the Jews to freedom. God wanted you to leave your quiet life and return to Egypt, a place you had only narrowly escaped from years before.

At first, you were reluctant to accept God's call. You were afraid. You feared that the pharaoh would kill you if you returned. However, God promised:

'I will be with you and I will help you.'

God gave you the power to work miracles and the confidence you would need to force the pharaoh to set the Jews free. So, you agreed to do as God asked. Soon afterwards, you left your old quiet life and set out for Egypt.

As you journeyed there you thought back over all you had learned from your encounter with God. You had learned that:

- God is far greater than we can possibly imagine.
- God can do things that are completely beyond our capacity to ever understand.
- God is not remote and uninterested in us – God loves and cares for each one of us.
- God has a plan for the world and invites each one of us to play a role in it.
- We can hear God's voice only when we open our hearts and are willing to listen.

In this extraordinary event, Moses was given important insights into who God is and what God wants from us. These insights could never have been worked out on their own by either Moses or any other human being. These insights became known to us only because God let them be known.

This way in which God chooses to communicate with human beings is called **revelation**.

> **REMEMBER!**
> **Revelation** is the way in which God reaches out to us and gives us insights into life that we could never discover if left to our own efforts.

Communities of Faith   SECTION A

ACTIVITIES

1. Wordsearch

Find each of the following words:

Earth
When
Mystery
Prophetic
Extinction
Where
Religion
Questions
Differences
Who
Wisdom
How
Seer
What
Why
Problem
Moses
Pharaoh
Burning bush
Revelation

X	N	I	W	V	X	Y	G	Q	E	H	C	L	R	P
P	U	O	O	I	R	C	U	C	A	S	O	S	E	W
G	D	V	I	E	S	E	R	V	R	T	J	W	V	F
T	J	I	T	G	S	D	A	Q	T	D	M	W	E	Z
M	E	S	G	T	I	Q	O	R	H	S	E	H	L	E
K	Y	X	I	T	G	L	E	M	E	J	L	Y	A	T
M	N	O	T	W	A	E	E	C	O	S	B	H	T	M
J	N	T	H	I	S	H	N	R	A	V	O	W	I	R
S	A	E	P	E	N	E	W	P	H	A	R	A	O	H
E	R	U	W	C	R	C	W	H	O	H	P	R	N	N
E	P	X	K	E	E	U	T	S	E	S	O	M	L	E
N	W	Z	F	B	U	R	N	I	N	G	B	U	S	H
I	S	F	C	I	T	E	H	P	O	R	P	Z	T	W
V	I	Z	D	S	F	G	D	O	L	N	P	J	N	W
D	S	D	Z	I	W	J	L	O	R	R	N	R	O	K

2. Say what it means!

(a) A problem is _____ .

(b) A mystery is _____

_____ .

(c) Revelation is _____

_____

_____ .

3. Tick the box!

Read the following questions. In each case, say whether it is a **problem** or a **mystery**.

	Problem	Mystery
1. How do bees fly?		
2. How do homing pigeons find their way?		
3. Is there life after death?		
4. What caused the extinction of the dinosaurs?		
5. Does God exist?		
6. What causes a disease?		
7. When did life on Earth begin?		
8. What causes tornadoes?		
9. Where can I find true and lasting happiness?		
10. Is there intelligent life elsewhere in the universe?		
11. Why do bad things happen to good people?		
12. Why are there so many different languages?		

39

LIGHT THE WAY

4. Tick the box!

In each of the following, say whether it is true or false.

		True	False
1.	If human beings disappeared off the face of the Earth, within seven years all of the 600 million automobiles in the world would have rusted into barely recognisable heaps of metal.		
2.	Within 100 years all metal bridges and towers would have collapsed.		
3.	Within 500 years all residential neighbourhoods would have become rain-forests.		
4.	Within 1,000 years there would be hardly any trace left to show that human beings had ever existed. All our great cities and all their contents would have turned to dust and crumbled away.		
5.	Asking questions is an essential part of being human. Without them we cannot learn and grow as individuals.		
6.	Human beings are not the only creatures on Earth that can think about life and ask questions about it.		
7.	Usually, as we grow older, our experiences of love and hatred, health and illness, gain and loss, birth and death prompt us to ask questions about the meaning of life.		
8.	As an infant, Moses escaped death because his mother placed him in a wicker basket and hid him among the thick reeds along the banks of the river Tiber.		
9.	Moses fled from Egypt to Midian after deliberately killing a man.		
10.	God appeared to Moses in the form of a bush that was being burned up by fire.		
11.	God told Moses that he was sending him back to Egypt to free the Jews from slavery.		
12.	Moses refused to return to Egypt as God had asked.		

5. Think about it!

(a) What kind of experiences can lead us to ask questions about the meaning of our lives?

(b) Why do you think these experiences can have such an effect on us?

(c) Suppose someone were to say 'All religions are the same!'

   Would you agree or disagree with this statement? Explain your answer.

(d) What insights did Moses receive about God through his experience at the Burning Bush?

Communities of Faith SECTION A

CHAPTER 5   THE FOUNDERS

The Importance of the Founders

Suppose you are a famous actor or artist or singer or writer. There are photographs of you on the cover of countless glossy magazines. You are frequently mentioned on radio and television programmes. Lots of people know who you are – today. But for how long will this last?

If, a century after your death, a movie you made is still being watched in a cinema, a painting you produced is still being viewed in an art gallery, music you composed is still being listened to or a book you wrote is still being read, you will be a member of a very small and select group. For fame is a passing thing.

How many people, alive today, will historians even consider worth mentioning a hundred, a thousand or two thousand years from now?

To be remembered long after your death, you must have said and done things that have had a lasting impact, not only on the lives of people in your own time, but also on all the generations that followed afterwards. You would have had to be a remarkable person. **The founders** of the world's religions were just such remarkable individuals.

> **REMEMBER!**
> **A founder** is someone who set up a religion.

Naming the Founders

Read encyclopaedia entries about the different world religions. They tell you that, today, some of these religions have millions of members, while others have more than a billion. However, it was not always like this. All these different religions started out as small groups of men and women who committed themselves to following the teachings of their founder.

NAME OF THE RELIGION	NAME OF THE FOUNDER
Judaism	Abraham
Buddhism	Siddhartha Gautama
Christianity	Jesus Christ
Islam	The Prophet Muhammad
Sikhism	Guru Nanak

The Appeal of the Founders

Imagine you are faced with an important decision. You need advice as to the best course of action to take. Usually, you will look to someone you trust for good advice.

The best advice comes from those who have followed their own advice and can show that it has worked in their own lives. This was an important part of the wide appeal each of the founders had in their own lifetimes and beyond.

Each founder got his message across, not just by his words but by his actions too. The message each founder gave was '**Do as I do**'. It was not merely '**Do as I say**'. There was no difference between how the founder lived and what he taught.

The Role of the Founders

During his lifetime, each founder built up a small community around him. These early communities were crucial to the lasting impact of the founder's life on later generations.

41

LIGHT THE WAY

Each of these early communities was made up of dedicated followers of the founder. They were attracted by his **inspiring vision**.

This inspiring vision is what encouraged those followers to continue the founder's work even after his death.

> **REMEMBER!**
> **An inspiring vision** is the message of hope for a better life that the founder gives to his followers.

Did You Know?

Not every religion can trace its origins back to one historical figure. Despite years of searching, historians have been unable to discover any single founding figure for Hinduism. It is now thought that a group of **rishis** (i.e. holy men) were responsible for spreading Hindu beliefs across the Indian subcontinent 4,000 years ago.

ACTIVITIES

1. Say what it means!

(a) A founder is _____ .

(b) An inspiring vision is _____

_____

_____

2. Crossword

Across

2. You write it for others to read it.
3. It is a passing thing.
5. You can view it in an art gallery.
7. The group of holy men who spread Hinduism across the Indian subcontinent.
8. He founded Christianity (2 words: 5, 5).
9. Prophet _____ founded Islam.
10. You compose it. People listen to it.
11. He founded Sikhism (2 words: 4, 5).

Down

1. You can watch it in a cinema.
4. He founded Judaism.
6. Siddhartha _____ founded Buddhism.

3. Think about it!

(a) Name one famous person living today who you think will still be remembered by people a hundred years from now.

(b) Why do you think that he/she will still be remembered a century from now?

Communities of Faith   SECTION A

SPOTLIGHT ON A FOUNDER: WHAT BUDDHISTS BELIEVE ABOUT SIDDHARTHA GAUTAMA

Early life

Siddhartha Gautama (sometimes written as **Siddatta Gotama**) was the founder of Buddhism. He was born in Lumbini in modern-day Nepal around 563 BCE.

We don't have any writings about Gautama that survive from his own time. The only historical sources for his life come from texts written by his followers about 400 years after his death. So we cannot be certain about the exact details of his life.

We are told that Gautama was born into royalty. His mother, Queen Maya, died a few days after his birth, so he was raised by his father, **King Suddhodana**. Gautama's father wanted him to become a great king. So he raised his son within the luxurious rooms and gardens of his palace. The young prince had no contact with the outside world. He was shielded from all knowledge of human suffering. His father believed that this would help him to grow up to be a strong king.

At sixteen, Gautama married a beautiful princess named **Yosodhara**. For ten years they lived happily together. They had a son named **Rahula**. They wanted for nothing. Gautama's life seemed complete.

Statue of Buddha in Hong Kong.

Inspiration

Despite his best efforts, Gautama's father failed to completely cut his son off from all contact with the harsh realities of life. On several occasions, Gautama had to travel outside the palace. Whenever this happened, his father ordered servants to go ahead of his son and try to clear away all evidence of suffering and death along his route. However, despite these precautions, Gautama still saw things that deeply shocked him.

We are told that Gautama went on four journeys. On each journey he saw something that challenged his whole understanding of life. Buddhists call the things he saw **the Four Sights**.

- **The First Sight**
  Gautama saw a man bent over and struggling to walk. A servant told him that this was **old age**. It is inevitable.

- **The Second Sight**
  Gautama saw a man suffering from leprosy lying by the roadside. A servant said that this was **illness**. It afflicts many people.

- **The Third Sight**
  Gautama saw a funeral procession taking a body to be cremated. He was told that this was **death**. No one escapes it.

- **The Fourth Sight**
  By now, Gautama was deeply troubled by what he had seen. Human life was far more fragile than he had ever realised. This led him to think about the meaning of suffering and death.

  Then, Gautama met a wandering **ascetic** (i.e. someone living a life of self-denial). Though homeless, and having very few possessions, this man looked happy. Gautama wanted to know why.

43

LIGHT THE WAY

These Four Sights turned Gautama's cosy, self-satisfied little world upside down. He was twenty-nine years old and deeply unhappy with his whole way of life. He had everything and yet he felt that he had nothing. He decided that the only thing that would make his life worth living was to discover the meaning of life, happiness, suffering and death.

Inspired by the example of the wandering ascetic he had met, Gautama decided that the only way to find the answers he was seeking was to give up his comfortable way of life. So, one night, Gautama quietly slipped unnoticed out of his palace. Next, to show his complete commitment to his mission, he cut off his long, flowing locks of hair, as these identified him as a nobleman. Finally, he traded clothes with a beggar before setting out on his quest. He would never return to his palace, nor would he see his wife and son again for many years.

Buddhists celebrate this event. They call it '**the Blessed Night of the Great Renunciation**'. This was the moment Gautama turned his back on comfort, power, security and wealth. From this point on he devoted all his energy to achieving **enlightenment**.

Seeking Enlightenment

Gautama spent the next six years travelling across India. He lived on whatever food he could get by begging in the streets. He looked for guidance from the most respected **gurus** (i.e. religious teachers) of the time. He followed their advice. He learned how **to meditate**.

Gautama studied the writings of Hindu holy men. He fasted and prayed to the Hindu gods. However, despite all this, he still felt no nearer to finding the answers he was looking for. Finally, he decided to take a whole new approach. He turned his back on Hinduism. He decided that he would try to work out the meaning of life on his own.

At the age of thirty-five, Gautama wandered into the village of Buddh Gaya in Bihar. There he sat down under a banyan tree. After receiving a gift of some rice pudding from a local girl, he began to meditate on all that he had learned so far. He stayed there for forty-nine days. Finally, on **the Sacred Night**, he found the answers he had been looking for and gained enlightenment.

Spreading Enlightenment

The Buddha spent the next forty-five years journeying by foot along the banks of the Ganges River. He attracted people from every walk of life and convinced many of them to accept his teachings.

The Buddha said that all suffering is caused by **selfish desire** (i.e. wanting things you do not really need). You can only free yourself from suffering by not desiring anything and living a good life. Only then can you achieve **nirvana**.

> **REMEMBER!**
> **Enlightenment** means gaining a deep understanding of the meaning of life.

> **REMEMBER!**
> **To meditate** means to still your mind so that you can be calm, focused and able to reflect on something important.

Did You Know?

The Sacred Night was the moment when Gautama achieved enlightenment.

The banyan tree Gautama sat under has been known ever since as **the Bo** (i.e. **wisdom**) **Tree**.

Gautama gave his first public sermon in the Deer Park at Benares. He soon attracted many followers. His wife and son joined him. To show how much they respected him, people began calling Gautama by a new name – **the Buddha**.

Communities of Faith SECTION A

> REMEMBER!
> **Nirvana** is a state of complete happiness and inner peace.

Did You Know?
The title '**Buddha**' means **the Enlightened One**.

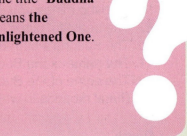

The Buddha died at the age of eighty in 483 BCE. Shortly before his death, he chose to share a meal with a poor peasant woman rather than accept a dinner invitation from a wealthy prince. The Buddha did so because he believed that wealth and status are not the most important things in life.

The Buddha passed away in a grove of trees at Kushingara. His body was cremated. Then his ashes were divided up and placed in **stupas** (i.e. burial mounds) built at different locations dotted across India. However, his teachings lived on. Today, they are followed by millions of Buddhists across the world.

ACTIVITIES

1. Say what it means!
(a) Enlightenment means _____.
(b) To meditate means _____.
(c) The Sacred Night was when _____.
(d) The title 'Buddha' means _____.
(e) Nirvana is _____.

2. Think about it!
(a) What do you think the Buddha meant by 'selfish desire'?
(b) Look at recent news stories. How much suffering do you think is caused by what the Buddha called 'selfish desire'? Explain your answer.
(c) What advice would the Buddha offer us today if we really wanted to reduce the suffering caused by our 'selfish desires'?
(d) How difficult would it be for us to follow the Buddha's advice? Explain your answer.

45

LIGHT THE WAY

3. Crossword

Across
5. Wanting things you do not really need (2 words: 7, 6).
8. The beautiful place in which the Buddha grew up, cut off from the harsh realities of life.
10. The Buddha's birth name was Siddhartha _____.
11. The name of the Buddha's son.
12. The name of the Buddha's mother.
14. Burial mounds in which the Buddha's ashes were placed.

Down
1. The name of the Buddha's wife.
2. The place in Nepal where the Buddha was born.
3. Name of the village where the Buddha found enlightenment (2 words: 5, 4).
4. The third sight.
5. The name of the Buddha's father.
6. The first sight (2 words: 3, 3).
7. Place in Benares where the Buddha gave his first public sermon (2 words: 4, 4).
9. The second sight.
13. Means 'religious teachers'.
15. Someone who lives a life of self-denial.

46

Communities of Faith   SECTION A

SPOTLIGHT ON A FOUNDER: WHAT MUSLIMS BELIEVE ABOUT THE PROPHET MUHAMMAD

> **REMEMBER!**
> **Islam** means **'peace through submission'**.
> A member of Islam is called **a Muslim**.
> Muslim means **'one who submits to Allah'**.
> **Allah** is an Arabic word meaning **'the (one and only) God'**.

Islam began in **Arabia**. Today, the harsh sun-scorched landscape of Arabia provides much of the oil that fuels our high-tech way of life. However, long before oil was discovered there, Arabia was important; merchants travelling between Africa and Asia passed through it.

Despite its importance as a trade route, early seventh-century Arabia was a dangerous, lawless place. There was no central government to keep order. Quarrels between different tribes frequently led to war.

One important city along the trade route was **Makkah** (or **Mecca**), located in a mountainous region of western Arabia. It was originally built there because of **the Zamzam**.

Did You Know?

The Zamzam is a deep well that provides fresh water to the people of Makkah.

At first, people went to Makkah to drink from the Zamzam. Later, they went there to worship at **the Ka'bah (or Kaaba)**.

> **REMEMBER!**
> **Ka'bah** means **'the house of God'**.

Muslims say that the Ka'bah was built by **Adam** – the first human being. However, it was later destroyed by the great flood in the time of Noah.

47

LIGHT THE WAY

The Ka'bah was then rebuilt by **Ibrahim (Abraham)** and his son **Ishmael**. They left us a simple, cube-shaped granite building, fifty feet high and about thirty-five feet wide. Today it stands, covered by a huge black cloth, at the centre of a massive walled enclosure called **the al-Masjid al-Haram mosque** in Makkah.

Ibrahim was also given the Black Stone by the Angel Jibril (or Gabriel). This was treated as a precious gift from Allah. It was set into the eastern corner of the Ka'bah, where it remains today.

Did You Know?

Islam teaches that **Abraham** was a Muslim. They say that all Arabs are descendants of Abraham's son **Ishmael**, while Jews are descendants of his other son, **Isaac**.

Muslims say that the Ka'bah was originally built as a place for worshipping Allah alone. However, in time, people forgot this and began to worship many different gods. By the seventh century CE, there were 360 idols (i.e. statues of different gods) in the Ka'bah. The different Arab tribes went to Makkah to worship at the idol of their own particular god.

Many people in Makkah were happy with this. They were earning a very good living by providing these people with food, clothing and shelter. However, some corrupt businessmen took advantage of this situation. They overcharged people so that they could make huge profits. Then they used this wealth to take control of the city.

One man grew increasingly unhappy with all of this. He became convinced that there had to be a better way to live. His name was Muhammad.

Muhammad was born in Makkah around 570 CE. He was a member of a powerful tribe.

Did You Know?

The name **Muhammad** means '**highly praised**'.
We have four sources of information about the life of **Muhammad**:
1. Islam's sacred text – **the Qur'an**.
2. A collection of Muhammad's sayings called **the Hadith**.
3. A collection of stories about Muhammad called **the Sunnah**.
4. **Biographies** written by Muslim scholars in the 8th and 9th centuries CE.
The account of Islam's origins that follows is based on these sources.

Tragedy touched Muhammad's life right from the start:
- His father died shortly before he was born.
- His mother became ill and died when he was only six years old.

Muhammad was adopted by his uncle, Abu Talib, who was a powerful figure within his tribe. He raised Muhammad as his own.

As a young man, Muhammad earned his living as a business manager, organising camel caravans to carry cargo throughout the Middle East. Then he married a wealthy widow named **Khadijah**. Theirs was a happy marriage. They had six children: four daughters and two sons (though sadly both boys died in childhood). Muhammad and Khadijah later adopted two boys.

Muhammad became a widely respected figure in Makkah. People began calling him '**Al-Amin**', meaning '**the trustworthy one**'. He and his wife used their own money to feed and clothe the poor in Makkah. However, Muhammad grew increasingly troubled by the corruption and injustice he saw all around him.

In order to figure out what to do about this, Muhammad began spending more and more time alone praying and meditating in a cave on Mount Hira, just outside Makkah. There, in 610 CE, something extraordinary happened. On **the Night of Power**, an angel named **Jibril** (Gabriel) appeared to Muhammad.

The angel held up a scroll and told Muhammad to '**recite**' (i.e. read) what was written on it. However, Muhammad said that he could not because he was **illiterate** (i.e. he had not learned to read or write). Then the angel left him.

Not knowing what to think about this, Muhammad returned home in a state of shock.

Later that night, the angel appeared to him again. He told Muhammad that Allah had chosen him to be his **prophet**.

Muhammad was told that he would be given the final and absolute word of Allah and must then teach it to the world. Since he was illiterate, Muhammad would have to memorise everything the angel told him. Then Muhammad would have to recite exactly what he had been told to scribes who would carefully record it, word for word.

After Muhammad's death, all these teachings were gathered into one volume – **the Qur'an**, Islam's sacred text.

> REMEMBER!
> **A prophet** is someone who receives messages from God and then passes them on to people.

Did You Know?

Muslims believe that Islam did **not** begin with the Prophet Muhammad. They say that the message of Allah was revealed to a number of other prophets who lived **before** Muhammad, such as Abraham and Moses.

However, Muhammad stands apart from these earlier prophets because he was the only one who accurately passed on **the complete truth** about God and the meaning of life to humanity. This is why Muslims accept Muhammad as **the final and greatest prophet** of all.

LIGHT THE WAY

For the next three years, Muhammad only talked to a small group of family and friends about what had he had experienced. His wife, their children and his best friend **Abu Bakr** were the first to accept his teaching and become Muslims.

Then, in 613 CE, Muhammad began openly preaching the message that Allah had entrusted to him. He taught that:

- We must accept Allah as the one and only God.
- We must treat one another as equals, be honest and show respect.
- We will be rewarded by Allah for any good we have done. We will be punished for any harm we have done.

Muhammad soon began attracting many Arabs to Islam, especially the young people of Makkah.

Then Muhammad demanded that all the idols be removed from the Ka'bah. This angered Makkah's powerful business community because he was threatening their large profits. However, Muhammad made these businessmen even angrier when he said that they had a duty to use their wealth to help the poor.

Muhammad's enemies tried to drive him out of Makkah. They only failed because he enjoyed the protection of his uncle. However, once his uncle died, Muhammad's enemies again put pressure on him to leave. He refused to be intimidated. Then he suffered a great loss when his wife Khadijah died suddenly in 619 CE.

> **Did You Know?**
>
> Muslims do **not** worship the Prophet Muhammad. They worship only Allah.

At this low point in his life, the angel Jibril once more appeared to Muhammad. This event is called **the Mi'raj** (i.e. **Night Journey**). The angel took him to Jerusalem. From there Muhammad was taken up into heaven, where he was brought before Allah. After this he was returned home to Makkah. Muhammad's faith in Allah was renewed and strengthened by this experience. He felt he was now ready for the challenges that lay ahead.

By the summer of 622 CE, Makkah had become a dangerous place. Several Muslims had been murdered. Muhammad was forbidden to preach in public. Then the neighbouring city of Yathrib offered the Muslim community a new home. Muhammad accepted their invitation.

Muhammad's move from Makkah is known as **the Hijrah** or **Hegira** (meaning '**the departure**').

Once in Yathrib, Muhammad took control of the city's government and reformed it. He proved to be a wise and inspiring leader. He made sure the poor, the sick, widows and orphans were cared for. Finally, he united its people under one religion – Islam.

People began calling Muhammad **the Rasul** (meaning '**the Messenger of Allah**'). In his honour, the city of Yathrib was renamed **Madinah** (meaning '**the City of the Prophet**').

Muhammad's enemies in Makkah twice sent an army to force him out of Madinah. On both occasions, Muhammad's smaller force defeated them. Finally, in 630 CE, Muhammad conquered Makkah. However, he achieved it without any bloodshed. His opponents' resistance simply crumbled away.

Muhammad's first act as ruler of Makkah was to remove all the idols from **the Ka'bah**. From now on it would be used only for the worship of Allah.

Some Arab tribes still opposed Muhammad but he soon defeated them. By 631 CE, most Arabs had accepted his leadership and become Muslims. Muhammad had brought peace to Arabia by uniting its tribes around a common religious faith – Islam.

Then, in 632 CE, Muhammad fell ill, probably with pneumonia, and died soon afterwards. He was buried in a tomb at the mosque in Madinah.

Muhammad's successors continued what he had begun. Within a century of his death, Islam had spread as far west as Spain and as far eastward as India. Today, it is the world's second largest religion.

Did You Know?

To show how important the **Hijrah** was, Muslims begin their calendar with this event – Muhammad's departure from Makkah. Therefore, 622 CE is the **first** year of the Muslim era.

Did You Know?

Today, Muslims show their love and respect for Muhammad by writing the letters *pbuh* after his name. These letters stand for '**peace be upon him**'.

Muslims praying together at Makkah.

LIGHT THE WAY

ACTIVITIES

1. Crossword

Across
5. He rebuilt the Ka'bah with his son Ishmael.
7. Where Islam began.
9. His name means 'highly praised'.
10. Title meaning 'the Messenger of Allah'.
12. Means 'the House of God'.
13. The wife of Muhammad.
15. Means you have not learned to read or write.
16. A collection of Muhammad's sayings.
18. A well that provides fresh water at Makkah.

Down
1. Where Muhammad prayed and meditated alone in a cave (2 words: 5, 4).
2. Where Muhammad is buried.
3. It means 'the Night Journey'.
4. On the Night of Power this angel appeared to Muhammad.
5. There were 360 of these in the Ka'bah until Muhammad had them removed.
6. It is set into the eastern corner of the Ka'bah (2 words: 5, 5).
8. A collection of stories about Muhammad.
11. It means 'the departure from Makkah'.
14. Means 'the trustworthy one' (2 words: 2, 4).
17. He originally built the Ka'bah.

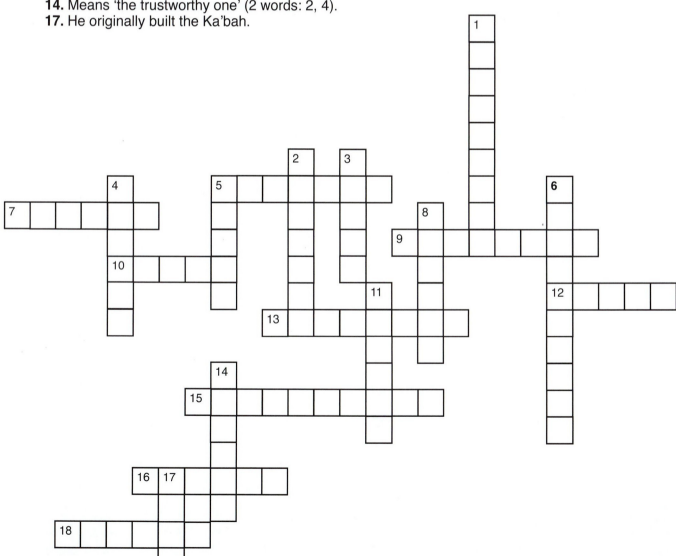

52

Communities of Faith SECTION A

2. Say what it means!

(a) Islam means _____ .

(b) Muslim means _____ .

(c) Allah means _____ .

(d) A prophet is _____

_____ .

3. Think about it!

(a) Why was early seventh-century Arabia a dangerous, lawless place?

(b) Who do Muslims worship?

(c) What do Muslims believe happened to Muhammad in a cave on Mount Hira in 610 CE?

(d) Why do Muslims accept Muhammad as the final and greatest prophet?

(e) How did Muhammad bring peace to Arabia by the time of his death?

(f) Why do Muslims write the letters *pbuh* after Muhammad's name?

LIGHT THE WAY

CHAPTER 6 WHAT IS A SACRED TEXT?

The Importance of Reading

In the film **Black Robe**, a Catholic priest tries to persuade a Native American chief to let him teach his tribe how to read and write. The chief refuses. He does not see any benefit to be had by learning how to make marks on paper. So the priest decides to give him a demonstration. '**Tell me something I do not know**,' he says. The chief thinks for a moment and replies, '**My wife's mother died in snow last winter**.'

The priest writes this sentence down on a piece of paper and walks some distance over to where another priest is standing. Without saying a word, he passes the note to him. The other priest glances at it and then says to the chief, '**Your mother-in-law died in a snowstorm?**' The chief is amazed. How could this be? The two priests had not spoken to one another. The chief had just encountered the great power of writing. This remarkable invention allows knowledge to jump across space and time and travel in silence through the marks we make on a page or a screen.

The invention of writing was one of the most important events in history. Indeed, it has made our whole complex modern civilisation possible. Think about it. Before the invention of writing, important stories and valuable information had to be passed on verbally, from person to person. But the story was only as reliable as the storyteller. Over time, distortions could be introduced, as stories passed on verbally were either added to or subtracted from. For example, it is said that before a battle in World War I, the following verbal message was passed down through a long line of troops: '**Send reinforcements; we're going to advance**.' However, by the time it got to the end of the line, this message had been changed to: '**Send three and four pence; we're going to a dance**.'

Writing prevented that kind of thing from happening. It preserved the original message exactly as it was expressed. Further, thanks to writing, stories and information could be recorded in books and read by people anytime and anywhere – whether in your school today or in another country years from now. You no longer had to communicate with someone face to face in order to find something out. You did not even have to live in the same century. Writing made it possible for people to communicate accurately over great distances of space and time.

Through books we have access to a vast storehouse of knowledge and ideas. This is why it is so important for us to develop the habit of reading.

There are so many good reasons for reading. These include:

- Entertaining yourself.
- Usefully passing the time on a journey.
- Learning more about places you have never been.
- Expanding your knowledge of our world and the people in it.
- Finding answers to life's great questions, namely, '**Who am I? Why am I here? How should I live? What happens when I die?**'

This final reason is why people read **sacred texts**.

The Importance of Sacred Texts

Each of the six major world religions has its own **sacred text**.

> **REMEMBER!**
> A **sacred text** is the holy book of a particular religion. It contains the most important stories and essential teachings of that religion.

54

Sacred texts were written because people wanted:

- To preserve the most important stories and teachings of their religion.
- To make sure this information would be passed on accurately from one generation to the next.

Name of the Religion	Title of its Sacred Text
Hinduism	The Vedas
Judaism	The Tanakh
Buddhism	The Pali Canon
Christianity	The Bible
Islam	The Qur'an
Sikhism	Guru Granth Sahib

Exploring a National Treasure

If you want to learn more about the sacred texts of the different religions, there is no better place to visit than the **Chester Beatty Library**. This is located in the grounds of Dublin Castle. It is said to be one of the finest museums in Europe. Admission is free and there are audio-visual programmes to help you make the most of your time there.

This library displays a vast array of sacred texts from every religion, in both book and manuscript form. These were collected during his lifetime by **Sir Alfred Chester Beatty**.

Born in New York in 1875, Beatty attended Columbia University, graduating as a mining engineer. He proved to be a brilliant businessman and soon amassed such great wealth that he became widely known as '**the Copper King**'.

After the death of his first wife, Grace, in 1911, Beatty moved to London. There he met and married his second wife, Edith, in 1913. They shared a great interest in art, books and travel. They journeyed throughout the Middle East and Asia, collecting beautifully decorated ancient manuscripts. However, Beatty did not merely want to own these priceless treasures. He also wanted to preserve them for their great historical value.

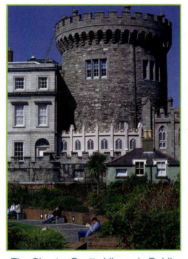

The Chester Beatty Library in Dublin displays a vast array of sacred texts.

For his contribution to the Allied war effort during World War II, Beatty was knighted by King George VI. However, in 1950, he decided to leave London and retire to Ireland.

Beatty built a library to house his collection on Shrewsbury Road in Dublin. It opened in 1954. Three years later, Beatty was made Ireland's first honorary citizen.

Upon his death, Chester Beatty left his entire, priceless collection to the Irish people. He generously turned his private library into a national treasure. The collection was subsequently moved from Shrewsbury Road to its present location in Dublin Castle. It has been open to the public there since 1999.

One of the museum's most beautiful sections is **the Sacred Traditions Exhibition**. It displays sacred texts that date back as far as 2700 BCE. Of particular interest are several examples of **papyrus**.

Did You Know?

Papyrus (plural: **papyri**) is a kind of paper that was used in ancient times. It is made from reeds that grow along river banks. You cut the stem of the reed into thin slices. Then these strips are pounded together to make sheets to write on.

LIGHT THE WAY

The **Chester Beatty papyri** date from between 200 CE and 400 CE. They contain some of the earliest known fragments of the Bible.

SPOTLIGHT ON THE BIBLE

The Bible is Christianity's sacred text. People tend to think of the Bible as being one book. However, this is not the case. The Bible is not really one book but a whole library of books, numbering 73 in all. These were written over a period of 1,000 years and finally bound together into a single volume by the early Christians.

The Bible is divided into two parts called 'testaments'. The word 'testament' means agreement or promise.

- The first part is the **Old Testament**. It contains forty-six separate books. These include history, law, poetry, prophecies and stories. These were mostly written in Hebrew, the language of the ancient Jews.
- The second part is the **New Testament**. It contains twenty-seven books, written in the latter half of the first century CE. These books were written in Greek, which was the most widely spoken language in the eastern Mediterranean region at that time.

Did You Know?
The name 'Bible' comes from the Greek word *ta biblia*, which means 'the books'.

How do I find a bible reference?

Each book of the Bible is divided into **chapters** and then subdivided into verses. For example:

The first letter to	The Christian community at Thessalonia in Greece	Chapter number	Verse number
1	Thessalonians	2:	13

The Bible is an important book. Think about this:

- For one-third of the human race, the Bible is 'the Word of God'. It teaches two important things:
  (a) Who God is; and (b) How God wants us to live.
- Over the centuries, the teachings contained in the Bible have inspired and strengthened many people to do great things or offered them consolation and encouragement in times of great sadness.
- The Bible has been a major source of inspiration too for artists, musicians and writers. You cannot understand much of the architecture, books, music, paintings, plays, poems and songs of the past without a knowledge of the Bible.

However, the Bible is open to different interpretations. Some people have used certain passages in it to justify wrongdoing, such as persecuting those who do not agree with them.

Yet, whether it has been used or abused, the Bible has done much to shape the world we live in today.

How to Treat a Sacred Text

If you are a member of a religion, you are expected to read its sacred text and think about what it says. Then you are supposed to apply any lessons you have learned from it to your everyday life.

However, you are also expected to treat any copy of the sacred text you are reading with great care. When you treat it with respect, it shows that you understand its importance.

One religion in particular – **Islam** – insists that its members show great respect for its sacred text – the Qur'an.

SPOTLIGHT ON THE QUR'AN

The title '**Qur'an**' means '**to recite**'.

The Qur'an is Islam's sacred text. Since it first appeared in the mid-seventh century CE, the Qur'an has rivalled the Bible as the world's most influential book.

The Qur'an has been described as '**the binding force between Muslims all over the world**'.

It is important because it sets out the teachings that unite all Muslims.

Muslims say that the words of the Qur'an are **literally** the words of Allah (God). They believe that the Qur'an was given to Muhammad by the angel Jibril (Gabriel) and that what the angel said came from Allah. Muhammad memorised everything the angel said. Then Muhammad recited (repeated) it all, word for word, to scribes. They wrote down exactly what Muhammad had said; not adding anything to it.

The Qur'an is written in **Arabic**. This is the language in which it was originally given to the prophet Muhammad. Muslim children everywhere must learn Arabic in order to read it.

The Qur'an consists of 114 **surahs** (i.e. chapters). Each surah is made up of a number of **ayats** (i.e. verses).

Did You Know?

Some Muslims try to memorise the entire text of the Qur'an. A Muslim who can accurately recite the whole text at a public examination is given the title **hafiz**.

Because they believe the Qur'an contains the actual words of Allah, Muslims say that every copy of it must be treated with great respect. Usually, copies of the Qur'an are beautifully bound and richly decorated with calligraphy to indicate the book's importance.

If you are a Muslim, you must always do the following:

- Wash your hands before touching or reading from **the Qur'an**.
- Place **the Qur'an** on a special stand when reading from it.
- Remain silent when listening to someone else reading it aloud. You should never eat or drink anything until the reading has ended.
- Store **the Qur'an** when not in use on a high shelf, keeping it covered and dust free.

LIGHT THE WAY

ACTIVITIES

1. Wordsearch

Find each of the following words:

Knowledge
Sacred text
Bible
Dublin Castle
Invention
Writing
Respect
Vedas
Quran
Civilisation
Books
Tanakh
Greek
Pali Canon
Arabic
Hafiz
Hebrew
Guru Granth Sahib
Chester Beatty

D	N	H	C	B	N	S	S	F	T	S	U	G	Q	B
U	O	E	E	I	G	O	A	A	A	A	N	K	I	Z
B	N	B	L	Y	V	B	I	C	D	I	N	H	H	A
L	A	R	B	N	U	I	R	T	T	E	A	A	R	I
I	C	E	I	H	N	E	L	I	N	S	V	A	K	K
N	I	W	B	C	D	N	R	I	H	E	B	I	H	H
C	L	K	Q	T	A	W	Y	T	S	I	V	O	A	S
A	A	J	E	R	E	Y	N	T	C	A	U	N	F	F
S	P	X	U	W	B	A	V	P	N	R	T	N	I	C
T	T	Q	P	Z	R	E	S	P	E	C	T	I	Z	E
L	V	M	E	G	D	E	L	W	O	N	K	L	O	M
E	Y	J	U	G	R	E	E	K	S	K	O	O	B	N
E	R	R	Q	U	Z	M	W	K	I	U	Y	D	G	Y
D	U	C	H	E	S	T	E	R	B	E	A	T	T	Y
G	G	M	Y	F	X	Z	H	W	A	O	U	V	G	Z

2. Say what it means!

(a) A sacred text is _____ .

(b) The name 'Bible' comes from _____ .

(c) The word 'testament' means _____ .

(d) Papyrus is _____ .

(e) The title 'Qur'an' means _____ .

3. Fill in the missing information!

Name of the Religion	Title of its Sacred Text
Buddhism	
Christianity	
Islam	
Sikhism	
Judaism	
Hinduism	

58

Communities of Faith   SECTION A

4. Tick the box!

		True	False
1.	The invention of writing made our entire complex civilisation possible.		
2.	Writing makes it possible for people to communicate accurately over great distances of space and time.		
3.	Sacred texts preserve important stories and teachings of a religion.		
4.	The Chester Beatty Library is now located at Shrewsbury Road in Dublin.		
5.	Alfred Chester Beatty amassed such wealth that he became known as 'the silver king'.		
6.	Alfred Chester Beatty was made Ireland's first honorary citizen in 1957.		
7.	The Sacred Traditions Exhibition displays sacred texts written on papyrus.		
8.	The Bible is not really one book but a whole library of books.		
9.	The Bible is divided into three parts, each called 'testaments'.		
10.	For the whole human race, the Bible is 'the Word of God'.		
11.	The Bible is open to different interpretations.		
12.	The title Qur'an means 'to repeat'.		
13.	The Qur'an is 'the binding force' between Muslims all over the world.		
14.	Muslims believe that the Qur'an was given to Muhammad by the angel Jibril.		
15.	The Qur'an is written in Greek.		
16.	The Qur'an consists of 114 ayats.		
17.	Muslims must wash their hands before handling a copy of the Qur'an.		

5. Think about it!

(a) Why do people read sacred texts?

(b) Why were sacred texts written?

(c) Give three reasons why the Bible can be called 'an important book'.

(d) Why are the members of a religion supposed to treat their sacred text with respect?

(e) Why do Muslims say that every copy of the Qur'an must be treated with great respect?

CHAPTER 7   RELIGIOUS IDENTITY

The Importance of Identity

Imagine you wake up one morning to see that the sun is shining; you feel rested. However, there is just one problem – you cannot remember who **you** are.

Sure, you can use a computer, drive a car, calculate the interest on a loan and translate from one language into another. However, there is something important that you cannot do. You cannot answer the following questions:

- What is my name?
- Who are my loved ones?
- What do I believe in?
- What things are important to me?

These are the most basic questions you can ask yourself. These are questions about your **identity**.

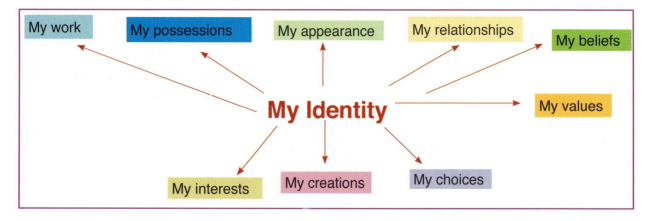

> **REMEMBER!**
> Your **identity** is your knowledge of what makes you **unique**.
> **Unique** means the ways in which you are different from everyone else.

Although you are unique, you don't live in isolation. You are a member of a family.

Think about your **surname** (i.e. **family name**). It not only says who you are here and now in the twenty-first century, it also says where you have come from. You are the latest member of a community whose story can be traced back over many centuries.

Your surname also represents your family living today. Think about how your relationship with other family members shapes your understanding of who you are. You are someone's son or daughter. You are someone's grandson or granddaughter. You may be someone's brother or sister. You may be an aunt, uncle or cousin to someone.

You are a member of other communities too. Remember, you live in a particular neighbourhood. You attend a particular school. You may be involved in an organisation such as a sports club, charity or musical/drama society. Through your involvement in them you can discover your particular talents and develop your own personal interests and hobbies.

In each of these community settings, you live out who you are – your identity – through your interaction with the people you meet. All your experiences of living with others combine to shape your identity – the way you look at life, how you think, speak and act.

This is why our need for community life is so great. We need one another to help us figure out who we are and how we can find happiness in life.

The Meaning of Religious Identity

Just like you, every religion has its **own** identity.

No two religions are alike. Each one has its own teachings about the meaning of life and its own rules about how to live a good life.

> **REMEMBER!**
> **A religious identity** is made up of all the things that distinguish one religion from another and make it unique.

Expressing your Religious Identity

People can express their religious identity in different ways. Here are two examples:

1. Using a religious symbol to show you belong to a particular religion

The most important symbols of the six major world religions are:

> **Did You Know?**
> **A religious symbol** is an image that identifies you as a member of a particular religion. It also says something important about what this religion stands for.

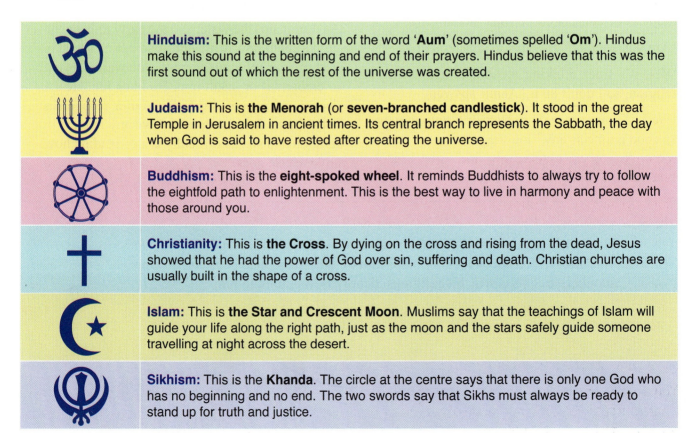

Hinduism: This is the written form of the word '**Aum**' (sometimes spelled '**Om**'). Hindus make this sound at the beginning and end of their prayers. Hindus believe that this was the first sound out of which the rest of the universe was created.

Judaism: This is **the Menorah** (or **seven-branched candlestick**). It stood in the great Temple in Jerusalem in ancient times. Its central branch represents the Sabbath, the day when God is said to have rested after creating the universe.

Buddhism: This is the **eight-spoked wheel**. It reminds Buddhists to always try to follow the eightfold path to enlightenment. This is the best way to live in harmony and peace with those around you.

Christianity: This is **the Cross**. By dying on the cross and rising from the dead, Jesus showed that he had the power of God over sin, suffering and death. Christian churches are usually built in the shape of a cross.

Islam: This is **the Star and Crescent Moon**. Muslims say that the teachings of Islam will guide your life along the right path, just as the moon and the stars safely guide someone travelling at night across the desert.

Sikhism: This is the **Khanda**. The circle at the centre says that there is only one God who has no beginning and no end. The two swords say that Sikhs must always be ready to stand up for truth and justice.

LIGHT THE WAY

2. Putting your religious beliefs into practice in your daily life

This can be quite a challenge when those around you do not share your religious beliefs. Think about the following situation:

'Hey, you've had too much to drink, Joe. I bet you can't walk in a straight line.'

'Of course I can, watch this!'

Joe tries to walk in a straight line across the room as if he were on a circus tightrope, but he loses his balance halfway and falls to the floor. Those around him burst out laughing.

Joe's new friend Aamir has to admit it was pretty funny, but he doesn't see this situation in quite the same way as everyone else in the room. This is because Aamir is a Muslim. His religion teaches that alcohol interferes with your mind, is harmful to your health and can lead you away from God. However, his friends do not share his religious beliefs, so not wanting to impose his own beliefs on them or ruin the happy mood, Aamir just smiles politely and says nothing.

'Man, I'm getting another beer,' Joe says. Then he turns to Aamir and asks: 'Hey pal, would you like a beer? I can get you one, it's no problem.'

'No thanks,' Aamir responds. After pausing for a moment he adds, 'I don't drink alcohol.'

'Are you serious?' Joe says in amazement.

'Yes, it's true; drinking alcohol is against my religion, so I don't do it,' Aamir answers.

'Well, if you ever want to start drinking, now is as good a time as any,' Joe suggests.

'No thanks, really,' says Aamir.

'Ah, it's not going to kill you, is it, bro?' Joe persists.

'Well, actually it might.'

'What do you mean?'

'I believe that our health is a gift from God and that alcohol is like a poison,' Aamir replies. 'It damages your health; that is why God forbids it. That and the harmful effect that drinking has on our society,' Aamir explains.

'Well, I don't think God would mind if you took a beer once in a while,' Joe says. 'I mean, I know it does me a lot of good, it helps me to relax – so why don't you have one too?'

'Look, thanks Joe, but I'm just not interested. I don't want a beer, I really don't need one to enjoy myself,' Aamir responds firmly, but with a smile on his face. 'Look we're all having a good time, so let's leave it at that, eh? Tell you what, I'll have a bottled water instead, OK?'

As Aamir sips the water and the party rolls on, he thinks about how difficult it is sometimes to stay true to your religious identity. Joe wasn't trying to embarrass or insult him. He likes Joe. He's a decent and generous guy, but Aamir recognises his attitude. Joe just doesn't have any interest in religion and so has difficulty understanding how anyone else does.

For Aamir, religion is not just about what you believe; it is about how you live your life. His religious identity helps him to understand who he is and how he should live. This is why his religious identity is important to him.

Communities of Faith SECTION A

ACTIVITIES

1. Say what it means!

(a) Your identity is _____

_____ .

(b) A religious identity is _____

_____ .

(c) A religious symbol is _____

_____

_____ .

2. Identify the religious symbol

In each of the following, identify the religion to which the particular religious symbol belongs and say what it means.

This is a religious symbol	Name of symbol	The meaning of this symbol
✝		
☬		
☪		
ॐ		
☸		
🕎		

3. Think about it!

(a) How did Aamir respond to Joe's first offer of a beer?

(b) Why did Aamir respond in this way?

(c) How did Joe react to what Aamir said?

(d) Why do you think Aamir politely refused Joe's repeated offering of an alcoholic drink?

(e) Why do you think Joe persisted in trying to get Aamir to accept a beer from him?

(f) What does this story tell you about the difficulty someone can face when trying to remain faithful to a religious identity in today's Ireland?

(g) What does it mean to say that 'religion is not just a set of beliefs but a whole way of life'?

CHAPTER 8   CHRISTIANITY TODAY

The Origin of Christianity

SPOTLIGHT ON A FOUNDER: JESUS CHRIST

Jesus was born a Jew in what is now Israel around 4 BCE. At that time, the area was a province of the Roman Empire. The Jews were divided among themselves as to how they should respond to Roman rule – some accepted it, while others rejected it. Those who opposed the Romans looked forward to the coming of a **messiah**.

Most Jews expected the messiah to set up an independent Jewish kingdom. However, Jesus had something very different in mind.

At around the age of thirty, Jesus began to preach a message of love, forgiveness and justice for all. He said that the most important thing in life is to love God and love one's neighbour as oneself. His own life was a perfect example of this. The people he dedicated his life to helping were the poor, the sick and any one in need. Further, he reached out not only to Jews but to non-Jews as well.

Jesus shocked his Jewish listeners by the way he talked about God. He referred affectionately to God as his **Abba**, i.e. **'Dear Father'**. Also, he claimed to have the power to forgive sins. When his critics doubted this, he demonstrated his power to do so by healing the sick, feeding the hungry and even restoring the dead to life.

However, the Jewish religious leaders of that time saw Jesus as a threat to their power. So they had him put on trial, tortured and executed by the local Roman governor, Pontius Pilate.

Whereas people of other faiths recognise Jesus as a great teacher, Christians believe that Jesus was far more than that. They say that, on the third day after his execution, Jesus rose from the dead and appeared to his **disciples** (i.e. followers). This event – **the Resurrection** – strengthened the faith of the disciples. They were now convinced that Jesus was more than the messiah. In Jesus, God had become a human being and lived on Earth.

Although Christianity grew out of Judaism, it very quickly developed into a religion with its own separate identity. Today, it is the world's largest and most widespread religious faith. There are more than two billion Christians scattered across the globe. They believe that Jesus conquered sin and death, and he lives today as the Lord of all creation.

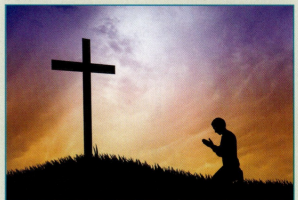

Did You Know?

Christianity is a religion founded on belief in and worship of Jesus Christ. Its members are called **Christians**.

Did You Know?

Messiah is a Hebrew word meaning 'the chosen one': in this case, someone chosen by God to do something great. The Greek word for **Messiah** is 'Christ'. Therefore, Jesus Christ means '**Jesus the Chosen One**'.

The Cost of Having Faith in Jesus Christ

For the first three centuries after Jesus's resurrection, it was dangerous to be a Christian in the Roman Empire. Emperors such as Nero and Diocletian insisted on everyone worshipping the Roman gods. When they refused, Christians were accused of being disloyal and rebellious. Many were tortured, burned at the stake, crucified or torn apart by wild animals in the arena.

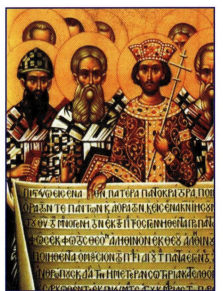

Icon depicting the Emperor Constantine and the bishops at the Council of Nicaea.

When faced with such terrors, some Christians lost their nerve. They abandoned their religion and chose to worship the emperor instead. However, most Christians did not give in. They remained loyal to their religion. Some suffered terribly for doing so.

Then, in 313 CE, something extraordinary and unexpected happened. The new emperor, **Constantine**, ended all persecution. He said that, from now on, Christians would be allowed to practise their religion in peace and safety. Indeed, Constantine himself later became a Christian and made it the official religion of the Roman Empire.

Constantine wanted peace among his subjects. However, he became worried about the bitter disputes developing among Christians. They disagreed about what you had to believe to be called a Christian.

Constantine invited all the leading Christians within the empire to come together and settle their differences at **a council** (meeting) at Nicaea in 325 CE. He asked them to talk with one another and agree upon a clear statement of what you had to believe to be called a Christian. He hoped that this would heal the divisions within Christianity and prevent any new ones arising.

If you were an onlooker at **the Council of Nicaea**, you would have been struck by two things right from the start. First, the 300 bishops who attended it were very serious-minded. They wanted to get things right. Second, you could see the reason for their attitude. Quite a few of these bishops bore the scars inflicted on them by a previous emperor's torturers. Some of them had empty eye sockets and disfigured faces. Others had limbs that were twisted or paralysed. These men had suffered terribly for their faith in Jesus Christ. The things they were going to discuss at Nicaea were the things that they had suffered for and had been willing to die for. Finally, after much prayer and lengthy discussion, the bishops agreed on what is called **the Nicene Creed**.

> **REMEMBER!**
> **Creed** comes from the Latin *credo*, meaning '**I believe**'.
> **A creed** is a prayer that sets out the beliefs shared by all the members of a religion.

What Christians Believe

The Nicene Creed is the most widely accepted statement of the Christian faith.

The Nicene Creed

I believe in one God, the Father almighty, maker of heaven and earth, of all things visible and invisible.

I believe in one Lord Jesus Christ, the Only Begotten Son of God, born of the Father before all ages, God from God, Light from Light, true God from true God, begotten, not made, consubstantial with the Father; through Him all things were made. For us men

LIGHT THE WAY

and for our salvation, He came down from heaven, and by the Holy Spirit was incarnate of the Virgin Mary and became man. For our sake He was crucified under Pontius Pilate, He suffered death and was buried and rose again on the third day in accordance with the Scriptures; He ascended into heaven and is seated at the right hand of the Father. He will come again in glory to judge the living and the dead and His kingdom will have no end.

I believe in the Holy Spirit, the Lord, the Giver of life, who proceeds from the Father and the Son, who with the Father and the Son is adored and glorified, who has spoken through the prophets.

I believe in one, holy, catholic and apostolic church. I confess one baptism for the forgiveness of sins and I look forward to the resurrection of the dead, and the life of the world to come. Amen.

SPOTLIGHT ON INTERPRETING THE NICENE CREED

1. Monotheism

There is **only one** God, who is beyond our human understanding.

2. The Holy Trinity

God is a **Trinity**, i.e. there are three divine persons in the one God. This does not mean that there are three Christian 'Gods'. Rather, these are the three different ways in which the one God has been shown to us, namely:

- **The Father** – who is the invisible, all-powerful creator of the universe; he lives and reigns forever.
- **The Son** – who is God made human in the person of Jesus; he is both fully human and fully divine. He was conceived in his mother's womb through the power of God, not by the actions of a human father. He really suffered and died on the cross. By rising from the dead he defeated the power of death over us. He is living now.
- **The Holy Spirit** – who is God's continuing presence working in the world today and sent to strengthen those who believe.

3. The final judgement

At a time known only to God, this world will end. Jesus will return to hold every one responsible for their actions. The good will be rewarded and the wicked punished.

4. The holy catholic church

Here, 'church' means the worldwide community of all those who have faith in Jesus Christ and who are baptised. Christians disagree among themselves as to who should lead it. However, they hope that one day it can be reunited again.

5. The communion of saints

The Christian community includes not only those who are alive today, but also all those who have died and now are with God in the afterlife.

Communities of Faith **SECTION A**

6. The forgiveness of sins

God's love has the power to overcome even the worst things we are capable of. If we are prepared to try, God will forgive our **sins** (i.e. wrongdoings). However, we must be genuinely sorry, want to put things right and be committed to leading better lives in future.

7. The resurrection and eternal life

Life does not end at death. Everyone is invited to share in the same resurrection as Jesus. Those who have unselfishly loved God and other people will be rewarded in the afterlife. There they will enjoy a happiness and peace that will last forever.

ACTIVITIES

1. Wordsearch

Find the following words:

Jesus
Constantine
Trinity
Catholic
Christianity
Messiah
Disciple
Creed
Saints
Abba
Nicaea
Father
Sins
Monotheism
Son
Forgiveness
Resurrection
Holy Spirit
Eternal life
Judgement

S	G	M	U	W	T	K	F	I	S	R	V	S	G	R
E	T	E	R	N	A	L	L	I	F	E	V	S	R	A
M	P	E	O	O	G	M	D	E	E	R	C	E	A	F
Y	O	S	N	R	W	Y	Q	J	W	H	Q	N	B	H
C	C	N	O	I	T	C	E	R	R	U	S	E	R	O
R	I	R	O	I	T	S	U	I	R	J	A	V	H	L
F	X	L	N	T	U	N	S	P	U	S	I	I	A	Y
P	A	I	O	S	H	T	A	D	P	N	N	G	I	S
A	R	T	F	H	I	E	G	T	N	I	T	R	S	P
T	B	J	H	A	T	E	I	E	S	S	S	O	S	I
K	P	B	N	E	M	A	N	S	R	N	A	F	E	R
H	V	I	A	E	R	U	C	X	M	R	O	C	M	I
V	T	G	N	E	L	P	I	C	S	I	D	C	D	T
Y	H	T	W	S	N	I	C	A	E	A	F	T	M	D
U	A	B	R	L	I	L	N	C	B	O	K	W	T	O

2. Say what it means!

(a) Christianity is _____

_____.

(b) Messiah means _____.

(c) Jesus Christ means _____.

(d) Abba means _____.

(e) A creed is _____.

(f) Church means _____.

LIGHT THE WAY

3. Tick the box!

Identify which of the following statements are true and which are false.

	True	False
1. Jesus was born a Christian in what is now Israel in 4 BCE.		
2. Jesus's followers were known as his 'disciples'.		
3. Jesus wanted to set up an independent Jewish kingdom.		
4. Jesus referred to God as his 'Dear Father'.		
5. The Jewish leaders were not threatened by Jesus.		
6. Pontius Pilate condemned Jesus to death.		
7. Christians believe that Jesus rose from the dead.		
8. Christianity grew out of Islam.		
9. There are more than three billion Christians scattered across the globe.		
10. Emperor Nero ended the persecution of Christians in 313 CE.		
11. Emperor Constantine called the Council of Nicaea in 325 CE.		
12. Monotheism means that there is only one God.		
13. The Trinity means that there are three Christian gods.		
14. Christians believe that life ends at death.		
15. The final judgement means that Jesus will return one day to hold everyone responsible for their actions.		

A Community Divided

Imagine you were to gather a sample group of Christians from all over the globe. Though drawn from a variety of different cultures, all of them would be united by their faith in Jesus Christ. However, you would soon notice that they each expressed this faith in different ways. This is because, over the centuries, groups of Christians have disagreed with and diverged from one another. This has led them to set up different **traditions**.

Christianity is divided into four traditions:

- **Catholic**
- **Orthodox**
- **Anglican**
- **Protestant**

Within each of these traditions there are different **denominations**.

> **REMEMBER!**
> **A tradition** is a distinctive way of thinking about and living out your religious faith. It is passed down over the centuries from one generation to the next.

> **REMEMBER!**
> **A denomination** is a particular branch of a Christian tradition.

Communities of Faith SECTION A

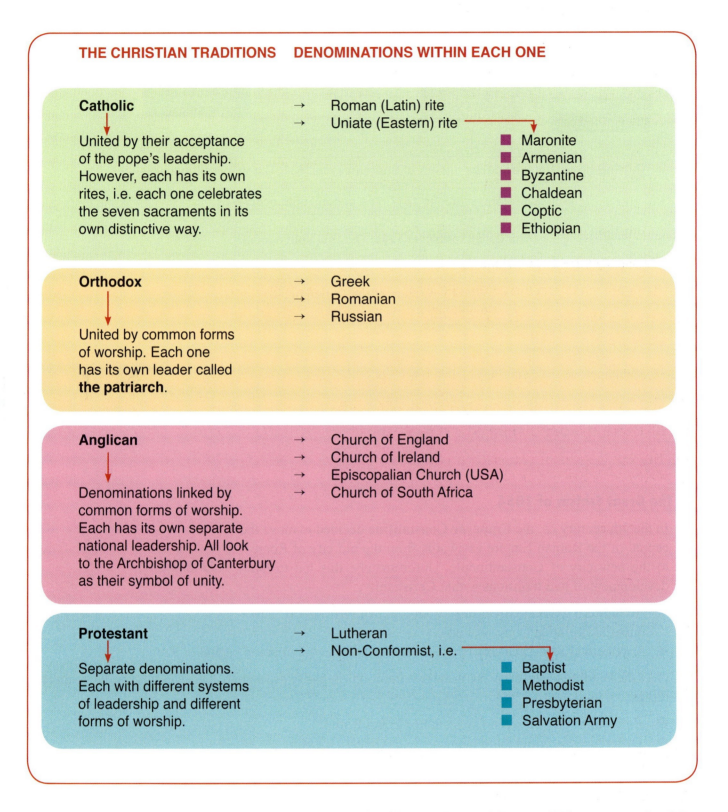

How do these traditions relate to one another? How should we understand them as **different strands of the one religion**?

One way is to imagine the worldwide Christian community as **a great tree**. The roots of this tree are firmly anchored in the life, death and resurrection of its founder – **Jesus Christ**. However, on three occasions in history, the trunk of this tree has branched off to produce the four different traditions we have today.

69

LIGHT THE WAY

How Christianity Became Divided

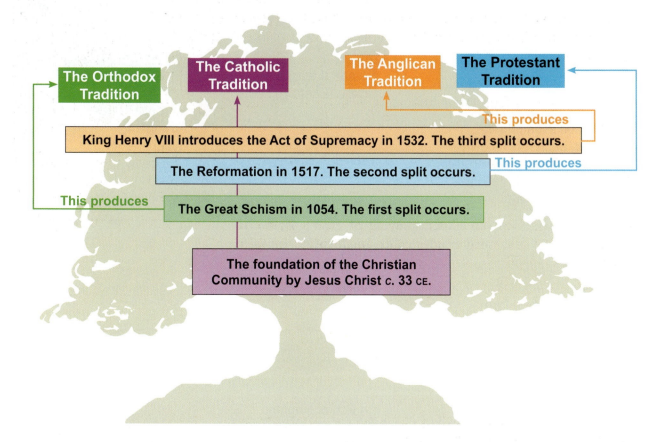

1. The Great Schism of 1054

In the 4th century CE, the **Emperor Constantine** decided to move the capital of the Roman Empire eastwards from the old city of Rome to the new city of Constantinople. Unfortunately, this led to the development of two traditions within Christianity:

REMEMBER!
Schism means 'a split'.

- An eastern (**Greek-speaking**) tradition centred on the new imperial capital at Constantinople.
- A western (**Latin-speaking**) tradition centred on the old imperial capital of Rome.

Over the centuries that followed, these two traditions began to grow apart. This was largely due to three things:

- Political rivalry between Constantinople and Rome.
- Differences in culture and language (e.g. Greek vs. Latin).
- Disagreement over who should lead Christianity – the east said it should be the emperor, while the west said it should be the pope.

Finally, in 1054, the whole issue of the leadership of Christianity erupted into a bitter quarrel between the eastern and western traditions. They separated from one another in an event known as **the Great Schism**. From this time on, Christianity was divided into two rival traditions:

The Catholic (meaning: **universal**) in the west and **the Orthodox** (meaning: **of right belief**) in the east.

2. The Reformation of 1517

In the period following the Great Schism, the Catholic tradition grew immensely powerful. However, with this great power came great temptation. Some leading church figures abused the power with which they had been entrusted. The result was a series of financial and sexual scandals.

By the early 16th century, many Christians were very unhappy with this state of affairs. They believed that too many of their leaders were ignoring the teachings of Jesus Christ. These men seemed interested only in accumulating power and wealth. There was a growing movement demanding reform. All it needed was a leader. It found it in **Martin Luther**.

Martin Luther was a Catholic monk who taught in the University of Wittenburg in Germany. After studying **St Paul's Letter to the Romans**, he developed an idea called **justification by faith alone**.

Martin Luther (1483–1546)

> **REMEMBER!**
> **Justification by faith alone** means that no one can earn God's mercy by doing good deeds. Human beings are saved only by the love and mercy of God.

Luther's acceptance of this teaching had important consequences. It led him into a direct confrontation with the pope.

In the early 1500s, **Pope Leo X** needed money to build the new St Peter's Basilica in Rome. The pope decided to authorise the sale of **indulgences** to raise these funds.

You could only get an indulgence if you did a good deed. The pope said that helping to pay for the construction of St Peter's Basilica was a good deed.

As he believed in justification by faith alone, Luther rejected the whole idea of indulgences. So when a Dominican friar named **John Tetzel** came to his area selling indulgences, Luther spoke out openly against him. He accused Tetzel of misleading people into believing that they could buy their way into heaven.

Luther thought that the pope would agree with him. However, Leo X did not. Luther was told to **recant** (i.e. take back) all he had said. Luther refused.

At this point, Luther said that he rejected both the authority of the pope and Catholic teaching on the sacraments. As a result, Luther was **excommunicated**.

In response, Luther set up the Lutheran Church. What had started out as a movement for reform had led to another division within Christianity.

> **Did You Know?**
> An 'indulgence' was a document that said all your sins were forgiven.

> **REMEMBER!**
> **Excommunicated** means being expelled from a religion.

> **Did You Know?**
> Luther established the **Protestant tradition**. It was called '**Protestant**' because Luther had **protested** against certain teachings and practices of the Catholic Church.

LIGHT THE WAY

ACTIVITIES

1. Say what it means!

(a) A tradition is _____

_____ .

(b) A denomination is _____

_____ .

2. Crossword

Across

3. This Christian tradition was given this name because Luther protested against certain teachings and practices of the Catholic Church.
4. The name of the monk who sold indulgences (2 words: 4, 6).
5. The language spoken by the western tradition.
7. It means 'of right belief'.
9. The west said he should lead Christianity.
12. It means 'universal'.
13. The roots of the Christian religion are firmly anchored in the story of his life, death and resurrection (2 words: 5, 5).
15. The name of the old imperial capital.
16. Being expelled from your religion.

17. This city became the new capital of the Roman empire in the 4th century CE.
18. It means a split.
19. The name of the pope who condemned Luther (2 words: 3, 1).

Down

1. The language spoken by the eastern tradition.
2. Name of monk who led the reformation of 1517 (2 words: 6, 6).
6. The number of Christian traditions.
8. To take back what you have said.
10. The east said he should lead Christianity.
11. Document that said all your sins had been forgiven.
14. He was the emperor who moved the empire's capital city east.

A Guide to the Christian Traditions in Ireland

1. SPOTLIGHT ON THE CATHOLIC CHURCH

Origins

The Catholic Church is the oldest institution in the Western world. Its origins can be traced back two thousand years to the time of Jesus Christ.

Importance

The Catholic Church is the largest Christian tradition. It has about 1.4 billion members worldwide. About 3.86 million Irish people identify themselves as Catholic.

> **REMEMBER!**
> The name '**Catholic Church**' means '**the universal community**'.

Organisation

The Catholic Church is organised as **a hierarchy**, i.e. it is made up of different levels, one above the other, with greater responsibility the higher up you go.

The Catholic Church explains the roles played by its different members as follows:

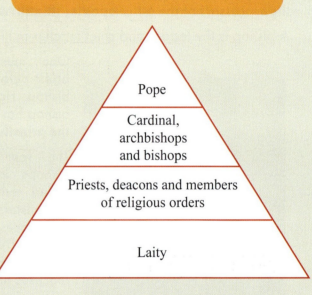

The pope

The title **pope** comes from a Latin word meaning '**father**'. Catholics address the pope as '**Holy Father**'. Catholics also refer to the pope as **the Vicar of Christ**, meaning '**Christ's representative on earth**'. The pope is called this because:

- He is the visible head of the Catholic Church on Earth and his authority extends to all its members.
- The Catholic Church is united through the power of the Holy Spirit under the leadership of the pope.

St Peter the Apostle was the first pope. Jesus Christ appointed him to the position (**Matthew 16:18–19**). Before his death, Peter passed on his authority to lead the Catholic Church to a man named **Linus**. He, in turn, passed it on to another and so on down to the present day. The current pope, Francis, is the 266th in this direct line of succession.

The First Vatican Council (1870) declared that the pope is **infallible**.

> **REMEMBER!**
> **Infallibility** is a gift the pope receives from the Holy Spirit. Under certain conditions, it helps him to define in clear terms what Catholics believe about essential matters of faith and morals.

The pope lives in Vatican City, Rome, Italy. This also serves as the worldwide headquarters of the Catholic Church.

LIGHT THE WAY

The cardinal

Every pope is chosen by **conclave** (i.e. an election held in closed session). The new pope is always chosen from among the members of the College of Cardinals. This is because only cardinals are entitled to attend a conclave and cast their votes to elect a pope.

Cardinals are selected by the pope from the ranks of the bishops. There are never more than 150 cardinals. Once a cardinal reaches the age of eighty he is no longer eligible to vote in a papal conclave.

In between elections, the cardinals help the pope to govern the Church; some serve as administrators in the Vatican. Most countries with a large Catholic population have at least one cardinal.

The bishop

As the pope is the successor to St Peter, so the bishops are the successors of the other apostles (**Matthew 28:18–20**).

A bishop is the leader and chief teacher in his **diocese**.

Archbishop of Dublin, Dr Diarmuid Martin.

One must become a priest before becoming a bishop. However, only a bishop has **the fullness of the priesthood**.

The four most senior bishops in Ireland are called **archbishops**. Each administers an area called an archdiocese. These are Armagh, Cashel, Dublin and Tuam. Each archdiocese has a number of dioceses linked to it.

Bishops are selected by the pope and are united under his leadership. To show this, each bishop must go to the Vatican every five years to make a report to the pope about his own diocese.

Did You Know?

A diocese is the geographical area over which a bishop has been given authority by the pope. The main church in a diocese, where the bishop has his base, is called **the cathedral**. Each diocese is sub-divided into **parishes** (i.e. local Christian communities).

Did You Know?

The fullness of the priesthood means that only a bishop can celebrate all seven sacraments; in particular, the Sacrament of Holy Orders. This is why only a bishop can perform an **ordination**. **Ordination** is where a bishop makes someone else a bishop, priest or deacon through the laying on of hands and saying the prayer of consecration.

The priest

A priest is a man who has been **ordained** by a bishop, i.e. he has received the Sacrament of Holy Orders. A priest must promise to remain **celibate** (i.e. unmarried).

Some priests are members of religious orders, while others are diocesan priests devoted to service in a particular diocese.

A priest's work includes:
- Celebrating the sacraments, e.g. baptising new members and marrying couples.

Communities of Faith   **SECTION A**

- Explaining the message of Jesus Christ through sermons and teaching.
- Offering leadership and giving good example by visiting the sick, helping the poor and counselling those in crisis.
- Acting as a chaplain in a school, hospice, hospital, prison or university.

A priest is only ordained after completing a lengthy period of study (usually a minimum of six years). The national **seminary** (i.e. priest training college) is at St Patrick's College, Maynooth, Co. Kildare. A student for the priesthood is called **a seminarian**.

The deacon

In the early days of the Catholic Church, deacons were those with a special responsibility for helping the sick and needy. In time, being a deacon became the final stage in training before being ordained a priest. In 1967, Pope Paul VI reestablished the role of a permanent deacon.

A permanent deacon is a man who is not called to be a priest. Only a bishop can ordain a deacon. Whereas a priest must be celibate, a deacon may be married. Often, a deacon has a full-time job outside the Catholic Church.

A deacon can read the Gospel and preach the homily during the Mass, as well as perform baptisms and conduct a marriage service. However, a deacon cannot preside (i.e. lead the congregation) at the celebration of the Sacrament of the Eucharist (i.e. the Mass).

The laity

The vast majority of Catholics are members of the laity. The term '**laity**' applies to all those Catholics who have not received the Sacrament of Holy Orders. However, all Catholics, no matter what roles they play – whether bishops, priests, deacons or laity – are **equal** members of the Catholic Church.

The laity are encouraged to play a variety of roles within a parish. They can be:

- Ministers of the Word (reading the sacred texts at the Mass)
- Ministers of the Eucharist (distributing Holy Communion)
- Altar servers (assisting when the sacraments are being celebrated)
- Catechists (preparing people to receive the sacraments)
- Counsellors (advising those in need)
- Members of Catholic charitable organisations (helping those in need)
- Choir members or musicians (enhancing the celebration of the sacraments).

ACTIVITIES

1. Say what it means!

(a) The name 'Catholic Church' means _____

_____ .

(b) Hierarchy means that the Catholic Church is _____

_____ .

(c) The title 'Vicar of Christ' means _____

_____ .

(d) A seminarian is _____

_____ .

LIGHT THE WAY

2. Crossword

Across

2. Someone who reads the sacred texts at the Mass is a Minister of this.
4. The name of the 266th pope.
6. An election held in closed session to choose a new pope.
8. Someone who advises those in need.
9. A priest training college.
13. Someone entitled to attend a conclave and cast a vote to elect a new pope.
14. Someone who distributes Holy Communion is a Minister of this.
18. Someone who prepares people to receive the sacraments.

Down

1. It means 'to remain unmarried'.
3. An ordained minister in the Catholic Church who can read the Gospel and preach the homily, perform baptisms and conduct a marriage service.
5. The name of the first pope.
7. The name of the second pope.
10. It is a gift the pope receives from the Holy Spirit. It protects him from error on matters of faith and morals.
11. Those who assist when the sacraments are being celebrated (2 words: 5, 7)
12. A geographical area over which a bishop has been given authority by the pope.
15. An ordained person who can celebrate all seven sacraments.
16. It means made up of different levels, one above the other, with greater authority the higher up you go.
17. Term that applies to all those Catholics who are non-ordained members of their Church.

76

Communities of Faith SECTION A

2. SPOTLIGHT ON THE CHURCH OF IRELAND

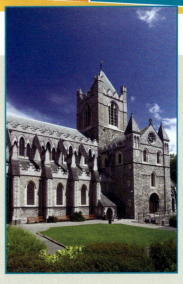

The Anglican Communion

The Church of Ireland is a self-governing member of **the Anglican Communion**. There are more than 80 million Anglicans worldwide.

The Church of Ireland is the second largest Christian tradition on the island of Ireland. It has about 400,000 members.

Fellowship

In addition to the Church of Ireland, the Anglican Communion also includes:

- The Church of England
- The Episcopalian Church in the United States of America
- The Church of Australia
- The Church of South India
- The Church of Nigeria
- The Church of Southern Africa.

These churches form **a fellowship**.

A fellowship exists wherever a group of independent churches have the following things in common:

- They believe the same things.
- They are organised in the same way.
- They worship God in the same way.
- They treat one another as equals.

> **Did You Know?**
>
> **The Anglican Communion** is an international fellowship of independent Christian churches. A member of the Anglican Communion is called **an Anglican**.

Leadership

All Anglican churches recognise **the Archbishop of Canterbury** in England as their spiritual leader and focus of unity. However, the Archbishop of Canterbury does not have the same authority as the pope in the Catholic Church. The different churches of the Anglican Communion are **not** under his control. For example, the Church of Ireland is led by **the Archbishop of Armagh**.

Origins

The Anglican Communion became a distinct Christian tradition due to the actions of **King Henry VIII** of England. He wanted to divorce his first wife and marry another woman. The pope would not agree. So, Henry rejected the pope's authority as leader of the Catholic Church. Instead, Henry VIII declared himself **'supreme governor'** of a newly established **Church of England** in 1532.

Despite breaking away from the Catholic Church, Henry VIII never saw himself as a Protestant. For instance, he celebrated the seven sacraments in the traditional Catholic way. Also, he persecuted anyone who promoted Protestant ideas in his kingdom.

The Most Revd Dr Richard Clarke, Archbishop of Armagh and Anglican Primate of All Ireland

77

LIGHT THE WAY

However, after Henry VIII's death, some of his successors introduced Protestant ideas into the Church of England. By the end of the 16th century, the Church of England had created a model that the other members of the Anglican Communion, including the Church of Ireland, would adapt to meet their local needs.

Did You Know?

The English monarch is still called 'the supreme governor' of the Church of England. However, he/she plays no role in either the Church of Ireland or any other member church of the Anglican Communion.

Identity

The Church of Ireland says that it is both **catholic** and **reformed**.

Catholic	Reformed
This means that…	This means that…
■ It is catholic in the sense of 'the catholic church' mentioned in the Nicene Creed, i.e. it is a member of the worldwide community of faith that was founded by Jesus Christ. ■ It traces its origins in Ireland back to the 5th-century church set up by St Patrick. It is the part of the Irish church that was influenced by the Reformation. ■ It has kept some pre-reformation elements of church life that the Protestant churches have rejected, such as: (i) A hierarchy with bishops and priests. (ii) The idea of sacrament.	■ It rejects certain teachings of the Catholic Church. For example: (i) It does not accept the pope as its leader. (ii) It does not accept the doctrine of transubstantiation, i.e. the Catholic belief that the bread and wine become the body and blood of Jesus during the Sacrament of the Eucharist. ■ It says that these Catholic beliefs are wrong because they cannot be found in the Bible. ■ It accepts the Protestant idea that the Bible contains all that you need to build a loving relationship with Jesus Christ so that you can be saved (i.e. enter heaven in the afterlife).

This is why the Church of Ireland/Anglican Communion is seen as **a middle way** between the Catholic tradition and the Protestant tradition.

Organisation

The Church of Ireland is divided into two provinces: Armagh and Dublin.

- Each province is led by an archbishop
- Each province contains several dioceses, each with its own bishop.
- Each diocese consists of a number of parishes, each with its own priest.

The archbishop

There are two Anglican archbishops – one in Armagh and one in Dublin.

Did You Know?

The Archbishop of Armagh is called **the Anglican Primate of All-Ireland**. He acts as the leader and chief spokesman of the Church of Ireland.

The bishop

There are twelve Anglican bishops. Each bishop is the leader of a diocese. In 2013 Patricia Storey became the first female bishop in the history of the Church of Ireland.

Communities of Faith   SECTION A

The rector

In the Church of Ireland, a priest is called **a rector**. In the Church of England, a priest is called **a vicar**. The rector's duties include:

- Celebrating the sacraments.
- Looking after the needs of his/her parishioners.

Anyone who wishes to become a rector must study at **the Church of Ireland Theological College** in Rathgar, Dublin. The title '**deacon**' is given to someone training to be a rector.

© Paul Harron - Church of Ireland Press Office

The Most Revd Pat Storey, Church of Ireland Bishop of Meath and Kildare.

The laity

As in all the other Christian churches, members of the laity play a vital role in the Church of Ireland. They may:

- Participate in Sunday worship through prayer, hymn-singing, reflecting on the Bible readings and receiving the Eucharist.
- Become **a lay reader**, i.e. be trained to preach and lead at prayer services.
- Be elected by their fellow parishioners to **the Select Vestry**, i.e. the group responsible for running a parish. These elections are held each year at Easter.
- Be elected to the House of Representatives of **the General Synod**.

The General Synod

The General Synod has two parts:

1. **The House of Bishops** – with twelve members.
2. **The House of Representatives** – with 216 clerical members and 432 lay members. All are elected by the people of their dioceses. They hold office for a three-year period.

Both houses come together to discuss important issues at the General Synod. The archbishop of Armagh acts as its **president** (or chairperson). He is expected to accept its decisions and implement them.

> ### Did You Know?
> The Church of Ireland ordains both men and women to the priesthood. They are free to marry and have a family.

> ### Did You Know?
> **The General Synod** is the Church of Ireland's chief decision-making body. It meets in May each year.

The Lambeth Conference

Every ten years, all the bishops of the Anglican Communion gather at **the Lambeth Conference** in London. This meeting is chaired (i.e. guided but not controlled) by the Archbishop of Canterbury. Important moral and religious issues are discussed at the Lambeth Conference. The bishops try to reach an agreement on what the Anglican Communion should teach about them.

However, the Anglican Communion is made up of **independent** churches. They do not automatically have to accept the statements of the Lambeth Conference. These statements must be debated by the General Synod of each member church. Then they can vote to either accept or reject the statements of the Lambeth Conference.

LIGHT THE WAY

ACTIVITIES

1. Crossword

Across

2. The number of bishops in the Church of Ireland.
7. His actions led to the Anglican Communion becoming a distinct Christian tradition (2 words: 5, 4).
10. King Henry VIII made himself 'Supreme _____' of the Anglican Communion.
11. The Archbishop of _____ is the leader of the Church of Ireland.
12. The title given to someone training to be a rector.
14. The Archbishop of _____ is the spiritual leader and focus of unity for Anglicans.

Down

1. The group responsible for running a parish (2 words: 6, 6).
3. It exists wherever a group of independent churches believe the same thing, are organised in the same way, worship in the same way and treat one another as equals.
4. The place in London where a conference of all Anglican bishops is held every ten years.
5. The title given to a priest in the Church of Ireland.
6. The Church of Ireland is a self-governing member of this communion.
8. The title given to a priest in the Church of England.
9. Someone trained to preach and lead prayer services (2 words: 3, 6).
13. The Church of Ireland traces its origins in Ireland back to the 5th-century church set up by him (2 words: 5, 7).

80

2. Say what it means!

(a) The Anglican Communion is _____
_____.

(b) The General Synod is _____
_____.

3. Fill in the missing words!

The Church of Ireland is Catholic…	The Church of Ireland is Reformed…
■ It is catholic in the sense of 'the catholic church' mentioned in the _____ Creed. ■ It traces its origins in Ireland back to the 5th-century church set up by _____ _____. ■ It has kept pre-reformation elements of church life such as: (i) A _____ with bishops and priests. (ii) The idea of _____.	■ It does not accept the _____ as its leader. It does not accept the doctrine of _____. ■ It says that these Catholic beliefs are wrong because they can not be found in the _____. ■ It accepts the Protestant idea that the Bible contains _____ that you need to build a loving relationship with Jesus Christ so that you can be _____.

3. SPOTLIGHT ON THE PRESBYTERIAN CHURCH

A Protestant denomination

The Presbyterian Church is a **Denomination** (i.e. branch) of the Protestant tradition. It is part of the World Alliance of Reformed Churches. There are about 75 million Presbyterians worldwide.

The headquarters of the Presbyterian Church in Ireland is located at **Church House** in Belfast.

Did You Know?

The name 'Presbyterian' comes from a Greek word meaning **an elder** (i.e. senior member) of a local Christian community.

Origins

The Presbyterian Church began with **John Calvin** (1505–1572). He became the leader of the Protestant community at Geneva, Switzerland during the Reformation. There he wrote a book called *The Institutes of the Christian Religion*. In it he set out his most important ideas about God, the sacraments and salvation (i.e. how we can get into Heaven). Calvin believed in **predestination**.

Did You Know?

Predestination is the belief that God has already decided, before you are even born, whether you will be saved (go to heaven) or be damned (go to hell).

Calvin's teachings were introduced to Scotland by **John Knox** in 1559. These were spread to Ireland in 1642 by Scottish chaplains serving with the British Army. Soon, many Scottish Presbyterians came to settle in Ireland, especially in Ulster following the plantations.

John Calvin (1505–1572)

LIGHT THE WAY

Today, many Presbyterians no longer accept all of Calvin's teachings. Indeed, there is now a wide range of views on religious matters within the Presbyterian Church.

Organisation

From the beginning, the Presbyterian Church rejected the idea of having a pope or a bishop as its leader. This was because Calvin claimed that he could not find a basis for the roles of pope or bishop anywhere in the New Testament. Instead, Calvin developed a system of church government where **a congregation** (i.e. a parish community) is led by a council of **elders**. Each elder is elected to that position by his/her fellow parishioners.

The council of elders is responsible for selecting a suitable minister. The minister's job is to look after the needs of the **kirk**.

> **REMEMBER!**
> **Kirk** is the name given to both a local Presbyterian community and its place of worship.

Any Presbyterian who wants to become a minister in Ireland must first study at Union Theological College in Belfast. Both men and women are entitled to become ministers.

Every minister is expected to:

- Lead the community in celebrating the only two sacraments recognised by the Presbyterian Church, namely: Baptism and Eucharist.
- Give sermons explaining how the teachings of the Bible can be applied to our daily lives.

The General Assembly

At national level, **the General Assembly** is the chief decision-making body of the Presbyterian Church in Ireland. Each year it elects a new **moderator**.

Did You Know?

The moderator acts as chairman of the General Assembly. The moderator also acts as the Presbyterian Church's principal spokesperson throughout the following year.

The moderator does **not** decide the Presbyterian Church's policy or direct its activities. These remain the responsibility of the General Assembly.

ACTIVITIES

Tick the box!

In each of the following, say whether it is true or false.

		True	False
1.	The Presbyterian Church is a denomination of the Orthodox tradition.		
2.	The headquarters of the Presbyterian Church in Ireland is located at Church House in Dublin.		
3.	The Presbyterian Church began with John Calvin in Geneva.		
4.	Calvin wrote a book called *The Institutes of the Catholic Religion*, in which he set out his most important ideas.		
5.	Salvation means how we get into heaven.		
6.	Predestination is the belief that God has already decided, before you are even born, who is to be saved and who is to be damned.		
7.	Calvin's teachings were introduced to Ireland by John Knox.		
8.	The Presbyterian Church accepts the idea of having a pope and bishops.		
9.	Each Presbyterian congregation is led by a council of elders.		
10.	Kirk is the name given to a Presbyterian minister.		
11.	Only men are entitled to become ministers in the Presbyterian Church.		
12.	The General Assembly is the chief decision-making body of the Presbyterian Church in Ireland.		
13.	The moderator of the Presbyterian Church is elected each year by the General Assembly.		
14.	The moderator decides the Presbyterian Church's policy and directs its activities.		

4. SPOTLIGHT ON THE METHODIST CHURCH

Origins

The Methodist Church is a denomination within the Protestant tradition. Today, there are about 70 million Methodists worldwide. There are about 53,000 Methodists in Ireland.

The Methodist Church began as a reform movement within the Anglican tradition. It was founded in the 18th century by two brothers, **John Wesley** (1703–1791) and **Charles Wesley** (1707–1788). Both men were priests of the Church of England.

The original aim of the Wesley brothers was to revitalise the Church of England. They believed that it had largely lost touch with the needs of ordinary working-class people in England at that time.

LIGHT THE WAY

From 1738 onwards, John Wesley put his great gifts as a communicator to use. He started preaching to people who had been largely ignored until then – such as coal miners and farm labourers. He told them that only by making a personal commitment to follow Jesus Christ could they be **saved** (i.e. go to heaven). This message filled many people with hope and a sense of purpose.

The Wesley brothers and their supporters did not want to break away from the Church of England. They saw themselves as reformers **within** it. They accepted most Anglican doctrines. However, they taught four things that were not acceptable to leading Anglicans at that time, namely:

- All people need to be saved.
- All people can be saved.
- Christians can reach a state of moral perfection in this life.
- The laity should have a greater role in the running of their church.

Finally the Church of England's bishops said that they did not approve of Wesley's preaching. They refused to let him use their buildings for worship. So, he spoke at outdoor venues instead. Large crowds came to listen to him. By 1739, Wesley had raised enough money to open his first church in Bristol.

By the time of John Wesley's death in 1791, the Methodists had been expelled from the Church of England/Anglican Tradition. Since then, the Methodist Church has been a separate denomination within the **Protestant** tradition.

Did You Know?

The name '**Methodist**' was originally a nickname given to a small group of Anglican students at Oxford University. They were called **Methodists** because of their **methodical** (i.e. highly disciplined) approach to prayer, the study of the Bible and life in general. The Wesley brothers were the leaders of this group.

Methodism comes to Ireland

The Wesley brothers attracted supporters in Ireland as early as the 1740s. Indeed, John Wesley frequently visited Ireland. As in England, Irish Methodists split from the Church of Ireland and formed a separate denomination here.

Organisation

The Methodist Church in Ireland calls itself **the Connexion**. This name reminds its individual members and local communities that together they form one community linked by a shared Christian faith.

A local Methodist community is called **a society**. There are more than 200 Methodist societies in Ireland. Each society is cared for by **a minister**. Both men and women can become ministers.

The Methodist Church in both Ireland and Britain is **non-episcopal**, i.e. it does not have bishops. The governing body of the Methodist Church is the annual conference. It elects the leader of the Methodist Church in Ireland, who is called **the President**.

Communities of Faith **SECTION A**

ACTIVITIES

Tick the box!

In each of the following, say whether it is true or false.

		True	False
1.	The Methodist Church is a denomination within the Anglican Tradition.		
2.	There are about 153,000 Methodists living in Ireland.		
3.	The Methodist Church began as a reform movement within the Catholic tradition.		
4.	The Methodist Church was founded in the 18th century.		
5.	The Methodist Church was started by two brothers – John and Charles Wesley – who were priests of the Church of Ireland.		
6.	Methodists were given this name because of their methodical (i.e. highly disciplined) approach to prayer, the study of the Bible and life in general.		
7.	John Wesley was a great communicator whose message gave people hope.		
8.	John Wesley taught that all people need to be saved and can be saved.		
9.	John Wesley did not want the laity having any say in the running of their church.		
10.	The Methodist Church in Ireland calls itself the Connexion.		
11.	A local Methodist community is called a society.		
12.	Each Methodist society is cared for by a priest.		
13.	Only women can become ministers in the Methodist Church.		
14.	The Methodist Church in both Ireland and Britain has bishops.		
15.	The leader of the Methodist Church in Ireland is called the President.		

85

CHAPTER 9 RELIGIOUS COMMITMENT

The Flying Scotsman

Imagine that you have been selected to represent your country at the Olympic Games. You are due to run in the 100-metres race. This is your best event. Then, you decide not to run. You do so because the race will be held on a Sunday. It is against your religious beliefs to compete on that day of the week. Instead, you decide to preach at the Scots Church on Rue Bayard. This is what **Eric Liddell** chose to do at the Paris Olympics in 1924.

Liddell was a science student at Edinburgh University between 1920 and 1924. Athletics and rugby played a major role in his life. In 1921 he ran for Edinburgh University's athletics team. He also played rugby for his university and, in 1922, won seven international rugby caps for Scotland. However, realising that he did not have enough time for both sports, Liddell chose running, concentrating on the 100-metres event at the Paris Olympics. In every race held in the year leading up to the Olympics, he had defeated all his rivals.

Liddell became known as **'the Flying Scotsman'** due to both his incredible speed and his awkward style of running. He ran with a huge sprawling stride, head thrown back and arms clawing the air. When some of his Olympic opponents first saw him running they simply doubled up with laughter and made the mistake of underestimating him.

However, Eric Liddell was more than just a great athlete. He was also a deeply religious man. He was a member of the Presbyterian Church. During his time in Edinburgh he had become a widely respected speaker who was much in demand.

When Liddell announced he would not run in the 100-metres Olympic final because it would be held on a Sunday, most Britons were puzzled by his decision. They were disappointed and could not understand why such a talented athlete would pass up such a great opportunity: he was the favourite to win the gold. Liddell's decision was widely criticised in the newspapers and even in the British parliament, but his mind was made up. He would not give in to pressure. Liddell simply said that he had his own priorities. Living according to his religious beliefs mattered more to him than winning a medal for his king and country.

Eric Liddell was known as 'the Flying Scotsman' due to his incredible speed and his awkward style of running.

Then Liddell surprised everyone by announcing that he would run in the 400-metres race. This was a distance in which he had performed well, but it was not his best. Also, Paris had been struck by a crippling heatwave, with temperatures regularly exceeding 40°C. These conditions did not help Liddell's tactics for the race. Most commentators did not rate him as having a chance of winning any medal, never mind the gold.

Then the draw for running lanes dealt Liddell another blow: he was given the outside lane. There he would be unable to see his rivals. So, he was left with no other option but to run as fast as he could for as long as he could.

On the day of the race, he went around and shook the hands of all the other contestants. He was not expected to win.

Liddell started well and covered the first 200m in 22.2 seconds. Just inside him in lane 5 was Horatio Fitch, the American who had broken the world record in the semi-final. **'I couldn't believe a man could set such a pace and finish,'** Fitch said afterwards. **'But Liddell pushed himself like a man possessed. He didn't weaken. With the tape only 20 yards away I again moved closer, but Liddell threw his head farther back, gathered himself together and shot forward.'**

Communities of Faith SECTION A

'**There was a gasp of astonishment when Liddell was seen to be a clear three yards ahead of the field at the half distance,**' reported the Press Association that day. '**Nearer the tape Fitch strained every nerve and muscle to overtake him, but could make absolutely no impression on the inspired Scot. With head thrown back and chin thrust out in his usual style he flashed past the tape to win what was probably the greatest victory of the games. Certainly there has not been a more popular win. The crowd went into a frenzy of enthusiasm.**'

The Scotsman sprinted through the tape six yards clear of his nearest rival, with a time of 47.6 seconds. He had not only won the gold medal but had set a new world record in the process. When asked about his medal win that day, Liddell said:

'**The secret of my success in the 400 metres is that I run the first 200 metres as fast as I can. Then, for the second 200 metres, with God's help I run faster.**'

Liddell returned to Britain a hero. One of his first duties was to attend his graduation ceremony at Edinburgh University. He was crowned with a laurel wreath by its chancellor, Sir Alfred Ewing. '**Mr Liddell,**' said Ewing, '**you have shown that none could pass you except the examiners.**'

Liddell spent a further year at Edinburgh, studying theology and preparing to be a Christian missionary in China, the country of his birth. This had long been his ambition; his father, James, had been a missionary in China before him.

Liddell's final race on British soil came less than a year after the Olympics, in June 1925, at the Scottish Amateur Championships at Hampden Park. Again, whenever he competed he won. A few weeks later a huge crowd of well-wishers turned up at Waverley Station as he left Scotland for China.

Liddell worked as a missionary in Northern China from 1925 to 1943. He returned for a few months to Scotland in 1932, where he was ordained a minister of the Presbyterian Church. He was asked if he ever regretted his decision to leave behind the fame and glory of athletics. '**It's natural for a chap to think over all that sometimes, but I'm glad I'm at the work I'm engaged in now,**' Liddell said. '**A fellow's life counts for far more at this than the other.**'

On his return to China, he met and married Florence Mackenzie, a Canadian missionary. They had three daughters, the last of whom Liddell would not live to see.

After the Japanese invasion of 1937, life in China became increasingly dangerous. Finally, all British nationals were advised to leave by their government. Liddell sent his pregnant wife and two children to safety in Canada, where they stayed with her family. He chose to stay behind to continue his work.

Liddell accepted a new job at a rural mission station in Xiaochang, a poor area that had suffered terribly during China's civil war. It had once more become a battleground following the Japanese invasion.

Liddell joined his brother, Robert, who was a doctor there. The station was severely short of help and the missionaries who served there were physically and mentally exhausted. There was a constant stream of local people who came at all hours seeking medical treatment. Liddell arrived at the station in time to relieve his brother who had become ill.

Once Japan attacked the USA in 1941, Liddell and other Westerners had their freedom of movement curtailed. In 1943, he and several thousand other Americans and Europeans were arrested by the Japanese army. They were held at the Weifang Internment Camp.

Liddell quickly emerged as one of the leaders among the internees. He worked tirelessly to help his fellow prisoners: taking care of the elderly, arranging games, refereeing football matches and repairing broken equipment. He set up a school and taught the children mathematics,

Eric Liddell is paraded around Edinburgh University after his Olympic victory.

religion and science. Soon the children began to call him 'Uncle Eric'.

Life in the camp was a daily struggle to survive. Food and medicines were in short supply. When some rich businessmen (mostly oil company executives) bribed the camp guards into giving them extra rations, Liddell found out and shamed them into sharing this food with their fellow prisoners.

One survivor of the camp said of Liddell: '**Often in an evening I would see him bent over a chessboard or a model boat, or directing some sort of square dance – absorbed, weary and interested, pouring all of himself into this effort to capture the imagination of these penned-up youths. He was overflowing with good humour and love for life, and had enthusiasm and charm. It is rare indeed that a person has the good fortune to meet a saint, but he came as close to it as anyone I have ever known**.'

In 2008 it was revealed by the Chinese government that, because he was a famous athlete, Liddell had been given an opportunity to leave the internment camp in a prisoner-exchange deal with the Allies. However, he turned this offer down and arranged for a pregnant woman to be released in his place. This information was released just before the Beijing Olympics and news of this remarkable act of self-sacrifice came as a surprise even to his family.

Liddell did not survive the war. On 21 February 1945, six months before the camp's liberation, he died of a brain tumour. He was buried in the garden behind the Japanese officers' quarters. His grave was marked by a simple wooden cross, with his name written on it in boot polish. The site was forgotten until it was rediscovered in 1989, in the grounds of what is now a school. A gravestone made of red granite was placed near the site in 1991.

Eric Liddell is remembered by many as a great sportsman. However, to many more he is remembered as a man of great courage and generosity. His whole life was a great example of **religious commitment**.

The Meaning of Religious Commitment

> REMEMBER!
> **A religious commitment** means making your best effort to live according to the teachings of your religion.

People show their religious commitment in two ways:

1. Worshipping God

If you are a Christian, you are expected to pray each day in private and regularly participate in the sacraments.

2. Doing good works

All religions ask their members to live according to the **Golden Rule**. This says: **Treat other people in the same way as you yourself would want to be treated.**

Communities of Faith   SECTION A

ACTIVITIES

1. Say what it means!

(a) A religious commitment means _____

_____ .

(b) The Golden Rule says _____

_____ .

2. Crossword

Across

4. The nickname the children of the camp gave Liddell because of his kindness (2 words: 5, 4).

7. The cause of Eric Liddell's death in February 1945 (2 words, 5, 6).

11. Liddell took a degree in this subject at Edinburgh University.

12. Liddell won seven caps for Scotland in this sport in 1922.

14. Liddell won this medal for his victory in the 400-metres final.

15. The country to which Liddell sent his wife and children to safety in 1941.

16. The camp where Liddell and others were interned by the Japanese in 1943.

17. Eric Liddell refused to run in the 100-metres final at the Olympic Games because it was being held on this day of the week.

18. The country whose armed forces invaded China in 1937.

Down

1. The lane in which Liddell had to run in at the 400-metre final.

2. Liddell was called the _____ Scotsman because of his great speed.

3. Eric Liddell married _____ Mackenzie in 1934.

5. The sport Liddell chose to follow in preparation for the 1924 Olympic Games.

6. The name of the Christian Church in which Liddell became a minister.

8. Eric Liddell's whole life was a great example of this kind of commitment.

9. The name of the rural mission station where Liddell worked with his brother.

10. The city where the Olympic Games were being held in the summer of 1924.

13. This rule means to treat others as you would want them to treat you.

15. The country where Eric Liddell worked as a Christian missionary.

89

LIGHT THE WAY

3. Think about it!

Read the following rhyme:

> *Mr Smith went to church,*
> *He never missed a Sunday.*
> *But all the wicked things he did,*
> *He did them on a Monday.*

(a) What does Mr Smith think is involved in making a religious commitment?

(b) Compare Mr Smith's understanding of religious commitment with that of Eric Liddell. What is the problem with Mr Smith's idea of religious commitment?

CHAPTER 10 VOCATION

Answering the Call

Gladys Aylward (1902–1970) felt sure that God was calling her to become a missionary.

The year is 1933. The location is a prison at Jincheng in Northern China. A riot has broken out among the prisoners. They are attacking each other and anyone else who gets in their way. The guards have withdrawn to the outer perimeter in fear. The warden has been injured. In desperation, he has called for help from a most unlikely source – a Christian missionary named **Gladys Aylward**. To her surprise, the warden asks her to go into the prison and stop the rioting. When she asks why he would want her to do such a dangerous thing, he says, '**You have been preaching that those who trust in Christ have nothing to fear**.' Though all too aware of the dangers, Aylward agrees to try. She pauses for a brief moment to pray for the strength to face this challenge. Then she walks out into the prison yard. She notices the bodies of the wounded lying strewn on the ground all around her. At the top of her lungs she shouts '**Quiet! I cannot hear when everyone is shouting at once. Choose one or two spokesmen, and let me talk with them**.' The prisoners are shocked to see her here; they all fall silent. Though she is a whisper-thin woman, about thirty years of age, standing only four foot ten inches tall, Aylward's voice and presence radiate an unusual calmness and authority. So the men drop their weapons and quickly select a representative.

After talking with the prisoners' spokesman, Aylward goes to the warden and says: '**You have all these men living in overcrowded conditions with absolutely nothing to do. No wonder they are so edgy that a small dispute set off this riot. You must give them worthwhile work to do. Also, you do not supply them with food. They only get to eat whatever their relatives can send them. No wonder they fight over food. We must set up looms so that they can weave cloth and earn money to buy their own food**.' As government funding is scarce, Aylward gets local businessmen to provide these looms. As the conditions quickly improve, there are no further riots in the prison. Soon, the local people begin to call Gladys Aylward '**Ai-weh-deh**', which means '**Virtuous One**'.

Who was this remarkable woman? How had she

> **REMEMBER!**
> **Virtuous** means you know what the right thing to do is and you have the courage to do it.

ended up in such an extraordinary situation?

Born into a working-class family in London on 24 February 1902, Gladys Aylward was the daughter of a postman and the eldest of three children. She had to leave school at fourteen to work as a wealthy family's maid. Although raised an Anglican, Aylward had little interest in religion until she was eighteen. Around that time she developed a great interest in her Christian faith. She became convinced that God was calling her to do something more than work as a domestic servant. She tried **to discern** what path she should follow in life.

> **REMEMBER!**
> **To discern** means to arrive at a decision about what is the right thing to do.

LIGHT THE WAY

Then Aylward heard a church sermon that planted the idea of becoming **a missionary** in her mind.

> **REMEMBER!**
> **A missionary** is someone who wants to convince others to become members of his/her religion.

But a missionary to where? Shortly afterwards, she came across a magazine article on China that sparked her interest. Now twenty-six years old, Aylward decided to study at the China Inland Mission Centre in London. However the principal told her that, in his opinion, she didn't have the ability to learn a difficult language like Chinese. They could not accept her as a missionary.

Though discouraged, Aylward refused to give up on the idea of missionary work. If this organisation would not send her to China, she would somehow make her own way there.

Then Aylward found employment as a maid with a retired army officer and his wife. They had lived for many years in the Far East and had an impressive library containing many books on China. She was encouraged to borrow whatever she wanted to read.

Four years later Aylward heard about a 73-year-old missionary, a widow named Jennie Lawson, who was looking for a younger person to carry on her work in China. She wrote to Mrs Lawson and was accepted, but only if she could get there on her own.

Aylward had been saving every penny she could for just such an opportunity. However she did not have the funds to travel by ship, the preferred method at that time for long-distance journeys. She had just enough to pay for an overland train ticket from London to Vladivostok.

On 15 October 1932, Aylward set off with a suitcase full of tinned food to sustain her on her long journey. She felt very much alone but believed she was answering God's call. It took her almost a month to reach Tianjin in China via the Trans-Siberian railway. However, there she discovered Mrs Lawson had moved on to another town. So Aylward had to set off on a dangerous 2-day journey by mule to the inland city of **Jincheng**, in the mountainous province of Shansi, south of Beijing, to find her. This was an area few Europeans had yet visited.

Mrs Lawson was delighted to see Aylward arrive safely. She became her mentor and helped her learn Mandarin Chinese. In time, and with great effort, Aylward came to speak it fluently, something she had been told was completely beyond her ability!

The two women decided to make Jincheng their home. They bought an old disused building, which the locals thought was haunted, and turned it into a hotel called **The Inn of the Eighth Happiness**. Since Jincheng was an overnight stop for mule caravans, the women would earn a living by offering the muleteers good food and a clean bed for the night at a fair price. As their guests ate their meals, the women told them stories from the Gospels about Jesus Christ. At first the muleteers distrusted the two women as foreigners and were not disposed to listen to them. However, in time they came to trust them, listened to their stories, and some became Christians.

Then tragedy struck. Mrs Lawson was seriously injured in a fall and died soon afterwards. With

After a month-long journey to China from England, Gladys Aylward had to travel by mule for a further 2 days to reach Jincheng, where Mrs Lawson lived.

Communities of Faith   SECTION A

the help of her Chinese cook, who had become a Christian, Aylward decided to continue her work. However she was on a financial knife-edge and just barely keeping the inn open. She wondered how much longer she could keep this up.

Then the **mandarin** of Jincheng came to see her.

Did You Know?

Mandarin was the title given to a town governor in China. He also served as the judge in the local law court.

The mandarin asked Aylward to work with him. The government had outlawed the practice of foot-binding. For centuries it had been the custom that a female's feet should be tightly wrapped in bandages from infancy, to prevent them from growing fully. Many Chinese men considered small feet attractive. However, women's foot-binding often led to deformities and crippling disabilities. Knowing the harm caused by this practice, Aylward agreed to act as his inspector. She travelled around the neighbouring villages enforcing the law. She also had the mandarin's permission **to preach** about Christianity as she did so.

> **REMEMBER!**
> **To preach** means to explain or to spread ideas.

In the days that followed, Aylward was successful because she won the local people's trust. Like them, she lived a simple life, wore the same kind of clothing, ate the same kind of food, spoke the same language and felt completely at ease in their company. Indeed, she so identified with them that in 1936 she decided to become a Chinese citizen. However, she never lost sight of her role as a missionary and succeeded in attracting a small but ever-growing number of converts to Christianity.

> **REMEMBER!**
> **A convert** is someone who chooses to join a religion.

It was at this time that the prison riot occurred. As we read earlier, Aylward persuaded the prisoners to put down their weapons, brought a swift end to the violence and negotiated better conditions for them. Afterwards, she regularly visited the prison to ensure that both sides were keeping their word. She also won some converts among the prisoners. One of these had been the leader of the rioters, a man named Feng, while another was the prison warden himself.

Soon after the riot, a chance encounter set Aylward's life on a new course. She saw a woman begging by the roadside, accompanied by a sick and undernourished five-year-old girl. The woman did not want the child and offered to sell her. Horrified by this attitude and worried about the child's safety, Aylward gave the woman what little money she had and took the little girl into her home. She named the child **Mei-en** (meaning 'Beautiful Grace'). She would be the first of one hundred unwanted children that Aylward would rescue from being abandoned or sold. All would find a loving home at The Inn of the Eighth Happiness.

Then in 1937 Japan declared war on China. Aylward offered her home as a place for wounded soldiers to recuperate. She helped care for between thirty and forty of them at a time, in addition to her other responsibilities.

Jincheng was thought of as too out of the way for the Japanese to attack it. However, in the spring of 1938, Japanese warplanes bombed the town, killing many inhabitants. As Aylward helped organise care for the wounded, word reached her that Japanese troops were on their way to kill anyone who had survived. She was also warned that the Japanese knew about her and had put a price on her head. The mandarin urged her to leave. Then he gathered the townspeople and told them to take refuge in mountain caves until the Japanese had left.

But what should be done to protect the nearly one hundred orphans, some of whom were mere infants, living with her at The Inn of the Eighth Happiness? Aylward was worried that the Japanese might decide to permanently occupy the town. If so, the children would starve in the mountains. She decided that the best thing to do was to take them to a place that was at a safe distance from the fighting. This meant taking the children on a journey of nearly 240 miles to the refugee centre at Xian, in the neighbouring province of Shaanxi.

LIGHT THE WAY

However, unable to use the roads or any motor transport, Aylward would have to lead them on foot over mountain ranges and somehow get them across the Yellow River.

One matter remained to be settled before she set out – what to do with the men still being held at the local prison. The traditional policy was to behead them all. The mandarin and prison warden asked Aylward for advice. She was horrified by the idea of mass executions. So she suggested that the prisoners' families should be responsible for them. This was accepted. All but one prisoner returned to their families. This was Feng, the leader of the riot, whom Aylward had befriended and who had become a Christian. He would be a great help to her on the long march to safety.

Walking at a pace the children could maintain meant that it took twelve days to cross the mountains. At one point Aylward narrowly escaped death when, scouting ahead of the children, she was fired on by Japanese troops. A bullet grazed her back but she was not seriously wounded. Despite several other such close-calls, she reached the Yellow River without losing a single child, though all were cold, exhausted and hungry. Then they faced another obstacle – all boats had been commandeered for military use. However, Aylward told their story to a sympathetic Chinese army officer and he organised a boat to take them across the wide river to safety.

A few days later, Aylward delivered the children safely to the refugee centre at Xian. There she promptly collapsed and remained in a semi-coma for several weeks. Doctors were amazed that she had managed to complete such a journey, as she had a temperature of 105 degrees and was suffering from typhus, pneumonia, malnutrition

When the Japanese attacked Jincheng in 1938, Gladys took the children on a 240-mile journey by foot to the refugee centre in Xian.

and complete exhaustion. At one stage she hovered close to death and had to remain in hospital for two months.

After she had recovered her strength, Aylward made sure that all the children were adopted by willing families. Then she started a Christian church in Xian and continued her work, caring for refugee children. She also opened a centre to care for people crippled by leprosy.

In 1947 Aylward returned to England for some badly needed rest. To her surprise she had become famous. Books were written about her exploits and even a Hollywood movie was made about her life. A modest person, Aylward did not enjoy all this media exposure. She decided to return to China but found that the new Communist regime would not allow her to go there. So she made her new home on the island of Taiwan, where many Chinese refugees fleeing the Communists had settled. She used her fame to obtain funds to open an orphanage and it soon filled with children, whom she happily cared for.

Gladys Aylward died peacefully in her sleep on 3 January 1970. Her work was continued by her friend and assistant, Kathleen Langton-Smith. Her body was buried in a marble tomb on a hill in the garden of Christ's College at Teipei, the capital of Taiwan.

In a letter to a friend, Gladys Aylward once referred to herself as someone who was '**insignificant and ordinary in every way**'. Yet her life was far from being either insignificant or ordinary. She had changed the lives of so many people for the better. Her Chinese friends had long ago acknowledged her goodness by calling her **Ai-weh-deh**, '**the Virtuous One**'.

The Meaning of Vocation

Read any interview with someone who is deeply committed to the kind of work Gladys Aylward did, such as:

- Caring for and protecting abandoned children
- Comforting the sick
- Giving shelter to the homeless
- Spreading a religion.

You will notice that they all have the same thing in common: a belief that this is something they were **called** to do. They will all say that they have **a vocation** for such work.

> **REMEMBER!**
> **A vocation** is a calling to do something worthwhile with your life.

Did You Know?

In the Catholic, Anglican and Orthodox traditions, you can fulfil your vocation in any of the following ways:

- as a single lay person
- as a married person
- as a bishop or a priest
- as a member of a religious order.

However, these vocations are of **equal** importance. No one vocation is superior to the other.

Regarding who can be ordained:

- The Catholic and Orthodox traditions do **not** ordain women to the priesthood. Both follow the traditional practice of accepting only men as candidates for the priesthood.
- The Anglican Communion ordains both men and women to the priesthood.
- Among Protestants, the following denominations have both male and female ministers: Baptists, Methodists and Presbyterians.

LIGHT THE WAY

ACTIVITIES

1. Say what it means!

(a) To discern means _____
   _____.

(b) Virtuous means _____
   _____.

(c) A vocation is _____
   _____.

2. Crossword

Across

2. The title given to a town governor in China.
6. The hotel where Aylward made her home and provided food and accommodation to the muleteers was called The Inn of the Eighth _____.
8. The name of the elderly widow who was looking for someone to carry on her work in China (2 words: 6, 6).
9. The name of the city in the mountainous province of Shansi where Aylward made her home for most of the 1930s.
10. A violent event that broke out among the prisoners.
13. The meaning of the Chinese name Ai-weh-deh (2 words: 8, 3).
14. He asked Gladys Aylward to end the violence in the prison.

96

Communities of Faith   **SECTION A**

Down

1. It means to explain or to spread ideas.
2. Someone who wants to convince others to become members of his/her religion.
3. Aylward was employed to enforce the laws against this harmful practice for women (2 words: 4, 7).
4. Gladys Aylward worked at this job to earn the money to travel to China.
5. The meaning of the Chinese name Mei-en (2 words: 9, 5).
7. Someone who chooses to join a religion.
11. The island where Aylward spent her final years caring for orphans.
12. The city in the Shaanxi province where Aylward led a hundred orphaned children to safety.

3. Think about it!

Do you think Gladys Aylward deserved to be called 'the Virtuous One'? Give reasons based on incidents in her life to support your answer.

CHAPTER 11   SECTARIANISM

The Destructive Power of Sectarianism

It is just past 2 a.m. Your home is in darkness. Everyone else is asleep. However, you are restless and cannot sleep. So, you quietly make your way downstairs to the kitchen to get yourself a glass of water.

Suddenly, a rock comes crashing through the glass panel beside your front door. It is followed by a petrol bomb. You have just enough time to find cover before it explodes.

The flames prevent you from going back upstairs. You can only shout warnings to the rest of your family. Fortunately, they hear you.

You escape through the back door. Your parents escape through a bedroom window. You all stand shocked but unharmed on the lawn at the back of your house.

You are forced to watch in horror as your home is totally consumed by the flames. You have lost everything in the fire.

For a few weeks afterwards you have to stay with relatives. Your insurance company assures you that it will pay the cost of rebuilding your home. You are grateful that no lives were lost. However, your peace of mind is shattered.

The police tell you that you were most likely targeted by someone who had never even spoken a single word to you. You and your family were chosen for this attack because the perpetrator (i.e. the one who did it) hates you for being who you are. This was reason enough for someone to try to burn you and your family to death.

This kind of violence is often the result of **sectarianism**.

REMEMBER!
Sectarianism is a hostile attitude towards anyone who does not share your beliefs or way of life.

Just imagine a place where people of different races, religions or politics do not talk to one another or mix in any way with one another. You know what will happen. Very quickly people begin to distrust one another. A mindset grows that divides people into '**them**' and '**us**'. Each side responds to any situation out of **prejudice**.

REMEMBER!
Prejudice means making up your mind before finding out the facts. It can also mean ignoring the facts altogether because it does not suit you to face the truth.

Wherever sectarianism thrives, rival groups form, with each side ready to take offence at the slightest incident. A tense situation easily turns into a violent confrontation. In this way, sectarianism gradually comes to dominate people's lives.

Sectarianism is always destructive. It has caused great misery in places as far apart as Afghanistan, Bosnia, Burma, Chechnya, Indonesia, Iraq, Nigeria, Northern Ireland, Somalia and Ukraine. Usually in sectarian conflicts the following things occur:

- People are murdered because they belong to a particular political, racial, religious or social group.

- People are forced off their land and have their property confiscated. They are intimidated in their workplaces and forced out of their jobs.
- People's homes, places of worship and schools are burned down to force them to leave a particular area.

The Need for Inter-Faith Dialogue

Certainly religious differences are one source of sectarianism and the violence that it can unleash. However a closer look reveals that this issue is more complex than it seems at first glance.

It is true that religion has often played a role in all sorts of conflict throughout human history. We cannot avoid the fact that in the hands of the wrong people, religion has been used to do great harm. Down through the centuries, such people have claimed it is right to:

- Persecute those whose beliefs differ from yours.
- Take part in so-called 'holy wars'.
- Support slavery and torture.

Often they do this despite knowing that such behaviour is **against** the teachings of their own religion.

It has been said that most of the wars in history have been caused by religious differences. But this is not true. In fact, the vast majority of wars have been fought for reasons that have nothing to do with religion. Think about it.

Why do people fight one another? Generally speaking, people kill for profit or power, to gain control over land and natural resources, to have their revenge or because they despise anyone who is in any way different from themselves. In these situations, religious differences are just one more ingredient to be thrown into a toxic mixture of anger, fear and hatred. Indeed, recent history, especially the horrors of the two world wars, has shown that people certainly do not need God as an excuse to do terrible things to one another.

All too often religion merely provides a useful cover for wicked individuals to hide their true motives. However, as people like Gladys Aylward and Eric Liddell have shown, religious belief can be an enormous force for good. It can inspire people to try to make the world a better place.

In the end, the ways in which some individuals have twisted religion to suit their own wicked ambitions really says more about human nature than it does about religion. This is why the Hindu holy man Mohandas Gandhi once remarked:

'The terrible crimes of history are the fault not of religion, but of the ungovernable brute in human beings.'

So, how should people of different religious faiths relate to one another? After all, each religion has its own beliefs and practices. That is not going to change. There will always be disagreements between them. As these differences have led to misunderstandings and given rise to unnecessary tensions in the past, there is a need to prevent them becoming a source of conflict in the future.

Today most leading religious figures agree with this. They want to avoid a situation where religious differences contribute to sectarian tension and violence. They want to live in a world where people of different faiths can live side by side in peace. This is why there is now such a great interest in **inter-faith dialogue**.

LIGHT THE WAY

> **REMEMBER!**
> **Inter-faith dialogue** is where the members of different religions meet to talk and exchange ideas with one another.

Encouraging Tolerance, Building Friendship

Chiara Lubich received The Unesco prize for Peace Education in 1996.

Chiara Lubich (1920–2008) was a Catholic lay woman. She worked as a school teacher in Italy before founding **Focolare** in the aftermath of World War II.

Did You Know?

Focolare means **'the family fireside'**. It is a worldwide organisation with two million members that works for greater friendship and understanding between people of all religious affiliations and none.

Lubich was convinced that everything possible should be done to prevent religious differences contributing to the outbreak of war. She drew her inspiration from Jesus Christ's prayer **'that they may all be one'** (John 17:21).

At first Lubich worked for greater unity among the different Christian traditions – Catholic, Anglican, Orthodox and Protestant. However, in time, she began to extend the hand of friendship to non-Christians too.

Lubich believed that all people of goodwill – whatever their religious affiliation – are united by a shared acceptance of **the Golden Rule**.

> **REMEMBER!**
> **The Golden Rule** says that you should always treat others as you would want them to treat you.

Lubich had no illusions that achieving a genuine dialogue would demand great patience and perseverance. She had to begin by breaking down long-standing barriers. However she believed that this common ground of commitment to the Golden Rule could serve as a starting point for dialogue between the members of the different world religions.

Lubich understood that inter-faith dialogue is **not** about trying **to convert** (i.e. to win over) people from one religion to another. Rather, **the purpose of inter-faith dialogue** is to break down the walls created by ignorance and mistrust. Only then can people come to understand one another, accept their differences, respect one another and live in peace.

Further, inter-faith dialogue is **not** an attempt to create some kind of 'world religion'. Chiara Lubich was a devout Catholic. She never wanted anyone to compromise their deeply held religious beliefs. However she saw a great potential for good if people of different faiths could meet and work together to solve shared problems.

Participants at the Genfest International Youth Meeting, organised by Focolare, gather in Budapest, 2012

100

Communities of Faith   SECTION A

Though rooted in Christianity, Focolare now includes members of many non-Christian faiths. The movement is united by the belief that, despite their differences, people of all faiths and none can work together to build a better world.

Today, Focolare continues the work begun by Chiara Lubich. Its members are actively involved in inter-faith events in 182 countries across the globe. The key to this inter-faith dialogue is tolerance.

Without tolerance, no worthwhile relationship can exist between people who hold different beliefs.

> **REMEMBER!**
> **Tolerance** means respecting the beliefs of others, even though you do not share them yourself.

Reaching Across the Divide

It is not unusual to turn on the evening news and see important political leaders – presidents and prime ministers – meeting with one another. Such events are often very useful. These face-to-face encounters can help world leaders. Think about the following:

- These leaders are encouraged to trust one another.
- Such meetings provide an opportunity for them to settle disputes peacefully.
- They can also help them to find ways to cooperate on areas of common interest.

These are the very same reasons why the leaders of the world's religions meet with one another to engage in dialogue. Their meetings can produce important benefits, such as:

- Increasing understanding and building friendships where before there was fear and mistrust between people of different faiths.
- Reducing tensions and helping to find peaceful solutions to disagreements that might otherwise encourage sectarianism and lead to conflict.
- Encouraging people of different faiths to work together on matters of common interest, such as ending wars, combating poverty and protecting the environment.

On several occasions since October 1986, the leaders of different religions – Christian and non-Christian – have come together for a day of prayer for peace. These meetings are held in the town of Assisi in Italy.

Assisi was chosen because it was the birthplace of **St Francis** (1182–1226). He wrote a prayer that has become the model to follow for all those who take part in inter-faith dialogue.

The Prayer of St Francis

Lord, make me an instrument of your peace.

Where there is hatred, let me sow love; Where there is injury, pardon;

Where there is doubt, faith; Where there is despair, hope;

Where there is darkness, light; Where there is sadness, joy.

O Divine Master, grant that I may not so much seek to be consoled, as to console;

Not so much to be understood as to understand;

Not so much to be loved as to love; For it is in giving that we receive;

It is in pardoning that we are pardoned; It is in dying that we are born to eternal life.

LIGHT THE WAY

At their 2002 meeting, representatives of the different religions agreed to the **Decalogue of Assisi for Peace**.

The first gathering at Assisi was hosted by **St John Paul II** (1920–2005). As pope, he was deeply committed to building bridges of understanding between the Catholic Church and other religions. In 2000, he visited Israel, where his heartfelt apology for centuries of Christian persecution of the Jews opened the way to a new era of respect and cooperation between Catholics and Jews. In 2006, his successor Benedict XVI (1927–) made the first official visit by a pope to a Muslim country, Turkey. Two years later he hosted the first joint gathering of Catholic and Muslim scholars at the Vatican to discuss ways of improving relations between their different faiths.

Did You Know?

The **Decalogue of Assisi for Peace** is a commitment to never again let religious differences be used as an excuse for violence.

Did You Know?

Sometimes, people are worried that inter-faith dialogue will in some way weaken their commitment to their own faith. However, this need not be the case. The whole idea of inter-faith dialogue is to develop in people the capacity to recognise and respect what is good and true in each other's beliefs. This does not mean that people should be any less committed to the teachings of their own religion.

Pope Benedict XVI visits the Blue Mosque in Istanbul. The pope, in an exceptional gesture, turned towards Makkah for a moment of meditation.

ACTIVITIES

1. **Wordsearch**

   Find the following words:

   Sectarianism
   Dialogue
   Tolerance
   Slavery
   Dominate
   Perpetrator
   Chiara Lubich
   Cooperate
   Politics
   Persecute
   Prejudice
   Holy war
   Gandhi
   Saint Francis
   Race
   Convert
   Violence
   Peace

H	B	P	Y	M	I	J	O	D	S	R	O	A	A	T
S	C	S	E	H	W	S	P	C	I	T	M	R	C	R
P	A	I	D	R	L	H	O	D	C	H	O	S	T	E
W	D	N	B	A	S	O	C	E	N	T	B	C	O	V
R	A	I	V	U	P	E	C	V	A	H	Y	I	L	N
G	A	E	A	E	L	N	C	R	R	J	O	T	E	O
M	R	C	R	L	E	A	T	U	F	J	K	I	R	C
Y	W	A	E	L	O	E	R	T	T	M	P	L	A	H
X	T	R	O	P	P	G	T	A	N	E	D	O	N	O
E	L	I	P	R	E	J	U	D	I	C	E	P	C	L
F	V	P	E	A	C	E	I	E	A	H	L	P	E	Y
V	M	P	B	U	N	X	K	Z	S	J	C	F	J	W
N	O	I	G	I	L	E	R	U	T	R	O	T	Y	A
M	S	I	N	A	I	R	A	T	C	E	S	I	G	R
R	Q	H	E	S	L	M	D	O	M	I	N	A	T	E

102

Communities of Faith   SECTION A

2. Say what it means!

(a) Sectarianism is _____

_____ .

(b) Prejudice means _____

_____

_____ .

(c) Inter-faith dialogue is _____

_____

_____ .

(d) The Golden Rule says _____

_____ .

(e) Tolerance means _____

_____ .

(f) The Decalogue of Assisi for Peace is _____

_____ .

3. Fill in the missing words!

Chiara Lubich (1920–2008) was a C _____ lay woman. She founded F _____ in the aftermath of World War II.

Lubich was convinced that everything possible should be done to prevent religious d _____ contributing to the o _____ of war. She drew her i _____ from Jesus Christ's prayer '**that they may all be one**' (John 17:21).

At first, Lubich worked for greater u_____ among the different Christian t _____. However, in time, she began to extend the hand of friendship to n _____ too.

Lubich believed that all people of g _____ are united by a shared a _____ of the Golden Rule.

Lubich believed that this c _____ g _____ of commitment to the Golden Rule could serve as a starting point for d _____ between the members of the different world religions.

Lubich understood that inter-faith dialogue is not about trying to c _____ people from one religion to another. Rather, its purpose is to break down the walls created by i _____ and m _____. Only then can people of different religions live in p _____.

Focolare is a movement u _____ by the belief that people of a _____ faiths can w _____ together to build a b _____ world.

4. Think about it!

(a) What is the danger of people developing a 'them' and 'us' mindset?

(b) Identify three things that happen in sectarian conflicts.

(c) '**Most of the wars in history have been caused by religious differences**.' Do you agree or disagree with this statement? Give reasons for your answer.

(d) '**Inter-faith dialogue is not about converting people from one religion to another**.' What do you think is the purpose of inter-faith dialogue?

LIGHT THE WAY

The Meaning of Ecumenism

It is not only differences between people of different religions that has led to conflict. This has also happened between people of the **same** religion. This is because each world religion has different traditions within it. Here we will look at efforts to improve relations between the different **Christian** traditions.

> REMEMBER!
> There are four Christian traditions: Catholic, Orthodox, Anglican and Protestant.
> All are called 'Christian' because they accept three essential teachings:
> - **The Trinity** – The belief that there are three divine persons in the one God.
> - **The Incarnation** – The belief that Jesus Christ is God made man.
> - **The Resurrection** – The belief that Jesus died on the cross and rose from the dead to a new and glorious life.

By the early 1900s, the divisions among Christians had become a matter of great concern to missionaries who were working in Africa and Asia. It was becoming a source of confusion for those whom they were trying to convince to become Christians.

In 1910, the World Missionary Conference was held in Edinburgh, Scotland. It brought together Anglicans and Protestants. They were concerned about the harm being done by poor relations between the rival Christian traditions. Their wish to improve these relations led to **ecumenism**.

> REMEMBER!
> **Ecumenism** refers to any project or event that brings Christians of the different traditions together to encourage greater understanding and promote unity among them.

The Aims of Ecumenism

At first some Christians treated the whole idea of ecumenism with suspicion. They thought that its aim was to do away with all the things that distinguish one Christian tradition from another. They feared that it would try to make everyone the same.

In time most Christians came to realise that this was not the case. They gradually understood that the aim of ecumenism is to encourage tolerance, understanding, respect and cooperation between the different Christian traditions. This can be achieved – at both local and international levels – when the members of the different Christian traditions:

- Pray together whenever and wherever possible.
- Work together to tackle important social issues such as:
  - Caring for the needs of terminally ill patients.
  - Providing for the needs of the disabled.
  - Helping the poor and disadvantaged.
- Meet to discuss the issues that divide them, such as:
  - The meaning of the Eucharist.
  - How the Christian community should be led.
  - The role women should play.

Communities of Faith   SECTION A

The World Council of Churches

The terrible experiences of the two world wars convinced many Christians that the time had come to let go of long-held prejudices and to extend the hand of friendship to the members of traditions other than their own. So, in 1948, representatives of the Anglican Communion and several Protestant churches met to set up **the World Council of Churches** (the **WCC**).

Young people at the WCC 10th Assembly in Busan, South Korea, 2013.

> **REMEMBER!**
> **The WCC** is a fellowship of independent Christian churches. It does not exert any control over the internal decision-making of any of these churches.

The **WCC** chose the city of Geneva in Switzerland for its headquarters because Switzerland is a neutral country and many other organisations (such as the World Health Organisation) have their headquarters there.

The **WCC** holds a general assembly every six years. This is attended by delegates who represent over 700 million Christians. They discuss issues of common concern, such as:

- war
- poverty
- the plight of refugees
- human trafficking
- child labour
- pornography
- the arms trade
- climate change
- the implications of recent advances in technology.

The **WCC** aims to encourage Christians of different traditions to live up to the words spoken by Jesus at the Last Supper:

> *'Father, may they all be one. As you Father are in me and I am in you, may they be one in us, so that the world may believe that you have sent me.'*
>
> John 17:21

At first, neither the Catholic nor the Orthodox traditions took part in the **WCC**. However the Orthodox became full members in 1961. While the Catholic Church has not yet become a member, it sends observers to the meetings of the **WCC** and cooperates with it on joint projects in the developing world, e.g. famine relief.

105

LIGHT THE WAY

The Secretariat for the promotion of Christian Unity is based in the Vatican, Rome.

Did You Know?

- In 1961, the Catholic Church set up the Secretariat for the Promotion of Christian Unity. It is based in the Vatican, Rome.
- In 1964, the Catholic pope and the Orthodox patriarch of Constantinople met and began a dialogue that has greatly improved relations and increased mutual understanding between these two Christian traditions.
- In 1969, the Catholic and Anglican traditions set up a joint commission to discuss a wide range of issues and clarify where each stands on them.

Christian Unity Week

Christian Unity Week is a time when:

- Christians are asked to pray for an end to the divisions within the worldwide Christian community.
- Christians are encouraged to develop a deeper understanding and greater respect for one another's point of view.

Christian Unity Week was first held in 1908. It was the idea of **Paul Wattson (1863–1940)**. He was an Episcopalian (Anglican) priest living at Graymoor, Garrison, New York. He chose to run it from 18 to 25 of January because:

- 18 January marked the feast of the Chair of St Peter
- 25 January marked the feast of the conversion of St Paul.

Reverend Wattson thought that it would be most appropriate to hold a week of prayer for Christian unity between the feasts celebrating the lives of two of Christianity's greatest saints.

To mark Christian Unity Week, parishes are encouraged to organise **ecumenical services**.

Usually, an ecumenical service consists of:

- Prayers
- Music and hymns
- Readings from the Bible
- A homily (i.e. sermon) on the theme of Christian unity.

Did You Know?

An **ecumenical service** is a joint act of worship involving members of the different Christian traditions.

106

That Little Springtime

Taizé is the name of a village that stands on a hill in Burgundy in central France. The village is surrounded by meadows, vineyards and woods. Here you can find the Taizé community. This is **an ecumenical monastic community**.

> **Did You Know?**
>
> **An ecumenical monastic community** is one where its members are drawn from the different Christian traditions.

The Taizé community was founded in 1940 by **Roger Louis Schutz-Marsauche** (1915–2005). The son of a Protestant minister, Roger grew up in Switzerland in the period between the two world wars. After completing his university education, Roger believed that he had a vocation to the monastic life. However, he fell ill with tuberculosis and so was unable to act immediately on his calling.

By the time Roger's health had recovered, World War II had begun in Europe. After reading accounts of the terrible chaos caused by the war, Roger felt he had to do something to help. Inspired by the example of his grandmother who had cared for refugees in World War I, Roger decided to do the same. He left the safety of neutral Switzerland and went to live in war-torn France. The country had been defeated and occupied by Nazi Germany in June 1940. Huge numbers of people had been forced out of their homes and had become refugees seeking shelter.

With a loan obtained from some friends, Roger bought a disused house and outbuildings in the village of Taizé, near the city of Lyons. He renovated them and began to shelter people left homeless by the war. Shortly afterwards, Roger's sister **Genevieve** arrived at Taizé to help him care for the refugees.

By the summer of 1942, Roger and Genevieve Schutz had attracted the unwanted attention of **the Gestapo** (the Nazi secret police). This was because they had been hiding Jewish refugees. However, thanks to a timely warning from a helpful local policeman, the brother and sister escaped arrest and went into hiding. It was not until the summer of 1944 that they could return to Taizé. By then, France had been liberated by the Allies.

However, now Roger and Genevieve Schutz were asked to do more than help refugees. They were asked to look after some of the many children left orphaned by the fighting.

Word of what was happening at Taizé soon spread. Several friends of Roger's were looking to do something more meaningful with their lives. They offered to join him and set up a monastic community.

On Easter Sunday 1949, the first group of brothers committed themselves by taking life-long vows of poverty, chastity and obedience. Roger Schutz became the first **prior** (i.e. leader of the community). From this point on he was simply referred to as '**Brother Roger**'.

Brother Roger in the Philippines.

Brother Roger drew up a rule for their community which said that all members must practise:

- Simplicity of life
- Celibacy
- Accepting the decisions of the community as expressed by the prior.

At first, all the brothers were drawn from different dominations within the Protestant tradition (e.g. Methodist, Presbyterian, etc.). In time, however, members of the Catholic and Anglican traditions also joined the Taizé community.

Brother Roger once admitted that he was surprised by the numbers who wanted to join

LIGHT THE WAY

their community. The monastery never actively recruited or advertised itself. However, a small but steady number were attracted by the opportunity to be a part of a welcoming community based on love and forgiveness.

In 1962, a new church was built at Taizé to meet the demands of the growing community and the expanding numbers of visitors from all Christian traditions. The church was built by volunteers, mostly from Germany. More than 100,000 people come to pray there each year.

Today, the ecumenical community of Taizé has about 100 members. These brothers are drawn from three different Christian traditions and come from more than thirty countries.

The brothers live simple lives. Following the ancient monastic tradition, the whole focus of each day is on prayer: the brothers come together to pray three times each day: morning, noon and evening. They dress as laymen but wear white hooded robes when in church.

The brothers do not accept donations. If a brother inherits something from his family, it is given up to the community to be sold to help the poor. The brothers earn their living making pottery and simple jewellery.

The brothers say that they want to show how peace and unity can come into people's lives through faith in Jesus Christ. They try to set an example for others to follow.

Brother Roger was a musician. He encouraged a unique style of worship that involves the repeated singing/chanting of short phrases from **the Psalms** (i.e. poems found in the Old Testament). This repetition is intended to help people **meditate**.

> **REMEMBER!**
> **To meditate** means to silently reflect on the meaning of something.

The music to which the Psalms are set was composed by the French musician **Jacques Berthier**, whom Brother Roger befriended in 1955.

The prayer services at Taizé are held by candlelight to create a calm, peaceful atmosphere in which to pray. The international flavour of the Taizé community is emphasised by the use of different languages in worship.

Icons, widely used by Orthodox Christians, are prominently displayed during worship at Taizé.

> **REMEMBER!**
> **An icon** is a richly decorated religious image painted on a wooden board.

Icons are thought to help people to meditate on the important teachings of the Christian religion.

Did You Know?

The brothers of Taizé have never tried to isolate themselves from the problems of the world outside the walls of their community. As early as 1962, they began to move out to establish other small **fraternities** (i.e. communities of brothers). These were set up in **deprived areas**, i.e. places where people suffer from the effects of poverty and division.

They help some of the most oppressed and poorest people on earth.

Since the late 1950s, the Taizé community has become an important place of pilgrimage for young Christians of all traditions. Each year, from early spring to late autumn, up to 5,000 young men and women, aged between seventeen and thirty, arrive in Taizé. They come from every corner of the globe to attend one of the week-long international youth meetings.

While in Taizé, these young people share in the simple lifestyle of the monks. They usually bring their own sleeping bags and camp in the fields around the monastery.

The schedule of a typical day includes:

- morning prayer
- breakfast
- group Bible study led by one of the brothers
- small group discussions where people share their own life experiences and insights in an atmosphere of openness and respect

Communities of Faith   SECTION A

- noon prayer
- lunch
- optional hymn practice
- practical tasks
- workshops
- dinner
- evening prayer.

© Ateliers et Presses de Taizé

The Taizé community is an important place of pilgrimage for young Christians of all traditions.

Prayer is the most important part of daily life. The aim of all this is to offer young adults an opportunity to reflect on their lives and to explore or rediscover their Christian faith. It is hoped that after their stay, people will try to live out what they have discovered in their own communities.

All who go to Taizé are reminded of the words of Brother Roger:

'It is not only the leaders of nations who build the world of tomorrow. The most humble and obscure of people can play a part in bringing about a future of peace and trust.'

Tragically, Brother Roger was stabbed to death by a mentally unbalanced woman at Taizé on 16 August 2005. His death shocked people of all religions around the world. He was succeeded as prior by Brother Alois, who is a German Catholic.

The community at Taizé remains dedicated to continuing Brother Roger's mission. They work tirelessly to help Christians of different traditions to understand and trust one another. It is because it is a place of peace and hope that St John XXIII once described Taizé as **'that little springtime in the Church'**.

ACTIVITIES

1. Say what it means!

(a) Ecumenism refers to _____

_____

_____ .

(b) The World Council of Churches is _____

_____

_____ .

(c) An ecumenical monastic community is _____

_____

_____ .

LIGHT THE WAY

2. Crossword

Across

2. The belief that there are three divine persons in the one God.
4. To reflect silently on the meaning of something.
7. This Christian tradition joined the WCC in 1961.
8. The World _____ of Churches is a fellowship of independent Christian churches set up in 1948.
10. 18 January marks the feast of this saint.
12. 25 January marks the feast of this saint.
15. A joint act of worship involving members of the different Christian traditions is called an _____ service.

Down

1. The WCC chose this city as the location for its headquarters.
3. The belief that Jesus died on the cross and rose from the dead to a new and glorious life.
5. The name given to a richly decorated religious image painted on a wooden board.
6. Paul _____ was an Episcopalian priest who had the idea of holding Christian unity week.
9. This Christian tradition has not yet become a member of the WCC, but it sends observers to its meetings.
11. The belief that Jesus Christ is God made man.
13. Jacques _____ was a French musician who set the Psalms to music for the Taizé community.
14. The World _____ Conference was held in Edinburgh, Scotland in 1910.

Communities of Faith   SECTION A

3. Fill in the missing words!

Taizé is the name of **an ecumenical m _____ community**. It was f _____ in 19 _____ by Roger Schutz-Marsauche.

After reading accounts of the terrible chaos caused by World War II, Roger felt he had to do something to h _____ and left his home in neutral S _____. He went to live in war-torn F _____.

Roger bought a disused house in Taizé, near the city of L _____. He renovated it and began to shelter people left h _____ by the war and, later on, children left o _____ by the fighting. His sister G _____ joined him to share in this work.

After much discussion, Roger decided to set up a m _____ community.

According to his r _____ all members of this community must practise:

- ■ S _____ of life.
- ■ C _____.
- ■ Accepting the d _____ of the community as expressd by the p _____.

Roger was elected the first p _____. From this point on he was simply referred to as 'B _____ R _____'.

At first, all the brothers were drawn from the P _____ tradition. In time, however, members of the C _____ and A _____ traditions also joined the Taizé community.

Today, the Taizé community has over a h _____ members. These brothers come from more than t _____ different countries.

The brothers live s _____ lives. The whole focus of each day is on p _____. They dress as laymen but wear w _____ h _____ r _____ when in church.

The brothers say that they want to show how peace and unity can come into people's lives through faith in J _____ C _____. They try to set an e _____ for others to follow.

The prayer services at Taizé are held by c _____ to create a calm, peaceful a _____ in which to pray.

Icons are prominently displayed during w _____ at Taizé. They are thought to help people to m _____ on the important t _____ of the Christian religion.

Each year, up to 5,000 young people arrive in Taizé. While there, they s _____ in the simple l _____ of the monks. They camp in the f _____ around the monastery.

After his tragic death in 2005, Brother Roger was succeeded as prior by Brother A _____.

The community at Taizé works tirelessly to help Christians of different traditions u _____ and t _____ one another.

111

LIGHT THE WAY

4. Think about it!

Produce an advertisement encouraging young people to visit Taizé. Be sure to include the following:
- A brief statement of what this community does
- The story of its founder
- The life of a brother
- What happens during a typical international youth meeting
- Illustrations of some or all of these features.

Section B

Foundations of Religion - Christianity

Chapter 1:	Daily Life in the Time of Jesus	114
Chapter 2:	Under Roman Rule	122
Chapter 3:	How We Know About Jesus	133
Chapter 4:	The Early Life of Jesus	144
Chapter 5:	The Public Ministry of Jesus	150
Chapter 6:	The Teachings of Jesus	158
Chapter 7:	The Miracles of Jesus	165
Chapter 8:	Conflict with Authority	172
Chapter 9:	The Passion and Death of Jesus	181
Chapter 10:	The Resurrection of Jesus	189
Chapter 11:	The Early Christians	196

LIGHT THE WAY

CHAPTER 1   DAILY LIFE IN THE TIME OF JESUS

The Holy Land

Before you begin studying the life of **Jesus Christ**, you need to learn about the time and place in which it happened. Thanks to the hard work of generations of archaeologists, we now have a detailed and reliable picture of what life was like in the time of Jesus.

Did You Know?

The land in which Jesus was born has had many names down through the centuries:

- In the time of Abraham, it was called **the Land of Canaan**.
- In the time of Moses, it was called **the Promised Land**.
- In the time of Jesus, it was called **Palestine** – a name taken from an ancient people who had once lived there.
- Today, it is called **Israel**, which can mean either 'Wrestles with God' or 'Ruled by God'.
- Since medieval times, Christians have called this area **the Holy Land**. This is because it was the place where the story of Jesus Christ unfolded.

In the time of Jesus, most of the Holy Land's population was Jewish. These were descendants of people who had first settled there around 1900 BCE.

Village and City Life

In the 1st century CE, most Jews lived in small towns and villages dotted across the landscape. Typically a town or village consisted of a few dozen houses and workshops. Usually these buildings were concentrated around a spring or well that provided the inhabitants with water. The most important building in every town or village was the local **synagogue**.

REMEMBER!
A synagogue is a Jewish place of worship. The name means 'a gathering of people'. Jews attended the synagogue to pray and to study **the Tanakh**.

Compared to the large and impressive Roman-built seaport city of Caesarea, Jewish-built cities were small by our standards. The average main street would not have stretched further than 200 metres. There was very little planning involved. A typical Jewish city was just a maze of houses, workshops and courtyards. Markets were held in an area just outside the city gates.

REMEMBER!
The Tanakh is Judaism's sacred text.

Most inhabitants of a Jewish city or town worked on nearby farms. They went out each morning to work in the fields and returned home each evening at dusk. The city/town gates were then closed behind them and sentries took turns standing guard throughout the night.

Jerusalem was the Holy Land's capital city. It was unique in having a large, paved open area within its walls known as **the Xystus**. This was located just below **the Temple**, in the lower right-hand corner of an area called 'the Upper City'. This was the wealthiest neighbourhood in Jerusalem. Markets were held regularly in the Xystus and it was a popular meeting place for the well-to-do.

Foundations of Religion - Christianity   SECTION B

As you can see on this map, the Holy Land is hemmed in by the Mediterranean Sea on one side and the vast Arabian Desert on the other.

The Geography of the Holy Land

Very little has changed since the time of Jesus. Consider the following:

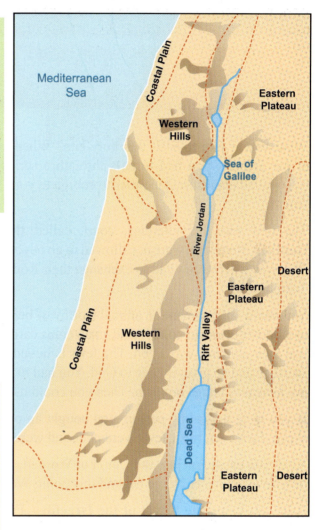

Size
The Holy Land measures:
- in length: approximately 230km
- in width: anywhere from 50km to 80km from its western coast to its eastern border.

Today, this entire area can be travelled easily from one end to the other by car in just a few hours. Indeed, a Jewish inhabitant 2,000 years ago could have walked the same distance in less than five days.

Climate
There are basically two seasons in the Holy Land:
- the hot, dry summer, which runs from May to September
- the cool, wet winter, which runs from October to April.

Landscape
The terrain falls into three almost parallel zones. From west to east, they are:
- the coastal plain
- the western hills
- the rift valley through which the Jordan River flows.

To the east of this lies a great plateau. Beyond this and to the south, there are vast expanses of scorching desert.

Land of contrasts
Although small in size, the Holy Land contains some remarkably diverse landscapes:
- The land around the Sea of Galilee in the north is generally green and fertile. This area remains home to many thriving farming and fishing communities.
- In contrast, the area around the Dead Sea in the south is a harsh wilderness with temperatures reaching 50 degrees centigrade.

115

LIGHT THE WAY

The Temple

Every Jew hoped to visit the Temple at least once a year. The busiest times at the Temple were during the great annual festivals, especially at **Pesach**.

> REMEMBER!
> **The Temple** was the Holy Land's most important place. It was the centre of Jewish religious life. It was where God was supposed to dwell. It was where the Jews offered **sacrifices** to God.
> **A sacrifice** is something valuable to you that you are willing to give up.

Jewish family celebrating Passover.

What was it like to visit this holy site? When you arrived at the Temple, you had to pass through a series of **courts** (i.e. walled enclosures) in order to complete your sacrifice to God.

Did You Know?

At **Pesach** or **Passover**, Jews celebrate the story of how God sent Moses to rescue their ancestors from slavery in Egypt and led them to freedom in the Promised Land.

The first was the outermost court, called **the Court of Gentiles**. Non-Jews were not allowed to go beyond this point. This was where Jews had to exchange their Roman coins for Temple coins.

You could not purchase an animal worthy of being sacrificed to God with Roman coins. All Roman coins carried an image of the Roman emperor. The Romans claimed that their emperor was a god. The Jews believed that if you used Roman coins it would 'contaminate' your sacrifice and so give offence to God. You had to exchange your Roman coins for Temple coins, as these did not have any image on them. Then you could use these Temple coins to buy an animal for sacrifice.

If you were a wealthy person, you bought an ox for sacrifice. Those who were less well-off purchased a sheep. However, most Jews were poor and were only able to afford a dove.

Next, you passed on into **the Court of Women**. Here women were expected to pray. A large sign stated that only Jewish men could go beyond this point. Women were forbidden to do so.

After this came **the Court of the Israelites**. From here, Jewish men were allowed to watch the Temple priests sacrificing their animals to God.

All animal sacrifices took place in **the Court of the Priests**. Only the priests could enter this part of the Temple. Sacrifices were carried out twice each day: in the morning and in the evening. The animals were killed and then burned on a large raised altar. While this happened, choirs sang from **the Psalms** (i.e. a book of poems found in the Tenakh).

The final part of the Temple was **the Holy of Holies**. This was a room located inside a large, square, windowless building that towered over the western end of the Court of Priests.

The Holy of Holies was sealed off from the rest of the Temple by a huge set of heavy curtains. Only **the High Priest** was allowed to enter the Holy of Holies. He could only do so once a year, at **Yom Kippur**. His role was to ask God to forgive all the sins the Jewish people had committed over the previous year.

> REMEMBER!
> **The High Priest** was the leader of the Jewish religion.
> **Yom Kippur** is the Jewish Day of Atonement, i.e. the day when Jews fast, pray and ask God to forgive their sins.

Foundations of Religion - Christianity SECTION B

There were two great Temples in the history of Judaism. The first was built by **Solomon** (961–922 BCE). This building was destroyed by an invading Babylonian army in 586 BCE. Construction of the second Temple was started around 521 BCE by **Zerubbabel**.

Under **Herod the Great**, the second Temple was completely rebuilt and greatly enlarged. Work began in 20 BCE. The new central complex was completed in two years and without any interruption of the Temple's rituals. Then the surrounding buildings and courtyards were built. This huge construction project was not finally completed until 64 CE.

Why Was the Temple So Important to the Jews?

The Jews believed that the Temple was special because it was where God dwelled. This does not mean that they thought God could be contained in a building. Rather, they saw the Temple as a meeting place between God and people. It was the best place in which you could ask for mercy and be forgiven, as well as the place to show your love for and gratitude to God.

When finished, the Temple was the largest building on earth. The entire complex covered an area equivalent in size to twenty-five soccer pitches. Sadly, this beautiful Temple was destroyed in 70 CE. It happened when Roman troops set fire to it while suppressing the Jewish revolt.

Did You Know?

The only part of the Temple which has survived down to the present day is a section of the perimeter wall. This is known as '**the Western Wall**'. For modern Jews, this is the holiest place on earth.

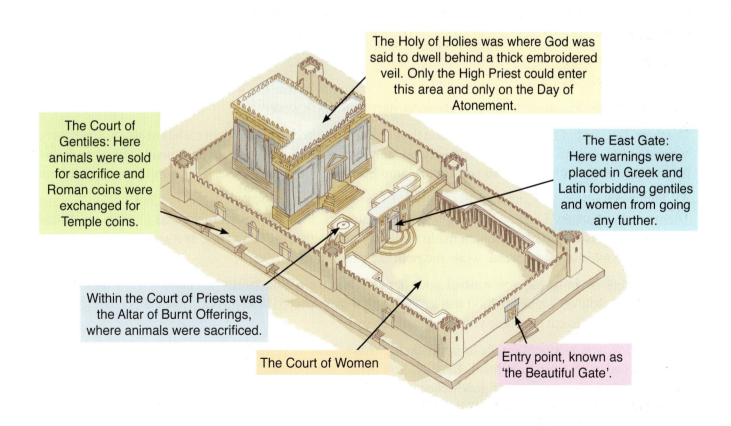

The Holy of Holies was where God was said to dwell behind a thick embroidered veil. Only the High Priest could enter this area and only on the Day of Atonement.

The Court of Gentiles: Here animals were sold for sacrifice and Roman coins were exchanged for Temple coins.

The East Gate: Here warnings were placed in Greek and Latin forbidding gentiles and women from going any further.

Within the Court of Priests was the Altar of Burnt Offerings, where animals were sacrificed.

The Court of Women

Entry point, known as 'the Beautiful Gate'.

LIGHT THE WAY

Visiting a Typical First-Century Jewish Home

For the average Jew, home was a simple, cube-shaped building made from clay bricks. There was only one entrance and exit point. Attached to the right-hand doorpost of every Jewish home was **a mezuzah**.

You always gently touched the mezuzah before entering and exiting your home.

> REMEMBER!
> **A mezuzah** is a small wooden box. It contains a tiny scroll with the words of a prayer called **the Shema** written on it.

A mezuzah

The walls of your house were whitewashed, both inside and out. There was only one room. This was divided in two: your family lived on a raised platform in one part, while the other part of the room served as a stable to keep your animals safe at night. There were no bathing or toilet facilities inside the house.

The house had a flat roof made from mud-caked reed mats. These mats were spread over and tied to the rows of parallel wooden beams that supported the roof. There was just enough of a slope to the roof to allow rain to flow into the gutters. There was a staircase providing access to the roof. Once washed, your clothes were hung out on the roof to dry in the sunlight.

There was no fireplace. Given the climate, it was rarely needed. If it became too cold you could light a charcoal brazier or use a little portable stove that burned straw and grass. However, as there was no chimney, once you lit a fire the interior would soon be filled with smoke.

There was very little furniture other than a few stools or chairs to sit on. You stored your clothes in wooden chests. Utensils were hung from hooks on the roof beams. Wine was stored in skins made from goat hides. Tools were stored on the roof. Water drawn from the local spring or well had to be carried to your house. There you stored it in porous earthenware jars. These kept the water cool by a process of slow evaporation. Other jars were used to store cooking oil and grain.

You slept on mats which were rolled up and stored when not in use. On warm summer nights you usually slept on the roof. You always got up at dawn to start your day's work.

The floor consisted of flat stones pressed into the earth and covered with a layer of rushes or straw. Since there were no windows and the door was the only opening, your house was cool but dark inside. To compensate for the lack of natural light, there was an oil lamp burning in a small alcove. This lamp was kept lit both day and night.

There was no kitchen. Usually, cooking was done outdoors. Most dishes were cooked in olive oil. Bread was the most basic food. The women made it by mixing flour, yeast and water. It was freshly baked each day. Rich people ate wheat bread, while the poor ate barley bread.

Before sitting down to eat, you washed your hands. Then the whole family sat cross-legged on the floor around a low table on which the food was served. You were expected to say a prayer of thanksgiving to God before you began to eat and once you had finished.

Unlike today, you were not served an individual portion. Instead you shared a common bowl. You always ate your food with your right hand. Usually, you broke some bread and dipped it into a dish. A typical Jewish family's diet consisted of goat's cheese, eggs, porridge, beans, lentils, onions, cucumber, dates, figs and pomegranates. Usually, you drank watered-down red wine and goat's milk with your meal.

If you lived near the sea, a lake or a river, you ate fish. Fish was dried and preserved in salt for use when needed. Unlike today, you did not eat much meat.

Jewish Attitudes to Children

Generally speaking, life was quite different for boys and girls.

A boy's life

Jewish fathers tended to place a greater value on a male child because he was expected to carry on the family name. Boys were expected to learn their father's trade, i.e. carpentry, farming, fishing, pottery and so on.

Once he was eight days old, a Jewish boy was formally named in a ceremony held at the local synagogue. The name chosen always had a meaning. Sometimes it said something about the kind of person the boy's parents hoped he would grow up to be. For example, **Joshua** means '**saviour**'. Other times, the name showed how the family felt about God. For example, **Isaiah** means '**God is salvation**'.

The father had the right to choose his children's names. However, these were usually agreed upon between the parents.

On the same day as a boy was named, he was **circumcised**, i.e. the top part of the loose foreskin over his penis was cut off. The Jews did this to remind themselves of **the covenant** (i.e. agreement) God made with the founder of their religion – **Abraham**.

Boys went to school at the local synagogue from the age of seven onward. They learned how to read, write and do basic mathematics. When a Jewish boy reached the age of thirteen, he was publicly examined on his knowledge of **the Tenakh**. Once he passed this test, he was declared **Bar Mitzvah** (meaning: '**Son of the Law**'). From this point on, he was recognised as an adult.

Parents with teenage son during his Bar Mitzvah.

A girl's life

In Jewish society, girls were generally seen as being less important than boys. However, unlike the Romans, the Jews did **not** allow new-born female babies to be killed if they were unwanted. This was because the Jews saw **all** children as a gift from God.

N.B. In a Jewish family, the father had the right to choose who his children would marry.

A Jewish girl did not go to school. She remained at home with her mother. She learned the skills needed to run a home and raise a family, e.g. cooking, spinning and weaving, caring for children and so on. However, by the time of Jesus, some rabbis had started to encourage Jewish fathers to educate their daughters.

Everyday Clothing

In the first century CE, Jewish men and women both wore versions of the same simple type of clothing – a linen undergarment and a woollen tunic on top of this which covered the body from the lower neck to below the knees. Over this they draped a cloak that could serve as a coat, a blanket or a bedroll. To keep this wide tunic from billowing awkwardly, men and women tied it with a leather belt.

Even the poorest Jews thought footwear was a necessity. Most wore sandals made from camel hide and wood.

LIGHT THE WAY

ACTIVITIES

1. Wordsearch

Find the following words:

Palestine
Israel
Holy Land
Arabian Desert
Caesarea
Synagogue
Tenakh
Jerusalem
Xystus
Temple
Court
Gentile
Sacrifice
Priests
Psalms
Pesach
Yom Kippur

Y	D	T	Q	S	Z	S	Q	T	Z	L	H	V	E	S
O	A	E	R	C	A	Y	F	H	R	O	F	U	U	T
M	D	M	E	E	M	C	A	X	L	U	G	M	B	S
K	A	P	N	U	S	L	R	Y	Y	O	O	S	N	E
I	D	L	I	E	Z	E	L	I	G	S	K	C	U	I
P	F	E	T	F	L	A	D	A	F	R	T	L	F	R
P	N	S	S	Z	N	I	N	N	C	I	E	U	T	P
U	Z	Y	E	D	M	Y	T	D	A	A	C	I	S	N
R	G	S	L	D	S	Q	I	N	R	I	I	E	E	P
A	E	R	A	S	E	A	C	S	E	D	B	D	S	D
G	S	M	P	J	B	E	I	N	D	G	K	A	H	Y
J	E	R	U	S	A	L	E	M	V	O	L	I	R	Q
L	V	J	I	T	E	N	A	K	H	M	I	O	K	A
H	C	A	S	E	P	R	B	F	S	D	N	S	V	Q
I	L	M	O	C	W	K	J	E	I	Z	Y	U	Y	F

2. Say what it means!

(a) A synagogue is _____.

(b) The Tenakh is _____.

(c) A sacrifice is _____

_____.

(d) A mezuzah is _____

_____.

3. Tick the box!

In each of the following, say whether it is **true** or **false**.

	True	False
1. We do not have a reliable picture of what life was like in the time of Jesus.		
2. The present-day name for the Holy Land is Israel.		
3. The name Israel means 'the Promised Land'.		
4. Since medieval times, Christians call Israel the Holy Land because it was the place where Jesus's story unfolded.		
5. The Holy Land is hemmed in by the Red Sea on one side and the Arabian Desert on the other.		
6. In the time of Jesus, most of the Holy Land's population was Jewish.		
7. The Holy Land was approximately 300 kilometres in length.		
8. There are basically four seasons in the Holy Land's climate.		
9. A Jewish inhabitant of Palestine 2,000 years ago could have walked the entire length of the country from north to south in less than five days.		
10. The River Jordan flows through the Rift Valley.		
11. The area around the Sea of Galilee is a harsh wilderness with temperatures reaching 50 degrees centigrade.		

Foundations of Religion - Christianity   **SECTION B**

	True	False
12. Two thousand years ago, most Jews lived in large cities dotted along the coast.		
13. Usually, a Jewish town or village was built around a spring or well.		
14. The most important building in every Jewish town and village was the local temple.		
15. In the 1st century CE, Caesarea was the Holy Land's capital city.		
16. The Xystus was a large, paved, open area within the walls of Jerusalem where markets were held.		
17. The walls of a typical Jewish house were whitewashed and there was just one room inside.		
18. Jews only touch the mezuzah when leaving their homes.		
19. In the 1st century CE, a Jewish father placed greater importance on a female child than on a male child.		
20. When a Jewish boy was eight days old, he was circumcised.		
21. When a Jewish boy reached the age of twelve, he was publicly examined on his knowledge of the Bible.		
22. For a Jewish boy to be declared Bar Mitzvah meant that from then on he was recognised as an adult.		
23. The Jews permitted female babies to be killed if they were unwanted.		
24. Even the poorest Jews wore sandals made from camel hide and wood.		

4. Fill in the missing words!

(a) The Temple was where G_____ was supposed to dwell. Every Jew hoped to visit the Temple at least o_____ a year.

(b) When you arrived at the Temple, you had to pass through a s_____ of courts. The first was the outermost court, called the Court of G_____. This was where Jews had to exchange their R_____ coins for T_____ coins in order to purchase an a_____ the Temple priests declared w_____ of being sacrificed to God.

(c) Next, you passed on into the Court of W_____. A large sign stated that only m____ could go beyond this point.

(d) After this came the Court of the I_____. From this place, Jewish men were allowed to watch the Temple priests s_____ their animals.

(e) All animal sacrifices took place in the Court of the P_____. The animals were killed and then b_____ on a large raised a_____.

(f) The final part of the Temple was the Holy of H_____. This was sealed off from the rest of the Temple by a huge set of heavy c_____. Only the H_____ Priest was allowed to enter it. He did so only o_____ a year, at Y_____ K_____.

(g) There were t____ great Temples in the history of Judaism. The first was built by S_____.

(h) Under H_____ the Great, the second Temple was rebuilt. When finished, the Temple was the l_____ building on Earth. The Temple was d_____ during the Jewish revolt in _____ CE.

(i) The only part of the Temple which has survived down to the present day is known as 'the W_____ Wall'.

5. Think about it!

(a) Identify five ways in which a 1st-century Jewish house differs from a house in 21st-century Ireland.

(b) Identify four ways in which the life of an Irish girl growing up in 21st-century Ireland differs from that of a Jewish girl growing up in the 1st-century.

LIGHT THE WAY

CHAPTER 2   UNDER ROMAN RULE

The Story of the Jews

Judaism is the world's oldest monotheistic religion. Its members are called '**Jews**'. However, originally they were called '**Hebrews**'. Their story began almost 4,000 years ago. This was the time of **the patriarchs**.

Abraham was the first patriarch. He was born in Mesopotamia (modern Iraq) sometime around 1850 BCE. God inspired him to leave his homeland with a small group of followers. Eventually, they settled down in what was then called '**The Land of Canaan**'. Once there, God made **a covenant** with Abraham and all his descendants.

> **REMEMBER!**
> **The patriarchs** were the founding fathers of Judaism.

> **REMEMBER!**
> **A covenant** is a solemn agreement in which both sides make a commitment that must not be broken.

What did they promise each other?

- God promised that the Hebrews would always own the land they had settled on. This is why the Hebrews called it '**the Promised Land**'.
- In return, the Hebrews promised to worship only the One God.

> **Did You Know?**
> Since ancient times, all Hebrew males have been circumcised to remind them of the covenant God made with their ancestors.

However, life in the Promised Land did not turn out as the Hebrews had hoped. Long droughts forced them to migrate to the kingdom of Egypt.

At first, the Hebrew people were welcome because Egypt was suffering from a labour shortage. **The pharaoh** (i.e. Egypt's king) employed the Hebrews as builders. However, after a series of political crises within Egypt, the Hebrews were forced into slavery.

Over the next three centuries, the Hebrews suffered terrible hardships. However, they did not lose hope. They continued to believe that God would rescue them. Eventually, a man named **Moses** came forward. He said that God had sent him to lead the Hebrews to freedom.

Moses confronted the pharaoh. He demanded that the Hebrews be set free. When the pharaoh refused, Egypt was struck down by one terrible plague after another.

These events shocked the pharaoh. He gave in to Moses's demand. He set the Hebrews free and let them leave Egypt. The journey of the Hebrews back to the Promised Land is called **the Exodus**.

On their journey home to the Promised Land, God renewed his covenant with the Hebrews. To regain control of the Promised Land, they would have to keep **the Ten Commandments**.

> **REMEMBER!**
> **The Ten Commandments** are ten short rules for how to live a good and worthwhile life.

Over the next two centuries, the Hebrews fought a series of wars to gain control of the Promised Land. Finally, around 1000 BCE, they set up their own independent kingdom and called it **Israel**.

For about a century, Israel thrived. Its most important kings were **David** and his son **Solomon**. David founded Israel's capital city, **Jerusalem** (meaning: '**the city of peace**'). Solomon built a beautiful Temple in Jerusalem. **The Ark of the Covenant** was kept in the Holy of Holies at the centre of the Temple complex.

122

Foundations of Religion - Christianity   SECTION B

Did You Know?

The Ark of the Covenant was a beautifully decorated casket. It contained two stone tablets. It was said that God had written the Ten Commandments upon them.

After Solomon died, the Hebrews could not agree on who should succeed him. So, his kingdom was split in two:

- The ten northern tribes formed their own kingdom, keeping the name **Israel**.
- The two southern tribes formed the kingdom of **Judah**.

After they split apart, these two kingdoms quarrelled with one another. It was during this time that a number of **prophets** appeared.

The prophets warned the Hebrews about the dangers of fighting among themselves.

Unfortunately the two Hebrew kingdoms became totally absorbed with in-fighting. They refused to listen to any warnings. They ignored the danger of attack by their powerful neighbours. Eventually, both kingdoms were invaded and conquered:

REMEMBER!
A prophet is someone who receives messages from God and passes them on to others.

- In 721 BCE, the northern kingdom of Israel was overrun by the Assyrians. Its people were marched away into captivity. None of them ever returned home. We do not know what happened to them.
- In 587 BCE, the southern kingdom of Judah was invaded by the Babylonians. They marched the people of Judah – who from then on were known as **the Jews** – eastwards. They became slaves in the great city of Babylon.

Then, in 539 BCE, **King Cyrus of Persia** conquered the Babylonian Empire. He freed the Jews from slavery and let them return to the Promised Land. However, in the centuries following their return home, the Jews suffered many setbacks. Their land was invaded by a succession of great powers – Persia, Greece and Egypt.

In 160 BCE, **Judas Maccabeus** led the Jews to freedom. However, their independence lasted less than a century. In 63 BCE they were conquered once more – this time by the Romans. From then on, the Holy Land was called **Palestine**. It became just another province of the mighty Roman Empire.

Why Did the Romans Want to Control Palestine?

In one word – **location**. Although it covered only a small area, Palestine was the meeting point for three continents – Africa to the south, Asia to the east and Europe to the north. Palestine sat at a crossroads where all the vital overland trade routes linking these three continents met. Whoever owned it controlled all the trade that flowed through it.

123

LIGHT THE WAY

The Political Map of Palestine in the Time of Jesus

The Romans divided Palestine into a number of administrative regions.

The principal political regions of Palestine
These were:

- Galilee in the north
- Samaria in the centre
- Judaea in the south.

Communities
People lived in one or other of the following:

- the long-established Jewish cities (e.g. Jerusalem) and towns (e.g. Nazareth)
- the more recently built Roman cities (e.g. Caesarea)
- the small farming villages built around wells that dotted the more arable areas.

The languages of Palestine
There were four different languages spoken:

- **Latin:** the official language of the Roman Empire.
- **Koiné:** a form of Greek spoken throughout the eastern Mediterranean and used by merchants as the language of business.
- **Aramaic:** the language spoken by the Jews in everyday life in Palestine.
- **Hebrew:** the ancient language of the Jews, now used only in their religious rituals.

Caesarea
Recent Roman-built city port where the Roman procurator lived for much of the year.

Jerusalem
The capital city of Palestine. Also its religious centre because the Temple stood there.

Decapolis
This consisted of ten cities founded by Alexander the Great.

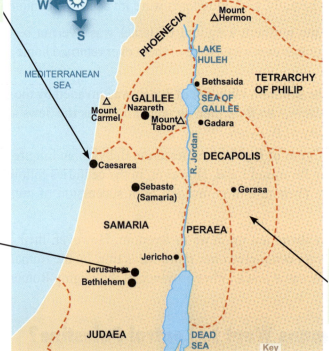

124

Foundations of Religion - Christianity   SECTION B

ACTIVITIES

1. Wordsearch

Find the following words:

Judaism
Hebrew
Patriarch
Abraham
Covenant
Pharaoh
Moses
Exodus
Renew
Commandment
Israel
David
Solomon
Temple
Ark
Split
Judah
Jew
Prophet
Babylon
Cyrus
Romans
Palestine
Location

T	M	L	H	N	T	Z	A	Q	E	I	T	Y	V	J
U	N	D	O	E	O	B	W	N	A	S	E	H	O	U
S	Y	E	M	C	R	M	I	K	D	R	H	C	Y	D
N	E	P	M	A	A	T	O	I	L	A	P	R	C	A
M	L	S	H	D	S	T	V	L	B	E	O	A	J	H
E	L	A	O	E	N	A	I	K	O	L	R	I	U	A
M	M	F	L	M	D	A	H	O	A	S	P	R	D	U
H	O	A	R	A	H	P	M	E	N	U	M	T	A	Y
V	P	S	U	R	Y	C	O	M	X	P	N	A	I	W
S	N	A	M	O	R	M	K	U	O	O	D	P	S	E
R	B	T	W	I	Z	N	O	R	L	C	D	R	M	N
C	O	V	E	N	A	N	T	Y	A	Z	Z	U	B	E
R	P	F	J	J	B	U	B	S	P	L	I	T	S	R
X	Q	M	H	N	U	A	H	E	B	R	E	W	B	N
E	X	W	B	V	B	H	V	Z	U	K	T	S	K	O

2. Say what it means!

(a) The patriarchs were _the founding fathers of jews_ .

(b) A covenant is _a solemn agreement in which both sides make a commitment that should not break_ .

(c) The Ten Commandments are _ten rules made by god_ .
~~make a commitment~~

(d) The Ark of the Covenant was _a casket carring the Ten commandments_

_____ .

(e) A prophet is _someone who recieves messages from_

_____ .

3. Tick the box!

In each of the following, say whether it is **true** or **false**.

	True	False
1. Judaism is the world's oldest polytheistic religion.		
2. Moses was the first patriarch.		

125

LIGHT THE WAY

		True	False
3.	Around 1850 BCE, Abraham and his followers settled in the Land of Canaan.		
4.	Jews believe that God made a covenant with Abraham and all his descendants.		
5.	The Jews were originally known as the Hebrews.		
6.	The Hebrews called the land they settled on 'the Promised Land'.		
7.	In the covenant, the Hebrews promised to worship many different gods.		
8.	All Hebrew males are circumcised to remind them of the covenant God made with their ancestors.		
9.	Long droughts forced the Jews to migrate to Ethiopia.		
10.	Once they reached Egypt, the Hebrews were immediately forced into slavery.		
11.	Moses led the Hebrews out of slavery to freedom in the Promised Land.		
12.	The name Jerusalem means 'City of God'.		
13.	The Ark of the Covenant was kept in the Holy of Holies.		
14.	After David died, his kingdom was split in two.		
15.	In 721 BCE, the northern kingdom of Israel was overrun by the Babylonians.		
16.	The name 'Jews' was first given to the people of the southern kingdom of Judah.		
17.	Between 587 and 539 BCE, the Jews were captives in the city of Babylon.		
18.	In 160 BCE, King Cyrus conquered the Babylonian Empire and let the Jews return home.		
19.	In 63 BCE, the Jews were conquered by Judas Maccabeus.		
20.	Palestine was a province of the Roman Empire.		

4. Fill in the missing words!

The Romans wanted to c_____ Palestine because of its l_____. Although it covered only a small a_____, Palestine was the meeting p_____ for three c_____ – Africa to the south, A_____ to the east and E_____ to the north. Palestine sat at a c_____ where all the vital overland t_____ routes linking these three continents met. Whoever o_____ it c_____ all the trade that flowed t_____ it.

How the Romans Governed Palestine

1. Herod the Great and his family

After conquering Palestine, the Romans handed the running of it over to an ambitious local who called himself '**Herod the Great**'. He ruled the province on behalf of the emperor. As long as Herod kept the peace and collected the taxes, the Romans did not interfere in Palestine.

Herod was cruel and ruthless. He murdered anyone he suspected of disloyalty, including his wife and his two eldest sons. In an attempt to gain popularity Herod began a massive reconstruction of the Temple in Jerusalem. However this did not work. Why not?

Foundations of Religion - Christianity   SECTION B

Firstly, Herod was not a Jew. He was from Idumaea, a region south of Palestine. Secondly, the Jews knew he was just a Roman henchman. So, he could never win their trust; they despised him.

When Herod died in 4 BCE, Palestine was divided among his three sons:

- **Archelaus** was given Judaea and Samaria.
- **Herod Antipas** received Galilee and Peraea.
- **Philip** got Trachonitis.

Each son was given the title **tetrarch**, which means '**controller of a part of a province**'.

2. The Roman Procurator

When Archelaus proved himself unsuited to the job, the emperor replaced him with a **procurator** (i.e. a Roman governor). The procurator's duties were:

- To keep the peace.
- To collect the taxes.
- To keep the trade routes open.

Pontius Pilate was appointed procurator of Judaea and Galilee in 26 CE. He soon discovered that it was a difficult place to govern. Why?

The Romans had brought security and created many new jobs by building roads, towns, ports and aqueducts. However most Jews deeply resented their presence. The Jews were fiercely independent. Most never saw the Romans as anything other than invaders. So, the atmosphere in Palestine was always tense. There was always a danger of revolt.

Pilate wanted to avoid a revolt. It would cost him his job. Also, he commanded a garrison of only three thousand soldiers. The nearest reinforcements were hundreds of miles away in either Egypt or Syria. Yet, as procurator, he was expected to keep control over three quarters of a million Jews. So how was he able to do it?

Firstly, Pilate used a network of spies to infiltrate and betray Jewish rebel groups. Secondly, he got the most important Jews in Palestine to help him govern it. This is why most ordinary Jews thought that they had no choice but to accept Roman rule.

3. The Sanhedrin

The Romans understood that religion played a very important role in Jewish life. This is why, to keep the peace, they let the Jews practise their religion with as little interference as possible. They also let the Jews keep **the Sanhedrin**.

> **REMEMBER!**
> **The Sanhedrin** was the ruling council of the Jewish religion.

The Sanhedrin helped the Romans to govern Palestine.

The Sanhedrin was made up of seventy members, plus **a president** (i.e. leader). **The High Priest** acted as its president. Usually, the Sanhedrin met twice a week. These meetings were held in **the Chamber of Hewn Stone**, inside the Temple complex.

The Romans allowed the Sanhedrin to:

- Make religious laws that all Jews had to obey.
- Use the Temple police to enforce these laws.
- Punish Jews who broke these laws.

However, the Sanhedrin did not have the power to sentence someone to death. Only the Roman procurator could order it. This reminded the Sanhedrin that, like everyone else, it too took its orders from the emperor.

The Sanhedrin was not a united body. It was divided into two rival groups: **the Sadducees** (who were in the majority) and **the Pharisees** (who formed the minority). They rarely agreed with one another. This situation suited the Romans. As long as the Jews were divided and quarrelled among themselves, they were easier to control and less likely to rebel.

4. The High Priest

The High Priest was the leader of the Sanhedrin. He was always chosen from one or other of the wealthy Sadducee families who controlled it. However, the Sanhedrin's choice for High Priest had to be submitted to the Romans. He could not become High Priest without their approval.

The High Priest was easily recognisable during religious rituals because he wore an elaborate costume decorated with precious stones. Only the High Priest was allowed to enter the Holy of Holies and come into the presence of God, no one else.

5. The tax collectors

Just as in every other occupied land throughout history, there were some Jews who were happy to **collaborate** (i.e. work with the Romans). These men and women were hated by their fellow Jews. However, the most despised of all these collaborators were **the tax collectors**.

Today our taxes are collected directly by the state authorities (i.e. the Revenue Commissioners). However, in ancient Rome, the job of collecting taxes was put out to private tender. A tax collector had to pay a large lump sum to the emperor in advance. Only then was he given the authority to collect taxes in a province like Palestine.

Most Jews earned just enough money to provide for their basic needs – food, clothing and shelter. Few were wealthy. However, tax collectors usually made inflated assessments of what people could afford to pay. This ensured that they made huge profits for themselves. People did not dare challenge a tax collector, as he had Roman soldiers to back him up.

Given all of this, it is no surprise that most Jews treated tax collectors as social outcasts. For example:

- Tax collectors were not permitted to hold any religious office.
- Tax collectors were not allowed to give evidence in a Jewish court.

Most Jews could never trust a tax collector because they believed that only a cheat and a liar would become a tax collector in the first place.

The Gospels say that Jesus horrified many of his followers and angered his critics when he invited a tax collector named **Matthew** to become one of his Apostles (i.e. closest friends).

Jewish Hopes about the Messiah

Even after decades of Roman rule, the Jews never gave up hope that, one day, they might regain their freedom. They believed that, in the past, God had helped their ancestors. For example:

- God sent Moses to free the Jews from slavery in Egypt.
- God chose David to set up the Kingdom of Israel.

This is why the Jews developed **a messianic expectation**.

> **REMEMBER!**
> **A messianic expectation** is the belief that, one day, God will send **a messiah** to save you.

Did You Know?

The title **'messiah'** comes from the Hebrew word *moshiach*. This means **'an anointed one'**. In earlier times, Jewish kings were anointed with scented oil. So, being anointed meant that you had been chosen by God to do something important. In the case of the Jews, it meant freeing them from Roman rule.

The Jews disagreed among themselves about the kind of messiah they should expect. However most hoped that the messiah would do three things:

- Bring God's peace and justice.
- Free the Jews from foreign control.
- Establish a new, independent Jewish kingdom.

Devout Jews looked forward eagerly to the coming of the messiah. Every day they recited the following prayer:

'I believe with perfect faith in the coming of the Messiah and, even if he delays, still will I await his arrival every day.'

By the 1st century, four distinct groups had emerged among the Jews in Palestine. Each one had its own ideas about the messiah.

1. The SADDUCEES

- They claimed to be descended from **Zadok**. He was the High Priest at the time of David and Solomon.
- They were wealthy priests and landowners.
- They formed a majority in the Sanhedrin and so controlled it.
- They decided who became High Priest. However, he also had to be approved by the Romans.
- They accepted only the first five books of the Tenakh. They said it had to be understood literally.
- They refused to accept new ideas, such as belief in life after death.
- They placed great importance on offering animal sacrifices to God in the Temple.
- They had no interest in helping the poor.

The Sadducees did **not** expect a messiah to free them from Roman rule. They happily cooperated with the Romans. Some even adopted Roman clothing and lifestyles. All this made the Sadducees very unpopular with their fellow Jews.

2. The PHARISEES

- They were middle-class laymen, not priests. They included merchants, craftsmen and scribes (i.e. lawyers).
- They controlled the local synagogues.
- Their name means **'the interpreters'**. However their opponents said it meant **'the separated'** – this was because they refused to mix with non-Jews.

LIGHT THE WAY

- They became totally preoccupied with preserving 'the purity' of their religion.
- They despised anyone who disagreed with them.
- Unlike the Sadducees, they were open to some new ideas. They believed in an afterlife.

The Pharisees rejected Roman rule but they didn't resist it. Unlike the Sadducees, the Pharisees believed that God would send a messiah. They said that he would be Pharisee and a descendant of King David.

3. The ESSENES

- Their name means '**the dutiful ones**'.
- The Essenes believed that the Jewish religion had been corrupted by outside influences. They refused to have anything to do with gentiles (i.e. non-Jews).
- They called themselves '**the Sons of Light**'.
- They believed that they would be the only ones to be 'saved' by God.
- They retreated to remote parts of Palestine and set up monastic communities. They regarded other Jews as sinful.
- They refused to worship with other Jews in the Temple.
- They followed strict rules. They took an oath to keep their teachings and practices secret.

The Essenes rejected Roman rule but they didn't oppose it. They said that there would be **two** messiahs. One would be a priest and the other would be a mighty warrior.

4. The ZEALOTS

- They were deeply religious Jews.
- They may have been an off-shoot of the Pharisees.
- They said that violence was justified if it was to defend your religion or to free your homeland.
- They were inspired by the example of **Judas Maccabeus**. He led a successful guerrilla-style war which freed the Jews from Syrian control in the 2nd century BCE.

The Zealots rejected Roman rule. They formed a resistance movement. They ambushed Roman troops and assassinated collaborators, e.g. tax collectors. They believed that the messiah would be one of them. He would be a mighty warrior who would defeat the Romans and set up an independent Jewish kingdom.

ACTIVITIES

1. Say what it means!

(a) The Sanhedrin was _____ .

(b) A messianic expectation is _____

_____ .

Foundations of Religion - Christianity **SECTION B**

2. Identify them!

(a) I was not a Jew but I rebuilt the Temple. I was cruel and ruthless. I killed anyone I suspected of disloyalty. As long as I kept the peace and collected the taxes, the Romans did not interfere in Palestine.
My name was _____ _____ _____.

(b) After my father's death, I was given control of Judaea and Samaria. However, I proved to be un-suitable so the Romans fired me.
My name was _____.

(c) I was appointed procurator of Judaea and Samaria in 26 CE.
My name was _____ _____.

(d) We made up the majority in the Sanhedrin.
We were the _____.

(e) We made up the minority in the Sanhedrin.
We were the _____.

(f) I acted as the president of the Sanhedrin. I was the only one who was allowed to enter the Holy of Holies in the Temple.
I was given the title of the _____ _____.

(g) I was a tax collector whom Jesus invited to become one of his Apostles.
My name was _____.

(h) I was sent by God to free the Jews from slavery in Egypt.
My name was _____.

(i) I was chosen by God to set up the Kingdom of Israel.
My name was _____.

(j) The Jews believed that God would one day send me to free them from Roman rule.
The Jews called me the _____ .

3. Great expectations!

In each of the following, identify the particular Jewish group based on what its members believed about the messiah.

(a) We rejected Roman rule but we didn't oppose it. We said that there would be **two** messiahs. One would be a priest. The other would be a mighty warrior.
We were _____.

(b) We rejected Roman rule but we didn't oppose it. We believed God would send a messiah. He would be a member of our group and a descendent of King David.
We were _____.

(c) We rejected Roman rule. We formed a resistance movement. We believed that the messiah would be one of us. He would be a mighty warrior who would defeat the Romans and set up an independent Jewish kingdom.
We were _____ .

(d) We did not expect a messiah to free us from Roman rule. We happily cooperated with the Romans. Some of us even adopted Roman clothing and lifestyles. All this made us very unpopular with our fellow Jews.
We were _____.

131

LIGHT THE WAY

4. Crossword

Across

3. He was the High Priest in the time of David and Solomon.
6. The atmosphere in Palestine was very tense so there was always a danger of this happening.
8. They were wealthy priests and landowners who controlled the Sanhedrin. They decided who became High Priest. They did not believe in life after death.
10. They were laymen who controlled the local synagogues. They refused to mix with non-Jews. They believed in an afterlife.
12. They were deeply religious Jews who said violence was justified to defend your religion or free your homeland.
14. This title comes from the Hebrew word *moshiach*, meaning 'an anointed one'.
15. After conquering Palestine, the Romans handed the running of it over to me. I did this job until my death in 4 BCE (3 words: 5, 3, 5).

Down

1. He was the leader of the Sanhedrin. He wore an elaborate costume during religious rituals. He was the only one allowed to enter the Holy of Holies (2 words: 4, 5).
2. This title means controller of a part of a province.
4. The Sanhedrin was not allowed to sentence you to it. Only the procurator could order it.
5. It means to work with someone.
7. They refused to have anything to do with either other Jews or gentiles. They set up monasteries in remote places. They called themselves 'the Sons of Light'.
9. Herod _____ was put in charge of Galilee and Peraea after his father's death.
10. This title means 'a Roman governor'.
11. They made huge profits but were treated as social outcasts. They were forbidden from ever holding a religious office and were not allowed to give evidence in court (2 words: 3, 10).
13. The Romans used a network of these individuals to infiltrate and betray Jewish rebel groups.

Foundations of Religion – Christianity   SECTION B

CHAPTER 3   HOW WE KNOW ABOUT JESUS

Looking at the Evidence

Konstantin Tischendorf (1815–1874) was a German scholar who lived at a time when some writers were claiming that Jesus had never existed. Even some of those who accepted his existence said that we didn't have any reliable information about his life.

Tischendorf wanted to know if there was any truth in these claims. So, he did what any historian would do when trying to find out about some person or event long ago: he went looking for **evidence**.

> REMEMBER!
> **Evidence** is any kind of information that lets you know what happened in the past.

To find the evidence, we need to look at different **sources**.

As Jesus did not write books about his life and teaching, Tischendorf had to study what **other** people had written about him. He found that they had left us two kinds of sources:

> REMEMBER!
> **A source** is anything from the past that provides us with evidence. For example: a building, a document, a painting and so on.

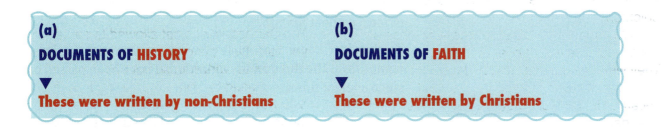

(a) **DOCUMENTS OF HISTORY**
▼
These were written by non-Christians

(b) **DOCUMENTS OF FAITH**
▼
These were written by Christians

All of these documents about Jesus were written between the years 50 CE and 115 CE.

When taken together, these sources provide us with a lot of information about **who Jesus was**, **what he said** and **how he lived**.

133

LIGHT THE WAY

Documents of History

> **REMEMBER!**
> **A document of history** is a source written by a non-Christian, i.e. a Jew or a Roman.

Source 1

The Antiquities of the Jews: This was written around 93 CE by a Jewish historian named **Flavius Josephus**. He said that:

- Jesus was a wise teacher.
- Jesus worked miracles.
- Jesus won followers among both Jews and **gentiles** (non-Jews).
- Jesus was condemned to death by **Pontius Pilate**.
- Jesus's followers claimed that he had risen from the dead.

Source 2

The Annals: This was written around 115 CE by a Roman senator and historian named **Tacitus**. He said that:

- The Roman authorities thought that Jesus was a trouble-maker.
- Jesus was executed during the reign of **the Emperor Tiberius** (who died in 37 CE).

Source 3

The Letter to the Emperor Trajan: This was written around 111 CE by a Roman procurator named **Pliny the Younger**. He said that:

- The followers of Jesus had spread throughout the Middle East and Asia Minor.
- His followers met every day before sunrise and prayed to Jesus '**as to a god**'.

IMPORTANT POINT!

These Jewish and Roman authors confirmed two things: (a) Jesus really existed; and (b) Jesus founded a new religion.

In fact, most scholars today agree that Jesus existed. But what about the claim that we do not have any reliable sources of evidence about his life?

Tischendorf knew that most of what we know about Jesus comes from **the documents of faith** that have been passed on since ancient times.

Documents of Faith

> **REMEMBER!**
> **A document of faith** is a source written by a member of the early Christian community.

Christianity's documents of faith can be found in **the New Testament**. This is a collection of twenty-seven books. All of them were written during the latter half of the 1st century CE.

134

How is the New Testament Organised?

The New Testament has four parts. They are:

1. The Gospels

These are four books that record the life and teachings of Jesus as remembered by those who knew him.

2. The Acts of the Apostles

This book tells the story of how Christianity spread beyond Palestine.

3. The Epistles

These include twenty-one letters written by leading Christians. They clarified important Christian teachings and helped settle disputes between Jesus's followers.

4. The Book of Revelation

This book explores the struggle between good and evil. It predicts that, in the end, good will triumph over evil.

Searching for Sources

Konstantin Tischendorf was an expert **authenticator**.

Tischendorf put his skills to good use as he travelled across the Middle East looking for ancient **manuscripts** of the New Testament.

> **REMEMBER!**
> **An authenticator** can tell you whether a document is genuine or a fake.

> **REMEMBER!**
> **A manuscript** is a handwritten document.

Finding the Codex Sinaiticus

The New Testament was written in the 1st century CE. However, Tischendorf discovered that all the original manuscripts had long since vanished. Some had faded due to normal wear and tear and had been discarded. Others had been destroyed during the persecution of the early Christians.

In February 1859, Tischendorf journeyed to Egypt. There he visited **the Monastery of St Catherine** at the foot of Mount Sinai.

The Monastery of St Catherine at the foot of Mount Sinai.

LIGHT THE WAY

Did You Know?

The Monastery of St Catherine on Mount Sinai in Egypt is the home to a community of Orthodox monks. It is one of the oldest working Christian monasteries in the world. It is also very remote. Tischendorf had to travel hundreds of miles across the desert to reach it.

The monastery was built in the 6th century by the Roman Emperor Justinian. Within the monastery is **the Chapel of the Burning Bush**. This is said to be the site where God first spoke to Moses.

At this stage, Tischendorf had been searching for manuscripts for twenty years. He went to Mount Sinai hoping to find something of value. He succeeded beyond his wildest dreams.

He spent several weeks searching through the old monastery's library, but found nothing. Then, on the evening before he was due to return home, he struck up a conversation with one of the monks. The monk asked him if he would be interested in looking at a copy of the Bible that he was reading. To humour him, Tischendorf agreed. The monk showed him a large volume, wrapped for safekeeping in a red cloth, and set it down in front of Tischendorf. When he opened the book, Tischendorf was stunned. It was an old manuscript of the Bible, a **very** old manuscript. It contained about half of the Old Testament but all of the New Testament.

Tischendorf was given permission to study this book. By the light of a small oil lamp, he sat up through the long cold desert night, reading and analysing its text. By the time dawn had broken, Tischendorf was sure he had made a priceless discovery. He called it *The Codex Sinaiticus*.

Tischendorf was amazed that the manuscript had been preserved for so long. However, he was worried about its future safety. He wanted to ensure its preservation. So, in 1869, Tischendorf persuaded the Tsar of Russia to buy it from the monks and preserve it for future scholars to study.

Did You Know?

The Codex Sinaiticus contains the oldest complete manuscript of the New Testament.

It is written in Greek. It was copied by Christian scribes from an earlier text around the middle of the 4th century CE.

When the Tsar was toppled from power by the communists in 1917, some Christian scholars persuaded the British government to buy it from them. It is now on display in the British Museum in London. For many Christian scholars, it is the most important and valuable book in existence.

Konstantin Tischendorf was a trailblazer. In the years since his discovery of *The Codex Sinaiticus*, other archaeologists have discovered **fragments** of even earlier copies of the New Testament. All of these were written on papyrus. The oldest of these fragments are:

The Rylands Papyrus

This is the earliest known fragment of the New Testament. It is a brief extract from the Gospel of John. It dates from around 135 CE. It is on display in the John Rylands Library at the University of Manchester, England.

The Chester Beatty Papyri

These fragments of the New Testament date from around 200 CE. They can be seen at the Chester Beatty Library, Dublin.

These different fragments have been very useful. When taken together with the *Codex Sinaiticus*, they confirm that our modern editions of the New Testament are **accurate**. They really do offer us faithful and reliable copies of what the first Christians recorded 2,000 years ago. It is from these manuscripts that our modern English translations of the New Testament have been made. So, they **do** offer us reliable sources of information about the life of Jesus Christ.

Foundations of Religion - Christianity   SECTION B

ACTIVITIES

1. Say what it means!

(a) A document of history is _____

_____ .

(b) A document of faith is _____

_____ .

2. Identify them!

(a) I was the German scholar who went looking for the ancient copies of the New Testament.
My name was _____ _____ .

(b) I was the Jewish historian who wrote *The Antiquities of the Jews.*
My name was _____ _____ .

(c) I was the Roman historian and senator who wrote *The Annals.*
My name was _____ .

(d) I was the Roman procurator who wrote *The Letter to the Emperor Trajan.*
My name was _____ _____ _____ .

(e) It is one of the oldest working monasteries in the world. It is home to a community of Orthodox monks. You can find it at the foot of Mount Sinai.
It is called _____ _____ _____ _____ _____ .

(f) It was written in Greek in the mid-4th century. It contains the oldest complete manuscript of the New Testament.
It is called _____ _____ _____ .

3. Tick the box!

In each of the following, say whether it is **true** or **false**.

	True	False
1. Evidence is any kind of information that allows you to find out what happens in the future.		
2. *The Annals of Tacitus* is a document of faith.		
3. *The Letter to the Emperor Trajan* was written by a Roman procurator named Pontius Pilate.		
4. The Gospels are documents of faith.		
5. The Acts of the Apostles tells the story of how Christianity spread beyond Palestine.		

137

LIGHT THE WAY

4. Crossword

Across

2. My job is to tell you whether a document is genuine or a fake.
3. The _____ Papyrus is the earliest known fragment of the New Testament. It is an extract from the Gospel of St John.
6. The title of the Russian ruler who bought *The Codex Sinaiticus* in 1869 to keep it safe.
8. This part of the New Testament includes twenty-one letters written by leading Christians in the 1st century. They helped to settle disputes between Jesus's followers.
9. The name of the Roman emperor who built the monastery of St Catherine in the 6th century CE.
10. The name given to four books about Jesus as remembered by those who knew him.

Down

1. A word meaning 'a hand-written document'.
4. It is the name for anything from the past that can provide us with evidence about some person or event.
5. Tacitus said that it was during the reign of this Roman emperor that Jesus was executed.
7. Flavius Josephus said that Pontius _____ was the one who condemned Jesus to death.

Exploring the Four Gospels

Every book of the New Testament tells us something about Jesus. However, our most important sources of evidence about him are the four **Gospels** of **Mark**, **Matthew**, **Luke** and **John**.

REMEMBER!
Gospel means '**good news**'.

The Gospels tell us about:
- Jesus's teachings.
- His miracles.
- His death and resurrection.

However, the Gospels do **not** offer us a biography of Jesus in the modern sense of the word. For example, you won't find a physical description of Jesus in them, nor do they say anything about his school days.

We need to keep in mind that the Gospels are **documents of faith**. This means that:

- The Gospels were written to record the important details of Jesus's life and teachings.
- However their authors were all committed Christians.
- They wanted to convince other people to believe in Jesus as they did.
- So their main focus was on explaining **the meaning** and **importance** of his life, death and resurrection.

The authors of the four Gospels are called **the evangelists**.

> REMEMBER!
> **An evangelist** is someone who announces 'the good news' about Jesus Christ.

Since earliest times, Christians have associated the four Gospels with the names **Mark**, **Matthew**, **Luke** and **John**.

According to Christian tradition:

- **Mark** was a missionary who travelled with St Peter to Rome.
- **Matthew** was one of the original twelve apostles.
- **Luke** was a Greek doctor who worked as a missionary with St Paul.
- **John** was one of the original twelve apostles.

Most scholars accept Mark and Luke as the authors of those Gospels. However, they think it unlikely that Matthew and John were written by the original apostles. It is more likely that these two Gospels were written by their students.

St Mark the evangelist.

Four Gospels but One Story

> REMEMBER!
> **A biography** tells us someone's life story.

If you read **the biography** of some famous athlete, entertainer, politician or soldier, you will expect to be told about the important events in that person's life. This is what the Gospels do; they tell us about the key moments in Jesus's life.

Each evangelist wrote his **own** version of this story. This is because each one tried to explain, as best as he could, the meaning of what Jesus had said and done. However, each evangelist saw the same person – Jesus – from his own particular point of view.

To understand this, think about **Mr Smith**.

LIGHT THE WAY

Mr Smith's wife sees him and thinks about him in her own special way – he is her **husband**.

His children see him as their **father** – a different role from that of husband.

Mr Smith's boss sees him from a different point of view too – as an honest, efficient and reliable **employee**.

However, as Mr Smith plays amateur soccer, his teammates have yet another view of him – as a good **goalkeeper**.

In each case, Mr Smith remains the **same** person, though each of these people see him differently, from their own particular point of view.

In the same way, each evangelist looked at Jesus from his **own** point of view. This led each one to think and write about him in a different way. This is why we can learn much from studying what all four Gospels say rather than by just reading one of them. Each of the four Gospels shows us different aspects of Jesus's life story. When combined, they help us to build up a fuller, richer portrait of this extraordinary person.

When the Gospels were Written

Christian scholars find it difficult to agree on exactly when each Gospel was written. However, they do agree that all were written within the latter half of the 1st century CE.

The Name of the Gospel	When it was written
Mark	Between 60 and 65 CE
Matthew	Between 65 and 85 CE
Luke	Between 60 and 85 CE
John	Between 85 and 100 CE

The Development of the Gospels

Introduction

The four Gospels were the end result of a three-stage process of development. You will notice that the spoken word came **before** the written word.

Stage 1: The public ministry, death and resurrection of Jesus

(27 CE to 30 CE)

From the start of his public ministry, Jesus called on the apostles to be witnesses to all that he had said and done. They saw Jesus show compassion to the poor and the outcast. They heard him teach great truths in a simple style that everyone could understand. They saw him feed the hungry, heal the sick and even restore the dead to life. They saw him suffer and die. Then, after his resurrection, Jesus appeared to them at different times and in different places. This led the apostles to believe that Jesus was the promised messiah. He had brought a message of salvation for **all** people.

Stage 2: The preaching of the apostles
(30 CE to 60 CE)

Before his ascension, Jesus told the apostles to:

> 'Go, make disciples of all nations …
> and teach them to observe all the commands I gave you.'
> Matthew 28: 19–20

At first, the Gospel message was passed on **orally**, i.e. from person to person by word of mouth.

The first Christians didn't see the need to record Jesus's story. This was because:

- They were mostly Jews. They preferred to memorise his story and teachings rather than write them down.
- Many of them thought that Jesus would return soon. They didn't think it necessary to write books about him.
- While the apostles were still alive there was no need to write books about Jesus. The apostles were seen as '**living books**' on which Jesus had written his message.

However, during this second stage, some Christians began to collect stories about what Jesus had said and done. They wanted to preserve them. Later, these collections were used when the Gospels came to be written.

Stage 3: The evangelists write the Gospels
(60 CE to 100 CE)

Years passed and the apostles began to die. Important information about Jesus was in danger of being lost to future generations if it was not recorded.

Working separately at different times and in different places, each evangelist studied the source material available to him, i.e. eyewitness accounts and collections of Jesus's sayings. Then each one produced his **own** version of Jesus's story. The first Gospel to be written was that of Mark.

By the early 2nd century, the four Gospels were being widely used by Christians. They proved very useful because:

- The Gospels provided a clear explanation of the Christian way of life.
- They cleared up any confusion over what Christians believed.
- They provided readings for use in Christian worship.

Did You Know?

Although written separately, three Gospels – **Mark**, **Matthew** and **Luke** – share so many similarities that they are known as **the Synoptic Gospels**.

Synoptic means '**seen together**'. The Synoptic Gospels agree on (a) what Jesus said and did; and (b) when this happened.

St John the evangelist

LIGHT THE WAY

Under Divine Inspiration

> **REMEMBER!**
> **Divine inspiration** means that:
> - God guided each evangelist as he wrote his own account of Jesus's story.
> - Each evangelist only recorded the things God wanted to reveal and in the way God wanted to reveal them.

Christians believe that the Gospels were written **under divine inspiration**.

However, this does not mean that everything Jesus said was recorded in exactly the same way as he had said it. Christians believe that God guided the evangelists to truthfully record **the meaning** of what Jesus had said.

Think about this modern example: a news report on a politician's speech

This will **not** give you a word-for-word account of what the politician has said. There is not enough airtime available to do that. Instead the reporter will give you a short **summary** of what was said. While the reporter might not use the exact same words the politician used when delivering the speech, the reporter will try to accurately pass on **the meaning** of what was said.

It was the same for the evangelists. They wanted to accurately pass on **the meaning** of what Jesus had said and done. They were less interested in the exact way in which he had said or done it. This is why Christians say that you can **trust** the Gospels to tell you the truth about Jesus.

ACTIVITIES

1. Wordsearch

Find the following words:

- Gospel
- Evangelist
- Mark
- Matthew
- Luke
- John
- Biography
- Version
- Orally
- Collect
- Sayings
- Record
- Synoptic
- Divine
- Inspiration
- Meaning
- Trust

S	S	E	W	M	U	S	V	B	T	O	L	N	D	I
O	G	X	K	P	O	E	Y	S	C	E	T	O	I	X
J	S	N	H	U	R	P	I	N	P	N	M	I	V	T
U	H	G	I	S	L	L	L	S	O	K	A	T	I	G
T	H	I	I	Y	E	Y	O	U	G	P	T	A	N	N
L	X	O	L	G	A	G	D	O	M	H	T	R	E	I
F	N	R	N	D	E	S	C	X	K	Z	H	I	Z	N
F	P	A	T	C	E	L	L	O	C	T	E	P	C	A
Z	V	O	R	A	L	L	Y	R	R	K	W	S	N	E
E	B	G	Z	W	N	K	C	U	E	C	J	N	H	M
K	Q	G	Z	U	F	N	S	M	P	C	D	I	O	Z
L	R	C	S	P	M	T	A	Z	U	B	O	F	J	A
B	I	O	G	R	A	P	H	Y	G	D	K	R	A	M
S	R	G	R	Z	O	Q	M	V	L	B	H	L	D	S
D	V	X	H	X	K	S	P	U	K	U	B	K	O	N

142

Foundations of Religion - Christianity   SECTION B

2. Say what it means!

(a) Gospel means _____ .

(b) An evangelist is _____

_____ .

(c) Divine inspiration means that _____

_____

_____

_____ .

3. Tick the box!

In each of the following, say whether it is **true** or **false**.

	True	False
1. The Gospels offer us a biography of Jesus in the modern sense of the word.		
2. Mark was a missionary who travelled with St Peter to Rome.		
3. Matthew was a Greek doctor who worked as a missionary with St Paul.		
4. Luke was one of the original twelve apostles.		
5. John was one of the original twelve apostles.		
6. The first Gospel to be written was the Gospel of Luke.		
7. All the Gospels were written in the latter half of the 2nd century CE.		
8. The Gospels of Mark and Luke were most likely written by their students.		
9. Each evangelist wrote his own version of Jesus's story.		
10. The main focus of the four Gospels is to explain the meaning and importance of Jesus's teaching, miracles, death and resurrection.		
11. The Synoptic Gospels do not agree on what Jesus said and did or when that happened.		
12. The Gospel of John is a Synoptic Gospel.		

143

LIGHT THE WAY

CHAPTER 4   THE EARLY LIFE OF JESUS

The Birth of Jesus

The story of Jesus's birth is one of the best known and most attractive stories ever written. It has been the inspiration for many great works of art, literature and music.

Only two evangelists, **Matthew** and **Luke**, tell us about Jesus's birth. If we combine what they wrote, we can offer the following account:

In the little town of Nazareth in Galilee, **an angel** appeared to a young girl named Mary and told her that she was going to be the mother of the messiah. Mary was a **virgin**. So, she would have **a virgin birth**.

Did You Know?
Christians use three different names when talking about the birth of Jesus. These are:
- **The Nativity** – This comes from a Latin word meaning 'the birth' (of Jesus).
- **Christmas** – This means 'Christ's celebration'.
- **The Incarnation** – This means that God became a real human being in Jesus Christ.

REMEMBER!
An angel is a messenger sent by God.
A virgin is someone who has not yet had sexual intercourse.
The virgin birth means that Jesus was conceived in Mary's womb through the power of the Holy Spirit, not by any human effort.

Shortly after this, the Emperor Augustus announced **a census** of the Jews. He wanted to find out how many of them were eligible to pay taxes. However, you could not fill out your census details in the place where you normally lived. Instead, you had to do it in your **ancestral home** (i.e. the place where your family originally came from).

By this time Mary was married to a man named Joseph. He was a descendant of King David who came from Bethlehem in Judaea. This meant that Mary and Joseph had to leave Nazareth and travel south to Bethlehem.

THINK!
Did the shepherds really visit the infant Jesus? We cannot say for sure. Some scholars think Luke wrote this to show that Jesus had come into the world to save people of all social classes, rich and poor alike.

When Mary and Joseph reached Bethlehem they could not find a room. They were forced to take refuge in a cave. There were many caves used to shelter animals in the limestone ridge on which Bethlehem is perched. It was in one such cave that Mary gave birth to Jesus.

The Gospel of Luke says that on the night of his birth, Jesus was visited, not by wealthy Jewish nobles, but by poor shepherds from the surrounding hills.

The Gospel of Matthew tells us that Jesus was also visited by **the Magi**.

144

Foundations of Religion – Christianity   SECTION B

> **REMEMBER!**
> **The Magi** is the name given to the **astrologers** who journeyed from lands somewhere to the east of Palestine, possibly modern Iraq. Their visit is remembered on the annual **Feast of the Epiphany**, celebrated on 6 January each year.
> **An astrologer** is someone who studies the movements of the stars and planets in the belief that they have an effect on our lives.

The Magi followed a star to Bethlehem, believing that it would lead them to a great king.

They brought with them three gifts. Each gift had a meaning:

- **Gold** – This was an expensive metal. It showed they recognised Jesus as a king.
- **Frankincense** – This was burned when worshipping God. It showed they had come to worship Jesus.
- **Myrrh** – This was a spice used to embalm bodies after death. It was a warning that Jesus would have to suffer much.

However, the Magi were not the only ones seeking Jesus. **King Herod the Great** had spies throughout his kingdom. He was always ready to strike down any rival who might threaten his grip on power. When he heard about the Magi and their search for a new-born king, he had them followed. After hearing they had found the child, he ordered his troops to kill all male children in Bethlehem aged two years or younger. However, Jesus escaped death because Joseph was warned of this danger in a dream. He took Mary and Jesus to safety in Egypt. They did not return to Palestine until after Herod's death.

> **THINK!**
> Were there really Magi? We cannot say for sure. Some scholars think that Matthew included the story of the Magi to show that Jesus's message was for **all** humankind; not just the Jews.

The Date of Jesus's Birth

We cannot be sure exactly when Jesus was born. This date was not recorded anywhere in **the New Testament**. However, there are **clues** in the Gospels. If we match them with non-Christian sources, we can say that Jesus was most likely born sometime between the years 6 BCE and 4 BCE.

Many Christian scholars accept this approximate date for the following reasons:

- **The Gospel of Matthew 2: 16**

    This says that Herod the Great ordered the massacre of all male children in Bethlehem up to the age of two. Since Herod died in 4 BCE, this would seem to indicate that Jesus was born sometime between 6 BCE and 4 BCE.

- **The Gospel of Matthew 2:1-10**

    This mentions a brilliant star. Chinese astronomical records say that this star shone brightly in the night sky during 5 BCE. Because Matthew says that this 'star' moved position, some scholars think that it was **a comet**. In ancient times comets were sometimes associated with the birth of a great king. Others say that what people saw was **a supernova**, i.e. the light given off by an exploding star far off in deep space.

145

LIGHT THE WAY

Christians in the Catholic, Anglican and Protestant traditions celebrate Jesus's birth on **25 December** each year. However, we can be reasonably sure that he was **not** born on that date.

Why?

Firstly, if there were shepherds present on the night of Jesus's birth, then it did not take place in the middle of winter. Even in first-century Palestine, winter nights could be cold. Animals were sheltered indoors at that time of year. So, Jesus was more likely to have been born in either spring or autumn.

Secondly, that date was not widely used to celebrate Jesus's birth until the early fourth century CE. Until that time, 25 December was known largely as the birth date of the Roman sun god, **Mithra**.

Christians may have **appropriated** (i.e. taken over) the date of 25 December in order to:

> ■ Discourage people from continuing to celebrate the older pagan festival honouring Mithra, the sun god.
>
> ■ Encourage people to believe in and worship Jesus, who is **the Son of God**.
>
> ■ Emphasise the deep mystery that God so loves human beings that God became one of us in the form of a helpless infant lying in a manger.

Did You Know?

The worship of **Mithra** started in Persia before becoming popular in ancient Rome. The Romans referred to Mithra as **Sol Invicta** or 'the invincible Sun'. Mithra's birthdate, 25 December, was celebrated near **the winter solstice** (i.e. the shortest day of the year). As the hours of sunlight grew stronger after the solstice, his followers believed that Mithra had begun to regain his strength for another year.

Growing up in Nazareth

Jesus grew up in the village of Nazareth in Galilee. Apart from a story Luke tells us about a trip Jesus took to Jerusalem with Mary and Joseph at the age of twelve (See: **Luke** 2:41-52), we know nothing of Jesus's childhood or young adulthood. It is likely that he was educated at the local synagogue like other young males and then served his time as an apprentice carpenter/builder in Joseph's workshop.

Although Joseph was not Jesus's father, the Gospels present him as a loving and caring husband and parent. We do not know when Joseph died. It may have happened when Jesus was a teenager. Being the family breadwinner would explain why Jesus did not leave home until he was around thirty.

While the evangelists were content to say so little about Jesus's childhood, others were not. From the second century onwards, some people used their imaginations to fill in these missing details. They wrote books called **Apocrypha**.

Some of these Apocrypha offer stories about Jesus's childhood. However, Christians reject them because these stories present Jesus as someone who used his powers to impress and even harm others. This is something the Jesus of the Gospels never did. It would have been completely out of character for him to act in such selfish and destructive ways.

REMEMBER!

Apocrypha are books that claim to be authentic sacred texts but are not accepted as genuine by Christians.

Did Jesus grow up in an isolated community, cut off from the rest of the world? No. Nazareth was only three miles from the thriving trading centre of Sepphoris. This city of 30,000 people served as the capital of Herod Antipas, Tetrarch of Galilee. He invested much of his wealth into impressive building programmes and Jesus would most likely have worked on them in Sepphoris. While there he would have met people from far and wide, both Jews and gentiles.

Foundations of Religion - Christianity SECTION B

What Jesus Looked Like

Our modern image of **Jesus** dates from the sixth century CE. Ever since, Western artists have painted Jesus as a fair-skinned man in his thirties. They have shown him as long haired with an oval-shaped face, bearded with a straight nose and penetrating eyes. However, it is unlikely that Jesus actually looked like this.

The New Testament does **not** give us a physical description of Jesus. No painting or sculpture of Jesus has been found that dates from the first century CE. There are two reasons for this:

- Most of Jesus's first followers were Jews. They thought that it was disrespectful either to paint an image of God or to offer a written description of God. So they avoided physical descriptions.
- The early Christians wanted to know **who** Jesus was, and what he said and did. They had very little interest in how he looked.

Given this, is there anything that we can say about Jesus's physical appearance? Yes, but only if we piece together a number of **clues** scattered throughout the four Gospels.

Think about this:

- Jesus was a carpenter or builder by profession. He worked out of doors in all kinds of weather. This means that his skin would have been leathered and heavily tanned by the sun.
- Because of his work, Jesus would have had a muscular build. If you shook hands with him you would have noticed both the strength of his grip and how calloused his hands were.
- Jesus was well used to walking long distances. He spent entire nights deep in prayer and fasted for long periods. This tells us that Jesus was physically healthy.

Whether Jesus was physically attractive by the standards of his time, we cannot say. However, forensic experts in Israel have spent years studying the remains of Galilean Jewish males dating from the first century CE. Their research has led them to claim that Jesus most likely had a broad, rectangular-shaped face. He probably had a hooked nose, a thick neck and a heavy jaw-line. This is the kind of face that is common today in parts of North Africa.

The face of Jesus in the Shroud of Turin, Italy.

LIGHT THE WAY

ACTIVITIES

1. Say what it means!

(a) The Incarnation means that _____
_____.

(b) Apocrypha are _____
_____.

2. Crossword

Across

1. Until the fourth century, 25 December was the birth date of this Roman god.
6. After Joseph's death, Jesus may have had to fulfil this role within his family.
11. He ordered his troops to kill all male children aged two years or younger (3 words: 5, 3, 5).
12. Chinese astronomical records say that this shone brightly in the night sky during 5 BCE.
13. Someone who studies the movements of the stars and planets in the belief that they have an effect on our lives.
14. The name of Mary's husband.
17. Joseph took Mary and Jesus to safety in that country until Herod died.
19. This means that Jesus was conceived in Mary's womb through the power of the Holy Spirit, not by any human effort (2 words: 6, 5).

Foundations of Religion - Christianity   SECTION B

Down

2. The light given off by an exploding star far off in space.

3. Name for a messenger of God.

4. The name of the city only three miles away from where Jesus grew up.

5. The name given to the astrologers who journeyed from lands to the east of Palestine to visit the infant Jesus.

7. The name of the town in which Jesus grew up.

8. The town where Jesus was born.

9. This was the job that Jesus did to earn a living.

10. The Emperor Augustus announced this to find out how many Jews were eligible to pay taxes.

15. It comes from a Latin word meaning the birth (of Jesus).

16. It means 'the celebration of Christ'.

18. They were the first people to visit the infant Jesus.

19. Someone who has not yet had sexual intercourse.

3. Think about it!

(a) '**Jesus was born sometime between 6 BCE and 4 BCE.**'
What evidence is there to support this claim?

(b) Why have Christians celebrated the birth of Jesus on 25 December since the fourth century CE?

4. Think about it!

(a) The early Christians were not interested in what Jesus looked like. Why?

(b) How have Western artists painted Jesus since the sixth century?

(c) Why, do you think, these artists have painted him looking like this?

(d) What do modern scholars think Jesus really looked like?

CHAPTER 5   THE PUBLIC MINISTRY OF JESUS

The Baptism of Jesus

When Jesus was about thirty years old, he left Nazareth and went to the Jordan valley to see his cousin, **John the Baptist**.

John was **an ascetic** and **a prophet**.

> REMEMBER!
> **An ascetic** is someone who lives a life of self-denial.
> **A prophet** is someone who receives messages from God and then passes them on to others.

John the Baptist was a well-known holy man. He often spent long periods fasting and praying in the hostile desert landscape of the Judaean wilderness. He wore a rough robe made from camel hair and survived by eating only locusts and wild honey.

Large crowds flocked to hear John speak. Some people wondered if John was the promised messiah, but he denied it. He said that he had been sent by God to warn his fellow Jews that the messiah had finally arrived. To prepare for the messiah, they all needed **baptism**.

Did You Know?

For John, **baptism** meant you were completely immersed by him in the waters of the river Jordan. This had to be done if you wanted to wash away your **sins** (i.e. the wrongdoings of your past) and have a fresh start in life.

Jesus went to John and asked to be baptised like everyone else. John was reluctant to do so because he realised that Jesus was the messiah and did not need to be baptised. Indeed, John felt so unworthy that he asked Jesus to baptise him instead. However, Jesus was adamant, so John relented and baptised him in the river Jordan.

According to the Gospels, when Jesus rose up from the water, the Holy Spirit descended on him in the form of a dove, and a voice from heaven declared, '**You are my Son, the beloved, my favour rests on you**' (Mark 1:11).

What happened? All four evangelists agree that Jesus's baptism was an extraordinary event. Somehow those who witnessed it found that God was present in a way that could be both seen and heard. This is why they mentioned the dove descending on Jesus. It was a way to represent the peaceful presence of God at this event.

Why Did Jesus Choose to be Baptised?

Christians believe that Jesus was **the Son of God**. He had never sinned. He did not need baptism. So why did he ask John to baptise him?

Jesus did so to show that:

- He would really share in all the daily struggles, the joys and sorrows, of the ordinary people around him.
- He would completely dedicate his life to doing what was right, even if that led to his suffering and death at the hands of his enemies.

The Temptations in the Desert

After his baptism, Jesus went alone into the barren wilderness east of the river Jordan. He spent forty days and forty nights there, fasting and praying. He wanted to prepare himself for the many challenges he knew lay ahead. However, he was not alone. The Gospels say that Jesus had unwelcome company. On three occasions, **Satan** visited Jesus. He tried to test his determination and convince him to abuse his power. By doing so, Satan hoped to divert Jesus away from fulfilling his mission.

Christians believe that:

- Satan is a **spirit**, i.e. a being without a physical body.
- Satan is **not** God's equal. Satan was created by God but abused the gift of free will and rebelled against God. In punishment, Satan was condemned to hell for all eternity.
- Satan is an evil, harmful and malicious being who wants to draw people away from God.
- Satan does not have the power to force anyone to do wrong. However, Satan has the power **to tempt** you to do wrong.

Did You Know?

Satan is a Hebrew name meaning '**the enemy**'. Its Greek equivalent is **Diablos** or **Devil**.

The Gospels say that Satan tempted Jesus three times:

- **In the first temptation**, Satan saw that Jesus was weak from hunger. So he tempted Jesus to use his power to turn stones into bread. Jesus refused. He told Satan, '**Man cannot live on bread alone**.'
- **In the second temptation**, Satan offered Jesus great wealth and power. He said that Jesus would need it to make people follow and obey him. The only thing Satan wanted in return was for Jesus to worship him. Again, Jesus refused. He told Satan, '**You must worship the Lord your God and serve Him alone**.'
- **In the third temptation**, Satan brought Jesus to the highest point on the roof of the Temple in Jerusalem. This was 450 feet above the ground. He tried to persuade Jesus to jump from there. Satan assured Jesus that it would be safe to do this, as God the Father would send angels to save him from harm. Also, everyone who saw this spectacular event would be so impressed that they would willingly follow Jesus. Once more, Jesus refused. He told Satan, '**You must not put the Lord your God to the test**.'

At this point, Satan gave up. He knew he had failed. So he left Jesus alone, until another opportunity arose. However, Satan would return again and again to tempt Jesus to abuse his power.

LIGHT THE WAY

Jesus Begins his Public Ministry

After his confrontation with Satan, Jesus was finally ready to begin his **public ministry**.

> REMEMBER!
> **The public ministry** of Jesus was the three years he spent preaching and working miracles.

When Jesus left the wilderness, he returned to his hometown of Nazareth (see **Luke 4:16–30**). On his arrival, Jesus went to the local synagogue. There he was asked to read aloud a passage from the book of Isaiah. After he had finished reading it, Jesus told his listeners that:

- He was the promised messiah.
- His message was for everyone – both Jews and gentiles.

Those who heard this were shocked by it. They refused to believe that Jesus could be the messiah. They expected the messiah to be a great prince or a mighty warrior. However, Jesus was only a local carpenter. When Jesus refused to apologise, his former neighbours became enraged. Some even threatened to kill him. Jesus knew it was pointless trying to reason with them. So he left Nazareth for good.

Jesus moved to the city of **Capernaum** on the shores of the Sea of Galilee. From there he travelled throughout the surrounding countryside, teaching and working miracles (see **Matthew 4:23**).

Did You Know?

Capernaum was an important trading centre in the time of Jesus. **Via Maris** (i.e. the main international trade route from Africa to Asia) ran through it.

Capernaum, on the shores of the Sea of Galilee.

The Personality of Jesus

What kind of person was Jesus? If you read the four Gospels carefully, you will find many important insights into **the personality** of Jesus (i.e. the kind of person he was). You will discover that:

- Jesus was very observant. He missed nothing **(Luke 5: 27-28)**.
- He was a great storyteller (**Mark 6:34**).
- He was wise and good humoured (**Mark 12:13–17**).
- He was modest and humble **(Luke 17:7-10)**.
- He had great courage (**Luke 4:28–30** & **John 18:4–11, 33–37**).
- He was honest. He had no time for hypocrites (**Mark 11:15–18** & **Luke 11:37–54**).
- He radiated a unique authority that made people immediately take him seriously **(Matthew 7:29)**.
- He treated everyone he met with equal respect, both men and women (**Luke 10:38–42**), adults and children (**Mark 10: 13-16**), Jew and gentile (**John 4:5–30**), saint and sinner alike (**Mark 2:15–17**).
- He cared for the sick (**Luke 13:10–13**) and the outcast (**Mark 1:40 –41**).
- He refused to give in to hatred or despair (**John 13:21–30**).

The Gospels say that Jesus was a uniquely good person. Christians believe that he was **God made man**. And, being human as well as divine, Jesus needed people to help him.

The Meaning of Disciples

Those who helped Jesus were called his **disciples**.

> **REMEMBER!**
> **Disciple** means '**student**' or '**follower**'.

This term is still used today. A disciple of Jesus is someone who follows his example and continues his work.

From the start of his public ministry, Jesus invited people to become his disciples. This was unusual. Why?

In the ancient world it was the normal practice for an intending student to select his own teacher. However, Jesus's disciples did not choose him, rather **he chose them**. He **invited** each of them to be his disciples. They were free to accept or reject his offer.

Becoming a Disciple of Jesus

The Gospels show that accepting Jesus's call to be one of his disciples was a huge step to take. Read the following account:

> One day Jesus was standing on the shore of Lake Gennesaret. The people pushed their way up to him to listen to the word of God. He saw two boats pulled up on the beach; the fishermen had left them and were washing the nets. Jesus got into one of the boats – it belonged to Peter – and asked him to push off a little from the shore. Jesus sat in the boat and taught the crowd.
>
> When he finished speaking, he said to Peter, 'Push the boat out further to the deep water, then you and your partners must let down your nets for a catch.'
>
> 'Master,' Peter answered, 'we worked hard all night long and caught nothing. But if you say so, I will let down the nets.' The men let them down and caught such a large number of fish that the nets were about to break. So they motioned to their partners in the other boat to come and help them. They came and filled both boats so full of fish that the boats were about to sink. When Peter saw what had happened, he fell on his knees before Jesus and said, 'Go away from me, Lord! I am a sinful man!'
>
> He and the others with him were all amazed at the large number of fish they had caught. The same was true of Peter's partners, James and John, the sons of Zebedee. Jesus said to them, 'Don't be afraid, from now on it is people you will catch.'
>
> They pulled the boats up on the beach, left everything, and followed Jesus.
>
> *Luke 5:1–11*

LIGHT THE WAY

The Apostles

The disciples closest to Jesus were called **the apostles**.

> REMEMBER!
> **Apostle** means 'one who is sent out'.

The apostles were sent out by Jesus to spread his message far and wide.

The choosing of his apostles was the first important act of Jesus's public ministry. There were **twelve** in all. Their names are recorded in the Synoptic Gospels. They were:

- Peter (whom Jesus appointed as the leader of the apostles)
- Andrew
- James, son of Zebedee
- John
- Philip
- Thomas
- Bartholomew
- Matthew
- James, son of Alphaeus
- Thaddeus (aka Jude)
- Judas Iscariot
- Simon the Zealot.

Did You Know?

The Catholic, Orthodox and Anglican traditions say that their bishops are the successors of the original apostles.

The apostles came from different backgrounds:

- Peter, Andrew, James and John were fishermen.
- Matthew had been a tax collector.
- Simon was a former Zealot.

The apostles were ordinary, flawed human beings. Christians of every era have readily identified with them. For example:

- Sometimes the apostles did not understand the meaning or grasp the importance of what Jesus had said (see **Mark 4:13**).
- Sometimes they quarrelled among themselves (see **Luke 9:46–48**).
- They all abandoned Jesus when he was arrested in the Garden of Gethsemane (see **Matthew 26:56**).
- One of them – Peter – publicly denied ever knowing Jesus (see **Luke 22:54–62**).
- Another – Judas Iscariot – betrayed Jesus to his enemies (see **Luke 22:1–6**).

Yet, Jesus saw a great potential for good in each of them. After Pentecost, the apostles justified his trust in them. They dedicated the rest of their lives to continuing the work he had begun.

Did You Know?

Jesus chose **twelve** apostles. This number had a special meaning for Jews. Originally, there had been twelve tribes in the ancient Jewish Kingdom of Israel. Jesus hoped that his twelve apostles would be the first members of a new kind of kingdom – **the Kingdom of God**.

Foundations of Religion - Christianity SECTION B

ACTIVITIES

1. Say what it means!
(a) An ascetic is _____.
(b) The public ministry of Jesus was _____
   _____.
(c) Disciple means _____.
(d) Apostle means _____.

2. Crossword

Across
1. The number of apostles.
2. Peter, Andrew James and John did this for a living.
3. The name given to the three Gospels where the names of the apostles are recorded.
4. It means the wrongdoings of your past.
7. It is a Hebrew name meaning 'the enemy'.
8. When Jesus was baptised, the Holy Spirit descended on him in this form.
10. Catholics, Orthodox and Anglicans say that these people are the successors of the original apostles.
13. This apostle betrayed Jesus to his enemies (2 words: 5, 8).
15. The number of years Jesus spent on his public ministry.
16. This apostle had been a tax collector.
17. The way John the Baptist was related to Jesus.

Down
1. Satan did this three times to Jesus.
5. This apostle was a former Zealot.
6. John the Baptist wore a robe made from this (2 words: 5, 4).
9. Jesus went to the synagogue in that town, after spending forty days and forty nights in the wilderness.
11. Jesus was about this age when he left Nazareth.
12. Jesus made him the leader of the apostles.
13. John said that you had to be completely immersed in the waters of this river in order to be baptised.
14. The city on the shores of the Sea of Galilee where Jesus lived after being forced to leave his hometown.

155

LIGHT THE WAY

3. Fill in the missing words!

In the first temptation, Satan told Jesus to turn stones into b_____. Jesus refused. He told Satan, '_____.'

In the second temptation, Satan offered Jesus great w_____ and p_____ if he would w_____ him. Jesus refused. He told Satan, '_____
_____.'

In the third temptation, Satan tried to persuade Jesus to j_____ from the top of the T_____. Jesus refused. He told Satan, '_____
_____.'

4. Think about it!

(a) Why do you think the Jews in the synagogue in Nazareth found it so difficult to accept that Jesus was the messiah?

(b) **'The apostles were ordinary, flawed human beings.'**
What evidence is there to support this claim?

(c) **Read the following story:**

God's Golden Acre

Heather Reynolds is a nurse. She lives in South Africa. Her early life was a great struggle. Her father's alcoholism made her childhood miserable. Her first marriage ended in divorce. She had lost her faith in people and was close to despair, until she rediscovered her faith in God.

Reynolds says that she found the comfort and support she needed in prayer. It gave her the strength to rebuild her life. It also gave her a new outlook on life. She learned to see **beyond** her own suffering. She became aware that many people around her badly needed her help.

Reynolds lived in Kwa Zula in the Natal province. It was an area badly affected by deaths from **HIV/AIDS**-related illnesses.

Heather Reynolds (2nd from left) with Jude Law and young Zulu warriors at the opening of a musical in London.

HIV/AIDS was first diagnosed in 1981. It destroys the human immune system. It leaves you defenceless against common infections. It has caused the deaths of millions of people worldwide. At its peak, more than 250 HIV/AIDS-related deaths were recorded each day in the Natal province.

One day, Reynolds came across a village where there were only children left alive. All the adults were dead. There was no one to help them, except her.

Reynolds felt that her whole life had led up to this point. She believed that God was calling her to care for these abandoned children. With the support of her second husband, **Patrick**, she used their life savings to set up **God's Golden Acre**. This is a charity that cares for children left orphaned by HIV/AIDS.

At the outset, Reynolds faced a lot of opposition. Some people were hostile towards her for highlighting a crisis that they would rather ignore. Others were indifferent to her, doubting that

Foundations of Religion - Christianity   SECTION B

anything could be done to improve the situation. However, with the help of generous donors, Reynolds provided a safe place for an ever-growing number of orphaned children. She rescued them from abuse, disease, poverty and starvation. Today, her organisation provides care for thousands of orphaned and abandoned children.

Heather Reynolds draws the inspiration and strength needed to do her work from her Christian faith. She believes that this is her vocation (i.e. what she is called by God to do). She is a modern-day **disciple** of Jesus Christ.

1. Jesus said that in order to become one of his disciples, you had to experience a **metanoia**, i.e. completely change your whole outlook on life. What evidence is there that Heather Reynolds experienced a metanoia?

2. Do you think Heather Reynolds deserves to be called '**a modern-day disciple of Jesus Christ**'? Explain your answer.

LIGHT THE WAY

CHAPTER 6   THE TEACHINGS OF JESUS

The Authority of Jesus

Imagine a group of science students sitting in a lecture theatre. They are all listening with great interest to an invited guest-speaker. He is a former student of their college. He is now a famous and wealthy inventor. He is here to share the story of his success with them. What he says is based on personal experience.

The students take what he says very seriously. After all, if he didn't know what he is talking about, he would never have become so successful, would he? He can tell them what they need to know if they too want to succeed.

In all areas of life, the most successful communicators are those who speak with **authority**.

> **REMEMBER!**
> **Authority** means knowing what you are talking about because you have put it into practice in your own life.

This was one reason why Jesus attracted so many disciples. His teaching wasn't just 'words' like that of so many other teachers. What he said was backed up by how he lived (see **Matthew 7:28–29**).

The Meaning of Parable

We all enjoy a good story, whether it is factual or fictional. We like thought-provoking, memorable tales. Jesus knew this too. He had important things to say. However, these were very difficult ideas for people to grasp. He didn't want people to simply learn by rote (i.e. know his teachings off by heart). He wanted them to think for themselves. This is why Jesus told stories. These stories are called parables.

> **REMEMBER!**
> **A parable** is an easily remembered story. It uses examples taken from everyday life to help us understand an important idea.

The parables make up about one-third of the total content of the Gospels. Each one contains an important part of Jesus's preaching about the Kingdom of God.

> **REMEMBER!**
> **To preach** means to **explain** or to **make known**.

To understand Jesus's parables, we need to learn about the time and place in which they were originally composed.

Did You Know?

Today we can have difficulties understanding Jesus's parables. Unlike his listeners in first-century Palestine, few of us earn our living from agriculture. We are not familiar with many of the examples Jesus used. He drew on things that were familiar to people at that time, such as the mustard seed, the sower in the field or the workers in the vineyard.

158

Foundations of Religion - Christianity SECTION B

Explaining the Kingdom of God

If you read the Gospels, this same phrase appears again and again – the **Kingdom of God**. This is not an easy teaching to understand.

To people today, a kingdom means a place marked out on a map. Most Jews in Jesus's time thought so too. They hoped that the messiah would set up and reign over an independent Jewish kingdom in the Middle East.

This was not what Jesus was talking about. The Kingdom of God is **not** a place on the map. So what is it?
Jesus never gave a precise explanation of what he meant by it. Instead, he offered memorable parables about it. He wanted to challenge people and set them thinking about what the Kingdom of God means.

Did You Know?

When trying to work out the meaning of a parable, you need to remember that it works on two levels:
On the surface – A parable is an interesting, easily remembered story. It uses images drawn from everyday life in first-century Palestine.

Beneath the surface – A parable is a story with a message contained within it. Jesus wants us to work this out, think about it and respond to it.

If we comb through Jesus's parables, we can build up a clearer picture of what he was talking about.

Let us begin by looking at two of Jesus's best-known parables. We will find clues in each of them.

Parable 1: The Good Samaritan   Read Luke 10:25–37

This is the story of how a Samaritan man rescues and cares for a Jewish man who has been viciously attacked, robbed and left for dead.

The Samaritans were a people who lived in Samaria. This was the part of Palestine located between Galilee in the north and Judaea in the south. The Samaritans were descendants of Jews who, long ago, had married non-Jews. The majority of Jews would not accept the Samaritans' mixed blood. So, they rejected and isolated them. For example:
- Samaritans were not allowed to worship in the Temple in Jerusalem. They had to build one of their own on Mount Gerazim.
- Samaritans could not give evidence in a Jewish court.

The Good Samaritan by Rafael Tejeo.

By the first century CE, the level of mistrust and hostility between Jews and Samaritans had become so great that they always kept apart. Indeed, Jews moving between Galilee and Judaea usually crossed over the river Jordan and travelled along its eastern bank, just to avoid any contact with Samaritans.

Jesus would have shocked his Jewish listeners with this parable. They would have expected the Samaritan to be the villain, not the hero of the story. However, Jesus did this to get two ideas across:
- There is no place for racial or religious bigotry in the Kingdom of God.
- Your neighbour is **anyone** who needs you or will help you.

159

LIGHT THE WAY

Parable 2: The Prodigal Son   Read Luke 15:11–32

Jesus told this story after the Pharisees had complained that he was spending too much time in the company of sinners and outcasts.

The chief character in this parable is **the father**, not the son of its title. The father represents **God**. He is shown to be extraordinarily forgiving towards **both** of his sons, as both were guilty of wrongdoing.

Think about this:

- The younger son was prodigal, i.e. wasteful of all his father had given to him.
- The older son was self-righteous and **unforgiving**.

Jesus makes it quite clear that the younger son represents the sinners and outcasts of society, while the older son represents the Pharisees.

Jesus wants his listeners to understand two things:
- God's love is always available to us.
- The Kingdom of God is open to anyone who is truly sorry and asks God for forgiveness.

Living in the Kingdom of God

The Kingdom of God is not about geography. It is about following Jesus's commandment to:

'Love God and love your neighbour as yourself.'

In order to live like this, Jesus said that you must start with **repentance**.

> **REMEMBER!**
> **Repentance** means being truly sorry for your sins and doing everything you can to live a better life.

Jesus's teaching about how you should live in the Kingdom of God can be found in **the Sermon on the Mount** (see **the Gospel of Matthew**, chapters 5 to 7).

The Sermon on the Mount.

> **REMEMBER!**
> **A sermon** is a talk that explains important religious teachings.

If you read the Sermon on the Mount, you will see that Jesus begins it with **the Beatitudes**.

> **REMEMBER!**
> **The Beatitudes** are the personal qualities you need to develop if you want to live in the Kingdom of God.

To enter the Kingdom of God you must be:

- **Repentant:** Truly sorry for your sins and determined to live a better life.
- **Humble:** Aware of both your strengths and your weaknesses. Ready to ask for God's grace (i.e. love and strength) to help you live a good life.
- **Compassionate:** Ready to forgive those who offend you.
- **Faithful:** Willing to enter dialogue but ready to stand up for what you believe.
- **Hopeful:** Have a positive outlook on life because you trust in God.
- **Confident:** At peace with yourself and others because you know God loves you.
- **Courageous:** Willing to do what is right rather than what is popular or profitable.

Foundations of Religion - Christianity   SECTION B

How do you become someone with these qualities? Jesus said that you must do three things:
- Love your enemies (**Matthew 5:38**).
- Do what is right without looking for recognition or reward (**Matthew 6:1–18**).
- Treat others as you would have them treat you (**Matthew 7:12**).

Clearly, Jesus set a very high standard for his disciples to follow. He himself lived up to it in every day of his public ministry. Let us look at two examples of how he put his teaching about the Kingdom of God into practice.

Example 1: Equality between the sexes

In today's developed world, women are guaranteed by law to enjoy the same rights as men. For example:
- Once eighteen, both men and women are eligible to vote.
- Both men and women can stand for election to public office.
- Women are entitled to equal pay for work of the same value.
- Both men and women may apply for any job, once they have the necessary qualifications.

However, such equal rights were not won until quite recently. Women in the developed world only achieved them after years of courageous and tireless campaigning. Most women in the developing world are still struggling to achieve them.

For much of human history, women have lived in **patriarchal societies**.

> REMEMBER!
> **A patriarchal society** is one where men dominate and women are treated as second-class citizens.

Jesus lived in a patriarchal society. He saw how women were generally looked down upon by men. Women were treated as the property of either their fathers or their husbands. Women were denied the right to choose how to live their own lives. For example, in first-century Palestine:
- A woman could be married off by her father without her consent. Her happiness was not considered important.
- A man could divorce his wife. However, a woman had no right to divorce her husband.

The evangelists show that Jesus was very different from other men of that time. He did not share their attitudes towards women. Instead, Jesus treated women as **equals**. For example:
- Jesus included women among his disciples (see **Luke 8:1–3**).
- Jesus had private conversations with women. He took what women said seriously and treated them with respect. In doing so, Jesus defied the social conventions of that time (see **John 4:5–42**).
- Jesus treated his male and female followers just the same (see **Luke 10:38–42**).
- Jesus readily accepted help from women and publicly thanked them for their help (see **Luke 7:36–50**).
- Jesus took a firm stand against the unjust and hypocritical treatment of women. For example, when he defended the woman accused of adultery (**John 8:1–11**) or when he healed the crippled woman on the Sabbath (**Luke 13:10–17**).

Jesus said that he had come into the world to free the oppressed, to raise up the humble and to give hope to those who are discouraged by life. He wanted to show that:
- The Kingdom of God breaks down all those barriers that divide people and cause so much injustice and unhappiness in this world.
- All human beings, whatever their gender, race or social class are equal in God's eyes.

Jesus set a high standard that he wanted his disciples to live up to.

161

LIGHT THE WAY

Example 2: Table fellowship

Today, we often celebrate important events in our lives – such as birthdays, weddings and anniversaries – by sharing a meal with family and friends. The same was true of people in first-century Palestine. For Jews, sharing a meal served two important functions:

- **Social:** When you extended hospitality to a fellow Jew, it was seen as an act of friendship.
- **Religious:** When you participated in the weekly Sabbath meal, it showed how you and your fellow Jews were united by your shared faith in God.

So, in the time of Jesus, sharing a meal was an event of great importance for Jews. Generally speaking, Jews were expected to keep two rules:

- Never to share a meal with non-Jews.
- Only share a meal with someone of the same social class as yourself.

However, the Pharisees took this even further. They would only eat with their fellow Jews after they had completed a series of strict handwashing rituals.

The Gospels say that Jesus shocked his critics by sharing meals with the poor, the outcast and gentiles. For example:

- Jesus angered the Pharisee who had invited him to dinner by pointing out how 'the woman who had sinned' had shown him far greater kindness and hospitality than his host (see **Luke 7: 36-50**).
- Jesus accepted an invitation to dine in the home of the tax collector Zacchaeus, who then became one of his disciples (see **Luke 19: 1-10**).

When Jesus shared these meals he offered his disciples examples of **table fellowship**.

REMEMBER!
Table fellowship means sharing a meal with others in a spirit of compassion, equality and friendship.

Through table fellowship, Jesus told his disciples that in the Kingdom of God:

- The poor are treated with compassion and respect.
- Those who repent and ask for forgiveness will receive it.
- Everyone is treated equally. There are no social classes and no outcasts.

The Kingdom of God is open to **everyone** – men and women, adults and children, Jew and gentile, rich and poor alike.

Foundations of Religion - Christianity   SECTION B

The Kingdom of God

A summary

By reflecting on what Jesus said and did during his public ministry, we can say that:

- The Kingdom of God began in Jesus's life and work. It continues today wherever people repent their sins and try to follow his example.
- Everyone is welcome in the Kingdom of God: men and women, adults and children, Jews and non-Jews, rich and poor alike.
- The Kingdom of God is a great mystery. We can gain insights into it through prayer, study and living good lives. However, only God will ever fully understand it.
- Jesus will bring the Kingdom of God to completion when he returns at the end of history.

ACTIVITIES

1. Wordsearch

Find the following words:

Authority
Preach
Parable
Kingdom of God
Samaritan
Prodigal
Unforgiving
Repentance
Sermon
Beatitudes
Merciful
Peacemaker
Courageous
Patriarchal
Equality
Fellowship
Compassion
Friendship

```
F E L L O W S H I P M G Q S R
P I H S D N E I R F Q I R U K
N Y M L H L P Y E A U E E O S
A P U E R Y A S C W P L Q E U
T Q U R R M T P G E N B U G K
I K D N E C R I N A R A A A C
R Q V C F K I T R H R R L R O
A J R C O O A F S O B A I U M
M Z N O J N R M U E H P T O P
A N Q D C C C G E L R T Y C A
S P R E A C H A I C H M U G S
P R O D I G A L V V A X O A S
S T I I Z U L G Q X I E Q N I
A S E D U T I T A E B N P P O
K I N G D O M O F G O D G F N
```

2. Say what it means!

(a) Authority means _____

_____.

(b) To preach means _____.

(c) A parable is _____

_____.

(d) A sermon is _____.

(e) The Beatitudes are _____

_____.

(f) A patriarchal society is _____

_____.

163

LIGHT THE WAY

3. Tick the box!

In each of the following, say whether it is **true** or **false**.

	True	False
1. Jesus simply wanted his followers to learn his teachings off by heart and not think for themselves.		
2. Jesus attracted many disciples because his teaching wasn't just 'words'. What he said was backed up by how he lived.		
3. A parable is a story with a deeper meaning contained within it.		
4. The Parable of the Good Samaritan tells the story of a Jewish man who rescues a Samaritan who has been robbed and left for dead at the side of the road.		
5. By the first century CE, Jews and Samaritans were on good terms with one another.		
6. Jesus would have delighted his Jewish listeners by telling the Parable of the Good Samaritan.		
7. In today's developing world, women are guaranteed by law to enjoy the same rights as men.		
8. Palestine in the time of Jesus was a patriarchal society.		
9. Jesus did not include women among his disciples.		
10. Jesus treated his male and female followers just the same.		
11. The Kingdom of God is all about geography.		
12. First-century Jews were allowed to share a meal with non-Jews.		
13. Jesus angered the Pharisees by sharing meals with sinners and outcasts.		
14. Jesus taught that the Kingdom of God is open to everyone.		

4. Think about it!

(a) Why would science students be willing to listen carefully to what a famous and successful inventor has to say to them?

(b) Why were many people in first-century Palestine willing to listen to what Jesus had to say?

(c) Why did Jesus use parables to communicate his teachings?

(d) Jesus said that to enter the Kingdom of God we need to do three things:
  1. Love your enemies.
  2. Do what is right without looking for recognition or reward.
  3. Treat others as you would have them treat you.

Why do people find it so difficult to live up to these standards of behaviour?

Foundations of Religion - Christianity   SECTION B

CHAPTER 7   THE MIRACLES OF JESUS

The Meaning of Miracle

Jesus's public ministry involved him not only teaching through parables, but also working miracles.

> REMEMBER!
> A **miracle** is a wonderful and awe-inspiring event. It has only **one** explanation – **God did it**.

Jesus's parables explained the Kingdom of God in ways people could understand. His miracles showed them that the Kingdom of God had begun in him.

Thirty-five miracle stories are recorded in the Gospels. They are organised as follows:

The types of miracle Jesus performed	An Example of this miracle is . . .	This miracle tells us that . . .
1. Healing miracle	The healing of the man afflicted with leprosy (Luke 5:12–14)	God has the power to conquer all those things that cause us harm and make us suffer.
2. Exorcism (i.e. casting out demons)	The Gadarene Demoniac (Mark 5:1–20)	God can overcome every form of evil that affects our lives.
3. Nature miracle	The calming of the storm (Matthew 8:23–27)	God can do marvellous things that are unexpected and beyond our understanding.
4. Restoration to life	The raising of Jairus's daughter (Luke 8:41–42 and 49-56)	The power of God is greater than death. Nothing can stand in the way of God's love for us.

Difficulties with the Idea of Miracles

Some people have difficulty accepting that Jesus worked miracles. They say that Jesus would be more acceptable without the miracle stories. However it is impossible to extract a miracle-free account of Jesus's life from the Gospels. Why?

Here are two important reasons:
- The story of Jesus's conception in Mary's womb is a miracle.
- Christianity itself is founded on the miracle of Jesus's resurrection.

The miracles of Jesus are as important to his story as his teachings.

The Evidence for Jesus as a Miracle-Worker

Our most important sources of information about Jesus's miracles come from the four Gospels. These accounts were written by Christians who had either witnessed the events themselves or had talked to those who had been there to witness them.

165

LIGHT THE WAY

However, in ancient times, several **non-Christian writers** also accepted that Jesus worked miracles. Here are three examples:

- The first-century Jewish historian **Josephus** described Jesus as '**a doer of wonderful deeds**', i.e. someone who worked miracles.
- A second-century opponent of Christianity named **Celsus** readily admitted that Jesus worked miracles.
- The third-century Jewish **Talmud** states that Jesus had the power to work miracles. However it claimed that Jesus had been given this power by Satan, not by God.

Jesus heals the sick.

Did You Know?

Hansen's disease is an illness which, if left untreated, can cause blindness, severe disfigurement and death.

Exploring the Healing Miracles

Example 1: The Healing of a Leper   Read: Luke 5:12–14

In this story, Jesus meets a man suffering from **leprosy** – or what is known today as **Hansen's disease**.

Modern medicine has discovered that leprosy is caused by a chronic bacterial infection. Two thousand years ago, people didn't know what caused leprosy. They only knew that, at that time, there was no cure for it. Naturally, it terrified them. They didn't know that only about 3 per cent of a population is at risk of contracting this disease. Nor did they realise that a person with leprosy is only infectious in the early stages of the disease. However, due to their ignorance, **lepers** were treated as social outcasts. They were ordered to keep apart from other people and forced to live as wandering beggars.

> REMEMBER!
> **A leper** was someone who was afflicted with leprosy/Hansen's disease.

The Jews dreaded leprosy. So, Jesus would have deeply shocked any onlookers by the way he responded to the man afflicted with leprosy. Not only did Jesus heal the man, but he actually **touched** him. By doing this, Jesus did something that no one else would have dared to do at that time. Indeed, the Temple priests, who were obsessed with cleanliness, went to any lengths to avoid physical contact with anyone suffering from this or any other disease. They did not allow the sick or the disabled to enter the inner courts of the Temple. At that time the physically disabled were not treated as real human beings. Jews were expected to either pity or despise them, but not to treat them as equals.

Jesus openly rejected such attitudes. He showed that, while other people may have rejected the man afflicted with leprosy, God had not. Jesus's actions in this story reveal that in the Kingdom of God no one is abandoned, demeaned, ignored and left to suffer alone.

Further, notice that the man is healed **instantly**. We cannot do this today. A lengthy course of treatment would be needed. Also, while we can now treat Hansen's disease, anyone afflicted by it would still be left with visible damage to the face, limbs and nervous system. Yet the man in this story was restored to full health. This is what Jesus meant when he told the man to '**show himself**' to the Temple priest. He had had all traces of the disease removed from his body.

Foundations of Religion - Christianity   SECTION B

Example 2: The Healing of the Paralysed man   Read: Luke 5:17–26

Jesus was teaching to a large crowd gathered at a disciple's house. The numbers present were so great that some men who had brought their friend to ask Jesus to heal him could not get through. The man had been unable to walk since birth and had to be carried everywhere on a stretcher. They showed some initiative by getting up on the roof of the house, making an opening in it and lowering their friend's stretcher right down in front of Jesus. To the amazement of all present, Jesus removed this man's disability and enabled him to walk for the first time in his life.

Jesus worked this miracle in response to the faith the paralysed man and his friends had in him. He did not do it to win over his most vocal opponents – the Pharisees.

Before Jesus healed this paralysed man, he told him that his sins were forgiven.

The Pharisees present were horrified by what Jesus had said. They would not accept that he had the power to forgive sins. They said that **only God** can forgive sins. They said that Jesus was claiming to be as important as God. So, they accused Jesus of **blasphemy**.

> **REMEMBER!**
> **Blasphemy** means showing great disrespect to God by what you say or do.

Jesus responded directly to their accusation. He insisted that he truly did have the power to forgive sins. He had not only healed the paralysed man out of compassion but also to show that he spoke only the truth.

To understand the full significance of what Jesus did in this miracle, you need to understand how people at that time understood illness and sin.

- Most Jews at that time tended to link illness and sin. So much so that many of them had little faith in doctors. Since God is the source of all life and well-being, most Jews believed that people only became ill or disabled because God had punished them for their sins.
- A first-century Jew suffering a long-term illness or disability was considered **impure**, i.e. not fit to worship in the Temple. Your illness or disability was taken as proof that God had rejected you.
- So, the Jews would only believe that the paralysed man's sins had been forgiven if they saw that his paralysis had been cured and that he had been restored to full health and mobility. Only then would they accept him back into society. Only then would he be allowed to worship in the Temple, as his relationship with God would be restored.
- Without such clear, solid evidence of Jesus's power over sin, suffering and death, his preaching about the Kingdom of God would have held little credibility with his Jewish audience. Christians believe that by healing the paralysed man Jesus showed that:
  (a) He had the power to forgive sins; and (b) **this power came from God.**

Above all, it means that what Jesus claimed about himself was true. He was indeed the promised messiah.

Exploring the Other Types of Miracles

The Gadarene Demoniac   Read: Mark 5:1–20

(Example of an Exorcism)
To modern ears, this is a strange tale. It tells of what happened when Jesus travelled to Gadara, a town on the southern shore of the Sea of Galilee, in an area known as the Decapolis. There Jesus encountered a man who was **possessed**.

> **REMEMBER!**
> **Possessed** means that you have freely chosen to put yourself under the control of a demon (i.e. an evil spirit).

This possessed man lived in one of the tombs at the local cemetery. He ran around naked, ranting and raving at people; threatening them with violence at the top of his voice. All the locals were terrified of him. His condition left him totally isolated from everyone.

167

LIGHT THE WAY

When Jesus met him, the man said that his name was 'Legion' because he had been possessed by so many demons. Jesus cast out these demons whom he then allowed to flee into a nearby herd of pigs. The entire herd became so agitated that it then ran off a cliff and drowned in the waters below. When the local inhabitants came to see what was causing such a disturbance, they found the man sitting fully clothed, calmly talking with Jesus. However, the locals were so disturbed by this whole episode that they asked Jesus to leave at once.

Some modern scholars wonder if it was mental illness rather than possession that had shattered this man's life and left him isolated. However, whether it was possession or mental illness, Jesus had restored him to his right mind. This man was able to rejoin his community and rebuild his life. By his actions, Jesus had demonstrated that in the Kingdom of God, isolation, rage and despair are replaced by community, peace and hope.

The Raising of Jairus's Daughter

Read: Luke 8:41–42 and 49-56

(Example of a Restoration to Life)

In this story, Jesus is asked by Jairus, an important official of a local synagogue, to save his young daughter's life. She is gravely ill. However, before Jesus can see her, news arrives that she has died. Despite this Jesus goes to Jairus's house and asks to see her. Those present who are mourning the family's loss mock Jesus when he refuses to accept that he is no longer needed. Surely there is nothing more to be done? What can he do now? Who does he think he is?

Only the girl's parents continue to have faith in Jesus. Their faith is rewarded. Jesus holds the young girl's hand and commands her to get up. At that, she is restored to life. Then Jesus asks that she be given something to eat. However, before he leaves, Jesus asks the family not to discuss this event with anyone else.

Jesus Christ raising Jairus's daughter.

Did You Know?

Jesus was often reluctant to perform miracles. He frequently told people he had helped not to tell anyone about what he had done.

Jesus always refused to use his miraculous powers to gain popularity or win followers. This was the very thing Satan had tried to tempt him to do during his forty days in the desert.

Jesus only worked miracles to strengthen or reward the faith of those who already believed in him.

Today, some people are sceptical of this Gospel story. They say that Jairus's daughter was not raised from the dead because she was never dead in the first place. Instead, she may have been in **a coma**.

REMEMBER!

A coma is where a person falls into a deep sleep and does not respond to either external stimuli (i.e. pinching or shouting) or internal stimuli (i.e. a full bladder).

Usually, a coma is the result of brain trauma caused by a head injury or due to an illness such as meningitis (i.e. where there is an inflammation of the brain's protective covering). These are serious conditions and they require urgent medical treatment. They are not easily or quickly treated. Yet, Jesus restored this girl to life and full health instantly.

Foundations of Religion - Christianity   SECTION B

Further, if Jairus's daughter was in a coma, she would still have been breathing or showing some roving eye movement. These show that there is still activity in the person's lower brain stem. However, this girl did not display either of these. This means that she had suffered total loss of brain function. She had died. She could only have been restored to life because Jesus worked a miracle.

ACTIVITIES

1. Wordsearch

Find each of the following words:

Miracle
Healing
Exorcism
Nature
Restoration
Josephus
Celsus
Talmud
Leprosy
Instantly
Blasphemy
Impure
Sins
Forgive
Possessed
Gadarene
Jairus
Coma
Dead
Alive

N	R	Y	G	Y	J	E	G	N	W	O	W	M	V	J
S	O	J	M	L	E	N	X	H	K	G	G	R	N	O
N	Y	I	E	T	R	V	N	O	A	C	Y	Q	E	S
I	V	V	T	N	C	E	I	D	R	M	P	V	T	E
S	W	D	W	A	R	E	A	L	E	C	I	B	P	P
M	A	S	U	T	R	R	L	H	A	G	I	P	W	H
G	V	W	M	S	E	O	P	S	R	B	C	S	Q	U
Y	N	R	K	N	O	S	T	O	U	D	R	A	M	S
S	B	I	E	I	A	Z	F	S	P	S	D	E	A	D
O	E	T	L	L	P	O	S	S	E	S	S	E	D	I
R	C	A	B	A	N	E	L	C	A	R	I	M	M	A
P	E	L	D	E	E	L	C	M	A	Q	N	P	M	K
E	G	M	I	R	N	H	H	G	D	V	U	O	N	H
L	X	U	W	N	A	T	U	R	E	R	C	Q	M	Z
E	J	D	S	U	R	I	A	J	E	T	D	Z	F	N

2. Say what it means!

(a) A miracle is _____
_____ .

(b) Blasphemy means _____
_____ .

3. Match it!

Match the type of miracle listed in Column **A** with the correct example in column **B**.

A. Type of miracle	B. Example
Healing miracle	The raising of Jairus's daughter
Exorcism	The calming of the storm
Nature miracle	The man afflicted with leprosy
Restoration to life	The Gadarene demoniac

169

LIGHT THE WAY

Fill in your answers in the spaces provided below.

A. Type of miracle	B. Example
Healing miracle	
Exorcism (i.e. casting out demons)	
Nature miracle	
Restoration to life	

4. Tick the box!

In each of the following, say whether it is **true** or **false**.

	True	False
1. Some thirty-five miracle stories are recorded in the Gospels.		
2. Jesus performed five different types of miracle.		
3. Jesus worked miracles to show that the Kingdom of God had begun in him.		
4. The story of how Jesus healed a Roman centurion's servant is an example of a nature miracle.		
5. The story of how Jesus walked on water is an example of a healing miracle.		
6. The story of how Jesus fed 5,000 people by multiplying five loaves and two fishes is an example of a nature miracle.		
7. The story of how Jesus raised his friend Lazarus from the dead is an example of a restoration-to-life miracle.		
8. Christianity is founded on the miracle of Jesus's resurrection.		
9. Leprosy is known today as Parkinson's disease.		
10. The Jews dreaded leprosy. Lepers were treated as social outcasts.		
11. Jesus shocked his fellow Jews by touching the man afflicted with leprosy.		
12. The man afflicted by leprosy was cured instantly and all traces of the disease were removed from his body.		
13. The Pharisees accepted that Jesus had the power to forgive sins.		
14. The Pharisees accused Jesus of blasphemy.		
15. For a first-century Jew, illness or disability was taken as proof that God had rejected you and was punishing you for your sins.		
16. The Jews would only believe that the paralysed man's sins had been forgiven if they saw that his paralysis had been cured and that he had been restored to full health and mobility.		

Foundations of Religion - Christianity **SECTION B**

	True	False
17. 'Possessed' means that a person has been forced to come under the control of an evil spirit.		
18. The possessed man Jesus met at Gadara said his name was Jairus.		
19. Jairus and his wife continued to have faith in Jesus even after their daughter had died and everyone else around them mocked Jesus.		
20. Jesus only worked miracles to gain popularity and win followers.		
21. Jesus only worked miracles to strengthen or reward the faith people already had in him.		

5. Think about it!

(a) Is it possible to extract a miracle-free account of Jesus's life from the Gospels? Give a reason for your answer.

(b) Read the following statement: 'There is strong evidence to support the claim that Jesus performed miracles during his public ministry.' Do you agree or disagree? Why?

LIGHT THE WAY

CHAPTER 8   CONFLICT WITH AUTHORITY

The Meaning of Martyrdom

Above the great west door of Westminster Abbey in London, you can see ten statues, all situated side by side. Each one is carved in the likeness of an extraordinary Christian man or woman. Their names were:

Dietrich Bonhoeffer (1906–1945) – A Lutheran minister
He was executed for being a member of the anti-Nazi resistance in Germany and for his involvement in the plot to assassinate Adolf Hitler in July 1944.

St Elizabeth of Russia (1864–1918) – A Russian Orthodox nun
She established a hospital and dedicated her life to helping the poor. She was executed by the Bolshevik government during its campaign to wipe out all traces of religious belief and practice within the Soviet Union (Russia).

Esther John (1923–1960) – A lay teacher of the Anglican Communion
She devoted her life to caring for the sick and educating the poor in Pakistan. She was murdered for being a Christian.

Martin Luther King, Jr. (1919–1968) – A Baptist minister
He dedicated his life to achieving civil rights for African Americans. He was awarded the Nobel Peace Prize for his work. He was assassinated by a racist gunman.

Maximilian Kolbe (1894–1942) – A Catholic priest
He was imprisoned at Auschwitz concentration camp during World War II. He offered his own life in exchange for the life of a fellow prisoner who had been condemned to death.

Janani Luwum (1922–1977) – An Anglican archbishop
He formed an alliance between Catholics and Muslims to peacefully oppose the cruel dictatorship of Idi Amin in Uganda. This cost him his life.

Manche Masemola (1913–1928) – An Anglican lay woman
A native of South Africa, she wanted to be baptised a Christian. She was murdered by non-Christian members of her own family who refused to let her become a Christian.

Oscar Romero (1917–1980) – A Catholic archbishop
He fearlessly exposed the cruelty of the armed forces in El Salvador. He was murdered by an assassin while celebrating Mass.

Lucien Tapiedi (1921–1942) – A lay teacher of the Anglican Communion
He bravely turned down an offer to be evacuated from Papua New Guinea after the Japanese invasion. He remained there to care for his fellow Christians, but was later betrayed and murdered.

Wang Zhimang (1903–1973) – A Protestant pastor
He openly opposed the cruel policies of Chairman Mao in China. He was executed on Mao's orders in a failed attempt to intimidate other Christians.

Statue of Manche Masemola, Westminster Abbey, London.

All these men and women were **martyrs**.

172

> **REMEMBER!**
> A **martyr** is someone who is willing to die for what he/she believes.

None of these men and women wanted to die. They all wanted to live out their lives. However, as devout Christians they were prepared to die for their religious faith. They all saw themselves as following in the footsteps of Jesus Christ, who gave his own life for what he believed was right and just.

Great Expectations

Jesus's disciples did not expect his public ministry to end in his death. They believed that it would end with him freeing them from Roman rule and setting up an independent Jewish kingdom. Indeed, as his closest friends, they all thought that they would become very important people.

This is why the disciples were overjoyed when, after three years of preaching and healing, Jesus told them that he was going to Jerusalem to celebrate the annual festival of Passover. They thought that, finally, Jesus was going to show everyone that he was the messiah.

Jesus knew what they were thinking. So, he tried to make them understand that he was not the kind of messiah they had been expecting. He was not here to create an independent Jewish kingdom. In fact, he warned them that he was going to his death (see **Luke 18:31–33**). However, the apostles did not want to hear this. They had their minds made up.

It was only **after** the events of **Holy Week** that his disciples came to understand the meaning of all Jesus had said and done during his public ministry.

Holy Week timeline

On Palm Sunday Jesus arrived in Jerusalem. His route was lined by cheering crowds. They waved palm branches to welcome him.

On Monday Jesus entered the Court of Gentiles at the Temple. This area was supposed to be set aside as a place where non-Jews could go to pray. However, now it was full of money-changers and traders who were over-charging pilgrims. Angered by this, Jesus overturned their tables and drove them out of the Temple precincts.

On Tuesday Jesus taught in the Temple. His enemies realised they could neither control him nor intimidate him. They agreed among themselves to find a way to have him put to death.

On Spy Wednesday Jesus taught in the Temple for the last time. Judas Iscariot volunteered to betray him.

On Holy Thursday Jesus shared the Last Supper with his disciples. He went to the Garden of Gethsemane where he was betrayed by Judas and arrested by the Temple guards. They brought him before the Sanhedrin, which interrogated him.

On Good Friday...

Jesus was accused of treason. He was tried by Pontius Pilate and condemned to death. He died on a cross. He was buried in a tomb nearby.

> **REMEMBER!**
> **Holy Week** is the name given to the last week of Jesus's public ministry.

On Palm Sunday, Jesus entered the city of Jerusalem seated on a colt.

LIGHT THE WAY

Palm Sunday

On Sunday morning Jesus arrived at Jerusalem. He was welcomed by enthusiastic people who formed a guard of honour up to the city gates. They shouted **'Hosanna!'** to show that they recognised him as **'the one who comes in the name of the Lord'**. Many waved palm branches in the air to salute him. This is why Christians call that day **'Palm Sunday'**.

Jesus's followers were excited by his arrival. They hoped that he would reveal himself to be the messiah. However, in their excitement, they did not pay attention to Jesus's reaction to what was happening. Though they cheered loudly, he said nothing. He made no speeches. He just calmly entered the city seated on a colt. This was another important clue that his followers missed. At that time, the colt was a symbol of peace, not of rebellion. Jesus was clearly signalling that he had no ambition to overthrow Roman rule.

The Romans watched all this with interest, but they didn't intervene. They don't seem to have considered Jesus a threat. However, they would be watching him, just in case.

Jesus at the Temple

On Monday morning Jesus went to the Temple. For Jews this great building was the holiest place on Earth. They believed that God was specially present in its innermost room, the **Holy of Holies**.

On arriving at the Temple, Jesus first had to pass through its outer courtyard, a place called the **Court of the Gentiles**. This was supposed to be where non-Jews could come to pray. But it was no longer available for this purpose. Instead, the whole courtyard was full of money-changers and traders selling animals for sacrifice. Jesus saw that the services they offered were ridiculously over-priced. They were cheating their customers. However, the pilgrims had no option but to go to them. Jesus said:

'They have turned it [the Temple] into a hideout for thieves.'

Luke 19:47.

He refused to let this go on any longer. Jesus went up to the money-changers and traders and began overturning their tables. Then he picked up a heavy piece of rope and used it as a whip to drive them all out of the Temple area.

Many onlookers cheered Jesus on. However the Temple priests were furious and embarrassed. Jesus had put an end to things that they should never have allowed to happen. By his courageous action, Jesus had made some very powerful enemies.

The next day, Tuesday, Jesus returned to the Temple. He spent the whole day preaching to huge crowds and healing long lines of people suffering from every kind of illness.

Given his popularity, the Temple priests decided not to openly confront Jesus. Instead they took a different approach.

Jesus overturns the money-changers' tables at the Temple.

They bribed some men to pretend they were sincere and they sent them to trap Jesus with questions, so that they could hand him over to the Roman procurator. These spies said to Jesus, **'Teacher, we know what you say and teach is right. We know that you pay no attention to anyone's status, but teach the truth about God's will for people. Tell us, is it against our law for us to pay taxes to the Roman Emperor, or not?'**

But Jesus saw through their trick and said to them, **'Show me a silver coin. Whose face and name is on it?'**

174

Foundations of Religion - Christianity **SECTION B**

'The Emperor's,' they answered.

So Jesus said, '**Well, then, pay the Emperor what belongs to the Emperor, and pay God what belongs to God.**'

Luke 20:20–25

With this answer, Jesus outwitted his enemies. He said you could be faithful in your duties both to God and to the state. They need not cancel each other out.

Jesus's enemies had underestimated him. However, he knew that they would not let him go on challenging them for much longer. He was now engaged in **a conflict with authority**.

> **REMEMBER!**
> **A conflict with authority** happens when you openly challenge or disagree with those who lead your community.

Anyone in conflict with authority in first-century Palestine knew they could expect no mercy if they were seen as a threat by those with wealth and power.

Jesus's Enemies Gather Against Him

The Pharisees

The Pharisees believed that they were the experts on Judaism. They did not like anyone else challenging their control of the local synagogues. However Jesus was not afraid of them. He had no hesitation in publicly disagreeing with them.

We know that a few Pharisees supported Jesus. For example, Nicodemus and Joseph of Arimathea defended him from criticism. However most Pharisees were completely opposed to Jesus. They claimed that he was a bad influence on people. They accused him of:

- Blasphemy because he claimed to have the power to forgive sins.
- Breaking the rules of their religion by healing people on the Sabbath.
- Being impure because he mixed with outcasts (e.g. lepers and tax collectors) and made friends with non-Jews.

The Pharisees ordered Jesus to be silent. He refused. He said that:

- As the **Son of Man** (a title used for the messiah) he had the power to forgive sins.
- As the **Lord of the Sabbath** he was not limited by the Pharisees' rules.
- His mission was to invite everyone to enter the Kingdom of God – Jew and non-Jew, saint and sinner alike.

These statements horrified the Pharisees. Jesus's teachings challenged everything they believed in.

Then Jesus went even further and called the Pharisees **hypocrites**.

> **REMEMBER!**
> **A hypocrite** is someone who pretends to be good but is not.

175

LIGHT THE WAY

Jesus claimed that the Pharisees were obsessed with rule-keeping. They had turned their religion into an unbearable burden for ordinary people to cope with. Further, they only talked about **fearing** God. Instead, Jesus talked about **God's love for us and our need to love God in return**.

Given these differences, a showdown between Jesus and the Pharisees was inevitable.

The Sadducees

During the three years of Jesus's public ministry, the Sadducees had heard stories about Jesus but took little interest in him. Some Sadducees enjoyed hearing about how Jesus embarrassed and angered their rivals, the Pharisees.

However, all that changed when Jesus arrived in Jerusalem. Only then did the Sadducees realise that he was threatening their power and status too.

When Jesus went into the Temple and drove the money-changers and animal traders out, he shocked the Sadducees. Jesus had shown them to be working with the money-changers and traders to rip off pilgrims. They were exposed as hypocrites who failed to live up to the high standards they demanded of everyone else.

No one else had ever dared to do this – to openly challenge the way the Sadducees ran the Temple. However the Sadducees took no immediate action against Jesus. What he did was very popular with the pilgrims. They didn't want to start a riot because the Romans wanted to avoid any situations that could get out of control and might lead to a rebellion.

The Sadducees realised that they had to do something soon to stop Jesus. Though they were not popular, the ordinary people feared the Sadducees' power. However, if Jesus got away with challenging them, it might encourage others to follow his example. Then they would lose their control over the people. So they decided to make an example of Jesus to prevent any future conflicts with authority.

Jesus is betrayed by Judas.

Jesus's enemies unite

The Sadducees and the Pharisees were bitter rivals. However neither group would tolerate anyone who publicly challenged their authority as Jesus did. This led them to unite against him.

The Sadducees and the Pharisees realised that Jesus could not be intimidated into staying silent. Nor could they hope to win him over to their point of view. So they decided that they had to find some way to have Jesus put to death.

Judas betrays Jesus

The Pharisees and the Sadducees were determined to find a way to silence Jesus once and for all. However they feared that arresting him in daylight would provoke a riot in Jerusalem. So they decided to arrest him after dark, in some place out of public view.

However they had a problem. No one seemed to know where Jesus stayed at night. In order to find and capture him, his enemies needed help from someone on the inside. This help came from **Judas Iscariot**.

The Synoptic Gospels say that Judas was the one who approached the Sanhedrin and not the other way around; he volunteered his help.

Judas's actions have puzzled scholars. He had been one of Jesus's close, inner circle of friends. Yet, despite this, he betrayed Jesus. Why?

Foundations of Religion - Christianity   SECTION B

In **Matthew 26:14-16** we are told that Judas did it for the money. However, thirty silver coins was the average purchase price of a slave or about four months of the average working wage at that time. This was a very small reward for Judas's treachery. Why did he accept such a small payment? Could it be that he didn't do it for the money?

Perhaps Judas thought that he needed to bring matters to a head. He may have thought that, if Jesus was forcibly brought before the Sanhedrin, he would work a miracle to convince the Pharisees and the Sadducees that he was the Messiah. If that was the case, then clearly Judas had completely misunderstood everything Jesus had said and done during his public ministry.

So, was Judas Iscariot greedy or misguided? Scholars cannot offer any definitive answer. However we are told that, when he learned that Jesus would be condemned to death, Judas was horrified. He returned the silver coins to the Sanhedrin and ended his own life.

ACTIVITIES

1. Say what it means!

(a)   A martyr is _____ .

(b)   Holy Week was _____

   _____ .

(c)   A conflict with authority happens _____

   _____

   _____ .

(d)   A hypocrite is _____ .

2. Match it!

Match the person listed in Column **A** with the correct description in column **B**.

A. Name of martyr	B. Description
Dietrich Bonhoeffer	He openly opposed the cruel policies of Chairman Mao in China. He was executed on Mao's orders in a failed attempt to intimidate other Christians.
St Elizabeth	A native of South Africa, she wanted to be baptised a Christian. She was murdered by non-Christian members of her own family who refused to let her become a Christian.
Esther John	She established a hospital and dedicated her life to helping the poor. She was executed by the Bolshevik government during its campaign to wipe out all traces of religious belief and practice within the Soviet Union (Russia).
Martin Luther King, Jr	He bravely turned down an offer to be evacuated from Papua New Guinea after the Japanese invasion. He remained there to care for his fellow Christians but was later betrayed and murdered.
Maximilian Kolbe	He was executed for being a member of the anti-Nazi resistance in Germany and for his involvement in the plot to assassinate Adolf Hitler in July 1944.
Janani Luwum	She devoted her life to caring for the sick and educating the poor in Pakistan. She was murdered for being a Christian.

LIGHT THE WAY

Manche Masemola	He formed an alliance between Catholics and Muslims to peacefully oppose the cruel dictatorship of Idi Amin in Uganda. This cost him his life.
Oscar Romero	He dedicated his life to achieving civil rights for black Americans. He was awarded the Nobel Peace Prize for his work. He was assassinated by a racist gunman.
Lucien Tapiedi	He was imprisoned at Auschwitz concentration camp during World War II. He offered his own life in an exchange for the life of a fellow prisoner who had been condemned to death.
Wang Zhimang	He fearlessly exposed the cruelty of the armed forces in El Salvador. He was murdered by an assassin while celebrating Mass.

Fill in your answers in the spaces provided below.

A. Name of martyr	B. Description
Dietrich Bonhoeffer	
St Elizabeth	
Esther John	
Martin Luther King, Jr	
Maximilian Kolbe	
Janani Luwum	
Manche Masemola	
Oscar Romero	
Lucien Tapiedi	
Wang Zhimang	

Foundations of Religion - Christianity   SECTION B

3. Tick the box!

In each of the following, say whether it is **true** or **false**.

	True	False
1. Maximilian Kolbe was a Protestant pastor in the USA.		
2. Oscar Romero was a Catholic archbishop in El Salvador.		
3. Manche Masemola was an Anglican lay woman in South Africa.		
4. Lucien Tapiedi was a lay member of the Anglican Communion in Papua New Guinea.		
5. Wang Zhimang was a Lutheran minister in Germany.		
6. Jesus's disciples expected his public ministry to end in his death.		
7. Jesus's disciples believed that his public ministry would end with him freeing them from Roman rule and setting up an independent Jewish kingdom.		
8. It was only **after** the events of **Holy Week** that Jesus's disciples came to understand the meaning of all he had said and done during his public ministry.		
9. Jesus's teachings challenged everything the Pharisees believed in.		
10. Jesus called the Pharisees hypocrites.		
11. The Pharisees told Jesus to be quiet and he agreed to do so.		
12. By challenging the power of the Sadducees and the Pharisees, Jesus was engaged in a conflict with authority.		
13. Joseph of Arimathea and Nicodemus were two Sadducees who defended Jesus.		
14. Jesus overturned the tables of the money-changers and drove them from the Temple precinct.		
15. The Sadducees did not know that the money-changers and the animal traders were working together to rip off pilgrims at the Temple.		
16. Although the Sadducees and the Pharisees were bitter rivals, they united against Jesus because he had publicly challenged them.		
17. The Sanhedrin feared that arresting Jesus in daylight would provoke a riot, so they decided to arrest him after dark.		
18. Judas Iscariot was forced by the Sanhedrin to betray Jesus.		
19. Judas was paid thirty pieces of gold for betraying Jesus.		
20. When Judas heard that Jesus had been condemned to death, he asked for more money.		

LIGHT THE WAY

4. Fill in the missing words!

Holy Week Timeline

On Palm Sunday… Jesus arrived in J_____. His route was lined by c_____ crowds. They waved p_____ branches to welcome him.

On Monday… Jesus entered the Court of G_____ at the Temple. This was supposed to be set aside as a place where n_____ could go to pray. However, now it was full of m_____ and t_____ who were over-c_____ pilgrims. Angered by this, Jesus o_____ their tables and d_____ them out of the T_____ precincts.

On Tuesday… Jesus t_____ in the Temple. His enemies realised they could neither c_____ him nor i_____ him. They a_____ among themselves to find a way to have him put to d_____.

On Spy Wednesday… Jesus taught in the Temple for the l_____ time. J_____ I_____ volunteered to b_____ him.

On Holy Thursday… Jesus shared the Last S_____ with his disciples. He went to the Garden of G_____ where he was betrayed by Judas and a_____ by the Temple guards. He was i_____ by the Sanhedrin.

On Good Friday… Jesus was accused of t_____. He was tried by P_____ P_____ and condemned to d_____. He died on a c_____. He was buried in a t_____ nearby.

5. Think about it!

'A conflict between Jesus and the Sanhedrin was inevitable.'

Do you agree/disagree?
Give reasons for your answer.

Foundations of Religion - Christianity   SECTION B

CHAPTER 9   THE PASSION AND DEATH OF JESUS

The Last Supper

Jesus is Betrayed and Arrested

On Holy Thursday evening before the feast of Passover, Jesus shared a private meal with his closest friends. This event is known as the Last Supper.

Jesus's friends were troubled and confused by the things he said during this meal. He forewarned them of his approaching death. Then he shocked them when he said that one of them was about to betray him. Though Peter promised to die alongside him, Jesus stunned him by predicting that, before sunrise, Peter would deny he had ever known Jesus, not once but three times.

Afterwards Jesus asked the apostles to accompany him to the Garden of Gethsemane. He wanted to find a quiet place to pray.

They were not there very long when Judas arrived, leading a large group of Temple guards. He had betrayed Jesus and was helping them to arrest him (**Matthew 26:47**).

Jesus confronted them, saying that they had no right to arrest him. He knew that they'd chosen the cover of darkness because they hadn't the courage to arrest him in daylight. (**Luke 22:53**).

Then one apostle drew a sword and cut off the right ear of the High Priest's servant. But Jesus stepped in and told his followers not to resist (**Matthew 26:51**). Then he healed the injured servant immediately (**Luke 22:49–51**).

At this point the apostles panicked. They all ran for their lives, except for Peter. He followed the Temple guards to find out what was going to happen to Jesus. The **passion** of Jesus had begun.

When the apostle Peter reached the Temple, he could not gain access to where Jesus was being interrogated. He had to wait in the courtyard outside.

As he stood in the courtyard beside a large fire to warm himself, he was asked if he was a friend of Jesus. Afraid that he too would be arrested, Peter said, '**No.**'

But others began to insist that he was one of Jesus's followers. He denied it again and then went so far as to say that he had never even met Jesus (**Luke 22:54–62**). At that point he turned around to see Jesus under guard nearby, looking right at him.

> **REMEMBER!**
> **The passion of Jesus** was the suffering Jesus endured from the time of his arrest until his death on the cross.

181

Only then did Peter realise what he had done. Earlier that evening he had promised Jesus that he would face death alongside him. Jesus had upset him when he had predicted that Peter would publically deny ever having known him (**Mark 14:29–31**).

Peter could not face Jesus. He turned and ran away into the darkness, leaving Jesus to face death alone.

Jesus is Interrogated by the Sanhedrin

Jesus was taken to the Hall of Hewn Stones. This was located within the Temple's inner court. He found himself standing before the seventy members of the Sanhedrin, who were seated in a large semi-circle. The High Priest **Caiaphas** was in charge (**John 18:13**).

> **REMEMBER!**
> **Treason** means being disloyal to the ruling political power, e.g. by rebelling against it.

This was an interrogation, not a trial. Its purpose was to find evidence, any evidence, to show that Jesus had committed **treason**.

Once such evidence was found, the Sanhedrin would send Jesus to the Roman procurator. He would put Jesus on trial for his life.

The Sanhedrin didn't treat Jesus fairly. It did things forbidden by Jewish law. For example:

- It didn't charge Jesus with an offence. Instead, attempts were made to trick him into admitting to treason.
- This interrogation was held secretly at night.
- Jesus was beaten both before and during his questioning, in an attempt to force him to confess to a crime he hadn't committed (**Luke 22:63–65** and **John 18:22**).

The reason for this was simple. The leaders of the Sanhedrin had already made up their minds: Jesus had to die. Why?

They wanted people to think it was because they were afraid Jesus would lead a rebellion against Roman rule, and that they only wanted to avoid the pointless bloodshed that would follow. But that was not the real reason. In truth, Jesus had openly challenged the power of both the Sadducees and the Pharisees. Worse still, he had proven them to be hypocrites who had betrayed the Jewish people's trust. They were not going to let him get away with this. They wanted to discourage anyone else from following his example.

As the interrogation progressed, the accusations against Jesus became more and more ridiculous. It was even claimed that he wanted to destroy the Temple. However, at this point, two Pharisees – Joseph of Arimathea and Nicodemus – spoke up in his defence.

Soon the whole interrogation descended into chaos as witnesses began to contradict one another. According to Jewish law, once witnesses disagreed in this way, then the questioning should stop. However Jesus's captors would not let him go free.

Throughout all of this, Jesus remained silent. He knew it was pointless saying anything. They would not listen. Their minds were made up.

As the night wore on, the High Priest, Caiaphas, got more and more annoyed. Jesus had refused to respond to any accusation made against him. Finally Caiaphas lost his patience and asked Jesus directly, '**Are you the Messiah, the Son of the Blessed One?**' (Mark 14:61).

Foundations of Religion – Christianity   SECTION B

At last Jesus chose to respond. He said **'I am. And you will see the Son of Man sitting at the right hand of the Mighty One and coming on the clouds of heaven.'** (Mark 14:62).

This answer infuriated his interrogators. Firstly, Jesus was saying he was the messiah. Secondly, he was claiming that the Sanhedrin didn't have the authority to question him.

Caiaphas declared that Jesus had committed **blasphemy**.

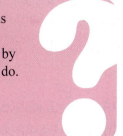

Did You Know?

Blasphemy means showing great disrespect to God by what you say and do.

Jesus's enemies wanted to have him put to death. However, they no longer had the power to impose the death penalty. Only the Roman procurator could have Jesus executed. They decided to bring Jesus before him.

Ecco Homo (Behold the Man) by Antonio Ciseri.

Jesus is Put on Trial

Pontius Pilate was the procurator of Judaea and Samaria. He was staying at the Antonia Fortress, not far from the Temple.

Shortly after dawn on Good Friday, a delegation from the Sanhedrin arrived with their prisoner – Jesus of Nazareth. Pilate knew about Jesus. His network of spies had kept him informed about Jesus's activities.

The delegates began by saying that Jesus was guilty of blasphemy. Pilate wasn't interested in that. That was a religious matter, and so had nothing to do with the empire. However, Pilate listened attentively when the delegates accused Jesus of treason.

He asked them for evidence to back up this charge. They said that:
- Jesus claimed to be the messiah.
- He said people shouldn't pay taxes to the emperor.
- He planned to lead a revolt.

Pilate was a lawyer by profession. Despite what they had said, the delegates couldn't offer any evidence to prove that Jesus had committed treason. So Pilate said that Jesus was innocent (**Luke 23:4** and **John 18:38**). However, the delegates angrily asked Pilate to reconsider his decision.

Although Pilate disliked the Sanhedrin, he needed its help to run Palestine. So, to avoid insulting its representatives, he tried to offload Jesus onto Herod Antipas, the tetrarch of Galilee (**Luke 23:6–12**). After all, Jesus was from Galilee.

Herod was staying nearby. When Jesus was brought before him, Herod tried to get Jesus to work a miracle for his amusement. When he refused, Herod had Jesus beaten and dressed in a purple robe. His soldiers made fun of the idea that Jesus was a king. They even placed a crown of thorns on Jesus's head before sending him back to Pilate.

This annoyed Pilate. He had met rebel leaders in the past, but Jesus was not one of them. However, to clarify matters beyond doubt, Pilate asked Jesus directly, **'Are you the King of the Jews?'** Jesus responded, **'Yes, I am a King'** (**John 18:37**).

LIGHT THE WAY

However, Jesus explained his answer by adding,

> **Mine is not a kingdom of this world; if my kingdom was of this world, my men would have fought to prevent my being surrendered to the Jews. But my kingdom is not of this kind.**
>
> **John 18:36**

Pilate was unsure how to respond to this. He found Jesus's calm manner both impressive and disturbing. As there was no case against him, Pilate decided to set Jesus free (**John 19:12**).

However the Sanhedrin delegates refused to accept this. They got angrier and angrier. They became more and more determined to get their way. So, in an effort to placate them, Pilate said,

> **As you can see, the man has done nothing that deserves death, so I shall have him scourged and then let him go.**
>
> **John 23:15–16**

Did You Know?

A **scourging** was a horrific ordeal. The victim was tied to a wooden post and struck again and again on the back by a many-stranded whip. Each strand of the whip had pieces of jagged metal inserted into it. The lashes not only cut the skin but also tore off strips of flesh each time they made contact. A severe scourging could kill even the strongest man. It would have left Jesus in a severely weakened condition.

After his scourging, Jesus was in a very bad way. He had lost a lot of blood and was barely able to stand. Pilate thought that this would be enough to satisfy the Sanhedrin. He was wrong. They wanted Jesus dead. It was as simple as that.

However Pilate still had one trick up his sleeve. Over the years it had become an accepted practice for the procurator to release one Jewish prisoner at Passover. So, Pilate offered the crowd gathered outside the Antonia Fortress a choice: he would let them choose the one to be released. He offered them either Jesus or a violent rebel named Barabbas. Pilate was stunned when the crowd shouted for Barabbas to go free. Some said afterwards that the crowd had been bribed to do this by the Sanhedrin (**Mark 15:11**). Regardless, Pilate was forced to set Barabbas free in order to avoid a riot. However his own officers and men were furious about this. Pilate was deeply embarrassed as he had been outwitted and made to look very foolish.

Pilate was still left with Jesus. He hesitated to condemn him, partly because he didn't want to give the Sanhedrin the pleasure of making him do their dirty work for them. Unfortunately, he underestimated how determined they were. The Sanhedrin's delegates even went so far as to directly threaten Pilate. They said:

> **If you let this man go, you are no friend of Caesar. Anyone who claims to be a king is an enemy of Caesar.**
>
> **John 19:12**

'Caesar' referred to the Roman emperor. They were threatening to complain directly to Pilate's boss in Rome. They were going to accuse him of failing to do his job by letting a rebel go free.

The emperor at that time was a man named Tiberius. He was ruthless and trusted no one. The mere suspicion that you were disloyal was all it took to end your career, and possibly even your life as well! Pilate decided not to risk the emperor taking such a complaint seriously. So he did what they wanted. He declared Jesus guilty of treason and sent him off to be executed.

However, before Jesus was led away, Pilate asked his servants to bring him a bowl of water and a towel.

He washed his hands in front of all those present and said, **'I am innocent of this man's blood'** (Matthew 27:24).

Pilate wanted to make it clear that any injustice done to Jesus was the Sanhedrin's responsibility, not his. However, try as he might to hide from it, Pilate had knowingly condemned an innocent man to death.

The Death of Jesus

Jesus was condemned to death by **crucifixion**.

The whole idea of crucifixion was to discourage people from rebelling against the empire. It was finally outlawed within the Roman Empire in 337 CE.

Many artists have shown Jesus carrying the whole cross to his place of execution. Actually, Jesus was given the wooden crossbeam to carry. However, a crossbeam was a heavy burden to bear and Jesus was already weakened by his injuries.

> **Did You Know?**
>
> **Crucifixion** was a method of execution used on non-Romans. It caused a condemned person to suffer a slow, agonising death by suffocation.

Wearing a crown of thorns, Jesus was forced to carry the crossbeam for a kilometre through the narrow winding streets of Jerusalem. Most of those who lined the route were horrified by what had happened. We are told that **'large numbers of people followed him, who mourned and lamented for him'** (Luke 23:27).

Jesus was condemned to death by crucifixion.

Jesus was led outside the city gates to a small hill named **Golgotha** (meaning: **'the place of the skull'**). There he was forced to lie on his back while nails were driven through his wrists to secure him to the crossbeam. Then the crossbeam was lifted up and slotted onto an upright post that stood permanently on the site. Once fixed in this position, Jesus's feet were nailed to the upright post and his body was tied to the cross with ropes to prevent it from tearing free.

> **Did You Know?**
>
> Jesus was hung by his arms, which put huge strain on his diaphragm. In order to breathe, he had to push down on the nails through his feet. This caused agonising pain and made breathing almost impossible. Jesus endured this torture for six hours.

Pontius Pilate was angry at the way the Sanhedrin had treated him. So, in retaliation, he ordered that a placard be nailed to the upright post above Jesus's head. It read **'Jesus of Nazareth, King of the Jews'**. The Jewish leaders were angered by this and demanded he change or remove it. However, Pilate refused.

The Gospels say that at around midday, a strange darkness descended across the whole land. This lasted until about three o'clock that afternoon.

Then a soldier offered Jesus a sponge soaked in vinegar diluted with water. This was held up to his lips to refresh him and keep him awake for as long as possible. But, after he had taken a drink, Jesus said:

> **'It is accomplished,' and, bowing his head, he gave up his spirit.**
>
> **John 19:30**

Most modern scholars think that Jesus died because his lungs had filled with fluid and he could no longer breathe. Also, it is very likely that his heart failed due to the enormous physical strain he was under.

The Jewish leaders asked Pilate to make sure that Jesus was dead. The normal practice was for Roman guards to break a prisoner's legs with a hammer so that he could no longer hold himself up to breathe. However when the guards came to Jesus they realised that he was already dead. In order to make sure that he had died, a Roman guard thrust a spear into his side (**John 19:34**). This pierced his lungs. Death was guaranteed.

The Burial of Jesus

Joseph of Arimathea was one of the few members of the Sanhedrin who had supported Jesus. Now he came forward to claim Jesus's body for burial. However Joseph had to get the permission of the Roman procurator. It was not usually allowed for a crucified rebel to be given a proper burial (**Luke 24:50–52** and **John 19:38**).

According to Jewish law, the body of an executed criminal could not be left unburied over the Sabbath (**Deuteronomy 21:22–23**). The Sabbath began at sunset (around six o'clock) on Friday evening. So the body had to be quickly taken down and buried.

The body of Jesus was quickly cleaned and wrapped in a linen shroud. It was **'put in a tomb, which had been hewn in stone in which no one had yet been buried'** (**Luke 23:53**). The tomb was sealed by rolling a large, heavy millstone, set in a channel, across its entrance. This little tomb was in a garden close to the city gates and **'near at hand'** (**John 19:42**) to where Jesus had been crucified.

As the Sabbath was about to begin, there was no time to embalm Jesus's corpse properly. So the women disciples decided that they would return on Sunday morning, once the Sabbath was over, to do this.

The Sacrifice of Jesus

Christians call Jesus's death **a sacrifice**.

> **REMEMBER!**
> A **sacrifice** is something (e.g. your life) given out of love to achieve something important.

The Synoptic Gospels say that when Jesus died **'the curtain hanging in the Temple was torn in two'** (**Luke 23:46**). This refers to the great curtain that hung over the entrance to the **Holy of Holies** (i.e. the sanctuary of the Temple).

This event may have happened just as it is written or it may have been a way of saying that, through Jesus's death, something great had occurred. Think about this:

Before Jesus's death on the cross…	After Jesus's death on the cross…
The Great Curtain separated people from the Holy of Holies. The Jews believed that this part of the Temple was the holiest place on Earth. It was the meeting place between God and the Jewish people.	All the barriers that separate human beings from God were removed.
Only the High Priest was allowed to enter the Holy of Holies and talk to God, and even then only once a year, at Yom Kippur.	The way to God was opened for everyone.

Foundations of Religion - Christianity SECTION B

Did You Know?

Christians believe that the sacrifice of Jesus marked the end of God's old covenant with only one people (the Jews), and the beginning of God's new covenant with all people.

ACTIVITIES

1. Say what it means!

(a) The passion of Jesus was _____

_____.

(b) Treason is _____.

(c) Blasphemy means _____.

(d) Crucifixion was _____

_____

_____.

(e) A sacrifice is _____

_____.

2. Fill in the missing words!

Before Jesus's death . . .		Christians believe that after Jesus's death...	
1.	The Great C_____ separated people from the Holy of H_____. The Jews believed that this part of the T_____ was the h_____ place on Earth. It was the m_____ place between G___ and human beings.	1.	All the barriers that s_____ human beings from God were r_____.
		2.	The way to G____ was opened for e_____.
2.	Only the H_____ P_____ was allowed to enter it and talk to God, and even then only o_____ a year, at Y___ K_____.	3.	The s_____ of Jesus marked the end of God's o___ covenant with the J_____, and the beginning of God's n___ covenant with _____ people.

3. Think about it!

(a) Why do you think Peter reacted the way he did and denied ever knowing his friend, Jesus?

(b) 'Jesus was not given a fair hearing by the Sanhedrin.' Do you agree/disagree with this statement? Give reasons for your answer.

(c) Why did Pontius Pilate give in to the demands of the Sanhedrin delegates and knowingly condemn an innocent man to death?

(d) 'There can be no doubt that Jesus died on the cross.' What evidence is there to support this statement?

(e) Why did Jesus's body have to be taken down from the cross before sunset and quickly buried?

LIGHT THE WAY

4. Crossword!

Across
3. Jesus did not carry the whole cross. He was given this part to carry.
5. The place carved out of rock in which Jesus's body was buried.
10. The name given to an agonisingly slow death on a cross by suffocation.
13. The name of the garden in which Jesus was arrested.
15. He promised to die alongside Jesus but later denied he even knew him.
16. The Sanhedrin delegates told Pilate that anyone who claims to be a king is an enemy of this important person.
17. The name of the place outside the city walls where Jesus was put to death.
18. He was the High Priest who led Jesus's interrogation in the Hall of Hewn Stones.
19. A Roman guard thrust this into Jesus's side to make sure that he was dead.
20. The Sanhedrin delegates told Pilate that Jesus was guilty of this serious crime.

Down
1. The name given to the day on which Jesus was tried and executed (2 words: 4, 6).
2. The name given to the private meal Jesus shared with his closest friends on Holy Thursday evening (2 words: 4, 6).
4. The name of the official post held by Pontius Pilate.
6. The apostle who betrayed Jesus.
7. This involved a man being tied to a post and repeatedly struck upon the back with a many-stranded whip.
8. The number of hours Jesus suffered on the cross before dying.
9. The man from Arimathea who claimed Jesus's body for burial.
11. Pilate asked Jesus if he was this and Jesus replied that he was (4 words: 4, 2, 3, 4).
12. The crowd chose to free him instead of Jesus.
14. Herod Antipas' men placed a crown of these on Jesus's head.

Foundations of Religion - Christianity   SECTION B

CHAPTER 10   THE RESURRECTION OF JESUS

The Meaning of the Resurrection

Christians believe that the story of Jesus did not end with his death on the cross. They say that, on Easter Sunday morning, **the resurrection** occurred.

> **REMEMBER!**
> **The resurrection** was when Jesus rose from the dead to a new and glorious life.

> **Did You Know?**
> The Gospels say that Jesus rose on **'the third day'**. This is because, at that time, people included the day on which Jesus died – Good Friday – as **day one**. So Easter Sunday was **day three**.

The Events of Easter Sunday Morning

All four Gospels agree that, once the Sabbath was over, some of Jesus's female disciples went to the tomb early on Sunday morning. They wanted to properly embalm his body. They were led by **Mary Magdalene**. They were surprised to find that the heavy millstone covering the tomb's entrance had been rolled back. The tomb itself was empty.

Resurrection was the last thing on the women's minds. At first they feared that someone had removed Jesus's body. However, to her shock and joy, Mary Magdalene met the risen Jesus. On his instructions she went immediately to the apostles and told them what had happened.

The apostles had been in hiding since Jesus's arrest. They were frightened and saddened by his execution. They were also deeply ashamed. They had all deserted Jesus and left him to suffer and die alone.

The Appearance of Christ to Mary Magdalene, Ivanov Aleksander Andreevich, State Russian Museum, St Petersburgh.

When Mary Magdalene told the apostles that Jesus had risen, **'they did not believe it'** (**Mark 16:1**). They dismissed her story as an hallucination, brought on by her grief over Jesus's death.

The apostles' reaction was understandable. At this point they thought that Jesus's public ministry had ended in complete failure. He was dead – it was over. All this talk of an empty tomb and a risen Jesus sounded to them like **'nonsense'** (**Luke 24:11**).

However Mary Magdalene insisted that she had met the risen Jesus. She was so insistent that some of the apostles began to wonder if it might be true.

Two of them – Peter and John – decided to risk going to the tomb. When they got there, they saw it was empty, just as Mary Magdalene had said. Jesus's body was gone and the linen cloths in which it had been wrapped were lying on the floor of the tomb (**John 20:3–9**).

LIGHT THE WAY

The apostles were still unsure about what had happened. It was only gradually, as other sightings of Jesus were reported back to them, that they began to hope that it was true. All their doubts were wiped away that Sunday evening when Jesus appeared to them **(John 20:19-20)**.

Did You Know?

At no stage did anyone claim to have actually seen Jesus rise from the dead. The Gospel accounts only deal with what happened **afterwards**.

The Appearances of the Risen Jesus

We are told that, in the forty days after his resurrection, a large number of people actually met and talked with the risen Jesus on several different occasions (see: **The First Letter to the Corinthians 15:5-7**). Each time, Jesus gave his disciples '**many demonstrations**' that he was truly alive (see: **Acts 1:3**).

According to the evangelists, Jesus's appearances followed this pattern:

- Before his first appearance Jesus's disciples were in a state of shock. They were confused and demoralised by what had happened. Jesus was dead. So, he was the last person they were expecting to see.
- Suddenly, without warning, Jesus appeared in the midst of them. He greeted his disciples with some reassuring words, such as '**Peace be with you**' **(John 20:21)**.
- At first the disciples were astonished and frightened when they saw him.
- However their fear quickly faded away. It was replaced by a great inner peace and joy. They realised that death had not destroyed Jesus. They now believed that he had risen, that Jesus was **alive**.
- The disciples were told to go and spread the good news of his resurrection (**Matthew 28:19**).

Jesus's disciples were shocked when he first appeared to them.

Understanding the Risen Jesus

The Gospels say that, at first, the disciples did not immediately recognise the risen Jesus. It was only **after** they heard him speak, touched his wounds or shared a meal with him that they were sure it was Jesus.

Yet we are told that the risen Jesus was the same person that the disciples had known before his death. Why was it that they did not immediately recognise him?

The reason was **Jesus was not alive in the same way after his resurrection as he had been before his death**.

Remember, the disciples had seen Jesus bring people back to life, e.g. Jairus's daughter, Lazarus and the widow of Nain's son. However, unlike these people, Jesus had not been restored to his former earthly life. Jesus had **changed**.

Those who met the risen Jesus said that he was no longer limited by the physical laws of our universe. For example:

- Jesus could suddenly appear within a room or immediately disappear from it, even if the doors were bolted and windows shuttered.
- Jesus could be in two places at the same time.

Foundations of Religion - Christianity SECTION B

> **REMEMBER!**
> **Transformed** means **completely changed**.

Christians believe that the risen Jesus could do those things because he had been **transformed**.

Christians believe that, after his resurrection, death no longer had any power over Jesus. He had conquered death. He was living a completely new kind of life. He would never die again. This is why Christians say that **Jesus is living now**.

Challenging the Resurrection

Over the centuries people have raised doubts about the resurrection. Let's look at some of the most important accusations:

1. Jesus did not die on the cross!

Yes, Jesus did die on the cross on Good Friday. How do we know that?

- First, the Jewish writer **Josephus** and the Roman writer **Tacitus** – both non-Christians – say that Jesus was put to death.

- His executioners were very thorough. They pierced Jesus's side with a spear, puncturing at least one of his lungs, to make sure he was dead (see: **John 19:34**).

- Jesus's executioners were strongly motivated to guarantee his death. Under Roman law, any soldier who failed to execute a prisoner would lose his own life too.

The burial of Jesus.

2. The tomb was empty because the disciples had stolen the body!

No. They didn't steal Jesus's body. How do we know that?

- We are told that at the request of the Sanhedrin, Pontius Pilate placed guards on Jesus's tomb to prevent this from happening (see: **Matthew 27: 62-66**).

- The disciples had all deserted Jesus. His death had shattered their confidence in him. They had not come forward on Good Friday to claim Jesus's body for burial. Instead, they had gone into hiding. Resurrection was the last thing on their minds. They feared for their lives.

- They would not have gone near the tomb to remove the body because to do so would have risked arrest and suffering the same horrible death as Jesus.

- They would have wanted to draw as little attention to themselves as possible, so that they could quietly return home to Galilee and try to get on with their lives as best they could.

3. What the disciples saw after Jesus's death was a ghost!

No. They did not see a ghost. The Jesus they encountered was not some **disembodied apparition**. How do we know that?

It's true that the Gospels say that Jesus could appear suddenly in a locked room and then vanish at will. At first hearing, this may sound like a ghost story. But it is not.

Remember, we are told that when Jesus appeared: (a) **he was tangible**, i.e. the disciples could touch Jesus and he ate food in their presence; and (b) **he interacted with them**, i.e. Jesus listened to what they had to say and spoke to them.

4. The story of the resurrection was a hoax!

No. It was not a hoax. How do we know that?

If the disciples had really wanted to commit a hoax, then they would have chosen a very different way of going about it, especially if they wanted to convince Jews living in the 1st century CE. Consider the following:

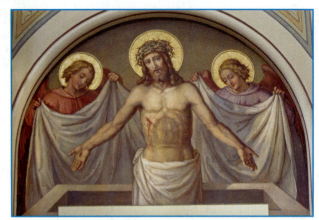
Fresco of the Resurrected Christ, Vienna.

- Firstly, those Jews who did believe in life after death thought that it would only take place at the end of time and be shared only by those people who had lived good lives. The idea of a single individual person rising from the dead would have been very difficult for most Jews to accept.

- Secondly, remember that the first witnesses to Jesus's resurrection were **women**. This would have immediately made many Jewish men wary of accepting this story. Why? Because according to Jewish law at that time, a woman had no credibility as a witness. Indeed, a woman was not allowed to offer evidence at a trial. So, if the disciples had wanted a hoax to succeed, they would never have identified women as the first witnesses to the resurrection.

The Importance of the Resurrection

The first Christians claimed that the resurrection of Jesus was a historical fact (see: **Acts 2:23-24**). Indeed St Paul wrote that, without the resurrection, Christianity would be meaningless and pointless (see: **First Letter to the Corinthians**). The belief that Jesus rose from the dead to a new and glorified life is the foundation of the whole Christian religion.

Christians believe that the resurrection of Jesus tells us five important things:

- There is life after death.
- Jesus is the promised messiah.
- The power of good will triumph over evil.
- What we do in this life has meaning and value.
- The good we do in this life will be rewarded by God in the next.

The Titles of Jesus

From the very beginning of Jesus's public ministry people had been asking: '**Who is he?**' (**Mark 1:27**). In the years following that first Easter Sunday, Jesus's disciples struggled with the very same question. They expressed their answers by using the following titles when referring to Jesus:

1. MESSIAH/CHRIST

This title was the one most often given to Jesus in the Gospels. **The messiah** was the saviour sent by God and promised by the Jewish prophets.

When the Bible was first translated from Hebrew into Greek, the Greek word used in place of the Hebrew **messiah** was '**Christos**'. From this we get the title **Christ**. So when someone says '**Jesus Christ**', it means '**Jesus the Messiah**'.

Many Jews still believe that the messiah will come at some time in the future. However, Christians believe that, in Jesus of Nazareth, the messiah has already come and will return again at the end of time.

2. The Son of Man

This is the only specific title that Jesus directly applied to himself. It was first mentioned in the Old Testament (see: **Daniel 7:13–14**). It referred to the messiah. Jesus used it to let his disciples know that he was the messiah they had been waiting for.

Jesus used the title '**Son of Man**' because:

- He wanted us to know that he was '**one of us**'. He went through the same ups and downs of life as we do. Jesus really suffered and died on the cross.
- He wanted to show us that he was '**God made man**'. He could do things only God could do. Jesus could forgive sins and restore life.

3. The Lord

The Jews believed that God's name was **Yahweh**. However, they believed that God's name was so holy that it should never be spoken aloud. Out of respect they substituted the title '**Adonai**', a Hebrew word meaning '**the Lord**', when talking about God.

Quite early on, the first Christians began calling the risen Jesus '**the Lord**' (see **Philippians 2:11**). They did so because they believed that Jesus had the authority to forgive sins and had power over death. Only God can do such things.

By calling Jesus '**the Lord**', the early Christians were saying that Jesus was the very God the Jews believed in and worshipped.

4. The Son of God

Jesus never called himself '**the Son of God**'. Other people gave him this title afterwards.

Sometimes, 1st-century Jews called an exceptionally good person '**a son of God**'. We can trace this idea back to the Old Testament books of **Hosea** and **Psalms**.

By the time **the Gospel of John** came to be written, the early Christians had had time to think about how often Jesus called God **his Father**.

Christians believed that Jesus was **not** simply **a** son of God. All that Jesus had said and done had shown him to have a totally **unique** relationship with God. Not even Abraham or Moses had enjoyed this kind of relationship with God. Jesus's whole life on Earth had shown that he was totally united in all that he had said and done with God, his Father.

So Jesus was not just a son of God. Jesus was *the* **Son of God**. This gave the early Christians a great insight into the mystery of God. This insight later led them to set out the doctrine of **the Trinity**.

> **REMEMBER!**
> **The Trinity** is the Christian belief that there are three divine persons – **the Father**, **the Son** and **the Holy Spirit** – in the one God.

LIGHT THE WAY

ACTIVITIES

1. Say what it means!

(a) The resurrection was _____
_____ .

(b) Transformed means _____ .

(c) The Trinity is _____
_____ .

2. Crossword

194

Foundations of Religion - Christianity   SECTION B

Across

1. The first Christians claimed that the resurrection of Jesus is a historical ____.
3. He was a Roman writer who said that Jesus died on the cross.
4. They were not allowed to give evidence in a Jewish trial.
5. After his resurrection, this no longer had any power over Jesus.
8. The female disciples went to the tomb to properly do this to Jesus's body.
10. The day of the week when Jesus rose from the dead.
12. He was a Jewish writer who said that Jesus died on the cross.
13. A title meaning a saviour sent by God and promised by the Jewish prophets.
14. They asked Pontius Pilate to place a guard on Jesus's tomb.
17. Jesus often called God this and said that he was his Son.
20. They believe that the messiah has already come and will return again at the end of time.
23. The Jews believed that God's name was so holy that it should never be spoken aloud. Out of respect, they substituted this Hebrew word when talking about God.
24. All talk of an empty tomb and a risen Jesus sounded to the apostles like this.

Down

2. At no stage did anyone claim to have actually seen Jesus rise from the dead. The Gospel accounts only deal with what happened _____.
6. To the surprise of the female disciples, this was empty on Easter Sunday morning.
7. St Paul wrote that, without the resurrection, this religion is meaningless and pointless.
9. The first Christians began calling the risen Jesus by this title. They did so because they believed that Jesus had the authority to forgive sins and had power over death.
11. The Jews believed that this was God's name.
13. The female disciples were led by this woman (2 words: 4, 9).
15. On the third day after Jesus's death this occurred.
16. A word meaning 'a disembodied apparition'.
18. They still believe that the messiah will come at some time in the future.
19. He instructed the women disciples to tell the apostles what had happened at the tomb.
21. Once this day was over, the female disciples went to the tomb.
22. This is the only specific title that Jesus directly applied to himself (3 words: 3, 2, 3).

3. Think about it!

(a) How would a Christian respond to each of the following claims:
1. Jesus did not die on the cross.
2. The tomb was empty because the disciples stole the body.
3. What the disciples saw after Jesus's death was a ghost.
4. The story of the resurrection was a hoax.

(b) Why is the resurrection so important for the Christian religion?

(c) Christians believe the resurrection tells us five important things. What are they?

LIGHT THE WAY

CHAPTER 11   THE EARLY CHRISTIANS

The Ascension

Jesus appeared to his disciples many times after his resurrection. Each time he talked about what he had said and done before his death. Gradually, the disciples began to see Jesus's words and actions in a new light. They finally came to understand their real meaning and importance. They believed that he really was the messiah.

Then, forty days after Easter Sunday, Jesus gathered his disciples on the Mount of Olives. Christians call this event **the Ascension** (see: **Acts 1:9**).

Jesus had done what he had set out to do. He had taught his disciples how to live and how to stand up for what they believed. Now it was up to them to continue his work.

However, before returning to heaven, Jesus assured his disciples that, '**I am with you always, to the end of time**' (**Matthew 28:20**). Although Jesus would no longer be physically present among his disciples, he promised to send them **the Holy Spirit** to guide and strengthen them.

> **REMEMBER!**
> **The Ascension** was when Jesus returned to his Father in heaven.

> **Did You Know?**
> During this period, the disciples chose a man named **Matthias** to replace Judas Iscariot as one of the twelve apostles.

Pentecost

Ten days after the Ascension, Jesus's disciples met in Jerusalem. Afterwards, they struggled to find words that could adequately express what happened next.

As they were praying, the disciples heard what sounded like '**a powerful wind**'. Then they saw what looked like tongues of fire descend on their heads, but they were unharmed by them. They called this extraordinary event **Pentecost**.

The seven gifts of the Holy Spirit include:

(1) wisdom
(2) understanding
(3) right judgement
(4) courage
(5) knowledge
(6) reverence
(7) awe and wonder.

> **REMEMBER!**
> **Pentecost** was when Jesus's disciples received the gifts of the Holy Spirit.

Whatever happened that day, Pentecost energised the disciples.
Instead of hiding away, afraid to speak out in fear of arrest, the disciples began openly preaching that Jesus was the messiah, that he had risen from the dead and that he would return at the end of time. Also, they began to heal the sick in Jesus's name.

The 7 gifts of the Holy Spirit.

Foundations of Religion - Christianity   SECTION B

The First Christian Martyrs

Pentecost was like a pebble dropped in a pool of water. In the years that followed, its effects rippled out across an ever-widening area, spreading outwards from Palestine to become a worldwide mission to spread the message of Jesus Christ.

Christianity spread rapidly thanks to the large network of Jewish communities that already existed in other parts of the Roman Empire. However, the real key to Christianity's success was the willingness of the disciples to go **beyond** their Jewish roots and reach out to **gentiles** (i.e. non-Jews).

> **REMEMBER!**
> **Jesus Christ** means '**Jesus the Messiah**'.
> **A Christian** is '**someone who has chosen to follow Jesus**'.

As more and more people became **Christians**, the Sanhedrin decided that it had to act. It arrested a young disciple named **Stephen** and put him on trial. However, his trial ended in a riot and Stephen was stoned to death by an angry mob. Stephen was to be the first of many Christian **martyrs**.

Did You Know?

Originally, '**Christian**' was a nickname given to the followers of Jesus by their non-Christian neighbours. This first happened in the city of Antioch, 300 miles north of Jerusalem, in Asia Minor (see: **The Acts of the Apostles 11:26**). At that time, Antioch was the third most important city in the Roman Empire.

Most of the original apostles later suffered martyrdom. It is believed that:

- **Peter** was crucified in Rome.
- **James** was beheaded in Jerusalem.
- **Philip** was executed at Phrygia in Asia Minor (modern Turkey).
- **Thomas** was put to death in India.
- **Jude** and **Simon the Zealot** were executed in Persia (modern Iran).

Only one apostle, **John**, is said to have lived to old age and died of natural causes.

St Peter the Apostle.

Becoming a Separate World Religion

From the outset, Christianity welcomed people of all races and social classes. So, quite soon, the early Christians faced an important decision: how should they treat **converts** who had become Christians but had not been Jews beforehand?

> **REMEMBER!**
> **A convert** is someone who chooses to join a religion.

197

LIGHT THE WAY

They wanted to know:

(a) Should these converts become Jews first **before** becoming Christians?
(b) Should all male converts be circumcised **before** being baptised?

Jesus had left no instructions about such matters. However, at **the Council of Jerusalem** in 49 CE, Christianity's leaders agreed that converts did **not** have to become Jews before becoming Christians. All that you needed to become a member of the Christian community was repentance for your sins and baptism (see: **The Letter to the Galatians 3:27–28**).

In the years following the Council of Jerusalem, Christians were no longer seen as a group within Judaism. Gradually, people came to realise that to be a Christian was to be a member of a new and separate world religion. By the end of the 1st century CE, Christianity had spread as far west as Spain, as far south as Ethiopia, as far north as the Crimea and as far east as India.

The Greatest Christian Missionary

The outstanding **Christian missionary** of the first century CE was **St Paul**.

> REMEMBER!
> **A Christian missionary** is someone who continues the work begun by Jesus Christ.

Paul (or in Hebrew **Saul**) was a Jew who was born at Tarsus in Asia Minor, around 5 CE. Before he became a follower of Jesus, Paul had been a devout Pharisee. For a time he had persecuted the Christian community in Jerusalem.

In 35 CE Paul was travelling to the city of Damascus in Syria. He had been sent by the Sanhedrin to persecute the Christians there. However, while on this journey, Paul underwent a dramatic **conversion** (see: **The Acts of the Apostles 9:1-9**).

> REMEMBER!
> **Conversion** means a sudden and complete change in how you think about and act towards God and other people.
> Usually **conversion** involves choosing to become a member of a particular religion.

St Paul underwent a dramatic conversion on the road to Damascus.

Instead of persecuting Christians, when Paul reached Damascus, he decided to convert and became a Christian.

What caused this sudden and unexpected change? Paul later said that it was due to an extraordinary event. While he was on his way to Damascus, the risen Jesus himself appeared to Paul and spoke to him (See **The First Letter to the Corinthians 15:8–10**).

Not surprisingly, once news of Paul's conversion reached Jerusalem, the Sanhedrin ordered that he be arrested on a charge of **heresy**.

Foundations of Religion - Christianity   SECTION B

However Paul avoided capture. He then spent some time with the apostle **Peter** learning more about Jesus.

In 38 CE, Paul set out on the first of three great missionary journeys. He followed the main trade routes around the eastern Mediterranean. He spread Jesus's message, baptised many new converts and set up Christian communities in every place he visited.

Later, Paul wrote a number of **epistles**. Thirteen of them have survived and they form part of the New Testament.

> **REMEMBER!**
> **Heresy** means accepting or spreading false ideas about God.

Did You Know?

Paul had not met Jesus during his public ministry. He doesn't seem to have been in Palestine at that time. Paul's first encounter with Jesus was when Jesus appeared to him on the road to Damascus.

> **REMEMBER!**
> **An epistle** was a letter offering advice to a new Christian community.

In the early days of Christianity, disagreements often arose over some important teachings. Paul wrote his epistles to clarify these teachings and settle any disputes.

Paul's epistles show that he played an enormous role in helping to spread the Christian message. However, Paul did not always work alone. He often worked with a team of missionaries. They included men such as **Barnabus**, **Luke** and **Mark**, and women such as **Lydia**, **Phoebe** and **Priscilla**.

Paul was uniquely well-equipped to spread the Christian message. Think about this:

- Paul was born a Jew but he was also a Roman citizen. This offered him certain protections under the law which he used to help spread Christianity.
- Paul spoke several languages (Aramaic, Greek and Hebrew). He could communicate with a wide variety of people, both Jews and gentiles.
- Paul was a deep-thinker and brilliant communicator. He made the message of Jesus relevant to people of different cultures, without ever changing its essential meaning.

Although not one of the original twelve apostles, Paul has been called '**the Apostle to the Gentiles**'. This is because he understood that the message of Jesus Christ was for **all** people, and he devoted his life to spreading it far and wide. Indeed, Paul played a key role in convincing the Council of Jerusalem that only baptism and repentance were needed to become a Christian.

The Acts of the Apostles ends with the story of how Paul was arrested and imprisoned in Rome. Historians believe that Paul was martyred around 67 or 68 CE on the orders of the Emperor Nero. However, because he was a Roman citizen, Paul was beheaded rather than crucified.

Persecution and Success

For almost 300 years after Jesus's death it was dangerous to be a Christian inside the Roman Empire. This was because the Romans persecuted Christians. Sometimes Christians were crucified, other times they were killed by wild animals in the arena. The worst persecutions were under the emperors Nero, Decius and Diocletian.

LIGHT THE WAY

Why were they persecuted?

At first the Romans saw Christianity as just another branch of Judaism. As such, they were content to leave Christians alone. However once the Romans realised that Christianity was a new and separate religion, Christians were no longer protected by the law that had freed the Jews from having to worship Rome's gods. So, when the Roman emperors began to claim that they too were gods who had to be worshipped, Christians were told that they had to offer sacrifices to them. When they refused, Christians were viewed as disloyal and dangerous (see: **Revelations 2: 10 and 13**).

Despite terrible periods of persecution and martyrdom, the Christian faith not only survived but thrived within the Roman Empire. Then, in 312 CE, a man called Constantine defeated his rivals and became emperor. The following year he granted freedom of worship to Christians. Finally, after almost three centuries of persecution, Christians could build their own meeting places (i.e. churches) and openly practise their religious faith without fear of persecution.

ACTIVITIES

1. Crossword

Foundations of Religion - Christianity   SECTION B

Across

2. Paul was journeying to this city in Syria when the risen Jesus appeared to him.
5. Paul was born there in Asia Minor.
7. The apostle who was put to death in India.
9. It means to undergo a sudden and complete change in how you think about and act towards God and other people.
12. At Pentecost, the disciples received seven of these from the Holy Spirit.
13. Thirteen of them survive and they form part of the New Testament.
17. The apostle who was crucified in Rome.
22. The sixth gift of the Holy Spirit.
24. The Roman emperor who granted Christians freedom of worship.
25. At Pentecost, the disciples heard this. It sounded powerful.
26. He appeared to his disciples many times after his resurrection.

Down

1. Forty days after Easter Sunday Jesus gathered his disciples at that place (3 words: 5, 2, 6).
3. The name of the city in which Jesus's disciples were first called 'Christians'.
4. The apostle who was beheaded in Jerusalem.
6. Before his Ascension, Jesus promised to send this person to guide and strengthen his disciples (2 words: 4, 6).
8. He was chosen to replace Judas Iscariot as an apostle.
10. This was Paul's Hebrew name.
11. The number of missionary journeys Paul set out on.
14. The young disciple who was stoned to death and became the first Christian martyr.
15. Tongues of this descended on the disciples at Pentecost, but they were unharmed.
16. A Christian who continues the work begun by Jesus Christ.
18. The only apostle said to have lived to old age and died of natural causes.
19. Because he was a Roman citizen, Paul was put to death in this way.
20. Where a council was held that established Christianity as a new and separate world religion.
21. The first gift of the Holy Spirit.
23. The fourth gift of the Holy Spirit.

2. Say what it means!

(a) The Ascension was _____

_____ .

(b) Pentecost was _____ .

(c) Jesus Christ means _____ .

(d) A convert is _____

_____ .

(e) Heresy means _____

_____ .

(f) An epistle was _____

_____ .

3. Think about it!

(a) How did Pentecost affect the disciples of Jesus?
(b) How far had Christianity spread by the end of the 1st century CE?
(c) Why was the Council of Jerusalem so important?
(d) Why was St Paul uniquely well-equipped to spread the Christian message?
(e) Do you think St Paul deserved to be called '**the Apostle to the Gentiles**'? Give a reason for your answer.

201

LIGHT THE WAY

4. Wordsearch

Find each of the following words:

Ascension
Holy Spirit
Pentecost
Wind
Fire
Gifts
Christian
Martyr
Stephen
Missionary
Paul
Convert
Heresy
Epistle
Aramaic
Greek
Hebrew
Apostle
Gentiles
Council
Jerusalem
Baptism
Repentance
Persecution
Nero
Diocletian
Constantine

Y	L	J	S	D	T	R	H	T	P	P	J	C	N	P
R	Q	A	N	E	Y	I	R	E	E	A	H	A	E	E
A	A	I	S	T	L	E	R	R	R	U	M	H	H	N
N	W	R	R	C	V	I	S	I	I	E	R	L	P	T
O	K	A	A	N	E	E	T	S	P	Y	S	G	E	E
I	M	E	O	M	C	N	T	N	E	S	I	Y	T	C
S	P	C	E	U	A	I	S	C	E	F	Y	P	S	O
S	A	G	T	R	A	I	N	I	T	G	V	L	K	S
I	P	I	X	N	G	A	C	S	O	G	G	Y	O	T
M	O	E	N	I	T	N	A	T	S	N	O	C	E	H
N	S	G	H	N	M	E	L	A	S	U	R	E	J	E
E	T	J	E	P	I	S	T	L	E	F	I	R	E	B
R	L	P	L	I	C	N	U	O	C	U	U	Q	P	R
O	E	D	I	O	C	L	E	T	I	A	N	E	N	E
R	B	A	P	T	I	S	M	O	D	E	E	R	F	W

Section C

Foundations of Religion - Major World Religions

Chapter 1:   **Being a Hindu** 204

Chapter 2:   **Being a Jew** 215

Chapter 3:   **Being a Buddhist** 228

Chapter 4:   **Being a Muslim** 242

LIGHT THE WAY

CHAPTER 1   BEING A HINDU

Origins

Hinduism is the oldest of the world's religions. It began in northern India around 2500 BCE.

Unlike the other major religions, Hinduism did not have a single, identifiable founder. Scholars believe that it was gradually spread across ancient India by **rishis**.

> REMEMBER!
> A **rishi** was a Hindu teacher of great holiness and wisdom.

Unfortunately, the names of these rishis have been lost over the centuries.

Beliefs

Hinduism does not have a single, widely accepted **creed**.

However most Hindus accept the following teachings:

Altar in a Hindu temple.

> REMEMBER!
> A **creed** is a statement of what the members of a religion believe in.

1. Polytheism

Hindus are free to worship many different gods. However, the three most important Hindu gods are:

- **Brahma** – the god who creates life.
- **Vishnu** – the god who protects life.
- **Shiva** – the god who destroys life.

However all these different gods point to something far greater than themselves. This mysterious something is called '**Brahman**'.

2. Brahman

Brahman is the supreme source of everything in the universe. Hindus believe that:

- It is **from** Brahman that all things come into existence.
- It is **through** Brahman that all things continue to exist.

However Brahman is not like the God of Christianity. Brahman is not a person. Brahman is **impersonal**.

Brahman is not only in all things but all things are in Brahman. This means that people, animals, insects, plants, rocks, rivers and even the gods themselves do not exist in their own right. They are all merely different ways in which Brahman expresses itself.

Brahma, the Hindu god who creates life.

204

As one Hindu text called *The Bhagavad Gita* puts it:

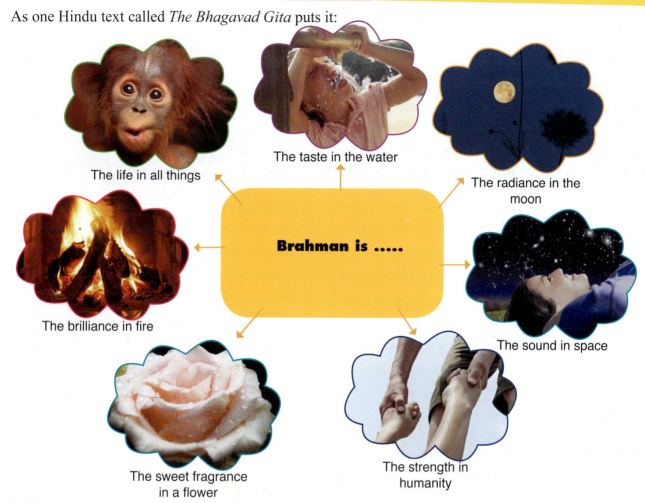

3. Atman

Atman is what gives life to your body. It is an invisible fragment of Brahman in you. Like Brahman, every atman is eternal. This means that while your body may grow old and die, the atman does not. Instead, the atman goes through **samsara**.

4. Samsara

When your body dies, your atman is **reincarnated**, i.e. it enters a new body. Then your atman goes on to live another life. This process happens over and over again throughout time. This repeating cycle of birth, death and rebirth is called **samsara**.

The atman must live through samsara many times before it can achieve **moksha**.

Did You Know?

Hindus believe that whenever evil threatens to take over the world, the god Vishnu comes down on earth to fight evil and restore order.

5. Moksha

Moksha is when your atman finally escapes from the cycle of birth, death and rebirth.

Moksha allows your atman to be reunited with Brahman. However, you can only do this when you have achieved **dharma**.

6. Dharma

Dharma is where you fulfil all your religious duties and live a good life. Dharma helps you to store up positive **karma**.

Vishnu, the Hindu god who protects life.

7. Karma

Karma means 'actions'. Hindus believe that the quality of your present life is decided by how you lived your previous life. So, if you consistently do good things in this life, you will be rewarded with a better life next time.

Eventually, if you live a life totally committed to doing only good, your atman will escape from samsara and be reunited with Brahman.

Did You Know?

Hindus believe that Vishnu has visited humanity nine times so far. He will make his tenth and final visit at the end of this cycle of history.

Each time Vishnu has come as a different being, called an **avatar** (meaning: **'one who descends'**). One of Vishnu's best-loved avatars is the warrior god **Krishna**.

The Castes

Hindu society is divided into **castes**.

There are four castes. In order of importance, they are:

REMEMBER!
A caste is the Hindu name for a social group.

1st	The Brahmin	These are priests.
2nd	The Kshatriya	These are rulers
3rd	The Vaishya	These are artisans, farmers and merchants.
4th	The Shudra	These are peasants and servants.

Over the centuries, the caste system developed into an entire way of life. Your status in your community was decided by the caste into which you were born. Even in today's India, if you are a member of one caste, it would be unusual for you to marry or socialise with a member of another caste.

Did You Know?

The lowest-ranking group in Hindu society is called **'the Untouchables'**. They are forced to do the most menial tasks, such as cleaning the streets and handling dead animals. Their fellow Hindus say that such work makes the Untouchables **impure** (i.e. unclean). As a result, Untouchables are forbidden to touch a member of the four castes or even to drink a cup of water from the same well.

One Hindu leader who tried to improve the treatment of the Untouchables was **Mohandas K. Gandhi**. He called them the **Harijans**, which means **'the Children of God'**. This was to remind people of their right to be respected.

Foundations of Religion - Major World Religions   SECTION C

The Vedas

Hinduism's sacred text is a collection of four books called the **Vedas**. These books were written during the third century BCE. They contain **Mantras**, **Brahmanas**, **Aranyakas** and **Upanishads**.

Did You Know?
Vedas means '**knowledge**'.

> **REMEMBER!**
> **Mantras** are chants or hymns.
> **Brahmanas** are explanations of those mantras.
> **Aranyakas** are guided meditations on important aspects of Hindu belief.
> **Upanishads** are poems offering insights into the meaning of life.

SPOTLIGHT ON THE MAHABHARATA

The Mahabharata is another important Hindu book. It is a great epic poem that describes the challenges faced by succeeding generations of two families. It explores the joys and hardships of human life.

Within the Mahabharata is a story called the **Bhagavad Gita**. Its title means **'the Song of the Lord'**. It is a poem written in the form of **dialogue**, i.e. an exchange of ideas between people.

The Bhagavad Gita's two main characters are the god **Krishna** (an avatar of Vishnu) and a warrior named **Arjuna**. The two are united on the side of good in the battle against evil.

By the end of their dialogue, Krishna has helped Arjuna to see that for an action to be truly good, it must be selfless, i.e. one where you do the right thing without seeking a reward in return.

Arjuna in a carriage behind Krishna who is mounted on a horse.

Worship

REMEMBER!
Puja means '**giving respect**'.

Puja is the Hindu word for worship. It should be performed twice a day, at sunrise and at sunset.

Did You Know?
A **Hindu shrine** consists of an image (i.e. picture or statue) of the particular god a family worships.

Worship in the home

Most Hindus worship in their own homes. Almost every Hindu home has its own **shrine**.

207

LIGHT THE WAY

Usually the mother arranges all the acts of worship for the family. She lights candles and burns incense sticks at the shrine. Then she sets out **the prasad**. This is an offering of food and flowers. It is placed in front of the image of a Hindu god. Such things are offered to show gratitude to **Brahma** (the creator god). Mantras are recited to summon the family's chosen god and texts from the Vedas are recited or sung.

Hindus pray for two reasons:
- To get the protection of their chosen god.
- To grow closer to this god in order to achieve moksha.

Prasad is an offering of food and flowers to show gratitude to Brahma.

Yoga helps you to gain greater control over both your body and your mind. It helps you to remove any trace of anger, greed and selfishness from your life. You need this to achieve inner peace.

Yoga is important because Hindus believe that it is only when you have reached a lasting inner peace that the cycle of reincarnation ends, allowing the atman to be finally reunited with Brahman.

Did You Know?
Yoga means **union**. It is a type of meditation popular among Hindus.

REMEMBER!
A mandir is a Hindu temple.

Worship in the mandir

Krishna Mandir, Nepal.

In India a typical **mandir** consists of a number of whitewashed buildings. These contain shrines to different gods. Usually there is an open courtyard where trees offer worshippers shade from the sun.

On entering a mandir you must:
- Remove your shoes to show you respect it as a holy place.
- Sit on the ground and pray facing a shrine containing the image of your chosen god.

There are three stages in Hindu worship:

- **Bhajans:** This involves reciting mantras, singing hymns and dancing.
- **Havan:** Here a **pandit** (priest) lights a fire and pours liquid butter onto the flame.
- **Arti:** Here a tray containing the symbols of the five elements (air, earth, ether, fire and water) is set out before the image of your chosen god. Then a red spot is made on both your own forehead and that of the image. Next, money is placed on the tray as an offering. After this you are given a mixture of dried fruit, nuts and sugar to eat.

Sometimes Hindus listen to a **pravachan** (i.e. a sermon) given by a visiting holy man.

Hindu Symbols

Aum (or 'Om')		Hindus believe that **Aum** was the very first sound made when the universe was created by Brahma. **Aum** is also the sound Hindus make when beginning and ending their prayers.
Lotus Flower		This symbol stands for purity, fertility, good fortune and progress.
Bindu		This is a coloured dot worn on the forehead of Hindu women. Married women wear a red dot. Unmarried women wear a black dot. Hindus believe it protects the wearer from evil.
The Cow	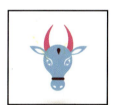	Hindus worship cows for their life-giving qualities (e.g. milk for food, hide for leather and dung for fuel). The cow represents humility and generosity. Hinduism rejects the whole idea of animal sacrifice. Hinduism teaches that we have a duty to protect all living things.

Rituals

1. Samskara

The first three samskara are celebrated while you are still a child in your mother's womb. You receive the fourth samskara shortly after birth. You are washed and the sacred symbol of Aum is marked on your tongue with honey from a golden pen.

You receive the fifth samskara when you are twelve days old. A Hindu priest prays with your family and announces your name.

You receive the sixth samskara when you are one year old. Your head is shaved to represent purity. You are now said to have left all the sins of your previous lives behind you.

> **REMEMBER!**
> **Samskara** is the religious ritual that introduces a Hindu into each new stage of life.

LIGHT THE WAY

2. Upanayana

This is also called 'the Ceremony of the Sacred Thread'. Usually, this ritual is restricted to boys who are members of the top three castes.

Traditionally upanayana took place when a boy left home to study with **a guru** (i.e. a religious teacher). Today it happens when they reach puberty. It marks the start of their formal religious studies.

> **REMEMBER!**
> **Upanayana** is the ritual where you become a full member of the Hindu community.

The ritual itself takes place in front of **the sacred fire** (which stands for energy and purity). A priest prays that you will continue to grow strong in your religious faith. Then the priest blesses **a coloured thread** (i.e. a loop of cotton).

There is a different coloured thread for each caste. The thread is tied loosely with a special knot. This thread is then worn by you, from your left shoulder across to your right hip. It represents the idea that you are now beginning a new and pure life. From this point on you are considered a full member of your particular caste. This means that you must accept and fulfil all the responsibilities that go with it.

Every caste member is expected to do five things:

1. Worship the gods.
2. Respect gurus.
3. Respect their parents.
4. Help the poor.
5. Care for animals and the environment.

Festivals

There are hundreds of Hindu festivals. Here we will look at two of the most important ones.

Holi - the Festival of Colours. Hindus drench one another in red-coloured water – all in a spirit of fun.

Holi

This is also known as 'the Festival of Colours'. Holi is held over several days in the Hindu month of **Phalunga**. It celebrates the arrival of spring.

Holi takes its name from the story of the evil princess Holika. She tried to murder her young nephew Prahlad because of his devotion to the god Vishnu. Prahlad was saved because he repeated Vishnu's name. Holika was punished for what she had tried to do. She was destroyed in a great bonfire.

This story represents the Hindu belief that good will always triumph over evil. It is also the source of the traditional practice of lighting bonfires on the eve of Holi. These bonfires also represent the end of the old year and the start of the new.

On the first morning of Holi, Hindus are allowed to set aside some of their normal ways of behaving. They dress in white clothing and throw red-coloured water over one another and smear each other with paint. All this is done in a spirit of fun.

Divali/Diwali

This is the most widely known Hindu festival. It lasts for five days. It takes place in the Hindu month of **Kartika** (October/November).

Divali is also known as 'the Festival of Lights'. This is because it is a common practice for Hindus to thoroughly clean their homes and decorate them with oil lamps called diyas. These lamps are lit to welcome **Lakshmi** (the goddess of prosperity) into their lives.

Hindus celebrate Divali by:
- Having a meal with family and friends.
- Putting on firework displays and dancing in the streets.
- Exchanging gifts.
- Clearing all outstanding debts.
- Buying new clothes and new household items.

Yatra

Hindus go on pilgrimage:
- To fulfil a promise made to a particular god.
- To give thanks for the birth of a child.
- To **atone** (i.e. show you are sorry) for sins.
- To put aside pride and become more humble and generous.

REMEMBER!
Yatra is the Hindu word for pilgrimage.

Once Hindus reach a pilgrimage site, they must take a ritual bath, usually in a nearby river or lake. They pray that their sins will be washed away by these waters and that they can make a fresh start in life. After bathing, a male pilgrim has his head shaved. However, a female pilgrim only has to have one or two locks of her hair cut off.

Hindus have many places of pilgrimage. Some of these are places where it is said that a particular god or goddess came down on earth. For example:
- **Ajodhya** in northern India is called the birthplace of the god Rama.
- **Vrindavan** is where the god Krishna was born and grew up.

Another famous site is the city of **Varanasi**. It was built on the banks of the river **Ganges**.

Millions of Indians depend on the life-giving waters of the Ganges. Pilgrims to Varanasi light a small candle and float it down the river as an offering to the goddess Ganga.

Did You Know?
The Ganges is the most sacred river in India. It is named after the goddess Ganga.

Morning on the River Ganges, Varanasi, India

LIGHT THE WAY

ACTIVITIES

1. Say what it means!

(a) A rishi was _____.
(b) A mandir is _____.
(c) Samskara is _____
    _____.
(d) Upanayana is _____
    _____.
(e) Yatra is _____.

2. Crossword

212

Foundations of Religion - Major World Religions   SECTION C

Across

4. Name meaning 'one who descends'.
7. These are priests.
8. These are the artisans, farmers and merchants.
10. The Hindu word for worship.
13. A coloured dot worn on the forehead by Hindu women.
15. Where a tray containing the symbols of the five elements (air, earth, ether, fire and water) is set out before the image of your chosen god.
18. Means an exchange of ideas between people.
19. Hindu name for a religious teacher.
20. These are the peasants and servants.
21. The most sacred river in India.
24. An offering of fruit and flowers placed before the shrine of a Hindu god.

Down

1. This involves reciting mantras, singing hymns and dancing.
2. These are the rulers.
3. The god who creates life.
5. It means 'to show that you are sorry for your sins'.
6. The very first sound made when the universe was created.
7. The supreme source of everything in the universe.
9. The oldest of the world's religions.
11. The lowest ranking group in Hindu society.
12. The god who protects life.
14. The god who destroys life.
16. It is a type of meditation. It helps you to get control over your mind and body.
17. The Hindu name for a social group.
22. Title of Hinduism's sacred text.
23. A statement of what the members of a religion believe.

3. Tick the box!

In each of the following, say whether it is **true** or **false**.

	True	False
1. Hinduism had one identifiable founder.		
2. Hinduism does not have a single, widely accepted creed.		
3. Hindus are free to worship more than one god.		
4. Hindus say that Brahman is just like the Christian God. Brahman is a person.		
5. Hindus believe that people, animals, insects, plants, rocks, rivers and even the gods themselves do not exist in their own right. They are all merely different ways in which Brahman expresses itself.		
6. Atman is what gives life to your body. It is an invisible fragment of Brahman in you.		
7. Hindus believe that when your body dies, your atman is reincarnated, i.e. it enters a new body and goes on to live another life.		
8. The repeating cycle of birth, death and rebirth is called moksha.		
9. Hindus believe that the quality of your present life is decided by how you lived your previous life. So, if you consistently do good things in this life, you will be rewarded with a better life next time.		

213

LIGHT THE WAY

	True	False
10. Hindus believe that whenever evil threatens to take over the world, the god Shiva comes down on earth to fight evil and restore order.		
11. The highest-ranking group in Hindu society are the Untouchables.		
12. One Hindu leader who tried to improve the treatment of the Untouchables was Mohandas K. Gandhi.		
13. Mantras are chants or hymns.		
14. Aranyakas are explanations of these mantras.		
15. Upanishads are poems offering insights into the meaning of life.		
16. Puja must be performed only once each day.		
17. Usually the father arranges all acts of worship for a Hindu family.		
18. You remove your shoes before entering a mandir to show that you respect it as a holy place.		
19. A pravachan is a Hindu holy man.		
20. You receive the sixth samskara when you are one year old. Your head is shaved to represent purity. You are now said to have left all the sins of your previous lives behind you.		
21. The Ceremony of the Sacred Thread is a ritual restricted to girls who are members of the top three castes.		
22. Holi is known as 'the festival of lights'.		
23. Holi celebrates the arrival of spring.		
24. During Holi, Hindus dress in white clothing and throw red-coloured water over one another.		
25. Lakshmi is the Hindu goddess of prosperity.		
26. Once Hindus reach a pilgrimage site, they take a ritual bath and pray that their sins will be washed away.		
27. Ajodhya in northern India is called the birthplace of the god Krishna.		

Foundations of Religion - Major World Religions   SECTION C

CHAPTER 2   BEING A JEW

The Dead Sea Scrolls

One day in 1947, three young brothers were herding a flock of goats through the desolate wilderness near **the Dead Sea**. Their route took them through an area called **Wadi Qumran**. Bored by their job, the boys amused themselves by throwing stones into the openings of caves as they passed by. After one throw, they were surprised to hear the sound of something breaking, deep inside the cave. As they were short on time and afraid of entering the dark cave, they chose not to find out what had been broken.

A few days later the youngest boy, **Muhammad-edh-Dhib**, decided to go back to the cave and investigate. Inside the cave he found several tall terracotta jars. Each jar contained bundles of ancient manuscripts (i.e. handwritten documents). These manuscripts were sewn together in long scrolls and wrapped in linen.

The boy returned home and told his family. They returned with him to the cave and took the manuscripts. Thinking that the manuscripts might be valuable, his father sold them. The scholars who bought them quickly realised that they now possessed one of the greatest archaeological discoveries of all time. These manuscripts were 2,000-year-old copies of **Judaism's** sacred text.

Did You Know?

Judaism is the world's oldest monotheistic religion. It members are called '**Jews**'.

Three young brothers discovered the Dead Sea Scrolls in a cave in Wadi Qumran.

Over the next nine years teams of archaeologists explored the caves around the Dead Sea. They discovered around 800 more manuscripts, all stored in the same way. These ancient manuscripts became known as **the Dead Sea Scrolls**.

Did You Know?

The Dead Sea Scrolls give us the oldest known complete manuscript of Judaism's sacred text. They were written in three languages: Hebrew, Greek and Aramaic.

The Dead Sea Scrolls are thought to have been produced by a Jewish group called **the Essenes** (see: Section B, Chapter 2). They most likely hid these scrolls in caves to prevent their destruction by the Romans during the Jewish rebellion (66–73 CE).

Today, the Dead Sea Scrolls are housed in the **Sh**... **Book** at the Israel Museum in Jerusalem. These manuscripts show us that the Jews have ... the actual words of **the Tanakh** since

LIGHT THE WAY

The Tanakh was written in Hebrew. It consists of 24 books bound together into a single volume.

> **REMEMBER!**
> **The Tanakh** is the name of Judaism's sacred text.

Spotlight on the Tanakh

The Tanakh is organised into three sections:

1. The Torah

This means 'the Law'. It contains: (a) the story of the Jewish people from Abraham to the death of Moses; and (b) the 613 **mitzvot** (meaning rules for life).

2. The Nevi'im

This means '**the prophets**'. It tells the story of Judaism, from Moses's death up to the conquest of the Hebrew kingdoms.

When reading a scroll from the Kethuvim, you should follow the text with a yad, as you are not allowed to touch the scroll with your fingers.

3. The Kethuvim

This means '**the writings**'. It contains heroic stories (e.g. Daniel in the lion's den), **the Proverbs** (wise sayings) and **the Psalms** (poetry).

Jews are taught to treat the Tanakh with great respect. For example:

- Only copies handwritten on scrolls are used in Jewish worship.
- When you read a scroll, you are not allowed to touch it with your fingers. You must always use a **yad** (i.e. pointer) when following the text.

> **Did You Know?**
> It is from the initial letters of each of these three sections – **T, N** and **K** – that we get the title **Tanakh**.

Beliefs

All Jews share a common **creed**.

> **REMEMBER!**
> **A creed** is a set of beliefs.

Belief in God

- The Tanakh teaches that there is only one God who is the almighty and eternal creator of the universe.
- The Hebrew name for God is '**Yahweh**'. However, out of respect this name is not spoken. Instead, God is usually referred to as '**Adonai**', meaning '**Lord**'.

Belief in the covenant

- **The covenant** is the sacred agreement that God first made with Abraham and his descendants. God later renewed it with Moses.
- God promised the Jews that, if they faithfully followed his Ten Commandments, they would receive the Promised Land in return.

Foundations of Religion - Major World Religions   SECTION C

The Talmud

The Talmud is a fascinating book. Its compilers were just as interested in encouraging its readers to ask questions as they were in providing them with answers. It tackles a wide range of topics, such as:

- What is beauty?
- How should we enjoy the natural world?
- What is the value of argument and debate?

> **REMEMBER!**
> **The Talmud** is a book that sets out the rules covering all aspects of Jewish life and religious practice. Its title means 'the Teaching'.

The Talmud has played a very important role in helping Jews to preserve their religious identity over the centuries. However, this has been very difficult to achieve. Until the state of Israel was set up in 1948, Jews had long been a small minority in any society in which they had lived. Often they had been subjected to vicious persecution.

Prayer

Jews pray to show their commitment to keeping **the covenant**. This involves praying at least three times each day:

- **In the morning**, because **Abraham** always started each day by asking for God's guidance in what he had to do.
- **In the afternoon**, because this was when **Isaac** always stopped to pray. He did so to remind himself of what really matters in life.
- **In the evening**, because this was when **Jacob** stopped to thank God for the blessings (i.e. good things) he had received during the day.

However, Jews also pray before and after any significant daily event, such as a family meal.

Whenever praying, Jews must wear a **kippah** (i.e. a small cap) on their heads. This is a token of their submission to God.

Worship

According to the Tanakh, God created our world in six days and rested on the seventh (see: **Genesis 2:1–4**). Later, God commanded that the seventh day of the week should be a day of prayer and relaxation for all Jews (see **Exodus 20:8–11**). Jews call the seventh day of the week **Shabbat**.

Shabbat is celebrated both at home and in the synagogue.

> **REMEMBER!**
> **Shabbat** or the **Sabbath Day** is the Jewish holy day. It begins at sunset on Friday and ends at sunset on Saturday. It is a day of prayer and relaxation. Indeed, 'Shabbat' is the Hebrew word for 'rest'.

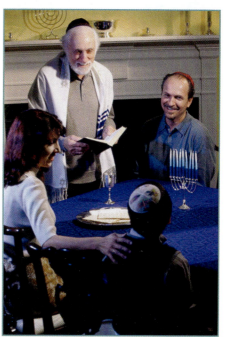

A Jewish family celebrate Shabbat.

LIGHT THE WAY

1. Worship at home – a Jew explains

The home is the main focus of Jewish life. This is because we see it as much more than the place in which we live. For us the home is a place where God is invited and welcomed. As such, we think of every Jewish home as a sacred place. The most visible symbol of this belief is **the mezuzah**.

> **Did You Know?**
>
> A **mezuzah** is a small parchment scroll. On it is written the first two paragraphs of a prayer called the Shema. This reminds Jews that there is only one God and that they must keep their side of the covenant.

The mezuzah contains two paragraphs of the Shema written on a small scroll.

A **mezuzah** is a sacred object. This is why we store it in a small decorated, protective container. As set down in **Deuteronomy 6:9**, this container is fixed to the upper third of all doorposts in our homes, with the exception of the toilet/ bathroom and the garage.

We touch the mezuzah every time we enter or leave a room to remind ourselves of what it means to be Jewish.

Our celebration of **Shabbat** begins at sunset on Friday. Our mother lights two candles and says a prayer to welcome Shabbat. Then our father says the **Kiddush**. This is a traditional prayer of thanksgiving to God. This is said over a cup of wine. This represents the sweetness and joy of Shabbat.

During Shabbat, challah bread is cut, dipped in salt and shared among the family.

Next, our mother says a blessing over **the challah** (a plaited loaf of bread). This recalls how God kept our ancestors alive as they travelled through the desert during the Exodus. The bread is cut, dipped in salt and shared out among us. After this our father blesses us and we eat the Shabbat meal.

At sunset on Saturday we celebrate **the Havdalah**. This ceremony marks the end of Shabbat. A plaited candle is lit to symbolise a return to work after a day of prayer and rest. Then, a box of sweet-smelling spices is passed around our family. We end with a prayer. We ask that the goodness of the Shabbat day will sustain us through the week ahead.

All **'creative'** work is forbidden during Shabbat. This is because God rested from creating things on the seventh day. For us, avoiding **'creative'** work means:

- Not buying or selling anything
- Not driving any kind of vehicle
- Not watching television
- Not using the internet.

We do this to have time to concentrate our minds on what really matters in life – doing God's will and loving one another.

Foundations of Religion - Major World Religions   SECTION C

2. Worship in the synagogue – a Jew explains

The fourth commandment says that we should '**Remember the Sabbath Day and keep it holy**' (**Exodus 20:8**). This is why we worship at the **synagogue** during Shabbat.

Usually, a synagogue serves three functions:
- It acts as a house of prayer
- It acts as a place of education
- It acts as a community centre.

> **REMEMBER!**
> **A synagogue** is a Jewish place of worship. Its name means 'a gathering of people'.

The synagogue became the focal point of our worship after the destruction of the Temple in 70 CE. Indeed, certain features of the modern synagogue recall Jewish worship in the ancient Temple.

For example:
- The layout of a synagogue is based on that of the Temple.
- The synagogue faces towards Jerusalem, where the Temple once stood.
- There are no images of God. We believe that such images are forbidden by the second commandment. Instead, our synagogues are decorated only with geometric patterns and Hebrew calligraphy.

A model of the Second Temple in Jerusalem, which was destroyed by the Romans in 70 CE.

However there is one important **difference**. The ancient Temple practice of sacrificing animals to God has never played any role in synagogue worship. Animal sacrifice ended with the Temple's destruction. Instead, our worship focuses on listening to the voice of God speaking to us through the Tanakh.

Jewish men are expected to attend their local synagogue as often as possible. This is because a full service involving public prayers can only be held if there is a **minyan** (i.e. a gathering of no less than ten adult males).

Leadership

In most Jewish traditions, only a man can become **a rabbi**. However, in the Reform tradition, both men and women can become a rabbi.

A rabbi is not a priest. The Jewish priesthood died out when the Temple was destroyed in 70 CE. A rabbi is **a lay person** who has studied for years to take up a leadership role in the Jewish community. A rabbi is free to marry and have a family.

> **REMEMBER!**
> **A rabbi** is someone employed by a Jewish community to lead it and run its synagogue. The title means 'my teacher'.

A Jewish rabbi is a lay person who has studied for many years to take up a leadership role in the Jewish community.

LIGHT THE WAY

The Stages of Life

As in other religions, Jews mark important moments in their lives with religious rituals.

Initiation – a Jewish boy explains

Our faith teaches us that children are a blessing and a gift from God. We have inherited the task of keeping the covenant God made with our ancestors.

As a new-born child, I was given my name at a ceremony held in the local synagogue. Every Jewish child's name has a religious meaning. My name is **Joshua**. It means '**saviour**'.

Then, eight days after my birth, the ritual of **Brit Milah** (or **the Covenant of the Circumcision**) took place. This was performed in our family home by a **mohel**.

> **REMEMBER!**
> **Male circumcision** means that the loose foreskin covering the penis is removed.
> **A mohel** is a man specially trained to carry out male circumcision.

We believe that God demanded this be done when he made the covenant with Abraham long ago (see: **Genesis 17:9–14**). Male circumcision **symbolises** (i.e. represents) the Jewish people's obedience to God's will.

After my circumcision, I was formally declared a member of our religion. My father recited a prayer of thanksgiving. Then my extended family came forward to offer me their best wishes for the future.

As we are Jews in the Reform tradition, my sister received her name at a special ritual held in the synagogue called **Zeved Habet** (meaning '**the gift of a daughter**'). This happened when she was seven days old.

Becoming an adult – a Jewish girl explains

Our religion recognises that girls mature earlier than boys. As a result, girls are considered adults at the age of twelve, while boys are declared adults at thirteen.

To mark the moment we become adults, we take part in rituals held at our synagogue. These are:

- **Bat mitzvah** (meaning: **Daughter of the Commandments**) when a girl is declared an adult.
- **Bar mitzvah** (meaning: **Son of the Commandments**) when a boy is declared an adult.

We spend years studying both the Hebrew language and the Tanakh to prepare for this day. These rituals have four parts:

- You stand at **the bimah** (reading desk) in the synagogue and read aloud in Hebrew a passage from the **Tanakh**. However, a girl is not allowed to read from the Torah, only from the other sections.
- Next you receive **a siddur** (prayer book) and **a tallit** (prayer shawl) for use when you pray in the synagogue.
- Then you put on **a tefillin** (a box tied to your left arm containing verses from the Tanakh) and read a chapter from the Torah.

- You end by reciting this celebratory prayer:

'Heavenly Father, on this sacred and solemn occasion in my life, I stand before thee in the presence of this congregation to fulfil my duty, to pray to thee every day and to keep thy Law that I may be a more worthy man/woman.'

After completing the ritual, you share a meal with family and friends to celebrate this important day.

The bar mitzvah and bat mitzvah are important to us. Through them we show our willingness to take responsibility for our relationship with God. We publicly commit to putting the teachings of Judaism into practice in our daily lives.

Diet

Jews have many rules about **diet** (i.e. what you may eat). These are called **kashrut**.

The rules of kashrut are set out in the **Book of Leviticus, Chapter 11**. Jews follow them to remind themselves to keep the covenant and help preserve their religious identity.

Did You Know?
Kashrut means 'fit, proper or correct'. It refers to the special diet all Jews must follow.

According to kashrut, all food belongs to either of two categories:
- Kosher – Permitted food.
- Treyfah – Forbidden food.

The following foods are **kosher**:
- All domestic fowl (chicken, duck, goose and turkey) and their eggs.
- All vegetables, fruits and grains.
- All fish with fins, tails and scales that are easily removed.
- Meat from animals that both chew the cud and have cloven (i.e. split) hooves (e.g. cow, deer or sheep).

However, all of these animals must be prepared for eating according to the rules of **shechita**.

For example, an animal must be killed by a single cut of a razor sharp blade across its throat, immediately severing its trachea and oesophagus. This causes a swift death. Then all blood is removed from the animal by broiling or salting.

Did You Know?
Shechita is a set of rules Jews must follow when preparing food.

LIGHT THE WAY

Jews believe that this is the most humane way to kill an animal. It is done by **a shochet**.

The following foods are **treyfah**:

- Animals that do not chew the cud (this rules out horsemeat, pork and rabbit).
- Animals slaughtered without having their throats cut and blood drained.
- Any animal that dies of natural causes.
- Shellfish.

> **REMEMBER!**
> **A shochet** is a butcher who is specially trained to slaughter animals according to shechita.

Jews are also forbidden to eat meat and dairy products together (see: **Exodus 23:19**). However, foods that contain neither meat nor dairy products may be eaten with either of them. Only cheeses certified as having been processed in a kosher manner may be eaten.

Jews must use separate utensils in kitchens when preparing meat and dairy products. This is why Jewish kitchens have two sinks and two sets of saucepans. Meat and milk products must not come into contact, not even accidentally.

Festivals

Festivals play an important role in Jewish religious life because they help to reinforce their separate religious identity.

There are **mitzvot** (i.e. rules) about how festivals should be celebrated. These state that:

- Celebrations must begin at sunset on the day before the festival.
- All daily activities must stop for major festivals, so you can have time to pray and celebrate with your family.
- Each festival has its own special foods that should be prepared and enjoyed.

Important Jewish festivals include:

Rosh Hashanah

This marks the start of the Jewish New Year. It is held in the autumn. **The shofar** (i.e. a ram's horn) is blown one hundred times in the synagogue. This is done to remind Jews that God told Abraham to sacrifice an animal instead of his son Isaac.

Yom Kippur

Also known as the **Day of Atonement**. This is the most holy and solemn day of the Jewish calendar. It lasts for a period of twenty-five hours. At Yom Kippur, Jews must **fast**, i.e. abstain from food and drink. You are not allowed to wash, wear perfume or leather shoes during this festival. This is a day for Jews to reflect on the direction of their lives and to seek forgiveness from God and from anyone they have offended.

Hanukkah

Also known as the **Festival of Lights**. Held around the Winter Solstice, this festival lasts eight days. Jews recall how an army led by Judas Maccabeus in 165 BCE regained Israel's independence from the Greeks. After this the Jews purified the Temple and rededicated it to God.

Foundations of Religion - Major World Religions   SECTION C

In Jewish homes, one candle is lit on the first night of Hanukkah, two on the second night and so on up to eight. Children receive presents and games are played.

Pesach

Also known as **Passover**. This is a celebration of the gift of freedom. For Jews in Israel it is a seven-day festival. For Jews living elsewhere it lasts eight days.

The name 'Passover' comes from the story of how the angel of death 'passed over' (i.e. left unharmed) the Hebrew children during the last of the ten plagues that struck Egypt. This forced the pharaoh to free the Hebrews. Then Moses led them home to the Promised Land.

Hanukkah is a Jewish festival that lasts for eight days.

SPOTLIGHT ON THE SEDER – A JEW EXPLAINS

The Seder is a special meal held on the first evening of **Passover**. It is a celebration of the **Exodus**, i.e. the story of how God sent Moses to free the Jews from slavery in Egypt and led them through the wilderness to the Promised Land.

To prepare for the Seder, we thoroughly spring-clean our homes. We also remove all traces of **hametz** (i.e. leavened/yeast bread) from it. Only special plates, glassware and cutlery that have had no previous contact with yeast bread are used during the Seder.

The Seder begins with the head of our household saying a prayer called the **Kiddush** over a glass of wine. Everyone eats some parsley that has been dipped in salt water. Then the head of our household takes the matzo (i.e. a loaf of unleavened bread) and shares it out among us.

During the meal, four small glasses of wine (for adults) or grape juice (for children) are consumed with the food. However, one glass of wine is poured out but left untouched. This symbolises our belief that, at some future time, the prophet **Elijah** will return and announce that the messiah is about to arrive.

The youngest person present asks, '**Why is this night different from all other nights?**' In response, the head of our household reads the **Haggadah** (i.e. the story of the first Passover and the Exodus). We remember the horror of slavery and give thanks to God for the gift of freedom.

After this, our main family meal is served. Then, any children present take part in a game to find the **afikomen** (i.e. a piece of matzo bread that has been hidden). The one who finds it receives a prize and the afikomen is shared out among all of us. We end the Seder with a prayer. We ask God to grant us the opportunity to share the Seder again next year.

A Jewish family celebrates the Seder.

LIGHT THE WAY

ACTIVITIES

1. Wordsearch

Find the following words:

Judaism
Torah
Adonai
Abraham
Shabbat
Bar Mitzvah
Kosher
Dead Sea Scrolls
Hebrew
Talmud
Isaac
Synagogue
Treyfah
Tanakh
Nevi'im
Kethuvim
Tallit
Seder
Yahweh
Creed
Rabbi
Shochet
Covenant
Kippah
Brit Milah
Tefillin
Passover

B	C	K	W	T	I	G	M	C	H	S	K	M	W	S
D	R	O	I	A	O	A	V	A	E	L	E	S	W	I
R	E	I	N	P	H	R	V	X	W	L	T	I	S	D
J	E	O	T	A	P	Z	A	H	H	O	H	A	H	D
M	D	V	R	M	T	A	E	H	A	R	U	D	O	U
A	I	B	O	I	I	B	H	C	Y	C	V	U	C	R
G	A	I	M	S	R	L	C	T	A	S	I	J	H	E
I	F	R	V	E	S	O	A	D	R	A	M	B	E	H
B	A	G	W	E	V	A	D	H	S	E	S	G	T	S
B	B	U	Y	E	N	L	P	J	W	S	Y	I	E	O
A	S	Y	N	A	G	O	G	U	E	D	Q	F	S	K
R	V	A	H	K	A	N	A	T	G	A	S	R	A	P
J	N	Q	M	N	I	L	L	I	F	E	T	T	H	H
T	S	H	A	B	B	A	T	S	E	D	E	R	R	B
T	A	L	M	U	D	D	D	S	T	I	L	L	A	T

2. Say what it means!

(a) The Tanakh is _____.

(b) The Talmud is _____
_____.

(c) The covenant is _____
_____.

(d) A synagogue is _____
_____.

(e) A rabbi is _____
_____.

3. Crossword

Across
4. The seventh day of the week for Jews. It is a day of rest.
7. The name of the Jewish group thought to have produced the Dead Sea Scrolls.
9. The story of how God sent Moses to free the Jews from slavery in Egypt and lead them through the wilderness to the Promised Land.
11. A Jewish prayer shawl.
13. A small cap Jews wear on their heads when praying.
14. A Jewish prayer book.
15. Hebrew word meaning 'the Law'.
16. This means 'permitted food'.
17. Where the Dead Sea Scrolls are housed at the Israel Museum in Jerusalem (4 words: 5, 2, 3, 4).

Down
1. Hebrew word meaning 'rules for life'.
2. Means handwritten documents.
3. This refers to the special diet all Jews must follow.
5. A small parchment scroll. On it is written the Shema. It is kept in a small decorated, protective container and fixed to the upper third of most of the doorposts of a Jewish home.
6. The special meal held on the first evening of Passover.
8. A box Jews tie to their left arm containing verses from the Tanakh.
10. Name of area near the Dead Sea where the scrolls were found (2 words: 4, 6).
12. This means to abstain from food and drink.
18. This means 'forbidden food'.

LIGHT THE WAY

4. Tick the correct box!

In each of the following, say whether it is **true** or **false**.

	True	False
1. Judaism is the world's oldest polytheistic religion.		
2. The Dead Sea Scrolls give us the oldest known complete manuscript of the Tanakh.		
3. The Tanakh was written in Greek.		
4. The Tanakh consists of twenty-three books bound into a single volume.		
5. The Torah means 'the Law'. It contains the story of the Jewish people from Abraham to the death of Moses as well as the 613 mitzvot.		
6. The Nevi'im means 'the writings'. It contains heroic stories, as well as the Proverbs and the Psalms.		
7. When Jews read a scroll they must not touch it with their fingers. They must always use a yak when following the text.		
8. The Hebrew name for God is 'Yahweh'. However, out of respect this name is not spoken.		
9. The covenant is the sacred agreement that God first made with Abraham and his descendants.		
10. The Kethuvim is a huge guidebook to Jewish life. It sets out all the rules that cover every aspect of Jewish daily life and religious practice.		
11. According the Tanakh, God created our world in five days and rested on the sixth.		
12. The Shabbat begins at sunset on Friday and ends at sunset on Sunday.		
13. There are no images of God allowed in a synagogue.		
14. A minyan is a gathering of no less than nine adult males.		
15. A rabbi is a Jewish priest.		
16. The bimah is a writing desk in the synagogue.		
17. The shofar is a plaited loaf of bread.		
18. The Havdalah is a ceremony that marks the end of Shabbat.		
19. A shochet is a man specially trained to carry out male circumcision.		
20. Bat mitzvah is a ceremony in which a Jewish girl is declared an adult.		
21. All domestic fowl and their eggs are considered kosher.		
22. Animals that do not chew the cud are considered kosher.		
23. Jews are allowed to eat meat and dairy products together.		
24. Yom Kippur marks the start of the Jewish New Year.		
25. Hanukkah is also known as the Festival of Lights. It is held around the Winter Solstice.		

Foundations of Religion - Major World Religions SECTION C

	True	False
26. The name 'Passover' comes from the story of how the angel of death 'passed over' (i.e. left unharmed) the Hebrew children during the last of the ten plagues that struck Egypt.		
27. The Seder celebrates the story of the messiah.		
28. To prepare for the Seder, Jews spring-clean their homes.		
29. Only special plates, glassware and cutlery that have had previous contact with yeast bread are used during the Seder.		
30. The glass of wine poured out but left untouched at the Seder symbolises the Jewish belief that, at some future time, the prophet Elijah will return and announce that the messiah is about to arrive.		

LIGHT THE WAY

CHAPTER 3 BEING A BUDDHIST

Origins

Buddhism was founded in the 6th century BCE by a holy man from Nepal named **Siddhartha Gautama**. He has been known ever since as the **Buddha**.

> REMEMBER!
> The title **Buddha** means 'the enlightened one'.

A statue of Buddha.

The Buddha turned his back on a life of luxury and security so that he could devote all his time and energy to achieving **enlightenment**.

> REMEMBER!
> **Enlightenment** means you have gained a deep understanding of the meaning of life.

Though it began in India, Buddhism spread gradually across much of eastern and southern Asia, finally reaching Tibet in the 8th century CE.

Basic Beliefs

Buddhists believe in **samsara**.

Whatever you say or do in your present life will decide what will become of you in your **next** life. This is because of **the Law of Karma**.

> REMEMBER!
> **Samsara** means that we must all go through a repeating process of birth, death and re-birth.

When you do something right you create **positive** karma. When you do something wrong you create **negative** karma. You may have to live through many lives on earth before you can gather enough positive karma to reach **nirvana**.

> REMEMBER!
> **The Law of Karma** says that from right action comes good and from wrong action comes evil.

If you want to reach nirvana you must begin by accepting the **Four Noble Truths**.

> REMEMBER!
> **Nirvana** is a state of complete and perfect peace of mind and body.

An artist's representation of Samsara, the cycle of rebirth.

228

The Four Noble Truths

Unlike other religions that are centred on the worship of a Supreme Being (i.e. God or Brahman), Buddhism is centred on the acceptance of four basic truths. These are:

1. Life is not perfect. All life involves suffering.

2. We are always left unhappy when we try to make our lives perfect. Our **desires** (i.e. wanting pleasure and wealth) are the cause of our suffering.

3. We must accept that all things are **impermanent** (i.e. do not last). Only then will we stop wanting things and look for a better way to find fulfilment.

4. To end our suffering, we need to achieve enlightenment. The only way to do this is to follow **the Eightfold Path**.

These teachings form the heart of the Buddha's message to humanity.

The Eightfold Path

This is also called '**the Middle Way**'. It sets out the Buddha's advice on how to live a good life. The eight steps are as follows:

Step 1: Right view
Follow the Buddha's teachings.

Step 2: Right thought
Avoid selfishness.

Step 3: Right speech
Avoid lies and gossip.

Step 4: Right action
Do not harm or kill any creature.

Step 5: Right livelihood
Earn your living honestly.

Step 6: Right effort
Try to do your very best.

> **REMEMBER!**
> **The Eightfold Path** consists of the eight steps you should follow if you want to do the following things: (a) free yourself of desire; (b) end your suffering; (c) achieve enlightenment; and (d) reach nirvana.

Step 7: Right mindfulness
Be responsible for yourself. Get control over your thoughts and moods.

Step 8: Right contemplation
Become a calm person through practising meditation.

LIGHT THE WAY

The Wheel of Law: The symbol of Buddhism.

Did You Know?

The symbol of Buddhism is **the Wheel of Law**. It is also known as '**the Eight-Spoked Wheel**'. This was the symbol used by the Buddha himself to explain his ideas.

During his first public sermon, the Buddha drew a wheel on the ground. He used it to represent the continuous cycle of birth, death and rebirth.

The Buddha said that there is only one way to escape from this repeating cycle and reach nirvana: You must follow his example and live according to the Eightfold Path in order to achieve enlightenment.

Schism

The Buddha did not choose anyone to succeed him after his death. Also, initially, his teachings were not written down and so were only passed on by word of mouth. This lack of a unifying leader and an agreed sacred text led people to develop different interpretations of his teachings. Within a century or so, there was a **schism** (i.e. split) within Buddhism. Two traditions emerged from this schism. They are:

- **Theravada Buddhism**.
- **Mahayana Buddhism**.

According to the **Theravada tradition**, the Buddha made two things clear:
- He was not a god and did not want to be worshipped as one.
- He was not a messenger for any God or gods.

Theravada Buddhists reject both monotheism and polytheism. They say that Gautama was an extraordinarily good and wise man, but nothing more. He generously dedicated his life to helping others achieve nirvana through enlightenment. He did this by his teaching and by the example of his life.

In contrast, the **Mahayana tradition** says that the Buddha was not merely a wise teacher. Influenced by Hinduism, Mahayana Buddhists believe that the Buddha was a god.

Foundations of Religion - Major World Religions SECTION C

	Theravada Buddhism	Mahayana Buddhism
Meaning	The Way of the Elders	The Universal Assembly
Outlook	Conservative. Demands strict faithfulness to the teachings contained in the Pali Canon.	Liberal. More open to outside ideas and influences.
View of the Buddha	He was a great holy man but not a god.	He was a kind of god who only appeared to be an ordinary man.
Teaching about life	We are on our own in the universe. There is no God. We can reach enlightenment only through our own efforts.	We are not alone in the universe. We can pray to the Buddha for guidance on how to reach enlightenment.

Sacred Texts

In time, both Buddhist traditions wrote down their own versions of the Buddha's teachings. Each one claims that its text is the only one that accurately passes on what he said.

The Pali Canon

This is the sacred text of **Theravada Buddhism**. **Canon** means an agreed set of teachings/writings.

The Pali Canon is made up of forty-five volumes. These are divided into three sections, known as **the Tripitaka**, which means '**the three baskets**'.

They are as follows:

The Vinaya Pitaka
- This means '**the discipline basket**'.
- It explains how you can live in peace.

The Sutta Pitaka
- This means '**the instruction basket**'.
- It sets out 'the Four Noble Truths'.

A Buddhist monk meditates.

> REMEMBER!
> **Pali** was an ancient language probably spoken by the Buddha himself.

231

LIGHT THE WAY

The Abhidhamma Pitaka
- This means '**the great teaching basket**'.
- It offers explanations of ideas such as karma and nirvana.
- It tells you about the most effective ways to meditate.

The Sutras

This is the sacred text of **Mahayana Buddhism**.

The most important of the Sutras is the **Lotus Sutra**. It contains poetry, sermons and stories. It also sets out the Mahayana teaching on **the Bodhisattvas**.

The Lotus Sutra examines the ways in which the Bodhisattvas try to help others reach enlightenment. Perhaps the best known Bodhisattva today is **the Dalai Lama**.

REMEMBER!
The title Sutras means '**threads**'.

REMEMBER!
A Bodhisattva is a perfect being who has gained enlightenment. However, out of compassion, he/she chooses to postpone nirvana and be reborn in order to serve humanity.

Did You Know?
Tibetan Buddhists believe that the current Dalai Lama is the 74th reincarnation of Avalokiteshvara, the Bodhisattva of compassion.

SPOTLIGHT ON THE DALAI LAMA

The Dalai Lama in Paris in 2003.

The title **Dalai Lama** literally means '**Ocean teacher**' or '**the teacher whose wisdom is as deep as the ocean**'. The Dalai Lama is the head monk of Tibetan **Buddhism**.

Buddhism was first introduced to Tibet around 750 CE by an Indian Buddhist monk named Padma Sambhava, author of *The Tibetan Book of the Dead*.

However, the institution of the Dalai Lama is a relatively recent one. There have been only fourteen Dalai Lamas in the entire history of Tibetan Buddhism. The first Dalai Lama was **Gedun Drub** (1391–1474).

The current Dalai Lama is **Tenzin Gyatso**. He was born on 6 July 1935 to a peasant farming family in northeastern Tibet. His followers believe him to be **the reincarnation** of the thirteenth Lama, **Thubten Gyatso**.

REMEMBER!
Reincarnation means that after this body has died, your soul passes on into a new body and begins a new life.

Foundations of Religion - Major World Religions   **SECTION C**

When the thirteenth Dalai Lama died, the most senior Tibetan monks began their search for his successor. They looked for a boy who was born at or shortly after the previous Dalai Lama's time of death.

After several months of searching, the monks located a two-year-old boy named Lhamo Thondup. In order to confirm his identity, the monks tested the child by asking him to identify certain personal items that belonged to the thirteenth Dalai Lama, to make sure that he really was his reincarnation. For example, the monks brought with them a number of items, such as prayer beads or a small bell. The boy was asked to identify those things that belonged to the previous Dalai Lama. If he chose the correct items, they would ask him to take more tests until they were sure that he really was the next Dalai Lama. If he failed the test, the monks would have left him and continued their search.

Dalai Lama Temple, Dharamsala.

Once the boy passed these tests, the monks changed his name to **Tenzin Gyatso** and proclaimed him the fourteenth Dalai Lama. Then he was taken to a monastery in Tibet to begin his years of training to prepare him to fulfil his role as the leader of Tibetan Buddhism.

While a student, the young Dalai Lama studied many subjects, including geography, mathematics, medicine and philosophy. He was fascinated by science and has since stated that, if he had not become a monk, he would have liked to have become an engineer.

At age 11, the Dalai Lama met Heinrich Harrer, an Austrian mountaineer, who became one of his tutors, teaching him about the outside world. The two remained firm friends until Harrer's death in 2006. The story of their friendship was recounted by Harrer in his book, *Seven Years in Tibet*.

In 1950, at the age of 15, the young Dalai Lama assumed his role as ruler of Tibet. However, soon afterwards, the People's Republic of China invaded Tibet. Following a failed uprising in 1959, the Dalai Lama was forced to leave his homeland, believing the Chinese leader Mao intended to assassinate him. He was followed by about 80,000 Tibetan refugees. They settled at **Dharamsala** in India and established a Tibetan government-in-exile there.

Since then, the Dalai Lama has set up schools and colleges to preserve the language, history, literature, music and religion of Tibet. He has supported the establishment of over 200 Buddhist monasteries and nunneries in Asia and elsewhere.

In 2011, the Dalai Lama announced that he has given up his role as Tibet's political leader. He says that the Tibetan people need to freely elect their own leader, not have one imposed upon them.

The Dalai Lama has focused his energy on his role as the spiritual leader of Tibetan Buddhism. As a **Bodhisattva**, he has committed himself to tackling urgent issues such as building a sustainable environment and finding peaceful resolutions to conflicts.

The Dalai Lama has written several books and addressed hundreds of international conferences on our need to respect the earth and have compassion for one another if our problems are to be resolved. He has held talks with many Western leaders and been actively involved in interfaith dialogue with the leaders of other religions. It is his hope that, one day, Tibet will become a place where its inhabitants, both Tibetan and Chinese, can peacefully co-exist.

In 1989, the Dalai Lama was awarded **the Nobel Peace Prize** in recognition of (a) his championing of a non-violent solution to the question of China's rule over Tibet; and (b) his support for sustainable solutions to our world's environmental problems.

LIGHT THE WAY

Rituals – A Theravada Buddhist Explains

We do not worship any gods. We do not worship the Buddha. Instead, we venerate (i.e. show our respect for) the **Three Treasures**. These are:

- **The Buddha's example** – It inspires us to live by his teachings.
- **The Dhamma** (the name given to the Buddha's teachings) – This is the medicine we need to rid ourselves of desire. These teachings guide us towards enlightenment.
- **The Sangha** (the community to which we belong) – It encourages and supports us to strive towards enlightenment.

For us, prayer means **meditation**.

> REMEMBER!
> **Meditation** is a method used to calm oneself in order to achieve inner peace and clarity of mind

We meditate for two reasons:
- It strengthens us so that we can resist evil thoughts and curb our selfish desires.
- It encourages us to have compassion for and show kindness to others.

We have two ways of meditating: saying a **mantra** and making a **mandala**.

Both methods help us to remove any distractions and focus our minds on what matters.

According to Buddhists, meditation encourages us to have compassion for others.

> REMEMBER!
> **A mantra** is a phrase repeated over and over again during meditation.
> For example: '**Om mani padme hun**'. This means '**The jewel of the lotus brings wisdom**'.

When Buddhist monks or nuns meditate together, they are led by a meditation master. His advice is based on years of personal experience. He shows you how to calm your mind and focus your attention on the meaning of the Buddha's teachings. However, we also believe that all Buddhists have the ability to guide their own lives if they follow the Eightfold Path.

This is a **mandala**. Great care is taken over the smallest detail. However, mandalas are not kept when they are finished. This is because Buddhists believe that, while we should do everything with great care, we should also be willing to let go of things and accept that nothing in life lasts for ever.

> REMEMBER!
> **A mandala** is a complex pattern with a meaning drawn in sand.

234

Foundations of Religion - Major World Religions   SECTION C

Initiation – A Buddhist Explains

Pravrajya is held just before the start of the rainy season. This is a time when monks and nuns tend not to travel far from their monasteries due to the bad weather.

> **REMEMBER!**
> **The pravrajya** is the Buddhist ritual of initiation.

This ritual is held when a young person reaches the age of eight. It marks their decision to enter a **vihara** to become a monk or a nun. Usually, this applies to more boys than girls.

> **REMEMBER!**
> **A vihara** is the name given to a Buddhist temple and its monastery compound.

Did You Know?
To fully follow the Eightfold Path to perfection means renouncing (i.e. giving up) family and ordinary life. This is possible only for a few. This is why Buddhism adopted the idea of monasteries.

Buddhist monasteries offer you a place where you can live in utmost simplicity, devoting all your time to meditation and studying sacred texts in your pursuit of enlightenment. The duty of monks and nuns is to master the ideas of the Buddha and pass them on to others through teaching and by the example of their lives.

Before entering the monastery, boys and girls have their heads shaved. This is done to remind them that monks and nuns must be humble and place no value on either appearances or possessions.

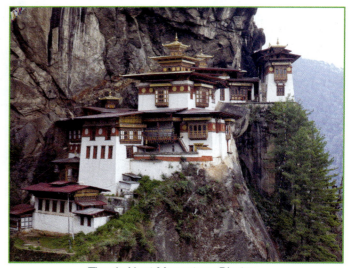

Tiger's Nest Monastery, Bhutan.

During this ritual, boys and girls wear specially coloured robes:
- In Sri Lanka and Thailand these robes are saffron-coloured.
- In Tibet they are maroon.
- In Japan they are black.

A new student is only allowed to keep what are called 'the eight requisites':
- A robe.
- A belt.
- A razor.
- A needle and thread.
- An alms' bowl.
- A walking stick.
- A water strainer.
- A toothpick.

LIGHT THE WAY

No one is forced to stay in a Buddhist monastery. Students are free to leave and return to ordinary life at any time they choose. Many young people only stay in the monastery to gain a basic education. However, those who choose to remain spend many years training both mind and body in order to become a Buddhist monk or nun.

Festivals – A Buddhist Explains

These are our main festivals:

Wesak

This is the most important day on the calendar for Theravada Buddhists. It is also known as 'Buddha Day'. Usually, we celebrate it on the first full moon in May. For three days, we recall the birth, enlightenment and death of the Buddha.

Wesak is a happy occasion. We clean our homes in preparation and decorate them in bright colours. Usually, we exchange gifts. Also, we are encouraged to make donations to charitable organisations that help the disabled, the poor and homeless.

Before dawn on the first day of Wesak we go to temples to meditate. We offer gifts to the monks and nuns. Our gifts are placed on altars to show our respect for the Buddha's teachings.

In some countries, we wash the statues of the Buddha. This is to remind us that we need to purify our hearts and minds to achieve enlightenment.

During Wesak, Buddhists offer gifts to the monks and nuns.

Dhamma Day

We celebrate this in July. Here we remember three important events in the life of the Buddha:
- When he took on his first followers.
- When he gave his first sermon.
- When he predicted the time of his own death.

Pilgrimage – A Theravada Buddhist Explains

As a Theravada Buddhist I do not worship the Buddha. Instead, I **venerate** (i.e. show respect for) his memory. I do so because he discovered the way to live in perfect peace and then dedicated his life to sharing his discovery with others.

I know of four main centres of Buddhist pilgrimage:
- Rummindei in Nepal – where the Buddha was born.
- Buddh Gaya in Bihar, India – where the Buddha achieved enlightenment.
- Sarnath in Uttar Pradesh, India – where the Buddha gave his first sermon to his disciples.
- Kushingara in Uttar Pradesh, India – where the Buddha died.

Foundations of Religion - Major World Religions SECTION C

I hope to visit at least one of these sites during my lifetime. I believe that going on pilgrimage to such sacred sites builds up positive karma. This will help me to have a better life in my next reincarnation.

Other popular places of pilgrimage include temples that contain stupas.

> REMEMBER!
> **A stupa** is a burial mound or casket that contains a relic of the Buddha.

Buddh Gaya in Bihar, India.

Temple of the Tooth relic, Sri Lanka.

A relic can be either the surviving physical remains of a deceased holy person, such a fragment of bone, or a personal effect such as a bell, book or piece of clothing.

The most famous stupa is **the Temple of the Tooth** in Kandy, Sri Lanka. This is said to hold a tooth belonging to the Buddha. Every August there is a special ceremonial parade of elephants held at this shrine. The largest elephant carries a golden casket containing the Buddha's tooth.

LIGHT THE WAY

ACTIVITIES

1. Wordsearch

Find the following words:

Buddhism
Enlightenment
Samsara
Karma
Nirvana
Theravada
Mahayana
Pali Canon
Sutras
Dalai Lama
Tibet
Reincarnation
Sangha
Mantra
Mandala
Pravrajya
Vihara
Wesak
Dhamma
Stupa

T	L	D	Q	S	V	M	B	N	A	P	A	T	N	S
G	N	Q	A	I	A	U	M	D	U	R	N	E	O	I
A	T	E	H	L	D	N	A	I	K	A	A	B	I	Y
D	R	A	M	D	A	V	G	A	V	V	V	I	T	O
A	R	A	H	N	A	I	S	H	X	R	R	T	A	M
A	M	I	S	R	E	E	L	M	A	A	I	B	N	M
J	S	R	E	M	W	T	J	A	G	J	N	O	R	A
M	N	H	A	G	A	R	H	G	M	Y	Z	A	A	N
J	T	Y	W	K	A	S	D	G	N	A	L	T	C	T
P	A	L	I	C	A	N	O	N	I	A	R	E	N	R
A	N	A	Y	A	H	A	M	K	D	L	M	V	I	A
S	U	T	R	A	S	G	Z	N	J	P	N	U	E	A
A	M	M	A	H	D	O	A	Y	D	C	G	E	R	S
T	U	Y	M	Z	S	M	L	I	S	T	U	P	A	P
M	O	C	H	W	L	Q	K	K	Z	O	H	F	O	B

2. Say what it means!

(a) The title Buddha means _____.

(b) Enlightenment means _____

_____.

(c) Samsara means _____

_____.

(d) The Law of Karma says _____

_____.

(e) Nirvana is _____.

(f) A Bodhisattva is _____

_____.

(g) Reincarnation means _____

_____.

(h) Meditation is _____

_____.

(i) A relic can be _____

_____.

Foundations of Religion - Major World Religions   SECTION C

3. Crossword

Across
4. The name given to the Buddha's teachings.
6. These things are the cause of our suffering.
9. To show respect for the Buddha's memory.
11. The only way to end suffering and achieve enlightenment is to follow it (2 words: 9, 4).
12. A Buddhist tradition whose name means 'the Universal Assembly'.
13. A burial mound or casket that contains a relic of the Buddha.
14. Buddhists believe that all life involves this.
15. A complex pattern with a meaning drawn in the sand.
18. A Buddhist tradition whose name means 'the Way of the Elders'.

Down
1. A perfect being who has gained enlightenment but who postpones it to serve humanity.
2. The title given to Siddhartha Gautama by Buddhists.
3. The symbol of Buddhism (3 words: 5, 2, 3).
5. Buddhism finally reached this country in the 8th century CE.
7. The title of this sacred book means 'threads'.
8. The most important day on the calendar for Theravada Buddhists.
9. The name given to a Buddhist temple and monastery compound.
10. An agreed set of teachings/writings.
14. The community to which Buddhists belong.
16. A phrase repeated over and over again during meditation.
17. An ancient language probably spoken by the Buddha himself.

LIGHT THE WAY

4. Tick the correct box!

In each of the following, say whether it is **true** or **false**.

	True	False
1. The Buddha turned his back on a life of luxury and security so that he could devote all his time and energy to achieving enlightenment.		
2. The Law of Karma says that whatever you do in your present life will decide what will become of you in your next life.		
3. When you do something right you create negative karma.		
4. Buddhists say that you only have to live through one life on earth before you can gather enough positive karma to reach nirvana.		
5. If you want to reach nirvana you must accept the Five Noble Truths.		
6. The Eightfold Path sets out the Buddha's advice on how to live a good life.		
7. The Buddha chose someone to succeed him after his death.		
8. According to the Theravada tradition, the Buddha was a god and wanted to be worshipped as one.		
9. The Sutta Pitaka sets out the Four Noble Truths.		
10. The most important of the sutras is the Lotus Sutra.		
11. Tibetan Buddhists believe that the current Dalai Lama is the 74th reincarnation of Avalokiteshvara, the Bodhisattva of compassion.		
12. The title 'Dalai Lama' literally means 'the jewel of the lotus'.		
13. The first Dalai Lama was Tenzin Gyatso.		
14. When the thirteenth Dalai Lama died, the most senior Tibetan monks began their search for his successor. They looked for a boy who was born at or shortly after the previous Dalai Lama's time of death.		
15. The fourteenth Dalai Lama's original name was Lhamo Thondup.		
16. After the Chinese invasion of Tibet, the Dalai Lama and his followers settled at Dharamsala in India and established a Tibetan government-in-exile there.		
17. In 2011, the Dalai Lama announced that he was going to continue in his role as Tibet's political leader.		
18. In 1989 the Dalai Lama was awarded the Nobel Peace Prize.		
19. Buddhists meditate because it strengthens them so that they can resist evil thoughts and curb their selfish desires.		
20. Mandalas are always kept when they are finished.		
21. The pravrajya is the Buddhist ritual of initiation. It is held when a young boy or girl reaches the age of eight.		
22. Pravrajya is held just before the start of the dry season.		
23. In Japan, boys and girls wear maroon-coloured robes during pravrajya.		
24. An umbrella is listed as one of 'the eight requisites' for a Buddhist monk or nun.		

Foundations of Religion - Major World Religions   SECTION C

	True	False
25. No one is forced to stay in a Buddhist monastery. Students are free to leave the monastery and return to ordinary life at any time they choose.		
26. Wesak is also known as 'Buddha's Day'.		
27. On Dhamma Day Buddhists remember three important events in the life of the Buddha.		
28. A Theravada Buddhist worships the Buddha.		
29. A Mahayana Buddhist venerates the Buddha.		
30. Rummindei in Nepal was where the Buddha achieved enlightenment.		
31. Sarnath in Uttar Pradesh, India was where the Buddha died.		
32. Buddhists visit pilgrimage sites to build up positive karma. They believe that it will help them have a better life in their next reincarnation.		
33. The most famous stupa is the Temple of the Tooth in Kandy, Sri Lanka.		

5. Look it up!

Find out about the visit of the Dalai Lama to Ireland in April 2012.

LIGHT THE WAY

CHAPTER 4   BEING A MUSLIM

Introduction

Islam is the world's second largest religion, with more than one and a half billion members.

> REMEMBER!
> **Islam** means '**peace through submission (to God's will)**'.
> A member of Islam is called a **Muslim**.
> This means '**one who submits to Allah**'.
> **Allah** means '**the (one and only) God**'.

Muslims make up the overwhelming majority of the population in most countries of the Middle East, Central Asia and North Africa. However, the majority of the world's Muslims now live in Southern Asia (e.g. Bangladesh, India and Pakistan) and in Oceania (e.g. Indonesia).

Islam is the world's second largest religion.

Name and Origins

It is often said that Islam was founded by Muhammad, a holy man who lived in Arabia during the 7th century CE. However, Muslims themselves say that Islam actually began with the first human being, **Adam**. He was the first **prophet**.

> REMEMBER!
> **A prophet** is someone who receives messages from God and then passes them on to people.

Muslims accept that Abraham, Moses and Jesus were prophets. However, Muslims believe that the Jews and the Christians who came after these holy men distorted what they had said. So, to set the record straight, Allah finally sent the Prophet Muhammad. He delivered God's true message to humanity in such a way that it could never again be distorted. He presented it in the form of a sacred text Muslims call the **Qur'an**.

The Qur'an is Islam's sacred text.

> REMEMBER!
> **The Qur'an** (or **Koran**) is Islam's sacred text. Its title means 'to recite'. It consists of 114 **surahs** (i.e. chapters).

Muslims believe that every line of the Qur'an is literally the word of Allah. They say that the Qur'an was first given by Allah to the Angel Jibril. Then the angel recited it to Muhammad. He, in turn, memorised everything the angel had told him and then dictated it all, word for word, to scribes who accurately recorded what he had said.

242

Foundations of Religion - Major World Religions SECTION C

The Six Beliefs

As a Muslim, you are expected to believe that:

1. Allah is the one and only true God.
2. Angels are the messengers of Allah.
3. The Qur'an is the final and complete revelation of Allah.
4. Muhammad was the last and the greatest prophet of Allah.
5. This world will be brought to an end by Allah on a day of his choosing.
6. Allah will reward the good by welcoming them into heaven and punish the wicked by sending them to hell.

> **REMEMBER!**
> Keep in mind that Muslims worship only Allah.
> Muslims do not worship Muhammad.

The way in which Muslims put these six beliefs into practice is by following the **Five Pillars of Faith**.

The Five Pillars of Faith

If you are a Muslim, it is essential that you fulfil these five **obligations**.

As a Muslim, you are expected to base your whole life upon the Five Pillars. They help to shape your ways of thinking and acting so that you can truly submit to the will of Allah. They are:

> **REMEMBER!**
> **An obligation** is a duty you must live up to.

1st Pillar – Shahadah

You must believe and openly proclaim, **'There is no God but Allah. Muhammad is the prophet of Allah.'**

2nd Pillar – Salah

You must turn toward Makkah and pray to Allah five times each day. You must attend the local mosque at midday each Friday to pray with your fellow Muslims.

3rd Pillar – Zakah

You must give generously to charity. You have two ways of doing this:
- Donate a sum of money on your own initiative.
- Have one-fortieth of your income collected each year to educate the poor and care for the sick.

4th Pillar – Sawm

You must fast to develop self-discipline. Do not eat or drink during the daylight hours of the holy month of **Ramadan** (i.e. the ninth month of the Muslim calendar).

A Muslim man turns towards Makkah to pray.

LIGHT THE WAY

5th Pillar – Hajj

If you are physically able, you must go on a pilgrimage to the holy city of Makkah at least once in your life.

The Mosque

The first mosque was built in Madinah by the Prophet Muhammad himself. He taught that the most important role of a mosque is to offer Muslims a quiet place where they can gather as a community to worship Allah.

The Islamic Cultural Office of Ireland, Clonskeagh, Dublin.

> **REMEMBER!**
> A **mosque** is a Muslim place of worship. The name comes from the Arabic word *masjid*, which means **'a place of prostration'**.

However, a mosque can serve other roles too:
- It can provide rooms for a **madrasah** (i.e. an Islamic school). Here children learn the Arabic language and study the Qur'an.
- It can offer facilities for community activities, such as running a youth club.

The most important officials in a mosque are:
- The muezzin – He calls Muslims to prayer.
- The khatib – He preaches the sermon at Friday prayers.
- The imam – He leads the community in prayer.

> **Did You Know?**
>
> **An imam** is not the same as a Catholic/Anglican/Orthodox priest. He is not ordained but employed by a committee that runs the mosque.
>
> An imam interprets the Shari'a, offers advice on how to be a good Muslim and helps young Muslims to understand their faith.

Salah – A Muslim Man Explains

The Prophet Muhammad taught that we must turn towards Makkah and pray five times each day – at sunrise, noon, mid-afternoon, sunset and early night. We usually begin praying this way around the age of seven.

> **REMEMBER!**
> **Salah** is an Arabic word meaning **'formal prayer'**.

When we pray, we remind ourselves that we must put obedience to the will of Allah before everything else in our lives. We believe that Allah sees all that we do and knows what is really in our hearts. We think that it is a serious sin for a Muslim

244

Foundations of Religion – Major World Religions   SECTION C

to deliberately decide not to pray. This is because we believe that we cannot succeed in life without the strength that only Allah can give us.

In countries where Islam is the religion of the majority, you will hear the call of the muezzin echoing out over your city or town five times each day. His job is to remind everyone that it is time to stop, put aside their earthly concerns and pray to Allah. He does so by calling out the **adhan** over a loudspeaker system from the balcony of a **minaret**.

> **REMEMBER!**
> **The adhan** is the prayer announcing that it is time for Muslims to pray.
> **A minaret** is a tall slender tower attached to a mosque.

The adhan goes like this:

> **Allah is the greatest.**
> **I bear witness that there is no God but Allah.**
> **I bear witness that Muhammad is Allah's messenger.**
> **Rush to prayer, rush to prayer.**
> **Rush to success, rush to success.**
> **Allah is the greatest.**
> **There is no God but Allah.**

Attendance at prayer in the mosque on Friday is **compulsory** (i.e. we must go there). Friday is our '**Day of Assembly**' (i.e. holy day). However, Friday is not a day of rest for Muslims as the Shabbat is for Jews. Our businesses and shops are only supposed to stay closed between the hours of twelve noon and two o'clock in the afternoon. Then they may re-open for business.

It is mostly Muslim men who pray at the mosque. When women go to the mosque to pray, they must sit in a separate area.

SPOTLIGHT ON PRAYING IN A MOSQUE

Washing place outside a mosque.

When we arrive at the mosque, we must take off our shoes and place them on a shoe rack. There is a washroom for **wudu** (i.e. ritual washing). We wash to prepare ourselves (both body and soul) for worship. Then we put on skullcaps before entering the prayer hall.

There are no pictures or statues in a mosque. The Qur'an forbids us to draw or paint any image of Allah. To attempt to do so is **shirk**.

> **REMEMBER!**
> **Shirk** or **blasphemy** means to offer insult to Allah, who is great and good beyond all compare.

However, we are permitted to decorate our mosques with **calligraphy** and **geometric patterns**.

LIGHT THE WAY

Did You Know?

The calligraphy displayed in a mosque consists of beautifully written verses taken from the Qur'an.

Geometric patterns are allowed because these angle and line drawings reflect the order and unity of Allah's creation.

These floral tiles decorate the Blue Mosque at Tabriz, Iran.

There are no seats in a mosque. The floor of the main hall is carpeted. There are markings on it to show where you should unroll your prayer mat. This means worshippers are organised into neat lines.

We always pray facing the holy city of Makkah.

During Friday prayers, **the khatib** (i.e. the preacher) goes to **the minbar** (i.e. a pulpit or raised platform) and gives **the khutbah** (i.e. the sermon). He may talk about social issues (e.g. crime) as well as religious ones.

After the sermon, the imam leads our community in prayer. We begin by saying the first surah of the Qur'an, which we all know by heart. As we say other verses, we make different gestures. Each gesture says something about our relationship with Allah. However, unlike other religions, we do not dance or play music in our place of worship.

Did You Know?

There is an alcove in one wall of every mosque that indicates the direction of Makkah. This alcove is called **a mihrab**.

Aqiqa – A Muslim Explains

We believe that the birth of a child is **barakah** (i.e. a blessing from Allah). The first word every baby should hear is the name of Allah. This happens when the father whispers **the adhan** (i.e. the call to prayer) into the child's right ear.

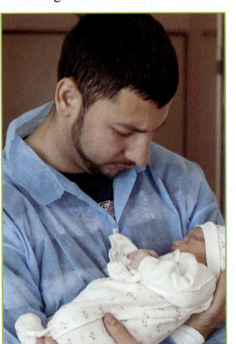

A week or so after you are born, the ritual of **Aqiqa** is held.

> REMEMBER!
> **Aqiqa** (pronounced **Aqee-qah**) is the Muslim naming ritual.

On that day, your head is shaved and your parents make a donation to the poor – by tradition gold or money equivalent to the weight of your hair. Then, your parents offer a sacrifice to Allah – two sheep for a boy and one sheep for a girl. This part usually takes place at a slaughterhouse. Then the meat is sweetened and divided out as follows:

- Two-thirds of it is shared among your extended family.
- One-third of it is shared with the poor in your community in a special meal.

Foundations of Religion – Major World Religions   SECTION C

After this, you are named. Usually, your parents choose your name in the following way:

- They may name you after either the prophet Muhammad himself, or a member of his family, such as Fatimah (if you are a girl) or Ali (if you are a boy).
- They may give you a name that reminds you of your duty to obey Allah, such as Abdullah (which means 'the servant of Allah').

Sometimes your parents may ask the local imam to suggest a name for you. Choosing the right name for a child is very important to us. We believe that your name influences the kind of person you will grow up to be.

Usually at Aqiqa, boys are **circumcised** (i.e. the loose foreskin covering the penis is removed). This is done at a hospital. It is necessary because all the prophets were circumcised.

Did You Know?

There is no special coming-of-age ceremony for Muslims. Boys and girls automatically take on adult responsibilities once they begin puberty. This means that boys and girls are not allowed to mix socially unless they are close relatives. From that time on, girls must follow Islamic dress code and wear **the hijab** (i.e. a veil that covers the head).

Festivals – A Muslim Explains

Islam has its own calendar which follows **the lunar cycle** (i.e. the phases of the moon). So, while our year has twelve months, it has only 354 days.

We also have our own way of dating events. The Muslim era began in 622 CE. This was when the prophet Muhammad emigrated from Makkah to Madinah. It is our Year One.

We have many different **festivals**.

> **REMEMBER!**
> **A festival** is a large-scale religious celebration where people come together to give thanks to God. The Arabic word for festival is '**Id**'. However, Muslims on the Indian subcontinent spell it '**Eid**'.

> **REMEMBER!**
> **Sawm** means you must fast during the hours of daylight during the holy month of Ramadan.
> **To fast** means that you do not eat or drink.
> **Ramadan** is the 9th month of the Muslim calendar.

Our main festivals include:

Ramadan

Sawm is the 4th pillar of Islam.

Ramadan is important to Muslims because it was during this month that Allah first sent the angel Jibril to Muhammad. We give thanks for the gift of the Qur'an. Many of us try to read all of the Qur'an at least once during this month.

We fast during Ramadan to show our devotion to Allah and to gain forgiveness for our sins. However, the following people are excused from fasting: the elderly; pregnant women; the mentally disabled; the incurably ill; and children below the age of puberty.

LIGHT THE WAY

Id-ul-Fitr

Ramadan ends when the next new moon rises. Then the festival of **Id-ul-Fitr** is held.

> **REMEMBER!**
> **Id-ul-Fitr** means 'the festival of breaking fast'.

A Muslim man reading the Qur'an.

We celebrate Id-ul-Fitr for three days. During this time we attend a special service at the mosque. After prayers, we greet one another with the words 'Id Mubarak'. This means 'Have a blessed festival'.

We celebrate Id-ul-Fitr not only to mark the end of a long period of fasting, but also to thank Allah for helping us to complete it. Also, to show our commitment to living out our Muslim faith, we also give our **Id zakah** to the mosque's officials.

A Muslim woman prepares a family meal during Id-ul-Fitr.

> **REMEMBER!**
> **Id zakah** is a compulsory charity tax that adult Muslims must pay once a year.

During Id-ul-Fitr, we decorate our homes, exchange cards, visit friends and hold a large family meal. We visit the graves of our loved ones and place flowers on them. We also buy new clothes to wear during this festival. Children receive presents. We also donate food to the poor.

Id-ul-Adha

This festival is held during **Dhul-Hijjah** (i.e. the twelfth month of the Muslim year).

It is a time to give thanks for Allah's goodness. Also, we think about what it means to be a Muslim and how we can live better lives.

> **REMEMBER!**
> **Id-ul-Adha** means 'the Festival of Sacrifice' or 'the Great Feast'.

During Id-ul-Adha, we remember how Ibrahim was told to sacrifice his son, Ishmael, to show that he was totally obedient to Allah. However, when Allah saw that Ibrahim was willing to do so, Allah stopped him. Allah accepted the sacrifice of a ram instead.

To show that, like Ibrahim, we are also ready to obey Allah without any hesitation, modern Muslims celebrate by sacrificing a sheep. One third of its meat is donated to the poor. We also exchange cards and give our children gifts.

We celebrate Id-ul-Adha over four days. It marks the end of **the Hajj**.

Foundations of Religion - Major World Religions   SECTION C

SP☉TLIGHT ON THE HAJJ – A MUSLIM EXPLAINS

Each year about two million Muslims take part in the Hajj between the 8th and the 13th day of Dhu al-Hijja.

Muslims do so to follow the example of the prophet Muhammad.

> **REMEMBER!**
> **The Hajj** is the 5th pillar of Islam. This states that if you are an adult Muslim who has both the health and the means, you must make a pilgrimage to Makkah at least once in your life.

> **Did You Know?**
> **Makkah** is the holiest place on Earth for Muslims. Non-Muslims are not allowed to enter the city precincts at any time.

Pilgrims after morning prayer, Makkah.

Before setting out on pilgrimage to Makkah, you are expected to:
- Settle all your outstanding debts.
- Take care of all your family commitments.

When you arrive in Makkah you must:
- Take a purifying ritual bath to show that you intend to complete the pilgrimage.
- Put on a plain white garment called the **ihram** and wear sandals. This shows that you accept that everyone is equal before Allah.

> **Did You Know?**
> For a man, the **ihram** consists of two pieces of plain white cotton – one piece is folded around the waist and the other hangs over the left shoulder.
>
> For a woman, the **ihram** is a long, white cotton dress that covers everything except the face, hands and feet.

All pilgrims to Makkah must wear the plain white garment called the ihram.

LIGHT THE WAY

The ihram is a great leveller. When you wear it, no one can tell if you are rich or poor.

As long as you wear the ihram, you must not tell lies or get angry. You must not wear perfume, make-up or jewellery. You must not look at your own reflection in a mirror, as to do so would show that you are thinking about yourself rather than about Allah.

We believe that, if you take part in the Hajj in a spirit of **reverence** (i.e. deep respect), Allah will forgive all your sins. Further, if you die while journeying to, attending or coming from the Hajj, you will be declared **a martyr** (i.e. someone who has died for your beliefs). Allah welcomes all martyrs directly into heaven.

Many Muslims say that their experience of taking part in the Hajj makes them more aware of the power and unity of Islam.

A Guide to the Hajj Route

Stage 1

You circle the **Ka'bah** seven times – three times quickly and four times slowly – in an anti-clockwise direction. You remember Adam, who built the Ka'bah. If possible, you try to kiss or touch **the Black Stone** as you pass by.

Stage 2

You walk between **the hills of Safa and Marwa** seven times. As you do this you remember Ishmael's mother Hagar, Abraham's second wife. She ran between these hills looking for water for her infant son who was dying of thirst. According to one version of events, Allah sent an angel who broke open the ground and revealed the **Zamzam** (i.e. a spring of water) to her. Today, you drink its water to remind you that, even when things seem very bleak, Allah will not abandon you.

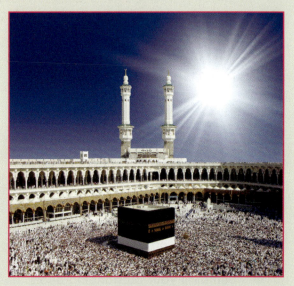

Pilgrims circling the Ka'bah at dawn.

Stage 3

Next, you go to the **Plain of Arafat**, near the Mount of Mercy. You pray there from noon until dusk. You confess your sins and ask for Allah's forgiveness. You also listen to a sermon that recalls Muhammad's final sermon. He gave it at this very place on his own pilgrimage.

Stage 4

After this you go on to **Mina**, a small uninhabited village. You spend the night there. You remember how **Shaytan** (i.e. Satan) tried to tempt Ishmael. He wanted to turn Ishmael against his father Ibrahim, just as Ibrahim was about to offer him as a sacrifice to God. However, Ishmael resisted the temptation. You throw forty-nine stones at three upright pillars to show that you too reject Shaytan's temptations and want to be faithful to Allah.

At this point a sacrifice of a camel, goat or sheep is made. You share this meat with the poor. This act recalls how Ibrahim offered an animal as a sacrifice to Allah, instead of his son, Ishmael.

Stage 5

Finally, you return to Makkah. You walk around the **Ka'bah** one last time. Then you go on to celebrate the feast of **Id-ul-Adha**.

The Divisions within Islam

Down through the centuries, devout Muslims have respected the Qur'an and tried to live according to the Five Pillars. However, after the Prophet Muhammad's death in 632 CE, disagreements arose as to who should be his **caliph** (i.e. successor). These disagreements eventually led to a schism (i.e. a split) within the Islamic community.

At first, the rival Islamic factions peacefully agreed that a representative group of elders should elect the caliph. Four successive caliphs were chosen in this way: **Abu Bakr**, **Umar**, **Uthman** and **Ali**.

The fourth caliph, Ali, was Muhammad's cousin and son-in-law. After Muhammad's death, an enthusiastic faction demanded that Ali be made caliph. They believed that only a descendant of the Prophet Muhammad should succeed him as leader of the Umma.

However, they were opposed by a more powerful group who thought that Ali should never have been made caliph at all. They thought that it would be better for **the Umma** to be led by a man of proven ability rather than a blood heir. They wanted the caliph to be chosen by agreement among the leaders of the Islamic community.

> **REMEMBER!**
> **The Umma** is the name given to the worldwide Islamic community.

When Ali was assassinated by a rival in 661 CE, the Islamic community split. Two rival traditions were formed – **the Sunni** and **the Shi'a**.

- **The Sunni** – This means '**the path shown by Muhammad**'. They make up about 90 per cent of the worldwide Islamic community.
- **The Shi'a** – This means '**the party of Ali**'. They make up about 10 per cent of the worldwide Islamic community.

The Sunni accepted the next caliph, **Mu'awiya**. However, the Shi'a supported Ali's descendants, beginning with his son **Husayn**. However, Husayn was later killed at Kerbala in Iraq in 680 CE.

> **Did You Know?**
> Every year, Shi'as celebrate **Al'Ashura** – the martyrdom of Husayn – with plays that recall his passion, i.e. his betrayal and death at the hands of a former follower.

For Shi'as, Kerbala, where Husayn died, is almost as important a pilgrimage site as Makkah.

Since the schism of the 7th century, members of the Sunni and Shi'a traditions have fought one another in bitter **fitna** (i.e. civil wars) on and off over the centuries.

Today, these two Islamic traditions still differ sharply on many issues. For example:

Sunni Muslims say that the Qur'an is the complete and unaltered record of all that Allah revealed to Muhammad. However, Shi'a Muslims claim that the text of the Qur'an was altered in some places by Sunnis. They say that Sunni scholars removed any statements that supported the Shi'a point of view.

LIGHT THE WAY

The Shari'a

When Muhammad established the first Muslim community at Madinah, his laws served as both the laws of the Arab state and the rules of the Islamic religion. The laws he set down became known as the **Shari'a**.

The Shari'a is a moral and legal code that sets out the way of life that Muslims should live.

The Shari'a covers all aspects of daily life, such as marriage, divorce, inheritance, business practice, diet and clothing.

Did You Know?
Today, the leader of the **Shi'a** majority in Iran is called the Ayatollah. This title means 'a sign of Allah'.

REMEMBER!
A literal translation of '**Shari'a**' is 'a way or path to the water'.

The Shari'a comes from three sources:
- The Qur'an (i.e. Islam's sacred text).
- The Hadith (i.e. the recorded sayings of the Prophet Muhammad).
- Court decisions handed down over the centuries by Islamic judges.

There is no single agreed version of the Shari'a. There are five different Islamic legal systems. Each one offers its own interpretation of the Shari'a. Four of these belong to the Sunni tradition and one to the Shi'a tradition.

In countries with a Muslim majority, the influence of the Shari'a can vary widely. For example:
- In Saudi Arabia and Iran, much of the Shari'a is enshrined in state law.
- In other countries, such as Morocco, only some aspects of the Shari'a (e.g. family law) are enshrined in state law, while most other aspects are not.

In countries where the legal system is based largely on the Shari'a, a wide variety of activities are usually **haram** (i.e. forbidden). These include:
- Adultery.
- Astrology.
- Gambling.
- Prostitution.
- Public dancing between men and women.
- The consumption of alcohol.
- The use of unprescribed drugs.

Did You Know?
Islam forbids both alcohol consumption and the use of unprescribed drugs because they can cause people to lose self-control.

Foundations of Religion - Major World Religions   SECTION C

Severe penalties can be imposed on those found guilty of offences under the Shari'a. Depending on the severity of the offence, punishment can range from public flogging to death by public stoning. For example:
- Repeated theft may lead to the amputation of a limb.
- Murder and rape are punishable by death.

For Muslims living in non-Muslim states, following the Shari'a is a matter of personal conscience. For example, a woman may choose to wear a veil or not.

In non-Muslim states, following Shari'a law is a matter of personal conscience.

Did You Know?

Non-Muslims living in Muslim states do not have to convert to Islam. However, non-Muslims must respect and obey the Shari'a. Also, they are subject to its penalties if they are found guilty of breaking it.

The Mosque

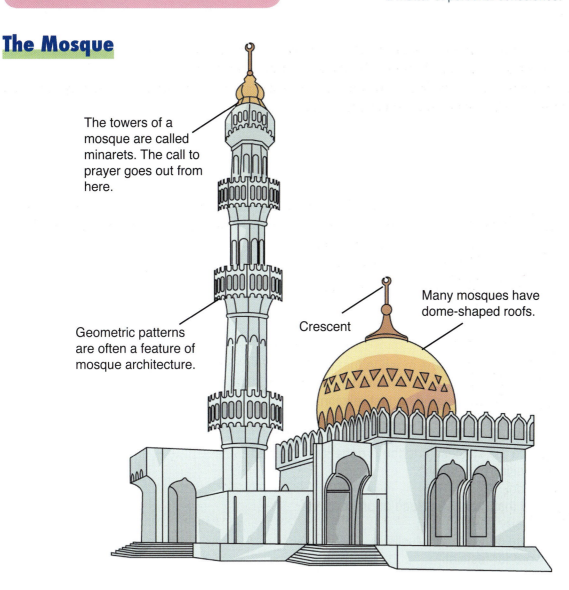

The towers of a mosque are called minarets. The call to prayer goes out from here.

Geometric patterns are often a feature of mosque architecture.

Crescent

Many mosques have dome-shaped roofs.

253

LIGHT THE WAY

ACTIVITIES

1. Wordsearch

Find the following words:

Islam
Muslim
Allah
Muhammad
Prophet
Quran
Obligation
Shahadah
Salah
Zakah
Sawm
Hajj
Mosque
Muezzin
Imam
Khatib
Minaret
Adhan
Wudu
Shirk
Mihrab
Aqiqa
Ramadan
Makkah
Ihram
Caliph
Umma
Sunni
Shi'a
Haram

T	K	Z	M	M	Q	N	N	H	A	M	H	I	Z	I
A	E	H	A	U	M	T	A	A	D	I	A	A	D	A
Z	I	R	A	K	H	L	D	L	H	H	I	L	J	Q
B	A	H	A	T	A	A	A	L	A	R	M	O	S	J
H	X	U	S	N	I	H	M	A	N	A	A	B	P	I
A	Q	I	Q	A	I	B	A	M	A	B	M	S	Y	I
S	A	L	A	H	L	M	R	M	A	C	Y	H	M	N
O	B	L	I	G	A	T	I	O	N	D	P	A	S	N
S	A	W	M	I	E	L	K	W	P	R	K	H	N	U
A	M	M	U	A	S	Y	U	T	O	K	I	A	L	S
F	Z	I	E	U	R	D	D	P	A	R	R	D	E	D
B	Y	Q	M	G	U	H	H	K	U	C	A	R	Z
H	P	I	L	A	C	E	I	Q	Q	Y	P	H	L	D
E	U	J	D	D	T	K	N	I	Z	Z	E	U	M	E
M	O	S	Q	U	E	B	S	Y	D	N	J	V	V	L

2. Crossword

Across

1. It is an alcove in one wall of the mosque that indicates the direction of Makkah.
3. This weekday is the Muslim Day of Assembly.
4. The name of the world's second largest religion.
7. He calls Muslims to prayer.
8. It means ritual washing.
10. The title given to the successor to the prophet Muhammad.
11. It means 'a blessing from Allah'.
14. An Islamic school.
16. An Arabic word that means 'a place of prostration'.
17. It means 'the party of Ali'.
18. The holiest place on Earth for Muslims.
20. The Arabic word for festival.
21. The third Pillar of Faith.

Foundations of Religion - Major World Religions SECTION C

Down
2. The ninth month of the Muslim calendar.
5. The Arabic word for formal prayer.
6. Muslims say that he was the greatest and final prophet of Allah.
7. A slender tower attached to a mosque.
9. He leads Muslims at prayers in the mosque.
12. The call to prayer for Muslims.
13. Islam's sacred text.
15. It means 'the path shown by Muhammad'.
17. The first Pillar of Faith.
19. Muslims say that this is the name of the one, the only true God.
22. Muslims say that he was the first prophet.

255

LIGHT THE WAY

3. Tick the box!

In each of the following, say whether it is **true** or **false**.

	True	False
1. The majority of the world's Muslims now live in the Middle East, Central Asia and North Africa.		
2. Muslims do not accept Abraham, Moses and Jesus as prophets.		
3. The Qur'an consists of 114 surahs.		
4. Muslims worship only Allah		
5. A Muslim must pray facing toward Madinah.		
6. A Muslim must pray five times each day.		
7. Zakah means fasting to develop self-discipline.		
8. Ramadan is the ninth month of the Muslim calendar.		
9. If you are a physically able Muslim, you must go on pilgrimage to the holy city of Jerusalem at least once in your life.		
10. The first mosque was built in Makkah by the prophet Muhammad himself.		
11. In a madrasah, children learn Arabic and study the Qur'an.		
12. The khatib preaches the sermon at Friday prayers.		
13. An imam is an ordained priest.		
14. Muslims believe that it is a serious sin to deliberately decide not to pray.		
15. A muezzin calls out the adhan from the balcony of a minaret.		
16. Attendance at Sunday prayers is compulsory for Muslims.		
17. When Muslims arrive at the mosque they must remove their shoes.		
18. Muslim men put on skullcaps before praying.		
19. There are pictures and statues on display in a mosque.		
20. Mosques are only decorated with calligraphy and geometric patterns.		
21. There are no seats in a mosque. You must unroll a prayer mat.		
22. The first word a new-born Muslim child should hear is the name of Allah.		
23. Aqiqa is held a year after a child is born.		
24. At Aqiqa, the child's head is shaved and the parents make a donation to the poor.		
25. The Islamic dress code says that, once they reach puberty, Muslim girls must wear the hijab.		
26. The Islamic word for 'festival' is Id.		
27. Sawm means you must fast during the hours of daylight of the holy month of Ramadan.		
28. The following people must fast during Ramadan: the elderly; pregnant women; the mentally disabled; the incurably ill; and children below the age of puberty.		

Foundations of Religion - Major World Religions   SECTION C

	True	False
29. Id-ul-Fitr means 'the Festival of Sacrifice'.		
30. Id zakah is a charity tax Muslims can choose to pay or not to pay.		
31. Muslims celebrate Id-ul-Adha over four days. It marks the end of the Hajj.		
32. Before setting out on pilgrimage to Makkah, a Muslim must settle all outstanding debts and take care of family commitments.		
33. When pilgrims arrive at Makkah they must take a purifying bath.		
34. The Zamzam is a spring of water that pilgrims to Makkah drink from.		
35. When they reach the Plain of Arafat, pilgrims throw forty-nine stones at three upright pillars to show that they reject Shaytan's temptations.		
36. The fourth caliph, Ali, was Muhammad's younger brother.		
37. When Ali was assassinated by a rival in 661 CE, the Islamic community split. Two rival traditions were formed: the Sunni and the Shi'a.		
38. The Sunni make up about 10 per cent of the worldwide Islamic community.		
39. The name Shi'a means 'the party of Ali'.		
40. The leader of the Shi'a majority in Iran is called the Ayatollah. This title means 'a sign of Allah'.		
41. A literal translation of the Shari'a is 'a way or path to the water'.		
42. The Hadith contains the recorded sayings of past Islamic judges.		
43. There is one single agreed version of the Shari'a.		
44. Islam allows both alcohol consumption and the use of unprescribed drugs.		
45. In Saudi Arabia and Iran, much of the Shari'a is enshrined in state law.		
46. Non-Muslims living in Muslim states must respect and obey the Shari'a.		

4. Say what it means!

(a) Islam means _____.

(b) Muslim means _____.

(c) Allah means _____.

(d) A prophet is _____

_____.

(e) An obligation is _____.

(f) A mosque is _____.

(g) Shirk means _____.

(h) To fast means _____.

LIGHT THE WAY

(i) The Hajj is _____ .

(j) The Shari'a is _____

_____ .

5. Think about it!

(a) What are the six things all Muslims must believe?

(b) Imagine that you are a Muslim who has returned home after successfully completing your pilgrimage to Makkah. Write an account describing your experiences there during the Hajj.

(c) What is the origin of the deep divide between the Sunni and the Shi'a traditions in Islam?

Section D

The Question of Faith

Chapter 1: **Religious Belief and Practice Today** . . . 260
Chapter 2: **What is Religious Faith?** 268
Chapter 3: **Religious Faith in Action** 279

LIGHT THE WAY

CHAPTER 1 RELIGIOUS BELIEF AND PRACTICE TODAY

Europe and the Wider World

For much of the last one and a half thousand years, most Europeans have been Christian. Indeed, Europe was once the global centre of the Christian faith. All aspects of European life – our art, architecture, literature, music, poetry, politics and theatre – show the influence of Christianity.

However, since the end of World War I there has been a great change. While Christianity has experienced enormous growth elsewhere in the world, in Europe it has seen a sharp decline in its membership. There have been dramatic changes in religious belief and religious practice among Europeans.

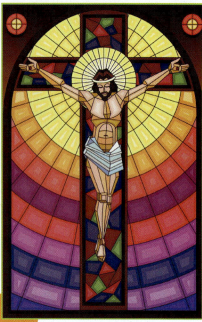

Stained-glass painting of crucifixion.

REMEMBER!
Religious beliefs are teachings about God and the meaning of life that the members of a religion accept as true.
Religious practices are the different ways in which you express your religious beliefs through your actions (i.e. what you say and do).

The consecration of the gifts.

The process that has brought this situation about is called **secularisation**.

REMEMBER!
Secularisation is the way in which religious belief and practice gradually lose their appeal to and significance for people.

Indeed, 21st-century Europe has one of the least religious populations in the world. Christianity is now a minority religion in much of Europe.

Did You Know?

According to successive Eurobarometer polls:
- Malta and Romania have the most religious populations in Europe.
- The Czech Republic and Estonia have the least religious populations in Europe.

The only religion in Europe to have seen steady growth in recent decades is Islam. It currently stands at about 4 per cent of Europe's overall population.

260

The Question of Faith   SECTION D

Today fewer and fewer Europeans look to Christianity for moral guidance. Also, compared to even forty years ago, the influence of the Christian churches on government policy in areas such as health and education has been greatly diminished.

The Situation in Ireland

Organised religion still has an influence on the **worldview** of many Irish people.

> **REMEMBER!**
> **A worldview** is your general outlook on life.

> **REMEMBER!**
> **A belief** is something you accept as true.

Your worldview is based on the **beliefs** you hold.

Your worldview is important because:

- It works in much the same way as a pair of spectacles or contact lenses. It helps you to make sense of events in the world around you.

- It provides you with a kind of chart that helps you to navigate your way through life. It helps you to decide what your priorities are (i.e. the things that are most important to you in life). Then it helps you to find a way to achieve them.

Recent surveys show that religion, particularly Christianity, remains a vital force in Irish life. In percentage terms Ireland still has one of the highest practice rates for Christians in Europe. Over the last two decades these Christians have been joined by a small but growing number of people who are committed members of other world religions. For instance, Muslims now form the third largest religious group in Ireland.

However, there is little doubt that rates of religious belief and practice are declining in Ireland. Church-going is increasingly seen as an activity practised by the middle-aged or elderly. The sharpest drop in religious belief and practice has been among young men and women. Often, the latter experience social pressure not to be actively involved in a religion nor to talk about any religious beliefs if they have them.

Religion, particularly Christianity, remains a vital force in Irish life.

Why has secularisation occurred in Ireland? A number of reasons have been offered:

The factors influencing the decline of religious belief and practice in Ireland
1. The loss of social supports

- In the past there was strong social pressure on people to attend religious services. Attendance at such services was closely associated with 'respectability'. By and large, this pressure has disappeared. The idea that religion is a purely private matter has become widespread.

261

LIGHT THE WAY

- Now, only people with deeply held religious convictions choose to participate in religious services.
- Many young people are no longer being encouraged to participate in religious services by their parents. They do not seem to miss what they have never known.

2. The range of choices

- Thanks to improved education and the impact of the mass media (e.g. internet), people are more aware of the wide variety of beliefs they can choose from, both religious and non-religious. This leads some to reject religious belief altogether, while leaving others confused about it.

3. The rise of materialism

- Many people are more focused on achieving success in this life. They are much less interested in questions about what happens to them in the afterlife.
- Shopping, socialising or involvement in a leisure activity (e.g. a sport) seem to be more attractive and worthwhile ways to spend your Sunday for many people.

4. The challenge of science

- Some people consider religious beliefs and practices to be unnecessary. They think that science can answer all the questions that really matter.

5. The impact of scandals

- The number and frequency of scandals involving the abuse of power by some members of the Catholic clergy has undermined some people's confidence in the Catholic Church.

The Non-Religious Worldview

A small but significant number of Irish people make sense of the world by accepting a **non-religious worldview**.

> REMEMBER!
> **A non-religious worldview** says that we can find happiness and fulfilment in our lives without any belief in God or an afterlife.

One of the most influential non-religious worldviews is that offered by humanists.

Norma McElligott, one of twelve accredited humanist celebrants in Ireland.

262

SPOTLIGHT ON HUMANISM

Humanists reject the beliefs and practices of the different world religions. Humanists are either **atheists** or **agnostics**. However, not all atheists or agnostics are humanists.

> **REMEMBER!**
> **An atheist** says that God does not exist.
> **An agnostic** says that there is no way for us to know if God exists or not.

Generally speaking, humanists believe that:

- This world is all that there is. There is no God and no afterlife.
- Human beings were not created by God. Instead, we are accidental products of the process of evolution.
- There is no meaning of life to be discovered. Each of us must make our own meaning.
- At best, religion is merely something left over from a time before modern science and it will fade away eventually. At worst, religion can be an instrument used to mislead and exploit gullible people.
- We should try to be positive and optimistic about life. We should trust in human goodness and make the best of whatever opportunities life offers us.
- Morality can be decided by reason alone without any reference to God.
- We do not need God to tell us how we should live. We are quite capable of working this out for ourselves.
- We can find happiness in this life if we are tolerant, generous and respectful towards one another.

The Humanist Association of Ireland was formed in 1993. Its members celebrate **Darwin Day** on 10 February and **World Humanist Day** on 21 June.

> **Did You Know?**
> Humanists have their own ceremonies for naming new-born children, as well as for performing marriages and conducting funerals.

Religious Freedom Today

The UN Declaration on Human Rights guarantees freedom of religion. However, despite commitments given, many governments fail to uphold this basic right. In too many parts of the world religious minorities suffer persecution.

> **Did You Know?**
> **Religious persecution** can range from **harassment** (i.e. being subjected to verbal abuse in public and prejudiced comments in the media) to **discrimination** (i.e. unfair treatment under the law) to **sectarian violence** (i.e. having your place of worship and homes attacked) to **genocide** (i.e. being deliberately and systematically targeted for murder).

LIGHT THE WAY

Research conducted by **the Pew Centre** in America shows that violence against religious minorities has grown steadily in many parts of the world, most notably in Africa (e.g. Nigeria and South Sudan), the Middle East (e.g. Iraq and Syria) and Asia (e.g. Afghanistan, Burma, India and Pakistan).

It is now estimated that about three-quarters of the world's population face some sort of restriction on their religious freedom. They live in countries where the government has imposed legal limits on worship, preaching and the display of religious symbols. For example, at present Christians face official hostility and limitations on their freedom to practise their faith in more than a hundred countries.

The six nations with the most government restrictions on religion are Egypt, China, Indonesia, Iran, North Korea and Saudi Arabia. North Korea is the most dangerous country on Earth for anyone holding any form of religious belief.

Another factor that negatively impacts on freedom of belief and practice has been the recent sharp rise in sectarian violence directed towards religious minorities in many African, Middle Eastern and Asian states. This has produced chronic refugee problems and great instability, leading to enormous misery and suffering for millions of people.

Did You Know?

Remarkably, Jews suffer hostility in 71 countries, even though they make up only 0.2 per cent of the world's population and about 80 per cent of them live in either Israel or the United States.

Our Need for Tolerance

In recent years, Irish society has come to place great value on **tolerance**.

> **REMEMBER!**
> **Tolerance** means respecting the right of others to hold beliefs different from your own.

This realisation of the necessity for tolerance is probably due to a combination of factors. These include:

- Our nation's experience of the harm caused by intolerance at different times in our history, e.g. the Penal Laws of the 18th century and the more recent sectarian conflict in Northern Ireland.
- The wider European reaction against intolerance following the terrible events of World War II. At that time, millions of people were murdered just because they happened to belong to a particular race or religion.

So what does it mean to be a tolerant person? Generally speaking, it means that:

- You recognise that other people hold a different worldview to yours.
- You accept that they have the right to do so.
- You respect their worldview even if you do not share it.
- You try to find some common ground with them.

In recent years, Irish society has come to place great value on tolerance.

264

The Question of Faith   SECTION D

However, tolerance does not mean indifference.

A tolerant person would never accept anything that might harm the community, such as propaganda promoting racism or violent acts of terrorism.

> **REMEMBER!**
> **Indifference** means not caring.

ACTIVITIES

1. Wordsearch

Find the following words:

Religion
Poetry
Secularisation
Persecution
Indifference
Art
Politics
Worldview
Harassment
Architecture
Theatre
Humanist
Discrimination
Literature
Belief
Atheist
Intimidation
Music
Practice
Agnostic
Tolerance

A	U	E	F	R	B	P	P	T	Q	S	I	P	N	I
H	R	Z	R	E	E	R	O	W	R	N	U	O	T	N
C	G	C	L	U	A	L	E	E	D	A	I	L	N	T
W	I	I	H	C	T	I	I	I	T	T	Z	I	E	I
T	E	T	T	I	V	A	F	G	A	R	T	T	M	M
F	H	I	S	D	T	F	R	S	I	S	Y	I	S	I
W	C	E	L	O	E	E	I	E	I	O	B	C	S	D
E	R	R	A	R	N	R	C	E	T	A	N	S	A	A
O	O	R	E	T	A	G	H	T	T	I	L	Z	R	T
W	W	N	G	L	R	T	A	U	U	J	L	L	A	I
L	C	U	U	V	A	E	E	M	J	R	M	E	H	O
E	N	C	T	S	I	N	A	M	U	H	E	C	S	N
K	E	N	O	I	T	U	C	E	S	R	E	P	M	W
S	D	I	S	C	R	I	M	I	N	A	T	I	O	N
Y	T	O	L	E	R	A	N	C	E	C	I	S	U	M

2. Say what it means!

(a)   Religious beliefs are _____

_____ .

(b)   Religious practices are _____

_____ .

(c)   Secularisation is _____

_____ .

(d)   A worldview is _____ .

(e)   Tolerance means _____

_____ .

(f)   Indifference means _____ .

265

LIGHT THE WAY

3. Crossword!

Across

5. They offer one of the most influential non-religious worldviews.
7. The most dangerous county in the world for anyone holding religious beliefs (2 words: 5, 5).
8. Humanists celebrate this on 10 February (2 words: 6, 3).
10. Your worldview is based on these things you hold.
11. It means verbal abuse.
13. The things that are most important to you in life.
16. A country in the Mediterranean that has one of the most religious populations in Europe.
17. Humanists say that we were not created by God. Instead, we are accidental products of this process.
18. Being systematically and deliberately targeted for murder.
19. A country in the Baltic region that has one of the least religious populations in Europe.
20. They say that God does not exist.
21. For most of the last 1,500 years, most of them have been Christians.

266

The Question of Faith   SECTION D

Down

1. Humanists say that this can be used to mislead and exploit gullible people.
2. Humanists say that we can find this if we are tolerant, generous and respectful towards one another.
3. It is now a minority religion in much of Europe.
4. They now form the third largest religious group in Ireland.
6. Humanists say that this must be decided by reason alone, without reference to God.
8. It means unfair treatment under the law.
9. This kind of violence happens when your places of worship are attacked.
12. They say that there is no way for us to know if God exists or not.
14. Humanists say that it is not there to be discovered. Each of us must make it for ourselves.
15. Means respecting the rights of others to hold beliefs different from your own.

4. Think about it!

(a) Think about the following survey findings:

- Despite a steep decline in weekly church attendance, a sizeable number of Europeans still attend carol services at Christmas.
- Significant numbers of Europeans still travel to places of pilgrimage such as to the Marian Shrine at Lourdes in France, or they follow the Camino (i.e. the Walk) to the shrine of St. James at Santiago de Compostela in Spain.
- Since their use as backing tracks to popular computer games, CDs of religious music (especially Gregorian chant) have been bestsellers in many European countries in recent years.

1. In each of these examples, say why you think this is the case.
2. What does this say about how many Europeans view the role of religion in their lives today?

(b) Here are five reasons often given for the general decline in religious belief and practice in Ireland:

- The loss of social supports
- The range of choice
- The rise of materialism
- The challenge of science
- The impact of scandals.

1. Which one of these do you think has had the most impact?
2. Why do you think so?

267

LIGHT THE WAY

CHAPTER 2   WHAT IS RELIGIOUS FAITH?

The Meaning of Religious Faith

During one of the terrible Luftwaffe night raids on London in 1940, a father, holding his small son by the hand, ran from a house that had just been rocked by a bomb blast. In the front yard was a deep crater. Seeking shelter as quickly as possible, the father jumped into the dark crater and held up his arms for his son to follow. Terrified, yet hearing his father's voice telling him to jump, the little boy replied, 'Dad, I can't see you!'

The father, looking up against a sky tinted red by burning buildings, called to the silhouette of his son, 'But I can see you. Jump!' The boy jumped, because he trusted his father.

Faith means putting your trust in someone or something.

One of the greatest compliments you can pay to another human being is to say 'I trust you'. When you trust someone it means that you believe that you can depend on that person. You believe that he or she will:

- Be honest with you.
- Act in your best interests.
- Help you when you are in need.
- Never let you down.

When someone enjoys your complete trust, you say that you have **faith** in him/her.

Faith is an essential part of all the important relationships in our lives. This is obvious when we think about our relationships with family and friends. However, we can easily underestimate the role faith plays in so many other important situations. Think about the following example:

> **REMEMBER!**
> **Faith** means putting your trust in someone or something.

Conor is four years old. However he is getting more and more unwell as each day passes. His local doctor recommends that Conor's mother brings him to see a specialist in the treatment of cancer and blood diseases at St Vincent's Hospital in Dublin.

The doctor conducts tests. He confirms that Conor has leukaemia, with only a fifty-fifty chance of recovery. Conor's mother is told about all the tests and treatments her child will have to undergo. Her ordeal will be almost as bad as her child's because she must stand by and watch him suffer, unable to do anything to relieve his suffering herself. Yet she is willing to do whatever is necessary to save her child.

Like her son, the first thing she must do is have faith in the hospital's medical team. His life is in their hands.

268

The Question of Faith SECTION D

It has been just such experiences of life, love, suffering and death that have led some people to say that they also need **religious faith** in their lives.

People who embrace religious faith say that it enables them to face life and meet death. This does not mean that they claim to know all the answers to life's mysteries, but they say that their religious faith gives them the strength they need to face up to the challenges each day may bring.

> **REMEMBER!**
> **Religious faith** means putting your trust in God because you believe that God loves you and only wants what is best for you.

Did You Know?

> Christians say that religious faith is a gift from God. We do not begin our relationship with God. It is God who starts it. God calls us to have religious faith. Each of us is free to decide whether or not to accept God's invitation.

Human Development

If you have a deep religious faith, you believe that your whole life is a journey. If you live it well, then your final destination is to share eternal life with God. As you go on this journey, you must pass through a series of stages. At each of these stages your body changes and grows. This is called **physical development**. It happens **automatically**.

However, you need to develop in other ways too. For example:
- You need to develop your **feelings** – this is called **emotional development.**
- You need to develop your **mind** – this is called **intellectual development.**
- You need to develop your **character** – this is called **moral development.**
- You need to develop your faith in **God** – this is called **spiritual development.**

A mature person is someone who is balanced, thoughtful and well-rounded.

The aim of all this development is to become a **mature person**.

> **REMEMBER!**
> A **mature person** is someone who is balanced, thoughtful and well-rounded.

However, this does not happen automatically. It requires consistent effort on your part to become a mature individual.

269

LIGHT THE WAY

The Roots of Religious Faith

There are three stages in the development of religious faith:

Stage 1: Childhood faith

Stage 2: Adolescent faith

Stage 3: Mature faith

Your image of God and your relationship with God differs from one stage to the next. The religious faith of an adult should differ from that of an adolescent, while the religious faith of an adolescent should differ from that of a child. However, as with your intellectual and moral development, you must **want** to advance from one stage to the next. It does not happen automatically.

As with any other aspect of your life, religious faith does not grow in a vacuum. It is a plant that grows out of the soil of your life experience. So a person's religious faith is shaped by all kinds of life experiences.

Think about all the people who have influenced your life up until now. Your relationships with these people have combined with important events in your life to influence who you are, how you think and how you live.

Let us take a closer look at two of these influences, especially as to how they may influence your attitudes towards religion.

1. The influence of your parents/guardians

Your parents/guardians have the biggest influence on your attitudes towards religion during childhood. It is said that religious beliefs and practices are '**more caught than taught**'.

Parents have a big influence on attitudes towards religion in childhood.

For instance:

- If your parents/guardians encourage you to have a positive view of religious faith, then you are more likely to think that it is worth having.

- Although you may not understand the meaning of the prayers you are taught as a young child, you are encouraged to see your relationship with God as important in your life.

- If your parents bring you to religious services (e.g. in a church, mosque or synagogue) when you are a child, this can help you to feel you belong as a member of a particular religion.

2. The influence of your peer group

As a young child you tended to accept without question what you were told by your parents, teachers and other adults whom you trusted.

However, as an adolescent (i.e. teenager), you are now capable of thinking at a deeper level. You may have begun to ask questions about the meaning of your life. One of these questions would be: '**If God really loves us, why do bad things happen to good people?'**

Also, you now feel a great desire to be more independent and self-reliant. You want to stand on your own two feet, do more things for yourself, think things through for yourself and be less dependent on your parents/guardians.

Clearly, adolescence is a time of great change in your life. It is when your **peer group** begins to play a very important role in how you see yourself and the world around you.

> **REMEMBER!**
> Your **peer group** is made up of those people who are of a similar age to yourself.

Adolescence is a time of great change in your life.

During adolescence, your peer group can have a greater influence on your attitudes to religious belief and practice than your parents/guardians. Perhaps this is because you feel that they are the only ones who really understand what you are going through.

Typically you draw much of your support and encouragement from the network of friends you have built up in your peer group. As an adolescent, it is only natural that you would want to be accepted by your peers and to fit in with them. However this can cause you to feel a strong pressure to conform to what your peers want you to believe and do. So, if you build friendships with people who are open to religious beliefs and see a value in religious practices, then you are more likely to do so too.

It is important to keep in mind that there is no need to agree in every respect with the views of your peers. If they really are your friends, then they should be willing to respect your choices on this issue. Within the broader context of taking greater responsibility for how you think and act, you have a responsibility to yourself to make your own mind up about the role religious faith plays in your life.

If you choose to take religious faith seriously, then you must make it your own. This means you must aim to develop a **mature religious faith**.

Did You Know?

Mature religious faith involves:
- Accepting that there are no easy answers to be had to life's most important questions.
- Giving up the idea that God is a remote figure who is '**above you**' and replacing it with one of God as a mysterious presence who guides and supports you.
- Putting your relationship with God at the centre of your life.
- Working out a clear idea of what you believe in and why you believe it.
- Respecting those whose beliefs differ from your own.
- Trying to live the best kind of life you can.

LIGHT THE WAY

The Relationship between Religion and Science

Despite what we have said so far about the meaning and importance of religious faith, there are a number of influential figures today who doubt if religious faith has anything worthwhile to contribute to our lives. They say that **science** can provide us with all that we need.

> **REMEMBER!**
> **Science** is knowledge of **how** the world works.

There are many different branches of science. The Junior Cycle Science syllabus concentrates on the basic discoveries of biology, chemistry and physics. Those who make an in-depth study of these important branches of knowledge are called scientists.

Scientists gain knowledge of how the world works by using **the scientific method**.

Did You Know?

The scientific method works this way:

You begin by carefully observing an event.

You offer an explanation for this event.

You do experiments to test your explanation.

If your explanation passes these tests, then you have gained knowledge of **how** the world works.

Our society depends on science for its very existence. If you try to think of what our society will be like in a hundred or a thousand years from now, your ideas will be based on what you think science will help us to achieve by then.

Closely linked to science is **technology**.

> **REMEMBER!**
> **Technology** is the practical application of scientific discoveries to our everyday lives.

Over the centuries, new developments in technology have transformed the way in which we live. Think about how we can now do things such as:

- Communicate with one another over vast distances.
- Gain access to a wide variety of information.
- Treat life-threatening illnesses/injuries.
- Develop disease-resistant foods.
- Manufacture goods in automated factories.
- Travel swiftly from one place to the next.

Clearly, the benefits of technology are enormous. If used wisely, they can enrich our lives in so many positive ways.

Unfortunately, very often in history, conflict between religion and science has arisen out of confusion over what each of them does. Think about the following examples from history:

Galileo

Galileo was a 17th-century Italian scientist. He used the newly invented telescope to show that the Earth revolves around the Sun. However, he was forced to recant (i.e. take back what he had said) by the Inquisition

The Question of Faith SECTION D

of the Catholic Church. This incident had the unfortunate effect of convincing some people that religion and science are in conflict and that if you accept one, you must reject the other. As we shall see, this is not the case.

Although the Catholic Church later accepted that the Earth revolves around the Sun, it took three centuries before a later pope, St John Paul II, apologised for Galileo's unjust treatment. All of this unnecessary conflict occurred because the Catholic Church had tried to defend an out-dated model of how the universe works.

Galileo used the telescope to show the Earth revolves around the Sun.

Charles Darwin

Charles Darwin was a 19th-century English scientist who put forward the **theory of evolution**. All evolution is driven by a process he called natural selection. This means that if a plant or animal can adapt (i.e. change) to better suit its environment, then it increases its chances of survival. If it fails to adapt to its environment, then it will become **extinct** (i.e. die out).

Darwin published a book entitled *On the Origin of Species* to explain his ideas. It caused an uproar among people who took the Bible literally. They thought that the Bible offered them a literal account of how life began. However, that was never the intention of the Bible's authors. They did not want to explain how the world was made. They wanted to explain **why** there is a world at all – because God made it. The evidence to support Darwin's theory of evolution by natural selection is now so great that its truth is no longer seriously doubted by the vast majority of scientists. Its chief opponents today are those who still try to defend an outdated explanation of how life developed here on Earth.

Evolution is driven by a process of natural selection (Charles Darwin).

REMEMBER!
The **theory of evolution** says that all the complex forms of life on Earth gradually developed over time from simpler forms of life.

In the case of both Galileo and Darwin, too many people failed to realise that when you want to know **how** something works, you should look to science for the answer, and not to religion.

273

LIGHT THE WAY

Scientists have made many important discoveries and solved many problems. This said, however, there are limits to what even science can explain. There are things that cannot be examined under a microscope, analysed by a computer, solved by a mathematical formula or viewed through a telescope. There are some questions that science cannot answer.

Think about the following questions:
- Who am I?
- Why am I here?
- Where is my life going?

There are some questions that science cannot answer.

These questions deal with life's mysteries. They touch on the meaning and purpose of our lives. These questions are not answered by science. They are answered by **religion**.

Providing Complementary Answers

Both religion and science search for **the truth**.

However, religion and science offer different approaches to the truth. Think about the following examples:

REMEMBER!
The truth is what really is the case, independent of how anyone feels or thinks.

Liberty Leading the People, 28 July 1830, Delacroix, The Louvre, Paris.

1. A Painting

- A scientific explanation of this painting would tell you about (a) the kind of materials used (e.g. the canvas and paints) and (b) the techniques used by the artist to produce it (e.g. perspective, sfumato and so on).

- However, there is far more to a painting than this. A painting can fire your imagination. It can cause you to stop and think about what it has to say about life. So, you need to look elsewhere to help you understand it.

- A religious explanation of this painting would look at its **meaning** (i.e. the message it contains). For instance, it would ask you to think about questions such as: What does the artist have to say about why people suffer? Why does God allow such suffering? Is there life after death?

2. A Gesture

- **A scientific explanation** of this gesture would describe how the nervous system and the muscles of the body work together to allow you to perform this action.
- **A religious explanation** of this gesture would explore its meaning. It would ask you to think about questions such as:
  - What message is contained in this gesture?
  - Why did Christians begin making this gesture?

As we can see from examples of a painting and a gesture above, the answers provided by both religion and science **complement** one another.

A gesture can have both scientific and religious explanations that complement one another.

> **REMEMBER!**
> When two things **complement** one another, they each contribute something of value and add to your understanding of the world.

We need both religion and science if we are to achieve a better understanding of the complex, rich and varied world around us. This is why Doctor Martin Luther King, Jnr. once declared:

> **Did You Know?**
> **Science** offers solutions to **problems**. It explains **how** things happen.
> **Religion** offers insights into **mysteries**. It helps you to understand the **meaning** of things.

'Science investigates; religion interprets. Science gives us a knowledge which is power; religion gives us wisdom which is control.'

LIGHT THE WAY

ACTIVITIES

1. Wordsearch

Find the following words:

Development
Spiritual
Peer group
Physical
Child
Science
Intellectual
Adolescent
Technology
Moral
Mature
Evolution
Trust
Faith
Truth
God
Gift
Meaning

D	W	T	W	L	T	K	U	I	T	A	M	S	K	W
A	E	B	U	R	A	S	P	E	C	D	T	C	B	H
P	P	V	U	O	X	R	C	H	E	O	M	G	D	I
N	U	S	E	C	M	H	O	L	O	L	A	S	O	Y
J	T	O	L	L	N	E	A	M	H	E	T	F	D	D
D	Z	I	R	O	O	C	A	T	R	S	U	N	L	R
A	L	S	L	G	I	P	U	N	R	C	R	O	I	A
Y	F	O	P	S	R	R	M	G	I	E	E	I	H	I
V	G	K	Y	T	T	E	G	E	C	N	V	T	C	D
Y	J	H	T	I	A	F	E	H	N	T	G	U	Z	Y
O	P	G	I	F	T	Z	C	P	E	T	M	L	S	S
I	N	T	E	L	L	E	C	T	U	A	L	O	A	C
S	C	I	E	N	C	E	V	Z	W	T	M	V	F	P
J	I	C	X	X	Y	A	X	Q	O	V	T	E	Z	L
L	A	U	T	I	R	I	P	S	X	N	R	E	I	U

2. Say what it means!

(a) Faith means _____.

(b) Religious faith means _____

_____.

(c) Science is _____.

(d) The truth is _____

_____.

3. Crossword

Across
2. You do experiments to test this.
5. This refers to the message contained in something.
6. It offers solutions to problems. It explains how things happen.
7. It means that you believe you can depend on someone.
8. The 19th-century English scientist who put forward the theory of evolution.
13. The practical application of scientific discoveries to everyday life.
15. Those who make an in-depth study of biology, chemistry and physics are called this.
16. The 17th-century scientist who showed that the Earth revolves around the Sun.
17. This development concerns your feelings.
18. Another word for 'teenager'.

276

The Question of Faith   SECTION D

Down
1. It offers insights into mysteries. It helps you understand the meaning of things.
3. This development concerns your mind.
4. This is made up of those people who are of similar age to yourself (2 words: 4, 5).
9. All of evolution is driven by this process (2 words: 7, 9).
10. This development happens automatically.
11. This development concerns your character.
12. Where two things each contribute something of value and add to your understanding of the world.
14. It is an essential part of all the important relationships in our lives.

LIGHT THE WAY

4. Think about it!

(a) Read the following story:

> Wilfred Grenfell was a doctor who cared for poor fishing communities along the Labrador coast. Once, in 1908, he found himself trapped on a drifting ice flow that was slowly headed out to sea. He was forced to kill three of his sled dogs, as mercifully as he could, to make a coat out of their hides to protect him from the intense cold. Then he put up a distress flag, lay down and slept. Later, after he was rescued, Grenfell said, 'There was nothing to fear. I had done all I could, the rest lay in God's hands.'

1. How is this story an example of religious faith?
2. What did Grenfell believe was his responsibility when faced with such a life-and-death situation?
3. What kind of God did Grenfell have faith in?
4. What insight about religious faith do you draw from Grenfell's reaction and response to the situation he faced?

(b) Read the following extract:

> I grew up in a home where religion was taken seriously. I was taught to pray at an early age. We prayed together as a family each morning and every night before bedtime. I was brought up to believe that God is there to guide and support me, in good times and in bad. I was encouraged to ask questions. My parents did their best to give me answers. If it wasn't for my parents, I doubt I would believe in anything. We don't agree about everything. I still have a lot of questions. But I think of myself as someone on a journey and I haven't arrived at my destination just yet.
>
> David, age 16

1. Identify those things David's parents did to encourage the growth of his religious faith.
2. How did David's parents try to help him to develop a mature religious faith?

(c) Who, do you think, has the greater influence on the religious belief and practice of adolescents: parents/guardians or the peer group? Give a reason for your answer.

(d) Explain how both religion and science have a different approach to the truth when explaining either (a) a painting; or (b) a gesture.

(e) Identify which of the following questions can be answered by religion and which can be answered by science:
1. Why do good people suffer?
2. How can heart disease be prevented?
3. How did animal life evolve on earth?
4. What causes earthquakes?
5. What is the purpose of human life?
6. Is there water on Mars?
7. How can we ensure an adequate supply of drinkable water to our population in the future?
8. Why do we find it so hard to do the right thing in life?
9. Why does the Earth rotate on its axis?
10. Is there life after death?

(f) Explain this statement: '**Religion and science complement one another.**'

The Question of Faith   SECTION D

CHAPTER 3   RELIGIOUS FAITH IN ACTION

Giving Witness to Faith

When World War II began in 1939, **Hugh O'Flaherty** (1898–1963) listened to what both sides were saying. The opposing sides – the Allies and the Axis – each accused the other of doing terrible things. Wary of being misled by **propaganda**, O'Flaherty was unsure what to believe at first.

> **REMEMBER!**
> **Propaganda** refers to ideas or statements that may be exaggerated or false but are spread in order to promote some cause, or to help a political leader achieve some goal.

Soon O'Flaherty began to hear shocking reports from reliable sources about what the Nazis were doing in areas they had occupied. He decided that he could not simply stand by and do nothing. He had to help their victims.

O'Flaherty was an Irish Catholic priest. A highly educated man with three doctorates (i.e. PhDs), he was fluent in French, German, Italian and Spanish. He was also an accomplished boxer and Italy's amateur golf champion. After his ordination to the priesthood in 1925, he had joined the Vatican's diplomatic corps. He served with distinction, first in Egypt and then in Haiti, where he had organised famine relief. After this, he spent two years in Czechoslovakia before being recalled to work in the Holy Office in Rome. He would spend the next quarter of a century there. In recognition of his efforts, the pope awarded O'Flaherty the title Monsignor.

In the early years of World War II, O'Flaherty toured all of the Allied POW (i.e. prisoner-of-war) camps in Italy. He tracked down prisoners who had been declared MIA (i.e. missing in action). Then he got word that they were alive back to their worried relatives via Vatican radio.

In September 1943, Italy surrendered to the Allies. In response, Hitler sent his elite Schutzstaffel to occupy Rome and to prevent the Allied armies from threatening his southern flank.

Hugh O'Flaherty (1898–1963)

In the chaos following the Italian surrender, thousands of Allied POWs were allowed to go free. Many of them remembered O'Flaherty from his visits to their camps. They made their way to Rome, seeking his help. They were not disappointed. He secured the help of many people – including monks, nuns, communist resistance fighters and foreign diplomats. They agreed to hide the escaped POWs in convents, monasteries, flats and farm buildings.

Then O'Flaherty set up an escape 'pipeline'. He used it to smuggle Jews and Allied POWs out of Italy and across the Alps to safety in neutral Switzerland.

This work was very dangerous. Inside the Vatican, the monsignor was relatively safe because it was neutral territory. However, once he stepped outside the Vatican he was putting his life at risk. The Nazis had learnt that this Irish priest was the leader of the escape organisation and were determined to stop him

> **Did You Know?**
>
> **The Schutzstaffel** or SS was an elite Nazi military force. Its members wore distinctive black uniforms with lightning SS insignia on their collars.
>
> The SS began as Hitler's personal bodyguard. However, by 1943 it had expanded into a massive combat force numbering over half a million men. Its members were fanatically loyal to Hitler. They carried out some of the worst atrocities of World War II. They set up and ran the concentration camps that murdered not only six million Jews, but also millions more opponents of the Nazi regime.

279

LIGHT THE WAY

In 1944, a thousand members of Rome's Jewish community were deported to Auschwitz Concentration Camp.

by any means necessary. In an attempt to persuade O'Flaherty to stop, the German ambassador warned him of this. O'Flaherty politely thanked him for the warning but continued on as before.

The chief of the German security force in Rome was **Colonel Herbert Kappler** of the SS. On his orders, suspected members of O'Flaherty's organisation were arrested, tortured and executed. However, none of these people ever betrayed O'Flaherty to the Nazis.

Colonel Kappler proved to be a ruthless opponent. When Italian resistance fighters killed thirty-two German soldiers in a bomb blast, Kappler randomly selected three hundred and twenty Italian civilians and had them executed in the Ardeatine Caves outside Rome.

Drawing on his considerable energy and ingenuity, O'Flaherty engaged in a continual battle of wits with Colonel Kappler. To avoid SS patrols that had been ordered to shoot him on sight, O'Flaherty became a master of disguise. At various times he presented himself as a beggar, a street cleaner, a coalman, a postman and even a German officer. On several occasions, O'Flaherty was almost caught and killed. Each time he used either his great physical strength or his quick wits to get him out of danger.

Then, in 1944, a thousand members of Rome's Jewish community were rounded up and deported to Auschwitz concentration camp. O'Flaherty reacted quickly. He hid the city's remaining 8,000 Jews in monasteries, convents, church colleges, private homes, the Vatican apartments and the pope's summer residence at Castelgandalfo. Some 400 Jewish men were even recruited into the papal guard. Elsewhere in Italy, another 40,000 Jews were given safe haven.

In desperation, Colonel Kappler tried to have O'Flaherty assassinated. The plan was for two undercover SS men to kidnap O'Flaherty just after he had finished saying Mass in St Peter's Basilica. They would manhandle him out of the Vatican to a place where he would be 'shot while resisting arrest'. But Kappler underestimated the monsignor. He had been tipped off. He organised a surprise for the SS men. They were arrested by the Swiss Guard and thrown out of the Vatican. O'Flaherty continued his work until Allied forces liberated Rome in June 1944.

Word of what O'Flaherty had done reached the US commander, **General Mark Clark**. When Clark met O'Flaherty he was surprised to hear the priest insist on proper care for the Germans who were now POWs. When asked about his interest in the welfare of his defeated opponents, O'Flaherty simply replied, '**God has no country**.' He believed that it was simply basic human decency to care for everyone, irrespective of their race or creed.

After the war, Colonel Kappler was caught, arrested and sentenced to life imprisonment at Gaela Prison near Rome. Only one person ever visited Kappler. Once a month, O'Flaherty came to see him.

Despite all that had happened, the two former opponents eventually became friends. Finally, in March 1959, Kappler asked for forgiveness for all he had done and was baptised into the Catholic Church by O'Flaherty.

O'Flaherty had the courage to do what he believed was right. He helped the needy despite the great personal risk it involved. But he also believed that as a Christian he was called to love his enemies and that he should show mercy, even to someone who had shown so little to others.

After World War II, O'Flaherty was awarded many honours, including the US Medal of Freedom. Some honours, such as the offer of a lifetime pension from the Italian government, he politely refused. He did not want any financial reward. In 2004, Israel's Holocaust Martyrs and Heroes Authority posthumously conferred on him the title '**Righteous among the Nations**'.

The Question of Faith SECTION D

In 1960, Monsignor O'Flaherty retired to Ireland. He served quietly as a priest in the Catholic diocese of Kerry. He never spoke to anyone about his wartime activities. However, when he died in 1963, news of his passing was reported on the front page of *The New York Times*.

In 1994, a grove of Italian trees was planted in Killarney National Park as a memorial to Hugh O'Flaherty. Beside these trees is a brass plaque which bears the legend:

To Honour Monsignor Hugh O'Flaherty (1898–1963)

In Rome during World War II, he heroically served the cause of humanity.

Hugh O'Flaherty understood that having religious faith means more than accepting a set of beliefs. It also means living by them. He understood that, at its heart, the Christian moral vision is based on two of Jesus's teachings:

- The Golden Rule: **'Do unto others as you would have them do unto you'** Matthew 7:27.
- The Commandment to Love: **'Love one another as I have loved you'** John 15:12.

Jesus made it very clear that his followers are called to give **witness** to their religious faith by putting these two teachings into practice.

As Hugh O'Flaherty shows, a Christian can give witness in the following ways:

- By being a friend to someone in need.
- By offering help when it is needed and not waiting to be asked.
- By supporting those who care for vulnerable people.

> **REMEMBER!**
> **Witness** means showing your love for God and for other people by the way you live your life.

The Meaning of Ministry

Christians say that whenever you give witness to your faith, you perform a **ministry**.

In the Catholic, Orthodox and Anglican traditions, there are two main types of ministry:

> **REMEMBER!**
> **Ministry** is any constructive activity that helps people in your community.

Formal ministry

This can be either:

- An ordained ministry – e.g. a bishop or a priest celebrating the sacraments.
- An institutional ministry – e.g. a member of the laity, who serves as a Minister of the Eucharist or a Minister of the Word.

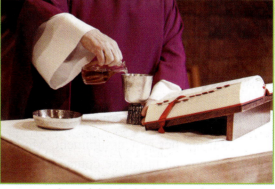

An ordained ministry – a priest celebrating the sacraments.

281

LIGHT THE WAY

Informal ministry

This refers to any situation in daily life – whether it is in the home, school or workplace – where Christians try to put their faith into practice.

For example:

- Supporting a classmate who is grieving after the death of a close relative or friend.
- Standing up for a classmate who is being bullied.
- Helping an elderly relative by doing some simple chores, such as cleaning, decorating, gardening or shopping.
- Fundraising to support the work of a charitable organisation.

Informal ministry – supporting a classmate.

Examples of Informal Ministry

No. 1. Mother Teresa and the Missionaries Of Charity

When **Mother Teresa** first visited London, one of the wealthiest cities in the world, she was saddened by what she found: people dying in the streets, and even in their own homes, alone and unloved.

It prompted her to say:

> 'You have a different kind of poverty in the Western world, a poverty of the spirit, of loneliness, and that is the worst disease in the world today. It is worse than tuberculosis or leprosy. We have to love one another.'

Mother Teresa worked with the poor in Calcutta.

Mother Teresa was born in Albania in 1910. Aged twelve she decided to become a Catholic nun. She spent six weeks in Ireland learning English. Then she was sent as a missionary to work in India. For several years she taught geography in a school for girls from wealthy families. Later, she became the school's principal.

Gradually, Mother Teresa came to believe that she was being called by God to do different work. She realised that her true **vocation** (i.e. calling) was to care for the poorest of the poor. So, she asked for permission from her religious superiors to work in the slums of Calcutta. They agreed.

Before starting her new assignment, Mother Teresa went to Patna to develop the skills she would need. There she took an intensive course in nursing. After completing her training she returned to Calcutta. In 1948 she opened her first slum school. It was in a small yard belonging to a poor family.

282

A year later, Mother Teresa was joined by a young Bengali woman who had been inspired by her example. They were the first members of a new Catholic religious order – **the Missionaries of Charity** – founded in 1950. Today, these sisters wear white saris edged with blue stripes. They have become a familiar sight since, not only in Calcutta but in many other poor communities around the world.

Whenever interviewed by the media, Mother Teresa asked people not to focus on her. She wanted them to focus on the message of Jesus Christ. She often quoted **the Parable of the Sheep and the Goats** (see: **Matthew 25:31–46**). Jesus's example inspired Mother Teresa to care for the dying and to rescue abandoned babies from dustbins.

Mother Teresa never worried about money; when needed it seemed to arrive. She believed that God would provide what was needed. When the Pope came to India, he gave her the car he had used during his visit. She raffled it and used the money raised to start a clinic for treating those afflicted with leprosy. Again, when she won the **Nobel Prize for Peace**, she used her prize money to clothe and feed Calcutta's poor.

Children play in a slum on a railway track in Calcutta, India.

Mother Teresa made great efforts to care for people who were left to die alone. This started when she found a seriously ill woman lying abandoned in the street. She was being eaten alive by ants and rats. Mother Teresa took her to several local hospitals, but all refused to help her. They said that care was only available to those with a hope of recovery. This woman was dying.

After this experience, Mother Teresa decided to open a place where she could take care of the terminally ill (i.e. people with no hope of recovery). The mayor of Calcutta offered her a disused Hindu temple. She accepted it. In the years since, this building has provided thousands of poor, terminally ill people with a place to die in peace and with dignity.

Mother Teresa also launched other services such as schools and rehabilitation centres for those recovering from leprosy. If leprosy is diagnosed early, it can be cured in less than two years.

When she first began her work, some people were dismissive of what Mother Teresa was doing. They doubted that her work could make any impact in such a vast sea of misery. However, she responded by saying that every human life is worth saving. She believed that the scale of the challenge she faced was no reason to give up. Eventually, most of her critics came to recognise her great influence for good.

It has been said of her that Mother Teresa had the ability to look at anyone, no matter how badly off, and make them feel special. One of her friends remarked that her eyes '**were not of a person of this Earth; she belonged to heaven**'.

When she died in 1997, Mother Teresa's passing was mourned by Christians and non-Christians alike. Today, the religious order she founded continues her work – building up the Kingdom of God on Earth. Inspired by her extraordinary example, more than 4,000 nuns and many more lay volunteers aid the poor, the lonely and the dying in more than ninety countries.

When asked at the Nobel Prize ceremony what could be done to promote world peace, she offered this simple answer: '**Go home and love your family.**'

LIGHT THE WAY

No. 2. Frederic Ozanam and the Society of St Vincent De Paul

The early 19th century was a time of great social unrest in France. Politicians, lawyers, trade unionists and academics all held sharply differing views as to how French society could be improved. Despite all their discussions, most French people continued to live in dire poverty.

Frederic Ozanam was a young law student at the Sorbonne University in Paris. During his teenage years, he had serious doubts about the role religion should play in his life. However, after much reflection, Ozanam decided to become an active member of the Catholic Church.

While a student, Ozanam took part in a series of vigorous public debates about the role of religion in society. It was during one of these debates that an opponent asked him:

'What do you do besides talk to prove the faith you claim is in you?'

Ozanam was stung by the implied criticism in this question. After some thought, he realised that:

'**Religious ideas have no value whatsoever if they are not practical and positive. Religion is meant to be acted on rather than talked about.**'

As he claimed to be a Christian, he decided that this meant that he had to follow the example set by Jesus himself. He would show his commitment to his religious faith by helping people in practical ways.

St Vincent de Paul has approximately 9,000 volunteers in Ireland.

Ozanam approached a Catholic religious order named the Daughters of Charity for guidance. He asked them to introduce him to poor families living in the Parisian slums. Then, in 1833, he and a group of six friends founded a new Catholic lay organisation – **the Society of St Vincent de Paul**.

The volunteers at the St Vincent de Paul offer advice on money management.

Did You Know?

The Society of St Vincent de Paul (the **SVP**) is an international Catholic lay organisation. It helps anyone in need, regardless of their religion.

After completing his studies, Ozanam became a university lecturer. He married Amelie Soulacroix in 1841. Within a few years his health began to suffer due to overwork, so he went with his family to Italy to rest and recover.

However, Ozanam soon returned to Paris at the request of the French government. They asked him to supervise the distribution of government aid to the poor following the chaos caused by the 1848 revolution.

Afterwards, Ozanam started up a newspaper called *The New Era*. It would campaign on behalf of the rights of the poor. However, his health rapidly deteriorated once more and he died in 1853.

Frederic Ozanam dedicated his life to following Jesus Christ's command to:

'Love God and love your neighbour as yourself.'

Matthew 22:36–39

Since his death, many others have been inspired by Ozanam's example. As members of the Society of St Vincent de Paul, they have tried to put their religious faith into practice by helping those in need. Today, there are over a million members who operate in more than 100 countries.

The Society of St Vincent de Paul has operated in Ireland since 1844. It consists of a nationwide network of conferences (i.e. local branches). These are based in parishes, schools and third-level institutions across the country. It has about 9,000 **volunteers** in Ireland.

Did You Know?

Ozanam gave the organisation this name because he himself was inspired by the example of **Vincent de Paul** (1581–1660). He was a Catholic saint who dedicated his life to helping the poor.

REMEMBER!

A **volunteer** is someone who chooses to give up free time to help others.

These volunteers are involved in a wide range of activities, such as:

- Visiting the poor at home, the sick in hospital, or inmates in prison.
- Providing educational grants, advice on money management, or affordable 'good-as-new' clothing through its shops.
- Providing counselling services for those in distress.
- Running crèches/pre-schools, homework clubs, youth clubs, community resource centres, hostels and refuges, visitor centres in prisons for families of inmates, and meals-on-wheels services.

St Vincent de Paul are involved in a wide range of activities, including counselling those in distress.

LIGHT THE WAY

ACTIVITIES

1. Wordsearch

Find the following words:

Propaganda
Kappler
Nobel prize
Conference
Allies
Jews
Informal
Peace
Volunteer
Axis
Golden rule
Mother Teresa
Dignity
O'Flaherty
Witness
Vocation
Ozanam
Vatican
Ministry
Calcutta
Vincent de Paul

E	S	S	E	N	T	I	W	K	V	N	M	R	P	Y
M	C	K	I	C	W	V	M	A	N	A	Z	O	R	T
B	O	A	I	D	N	L	M	P	P	C	V	D	O	R
Z	K	T	E	W	B	E	S	P	G	I	M	S	P	E
E	R	C	H	P	T	W	R	L	R	T	F	R	A	H
V	I	N	C	E	N	T	D	E	P	A	U	L	G	A
O	N	S	E	W	R	E	E	R	F	V	Y	O	A	L
C	M	I	N	I	S	T	R	Y	M	N	L	P	N	F
A	L	X	X	W	N	M	E	F	T	D	O	Z	D	O
T	O	A	E	U	S	F	A	R	E	I	I	C	A	O
I	C	J	L	V	E	X	O	N	E	H	N	S	Q	P
O	Y	O	U	T	I	J	R	R	G	S	M	G	J	H
N	V	L	E	N	L	U	J	A	M	I	A	V	I	L
E	Z	I	R	P	L	E	B	O	N	A	B	X	L	D
Y	P	A	Y	E	A	A	T	T	U	C	L	A	C	Y

2. Say what it means!

(a) Propaganda is _____

_____.

(b) Witness means _____

_____.

(c) Ministry is _____

_____.

(d) A volunteer is _____

_____.

3. Crossword

Across

5. This was Hugh O'Flaherty's occupation (2 words: 8, 6).
9. An abbreviation meaning 'missing in action'.
11. O'Flaherty set up an escape organisation to transport Jews and escaped Allied prisoners across the Alps to this neutral country.
14. The prison near Rome where Kappler was imprisoned for life after world War II.
16. It says, 'Do unto others as you would have them do unto you.' (2 words: 6, 4)
17. The sport in which O'Flaherty was Italy's amateur champion.

286

The Question of Faith   SECTION D

Down

1. The elite Nazi military force sent to occupy Rome in 1943.
2. After World War II O'Flaherty was awarded many of them, but he turned most of them down.
3. Name of the caves outside Rome where 320 Italian civilians were murdered in reprisal by the SS.
4. O'Flaherty became a master of this to fool the Germans and avoid capture while leading his escape organisation.
5. Where the pope has his summer residence. It was used to hide Jews from the Nazis.
6. A type of camp run by the SS during World War II in which millions of people were murdered.
7. An abbreviation meaning 'prisoner of war'.
8. The tiny neutral state from inside which O'Flaherty ran his escape organisation.
9. The pope awarded O'Flaherty this title.
10. The surname of the chief of the German security force in Rome.
12. Site of the National Park in Ireland where there is a memorial to O'Flaherty.
13. The number of doctorates O'Flaherty had.
15. The forces that liberated Rome in June 1944.

287

LIGHT THE WAY

4. Think about it!

Read the following:

> Take the case of someone who has never done a single good act but claims that he has faith. Will that faith save him? If one of the brothers or one of the sisters is in need of clothes and has not enough food to live on, and one of you says, 'I wish you well, keep yourself warm and eat plenty,' without giving this person these bare necessities of life, then what good is that? Faith is like that: if good works do not go with it, it is quite dead…Faith without good deeds is useless.

The Letter of St James 2:14–17 and 20

(a) What does this author say it means to have religious faith?

(b) Choose any one of the three extraordinary people discussed in this chapter. Then explain how he or she lived up to the Christian faith he/she claimed to have.

(c) Suppose someone were to tell you, '**It's pointless. One person cannot make any real difference with all the suffering in the world**.' In the light of the three stories you have read, how would you respond? Would you agree or disagree? Give reasons for your answer.

Section E

The Celebration of Faith

Chapter 1: **Prayer** 290

Chapter 2: **Sign and Symbol** 299

Chapter 3: **The Sacraments** 314

Chapter 4: **The Liturgical Year** 330

Chapter 5: **Pilgrimage** 340

289

LIGHT THE WAY

CHAPTER 1   PRAYER

The Meaning of Prayer

Clive Staples Lewis is best known as the author of the seven **Chronicles of Narnia** books. He was born in Belfast, Northern Ireland, in 1898. Tragedy struck early in Lewis's life. His mother died when he was only ten years old. Her death left him deeply saddened and confused. By age seventeen, Lewis no longer believed in God.

Lewis served as an officer in the British Army towards the end of World War I. He was wounded at the Battle of Arras in 1918. Fortunately, he managed to make a full recovery. However, his best friend, **Paddy Moore**, was killed in combat shortly before the war ended.

On his return to England, Lewis took up the scholarship he had been awarded at Oxford University. He excelled as a student and after graduation was appointed to a lectureship at Magdalen College, Oxford. There he taught courses on English language and literature.

From the late 1920s onwards, prompted by his experiences, Lewis began to think more and more about the existence of God and the value

The Chronicles of Narnia was one of C. S. Lewis's best-known works.

of religious faith. He became the close friend of another brilliant scholar, **J.R.R. Tolkien** (author of *The Hobbit* and *The Lord of the Rings*). Tolkien was a devout Catholic who, like Lewis, had fought in the trenches during World War I. The two men talked at great length about the meaning of life. Eventually, in September 1931, Lewis decided to become a Christian. He became a member of the Church of England (the Anglican Communion).

In his autobiography, *Surprised by Joy*, Lewis admitted that he did not make this decision lightly. He described himself as '**perhaps the most reluctant convert in all England**'. His decision shocked many of his fellow scholars at Oxford. They could not imagine why a man, said to be one of the finest minds of his generation, would choose to become a Christian.

Lewis now turned his attention to writing books and giving radio talks explaining the Christian message. Though a shy and reserved man, he proved to be a brilliant communicator.

Then, in the aftermath of World War II, Lewis's life took an unexpected turn. Most of his friends thought that he was a confirmed bachelor. To their surprise, Lewis met and fell in love with an American divorcée named **Joy Davidman**. They married in 1956. Their marriage was happy but tragically brief, as Joy died from bone cancer in 1960. After her death, Lewis wrote a short book entitled *A Grief Observed*. In it, he openly admitted to his own struggle to deal with his wife's death. He had loved her more than anyone else in his life.

The Celebration of Faith   SECTION E

After Joy's death, Lewis's own health began to decline. He died on 22 November 1963, the same day **President John F. Kennedy** was assassinated. As a result, Lewis's death received little media coverage at the time. However, his books continue to be read by new generations of people looking for answers to life's great questions.

It was in his last book – **Letters to Malcolm** – that Lewis dealt with the role **prayer** played in his life.

> **REMEMBER!**
> **Prayer** is a way of focusing your attention on, and communicating with, God.

Why People Pray

Lewis explained that people turn to God in prayer for many reasons.

You pray because...	This type of prayer is called...
You are awed by an encounter with the beauty of nature or because you experience the love of another person.	**Adoration:** You acknowledge God as the source of all goodness and beauty. You give praise to God.
You want to help someone who is ill or troubled.	**Intercession:** You ask God to help and support this person.
You experience suffering in your own life.	**Petition**: You ask God to ease your suffering or else grant you the strength to endure it.
You are sorry for acting selfishly and harming others.	**Penitence:** You admit your **sin** (i.e. the harmful thing you chose to do). You ask for God's forgiveness and try to do better in future.
You realise how fragile your health is and how easily your life can be ended.	**Protection:** You remember that God is there to guide you and that God's love is greater than the power of evil.
You are thankful that something important has gone well for you.	**Thanksgiving:** You express your gratitude to God for all the good things you have received but so often take for granted.

Ways of Praying

There are many different ways of praying.

> **REMEMBER!**
> **Vocal prayer** means using words to pray aloud.

1. Praying aloud

There are three kinds of **vocal** prayer:

- **Formal**, i.e. a prayer with a fixed format. A formal prayer's words are taken either from a sacred text (e.g. **the Lord's Prayer**) or decided upon by religious authorities.
- **Informal**, i.e. one that is very personal because you compose it yourself.
- **A hymn**, i.e. a song in which the lyrics give praise to God.

LIGHT THE WAY

2. Praying alone

> **REMEMBER!**
> **Personal prayer** is when you pray alone.

Jesus told his followers what this involves:

> '**When you pray, go to your private room and, when you have shut the door, pray to your Father who is in that secret place, and your Father who sees all that is done in secret will reward you.**'
>
> Matthew 6:6

3. Praying with others

Prayer is not only about your own, individual relationship with God. Prayer also concerns your relationship with other people. Why? Because having faith in God is not an isolated act. **No one can believe alone, just as no one can truly live alone**. This is why all religions encourage their members to take part in **communal prayer**.

> **REMEMBER!**
> **Communal prayer** is when you join together with other people to pray.

Praying with other members of your community helps you to keep your faith alive. It reminds you that prayer cannot be separated from the other parts of your life. You cannot grow in friendship with God if you ignore the needs of those around you.

4. Meditation

Meditation is a mixture of both vocal and silent prayer. It is not easy to meditate in our noisy, fast-paced world. It seems as if there is always some new distraction at hand. It is all too easy to become engrossed in a computer game or in a television programme. So many of us prefer noise over silence, motion over stillness, being scattered over being focused. However, for our own good, we all need to take some time out, to find a quiet place, to calm down and to get ourselves together. Without this **meditation** is impossible.

> **REMEMBER!**
> **Meditation** is a way to find inner peace. Only then can you focus your attention on something important.

Athletes use meditation to improve their performance in competitions. Doctors recommend meditation as a way of reducing your stress and lowering your blood pressure.

These are all good and worthwhile uses of meditation. However, as a form of prayer, **Christian meditation** has a different purpose. Its goal is to focus you on the mystery of God. As one **Old Testament** author put it, meditation must begin with your acceptance of God's command to:

> 'Be still, and know that I am God!'
> Psalm 46:10

Christian meditation is all about making room in your life for God and improving your relationship with God. It is not just about achieving better health or sharpening your mental focus.

SPOTLIGHT ON: HOW TO MEDITATE

If you have ever tried to empty your mind of thoughts, you will know how difficult it is to be still. It takes self-discipline, practice and patience to learn how to meditate.

The first step is to calm your body. You do this by consciously relaxing your muscles and breathing deeply and rhythmically. The second step is to focus your attention on God. You might slowly repeat the name of Jesus.

Alternatively, you might read a Bible passage and reflect on it. Here you might imagine yourself as one of the characters in a Gospel story. You could think about how you would feel or react to what Jesus had said and done if you were there.

The Importance of Prayer

C.S. Lewis believed that prayer can make a real difference in our lives, even in a technologically advanced society such as ours. He hoped that he might help other Christians who, like him, were struggling with prayer. However, Lewis did not set himself up as an expert on prayer. He was very modest about the value of what he had to say. He wrote:

'I write as one amateur to another, talking about difficulties that I have met, or insights I have gained, with the hope that this might at any rate interest, and sometimes even help, other inexpert readers. I am comparing notes, not presuming to instruct.'

Lewis agreed with **Saint Teresa of Avila** that prayer is:

'Nothing less than an intimate sharing between friends; it means taking time to be alone with God who loves me.'

The time for prayer could be any time. Lewis himself would pray while he walked from one college building to another.

Lewis believed that prayer is the way in which we deepen our **friendship** with God. He admitted that it did not make life any less challenging, but it helps to know that we are not alone when we face crises. He believed that God is always there to guide and support us. This is what gave him the strength to cope with illness and the loss of loved ones.

LIGHT THE WAY

However, Lewis reminded his readers that prayer cannot be detached from the other areas of our lives. As with all true friendships, our relationship with God must be outward-looking and unselfish. We can only build a strong friendship with God if we care about the welfare of other people.

Difficulties with Prayer

Lewis had a no-nonsense kind of religious faith. He had no time for sentimentality or wishful thinking. This is perhaps not surprising, given his life experiences – losing his mother as a child, experiencing combat in World War I, losing his best friend, and finally caring for his beloved wife as she slowly died from cancer.

Lewis understood that people have difficulty with the whole idea of prayer. He frankly admitted that he had experienced long periods of '**dryness**', i.e. times when he got no satisfaction from prayer. He even wrote that sometimes, '**I wonder if I am posting letters to a non-existent address**.' So why did he keep praying?

Lewis was well aware that, all too often, we turn to prayer only because we want something or are faced with a personal crisis. Common examples of this include:

- 'God, I know I didn't study, but please let me pass this exam!'
- 'God, please help me to get this job!'
- 'God, please cure me of this illness now!'
- 'God, please let me win the lottery!'

Typically, when such prayers go unanswered, we experience disappointment and resentment towards God. Often this leads us to ask:

- Does God really exist? Is there anyone there to hear and respond to my prayers?
- Why does God refuse to answer me? Is it because God is not interested in what happens to me?

Lewis said that these questions arise because we misunderstand our relationship with God and the whole purpose of prayer in our lives. This is rooted in our tendency to think that:

(a) God is some kind of heavenly magician.

(b) We have the right to demand he work a miracle to save us from the consequences of our own actions whenever we want.

As a Christian, Lewis believed that:

- God does exist.
- God loves and cares for each and every one of us.
- God only wants what is best for us.

However, he asked people to try to remember that:

- Not all the things you pray for are necessarily good for you. You should not expect God to give you something that would not be in your best interest.
- God has given you the gift of **freedom** (i.e. you can make your own choices).

What are the consequences of accepting this? Lewis said that it means the following:

1. **You must play your own part in achieving the things you want**

    Think about it: If you became seriously ill, you might pray to be healed or to get the strength to endure the pain and the worry it causes. However you should still go to the doctor, follow any medical advice given and undergo the prescribed treatment (e.g. medication and/or surgery). In other words, if you were facing this situation you might pray to God but you would also cooperate fully with those trying to treat your illness.

2. **You cannot expect God to stop you from acting on the choices you make, even if you might cause harm to yourself or to others**

    Think about it: You would be asking God to take away your freedom. God will not do this. Why? Because you cannot live a human life unless you are free to make your own choices.

3. **You cannot expect God to protect you from the consequences of your own actions**

    Think about it: You would be asking God to change all the physical laws of the universe. It would mean asking God to intervene constantly in your life. You could never have a traffic accident, no matter how recklessly you drove a vehicle, because God would always step in and prevent it! This would mean that you would never be held responsible for your actions. But responsibility goes hand in hand with freedom. You cannot have one without the other. Once again you would be asking God to take away your freedom. God will not take away your freedom, because without freedom you cannot live as a human being.

Approaching Prayer

Lewis said that the purpose of all prayer is to build a strong and lasting friendship with God. However, you can only really pray when you truly believe that God loves you, knows what your real needs are and does what is best for you. This is not easy but it is worthwhile.

Looking back on his own life experiences Lewis came to believe, reluctantly, that God works through our experiences of suffering and loss to teach us important lessons about what really matters in life. If we are willing to learn these lessons and integrate them into our lives, then we can build a strong and mature religious faith and find the courage to face life's challenges.

Lewis concluded that, if we really want to pray, we must stop living life on a selfish or trivial level. We must accept that God is **not** some kind of supernatural ATM who gives out wishes like cash. Prayer is not a matter of pressing a button and automatically having your request granted. Prayer is not about putting pressure on God to get what you want. It is not about bringing God around to see things your way. Rather, prayer is all about bringing yourself to accept what **God** wants for you.

This is why Lewis once told a friend:

'Prayer doesn't change God – it changes me.'

LIGHT THE WAY

ACTIVITIES

1. Wordsearch

Find the following words:

Lewis
Narnia
Oxford
Literature
Tolkien
Anglican
Communicator
Joy Davidman
Letters to Malcolm
Adoration
Intercession
Petition
Penitence
Protection
Thanksgiving
Vocal
Personal
Communal
Meditation
Freedom
Challenges

N	S	P	R	L	J	T	I	P	S	D	X	M	N	D	I
A	E	E	O	A	R	V	O	R	F	I	O	Y	E	S	P
M	G	N	T	C	O	E	X	O	O	D	W	P	I	C	N
D	N	I	A	O	Y	E	F	T	E	F	X	E	K	C	O
I	E	T	C	V	M	E	O	E	Q	D	Q	H	L	C	I
V	L	E	I	N	T	E	R	C	E	S	S	I	O	N	T
A	L	N	N	V	U	F	D	T	G	B	I	D	T	X	I
D	A	C	U	G	N	I	V	I	G	S	K	N	A	H	T
Y	H	E	M	P	E	R	S	O	N	A	L	I	J	A	E
O	C	L	M	D	U	L	A	N	U	M	M	O	C	M	P
J	G	N	O	N	A	C	I	L	G	N	A	R	N	I	A
M	L	O	C	L	A	M	O	T	S	R	E	T	T	E	L
L	I	T	E	R	A	T	U	R	E	Y	A	R	P	I	U
R	O	R	P	D	A	D	O	R	A	T	I	O	N	Y	Q
N	O	I	T	A	T	I	D	E	M	Y	Q	S	R	Z	I

2. Say what it means!

(a) Prayer is _____
_____ .

(b) Vocal prayer means _____ .

(c) Personal prayer is _____ .

(d) Communal prayer is _____ .

(e) Meditation is _____
_____ .

3. Fill in the missing words!

THE SIX TYPES OF PRAYER	
Adoration:	You _____ God as the source of all goodness and beauty. You give _____ to God.
Intercession:	You ask God to _____ and _____ someone.
Petition:	You ask God to _____ your suffering or else grant you the _____ to endure it.
Penitence:	You admit your _____. You ask for God's _____ and try to do _____ in future.
Protection:	You remember that God is there to _____ you and that God's _____ is greater than the power of _____.
Thanksgiving:	You express your _____ to God for all the ____ things you have received but so often take for _____.

4. Crossword

Across

2. Where Lewis was born in Northern Ireland.
3. The second step in meditation should be to focus your attention on this person.
5. The cause of Lewis's wife's death in 1960 (2 words: 4, 6).
9. The first name of the woman Lewis married.
10. The surname of Lewis's best friend who was killed in World War I.
12. A word that means you can make your own choices.
14. She died when Lewis was ten years old.
18. The first step in meditation is to calm this.
19. Describes a prayer that is very personal because you compose it yourself.
20. Lewis became a member of this Communion in 1931.
21. In Matthew 6:6 he told his followers about what is involved in personal prayer.

Down

1. They all encourage their members to take part in communal prayer.
4. Lewis was wounded in 1918 during a battle at this place.
6. The university to which Lewis was awarded a scholarship.
7. The surname of the brilliant Catholic scholar, author of *The Lord of the Rings*, who became a close friend of Lewis.
8. Lewis believed that prayer is the way that we deepen this with God.
11. Describes a prayer with a fixed format.
13. C. S. Lewis is best known as the author of seven books set in this place.
15. A song in which the lyrics give praise to God.
16. A harmful thing you choose to do.
17. The topic Lewis wrote about in his last book, *Letters to Malcolm*.

LIGHT THE WAY

5. Think about it!

(a) Read the following story:

Once there was a man who lived in a small town, situated on a riverbank, downstream from a huge hydroelectric dam. One day, disaster struck. The dam collapsed and a huge tidal wave swept down towards his town. The man did not panic. He prayed that God would save him.

When the police came to warn everyone to evacuate the area immediately, the man ignored their advice. Surely, he thought, God would save him.

Then the flood waters surged through the town and flooded the ground floor of his house, forcing the man to move upstairs. A rescue boat called on him to jump aboard but he refused. Surely, he thought, God would save him.

As the waters rose higher, the man was forced to sit up on the roof of his house. A rescue helicopter flew over the area, hovered above him and offered to airlift him to safety. But he refused. Surely, he thought, God would save him.

Eventually, the whole house collapsed and the man was plunged into the fast-flowing water. He was unable to swim and so he drowned.

The next thing the man knew, he found himself standing at the gates of heaven. However, he was angry. The angel who greeted the man noticed that he was angry and asked him why.

The man replied, 'I prayed. I asked God for help but he didn't listen to me. I'm dead and it's all God's fault.'

The angel looked puzzled by this statement. Then the angel said, 'I don't see why you should think that. Remember, God sent the police to warn you and a boat and a helicopter to rescue you. Surely your prayers were answered.'

Answer the following questions:
1. Why did this man think that God had **not** listened to his prayers?
2. How could he have avoided drowning?
3. What, do you think, is the lesson of this story?

(b) Read each of the following statements. Then say how you think a person of strong religious faith might respond to each of these statements and their attitude to prayer.
1. My favourite team was playing in the Champions League final. I put a large bet on them and prayed that they would win. They lost. Clearly, God didn't listen to me.
2. Though I didn't do any study, I prayed that I would pass my exams. I failed. So, it's safe to say that there's no point in asking God for anything.
3. I really wanted to win last Saturday's Lotto draw. I prayed that I would. I didn't, someone else did. I don't see any point in praying if God doesn't give me what I want.

(c) What do you think Lewis meant when he said that **'Prayer doesn't change God – it changes me'**?

The Celebration of Faith   SECTION E

CHAPTER 2   SIGN AND SYMBOL

The Importance of Language

One important difference between human beings and animals is that we use **language**, while they do not.

> **REMEMBER!**
> **Language** refers to the different ways in which we communicate with one another. We communicate through: **speech**, **gestures**, **images** and **writing**.

Notice how each way of communicating involves the use of our **senses**. For example:

- Words are spoken to be **heard**.
- Images are made to be **seen**.
- Handshakes are gestures made to be **felt**.

This is how it has to be, because we gain all our knowledge of the world around us through our senses. So, when we want to communicate our ideas to others, we need to use things they can see, hear or touch to get our message across. This is where **signs** and **symbols** play an important role.

Did You Know?

The words **sign** and **symbol** are often confused with one another. Sometimes they are used as if they mean the same thing. However, they do **not**.

The Meaning of Sign

Think about the following examples:

1. Traffic lights

This is a set of three lights used to direct the flow of pedestrians and vehicles at a road junction.
Each colour means **one and only one** thing:

- **Red** means '**Stop**'.
- **Amber** means '**Prepare to stop**'.
- **Green** means '**Proceed ahead if the way is clear**'.

2. Road signs

These are self-explanatory. They give motorists **one** clear instruction.

　This means, '**Parking prohibited**'.

　This means, '**Do not exceed the maximum speed limit of 110 kilometres per hour**'.

Both traffic lights and road signs help us to understand what **a sign** is.

299

LIGHT THE WAY

> **REMEMBER!**
> **A sign** is any image, word or gesture that communicates **one** and **only one** idea.

Some signs are more important than others. Think about the following:

- This means '**Advanced direction to motorway services**'. You can choose to ignore this sign if you do not wish to stop for something to eat and drink.

- This means '**Stop your vehicle at this point**'. Unlike the previous sign, you are **not** allowed to use your discretion when you see this sign; you must **always** obey it.

Clearly signs are very useful **abbreviations**.

> **REMEMBER!**
> **An abbreviation** is a shorthand way of communicating specific information.

Signs help us to avoid confusion. They allow us to give and receive clear, quick and sometimes life-saving messages that can be easily understood.

The Meaning of Symbol

A national flag is of great importance to every country. It stands for **many** different things. For example: the land itself, the people who live there and all the things they believe are important and worthwhile. For this reason, you expect your national flag to be treated with respect.

Let us turn to explore the meanings contained in two national flags:

1. The flag of the Republic of Ireland

The flag of the Republic of Ireland is known as **the Tricolour**. It was designed by **Thomas Francis Meagher**. He deliberately chose the three colours of **green, white** and **orange** to express a great hope for the people of Ireland. He believed that there could only be peace on this island when the members of both political traditions, Nationalist and Unionist, treated one another with respect.

Notice how each of the flag's three coloured segments are of **equal width**:

1. The **green** segment: This represents the **Nationalist** tradition.

2. The **orange** segment: This represents the **Unionist** tradition.

3. The **white** segment in the centre: This represents **peace** existing between these two traditions.

This flag was flown over the General Post Office in Dublin during the Easter Rising of 1916. It captured the popular imagination and was adopted as the national flag afterwards.

The founders of the Irish Republic hoped that ours would be a land where the members of both traditions – Nationalist and Unionist – would live together in friendship and peace.

2. The flag of the United States of America

This flag is popularly known among Americans as 'Old Glory', 'the Stars and Stripes' or 'the Star Spangled Banner'. It was officially adopted as the national flag of the United States in 1777.

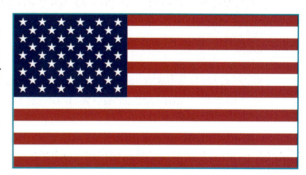

The design of this flag was intended to mark the beginnings and to chart the progress of the United States as a nation. How?

The flag has two parts:

1. **The thirteen alternating horizontal stripes:** These seven red and six white stripes of equal length represent the original number of founding states that declared their independence from the British Empire in 1776.

2. **The fifty white five-pointed stars in the blue rectangle:** These stars represent the extent to which the United States has grown as a nation since its founding. Each state is represented by a white star. As there are now fifty states, there are fifty stars on the flag.

The colours of this flag were chosen to express important ideas and qualities that the citizens of America should embody and uphold. These are:

1. **Red** represents strength and courage.

2. **White** represents purity and unity.

3. **Blue** represents justice, endurance and vigilance.

The flag of the United States is customarily flown all year-round at most public buildings. Many Americans like to decorate their homes with this flag, especially on national holidays, to show their pride in their country. There is a long-standing tradition around **Memorial Day** (held in the USA on the last Monday in May) of placing small versions of the national flag at war memorials and beside the graves of war veterans.

From these two examples we can see that a country's national flag is a **symbol**.

REMEMBER!
A symbol is any image, word or gesture that communicates **more than one** idea.

Did You Know?
You should try to be more aware of the role played by symbols. It will enrich your experience of everyday life. By looking **beyond** surface appearances, you will see the deeper meanings in things around you, whether it is in art, architecture, drama, literature, poetry or religion.

LIGHT THE WAY

The Role of Symbols in the World's Religions

Symbols play an important role in all religions. Think about the following:

1. Communication

A symbol, such as a lighted candle, can act as a **visible**, **tangible** link between you and the **invisible**, **intangible** God you worship.

> **REMEMBER!**
> **Visible** means 'can be seen'. **Invisible** means 'cannot be seen'.
> **Tangible** means 'can be touched'. **Intangible** means 'cannot be touched'.

When used during a religious ritual, a symbol such as a lighted candle can help **communicate** a belief in ways that words could never fully express.

> **REMEMBER!**
> **To communicate** means to share or exchange information or ideas.

For example:

A lighted candle represents the idea that God is the true source of all hope and all wisdom.

2. Identity

Symbols can be used to clearly establish your **religious identity**.

> **REMEMBER!**
> **A religious identity** consists of all the things that distinguish one religion from another.

For example:

 This is **the Aum**. It is the symbol of **Hinduism**.

 This is **the Eight-spoked Wheel**. It is the symbol of **Buddhism**.

 This is **the Menorah**. It is the symbol of **Judaism**.

 This is **the Star and Crescent Moon**. It is the symbol of **Islam**.

Christian Symbols

Christianity is rich in symbols. Here are some of the most commonly used symbols in Christian architecture, painting, sculpture and worship.

1. The Fish

This was the most popular symbol among the early Christians. The Greek word for '**fish**' is *Ichthys*.

Each letter of this word points to a name or title of Jesus. When these letters are combined, they offer us a basic statement of what Christians believe about Jesus:

- **I – Iesos:** Jesus
- **Ch – Christos**: Christ
- **Th – Theou:** Of God
- **Y – Yios:** Son
- **S – Soter**: Saviour

When re-arranged, this reads: '**Jesus Christ, God's Son, Saviour**'.

2. The Cross

The earliest Christian paintings preserved in the catacombs beneath Rome show that, at first, the early Christians focused on the idea of Jesus as 'the Gentle Shepherd' of his people. They were reluctant to show him on the cross because it was considered to be a shameful death to endure, one reserved for criminals and rebels.

By the 4th century CE, however, Christians had begun to publicly identify the cross as **the** Christian symbol above all others. Yet, they still considered crucifixion to be a cruel and vicious form of execution. So, why did Christians choose to adopt the cross as their symbol?

Perhaps it is because the cross gives us a powerful insight into the kind of God Christians worship. Christians believe that our world only exists because God made it. However, God is not a remote observer of events in human history. On the contrary, God so loves us that He came down to Earth and lived as one of us.

Did You Know?

Christians believe that in Jesus of Nazareth, **God became a human being**. They refer to Jesus as **the Incarnation** (meaning '**God in the flesh**'). The Gospels tell us that:

- **As God** – Jesus could work miracles, the greatest of which was his resurrection.
- **As man** – Jesus had a human mother who gave birth to him and raised him. This is why he suffered and died on a cross.

This does **not** mean that Jesus is part human and part divine. Rather, it means that Jesus has a fully human nature and a fully divine nature in the **one** person. Jesus is '**true God and true man**'.

303

LIGHT THE WAY

Christians accept the Incarnation as a very great **mystery**. It cannot be completely explained. It must be accepted on faith.

The Incarnation means that God is not distant. Christians have faith in a God who is very close to them. They worship a God who understands what it means to suffer. But more than this, by dying on the cross, God says to us:

'Not only do I know about your suffering, I have shared in it.'

For people who are themselves suffering from illness or injustice, having faith in a loving and forgiving God who has suffered too can be a lifeline. It can help them to:

- Find meaning in their suffering.
- Gain the strength to endure their suffering.
- Have hope that, one day, they will experience eternal peace and joy with God in a life beyond this, a life forever free from suffering.

The cross is always found in a Christian place of worship. There are also many different versions of the cross. Here we will look at just four different versions of it.

The Latin cross – This is a plain cross, i.e. one without any figure or image upon it. It emphasises the resurrection of Jesus, which Christians believe to be a promise of eternal life for them.

The Crucifix – This is a cross with a figure or image of Jesus hanging from it, either dead or in agony. It represents the suffering of Jesus, by which Christians believe they have been saved from sin and death.

The Celtic cross – This is a type of cross with a circle around its centre, representing the idea that Jesus is 'the Everlasting Light of the World'.

On large stone versions of this cross that still dot the Irish landscape, both the upright and crossbeam are decorated with scenes from the Bible carved into them. During early medieval times, these carvings were used as aids to help Irish monks teach the Christian faith to **the illiterate** (i.e. those who could not read).

In ancient times, a Celtic cross marked a holy place, but it was never used to mark the site of a graveyard. Originally, it was only used to mark a place associated with life, such as a pilgrimage site.

The St Brigid's cross – This cross is named after a 5th-century CE Irish saint. She established a monastery known as **Cill Darach** (i.e. Kildare). The feast of St Brigid is celebrated on 1 February each year.

Usually, this cross is made from woven rushes or straw. In rural Ireland, there was a tradition that a couple taking possession of a farm or homestead would nail a St Brigid's cross under their barn's eaves. It identified this place as under the protection of Jesus Christ.

304

The Celebration of Faith   SECTION E

Icons

Images play an important role in Christian worship. One particularly beautiful form of Christian image is **the icon**.

Icons depict either the Trinity, Jesus Christ, Mary, a saint, an angel or a combination of some or all of these figures.

> **REMEMBER!**
> An **image** can be any **likeness,** such as a carving, a mosaic, a painting or a sculpture.

The purpose of an icon is to help you to pray and so grow closer to God. Icons were first produced and displayed by artists in the Orthodox tradition. However, in recent times, icons have become popular among Catholics and Anglicans too.

> **REMEMBER!**
> An **icon** is a richly decorated religious image painted on a wooden board.

When looking at an icon you must remember two things:

- An icon does **not** offer a life-like portrait. It is deliberately painted out of perspective. Although there is a certain life-like quality to it, it has an otherworldly appearance. Its purpose is to get across a profound religious truth that is very hard to express in words.
- An icon tries to show the power, greatness and perfection of the invisible God. It tries to help you feel the presence of God and to focus all your attention on God.

Icons have been painted since at least the 5th century CE. An artist who paints icons is called **an iconographer**.

SPOTLIGHT ON: THE WORK OF THE ICONOGRAPHER

Traditionally, iconographers were Orthodox monks and nuns. Recently, this work has also been done by members of the laity.

To be an iconographer is to be more than an artist in the usual sense of the word. The work involved is said to be **a vocation** (i.e. a calling from God to do it).

An iconographer uses materials from this world (e.g. wood, paint, oils and cloth). However, his/her task is to produce an image that points you beyond the work itself, beyond this world altogether, onwards and upwards towards the almighty God who lives and reigns forever in heaven.

An iconographer must follow two rules:
- Before beginning to paint, you must fast and pray. You ask God to inspire you in your work.
- You must continue to pray while painting the icon. This allows the Holy Spirit to guide your brush strokes.

This is why icons are often called **'prayers captured in wood'**.

Did You Know?

One thing must be clearly understood: Christians do **not** worship icons. They do **not** pray to them.

When Christians kiss an icon or place a lighted candle in front of it, they are only paying their respect to the person **represented** in the icon, e.g. The Holy Trinity, Jesus or Mary. They do **not** believe that any divine power resides in an icon itself or in any other kind of sacred image.

LIGHT THE WAY

Interpreting an Icon

Example No. 1: CHRIST PANTOCRATOR

The title of this icon means '**Christ: The Ruler of the World**'. It was painted by an unknown iconographer around 1670. It is now preserved in the Kolomenskoye Museum in Moscow.

The gentle, wide-open, symmetrical eyes of Jesus gaze out of the painting to emphasise the belief that, unlike us, Jesus lives in a way that is beyond the limits of space and time.

The red colour of Jesus's inner garment symbolises the **humanity** of Jesus. The blue colour of his outer garment symbolises his **divinity**.

The fingers of Jesus's right hand are raised in a benediction (blessing). The fingers are gathered to form the initials of the monogram IC (Jesus) and XC (Christ).

The warm golden light of the halo around the head of Jesus suggests the joy, holiness and peace of heaven.

The cross superimposed on the halo bears the words 'He who is' and refers to God the Father.

Jesus's left hand holds an open copy of the Gospels. He displays the text of Matthew 25:35–36. This reminds us that, on Judgement Day, Jesus will recognise his true followers according to how they have sought to love their neighbours as themselves.

The icon is unsigned because the iconographer did not seek personal fame or glory for his work.

The clothes Jesus wears have neat folds to show the calm harmony of life in heaven.

Example No. 2: ST. NICHOLAS OF MYRA

The halo around his head and the brightness around his face reveal the presence of the Holy Spirit at work in him.

The firmness of the expression on his face symbolises his life-long commitment to preaching and defending the Christian faith.

He wears the cross-adorned vestments of a bishop.

His right hand is raised in a benediction (blessing). The thumb touching two fingers indicates the Christian belief in the Trinity.

The large eyes symbolise his desire to see beyond this world to heaven.

The large ears show his desire to listen to God's word.

The small mouth shows his desire to listen first and foremost to God and only speak when it is in the service of God.

His left hand is holding a closed copy of the New Testament because he dedicated his life to defending authentic Christian teaching against heresy.

306

St Nicholas is a very popular saint in the Orthodox tradition. Every city in Russia has a church dedicated to his memory. This icon of the saint was painted in the 13th century. It is now on display in the Russian Museum in St Petersburg.

Exploring a Place of Worship

The purpose of a place of worship is to help you get a sense of God's presence and encourage you to respond to God with gratitude, love and respect.

For nearly three centuries after Pentecost, Christians living within the Roman Empire were frequently subjected to brutal persecution for their beliefs. As a result, they had to gather in secret. Usually, they met in small groups at the home of a fellow Christian.

However, in 313 CE, the Emperor Constantine granted Christians freedom of worship. Finally, they could gather in public to worship without fear of harassment. This is why the earliest known **churches** date from the middle of the 4th century CE.

There are significant differences between the various Christian traditions regarding the layout and the contents of their particular places of worship. Here we shall look at two examples: a Catholic church and an Anglican church.

A church – a place of worship.

Did You Know?

For Christians, the word '**church**' has several different meanings, depending on the context. Here we shall use the word '**church**' to mean a building designed and used by Christians for the worship of God.

LIGHT THE WAY

Example No.1: The interior of a Catholic Church

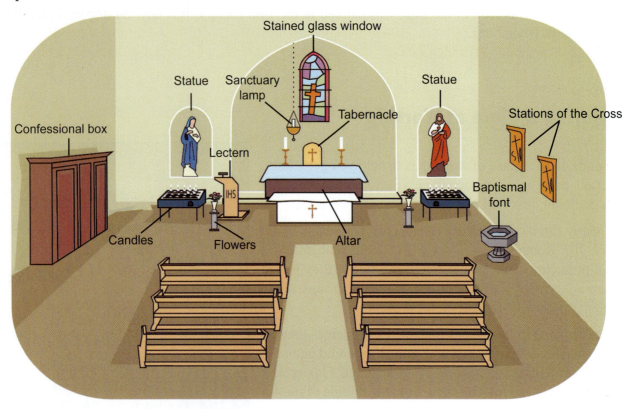

Example No.2: The interior of an Anglican Church

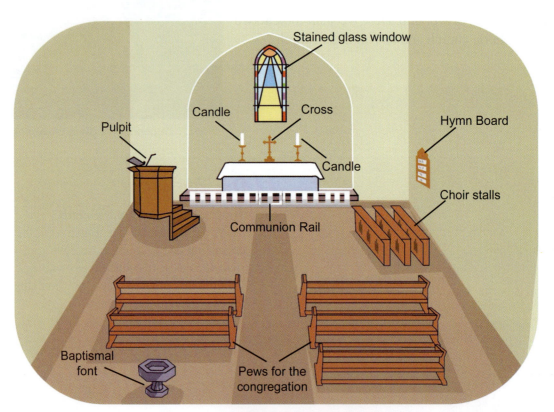

Did You Know?

Although different, both of these buildings serve the same purpose. They help worshippers to be more aware of God's presence and encourage them to respond to God with gratitude, love and respect.

The Celebration of Faith SECTION E

ACTIVITIES

1. Wordsearch
Find the following words:

Language
Image
Word
Gesture
Abbreviation
Sign
Symbol
Flag
Communication
Invisible
Intangible
Candle
Identity
Fish
Cross
Incarnation
Brigid
Icon
Church
Catholic
Anglican
Crucifix

I	F	E	L	B	I	S	I	V	N	I	B	G	B	Y
C	A	T	H	O	L	I	C	J	D	W	Z	I	I	T
C	O	M	M	U	N	I	C	A	T	I	O	N	H	I
A	E	L	D	N	A	C	E	N	F	G	T	C	C	T
E	B	J	E	K	D	G	L	L	B	A	N	A	R	N
A	U	B	Y	G	A	I	A	N	N	Z	X	R	U	E
S	N	U	R	M	A	G	G	G	O	I	G	N	H	D
I	E	G	I	E	R	U	I	I	F	C	S	A	C	I
G	S	G	L	N	V	B	G	I	R	Y	I	T	Z	T
N	Z	E	M	I	L	I	C	N	M	B	U	I	X	D
M	N	S	S	E	C	U	A	B	A	C	R	O	S	S
W	C	T	Q	R	R	A	O	T	W	L	J	N	X	M
N	U	U	V	C	I	L	N	G	I	O	H	S	I	F
V	B	R	U	Z	U	B	G	F	Q	O	R	G	V	J
P	H	E	K	R	S	F	A	Y	Y	N	N	D	G	B

2. Say what it means!

(a) Language refers to _____

_____

_____

(b) A sign is _____

_____

(c) A symbol is _____

_____

(d) To communicate means _____

_____

(e) An icon is _____

_____

LIGHT THE WAY

3. Crossword

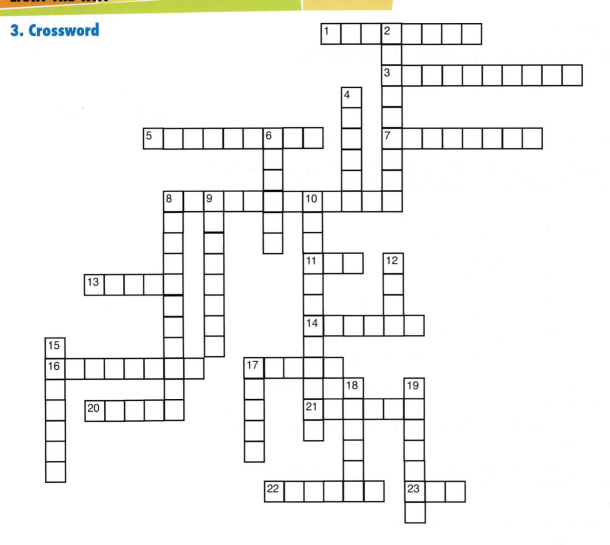

Across

1. Like a handshake, we use them to communicate with each other.
3. It means 'cannot be touched'.
5. It means 'cannot be seen'.
7. Human beings use it but animals do not.
8. Name given to an artist who paints an icon.
11. On the American national flag, this colour represents strength and courage.
13. At a traffic light, when this colour is displayed, it means 'prepare to stop'.
14. They are made to be seen.
16. The name for a cross with a figure or image of Jesus hanging from it either dead or in agony.
17. On the Irish national flag, this colour represents peace existing between the two traditions on this island.
20. On the Irish national flag, this colour represents the Nationalist tradition.
21. On the Irish national flag, this colour represents the Unionist tradition.
22. Communicating through speech, gesture, image and writing involves our use of them.
23. This is the symbol of Hinduism.

Down

2. The name given to the flag of the Republic of Ireland.
4. Name given to a building designed and used by Christians for the worship of God.
6. A cross is named after this 5th-century female Irish saint.
8. It means 'God in the flesh'.
9. Icons were first produced and displayed by artists in this Christian tradition.
10. It's a shorthand way of communicating specific information.
12. On the American national flag, this colour represents justice, endurance and vigilance.
15. The Greek word for 'fish'.
17. They are spoken to be heard.
18. When lit, it represents the idea that God is the true source of all hope and all wisdom.
19. This is the symbol of Judaism.

The Celebration of Faith   SECTION E

4. Tick the box!

In each of the following, say whether it is **true** or **false**.

	True	False
1. A sign and a symbol mean the same thing.		
2. Signs allow us to give and receive clear, quick and sometimes life-saving messages that can be easily understood.		
3. This image [image] is a symbol.		
4. This image [image] is a symbol.		
5. Thomas Francis Meagher designed the Irish Tricolour.		
6. Christians believe that God is tangible and visible.		
7. A religious identity consists of all the things that distinguish one religion from another.		
8. From the very beginning, the first Christians were happy to show Jesus on the cross.		
9. The Latin cross is a type of cross with a circle around its centre, representing the idea that Jesus is 'the Everlasting Light of the World'.		
10. An image can be any likeness, such as a carving, a mosaic, a painting or a sculpture.		
11. Icons depict either the Trinity, Jesus Christ, Mary, a saint, an angel or a combination of some or all of these figures.		
12. An icon offers a life-like portrait.		
13. An icon tries to show the power, greatness and perfection of the visible world.		
14. When Christians kiss an icon or place a lighted candle in front of it, they are paying their respect to the icon itself.		
15. Christ Pantocrator means, 'Christ the Ruler of the World'.		
16. There are no significant differences between the various Christian traditions regarding the layout and the contents of their particular places of worship.		

LIGHT THE WAY

5. Identify the features!

(a) A Catholic church

Identify each of the features numbered here. Write your answers in the spaces provided.

(b) An Anglican church

Identify each of the features numbered here. Write your answers in the spaces provided.

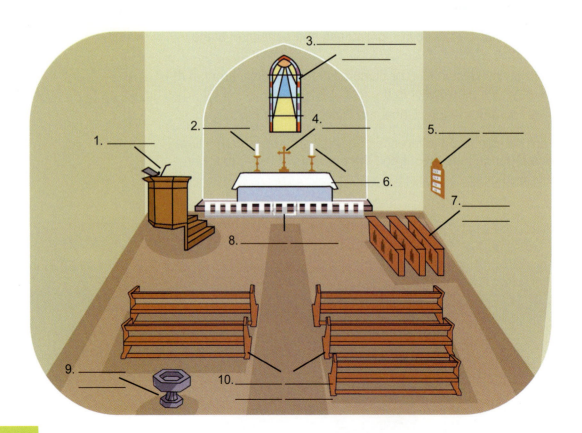

The Celebration of Faith   SECTION E

6. Think about it!

(a) Why is the work of an iconographer said to be 'a vocation'?

(b) Read the following story. It is set on the Last Day or **Judgment Day**.

> A group of people who had suffered terribly in their own lives complained that, as far as they could see, God had led a very sheltered life. They said that, in order to qualify as our judge, God would have to know what our lives are really like.
>
> God should have to live on Earth as a human being. They agreed that:
>
> **God should be born a Jew. He should be doubted by his family and betrayed by his friends. He should face false charges and be tried by a prejudiced jury in front of a hostile crowd. He should be mocked and tortured to death – and as he slowly dies, he should feel abandoned and alone.**
>
> When they had said this, a long silence followed. No one moved, for suddenly, they all realised that God had already served his sentence here on Earth.

What point does this story make about the Christian God?

LIGHT THE WAY

CHAPTER 3 THE SACRAMENTS

The Mystery of God

At the heart of Christianity is the awareness that, beyond the visible, tangible world in which we live, there is a **God** who gives meaning and purpose to our lives.

> **REMEMBER!**
> **God** is **the Supreme Being** who created and sustains the universe.
>
> To call God **the Supreme Being** means that no one is as great as or greater than God.

God is the most difficult topic we can ever think about. The following story illustrates this point:

Even Greater than the Ocean

One morning two Christian scholars went for a walk together along the coastline. As they walked on the sand, they discussed each other's ideas about God. Soon it became obvious that they did not agree.

Then they met a young boy playing by the water's edge. They saw that the boy had dug a small pit in the sand.

He kept running down to the sea, dipping his little bucket into the water and running back up the beach to empty the water into the pit. The two men found the scene amusing. So they went up to him and asked him what he was trying to do. The child pointed to the sea and told them, very seriously, that he was going to take all the water in the sea and pour it into the little pit that he had dug in the sand.

The two scholars wished him well and continued on their way, carrying on their discussion. Suddenly, one of them stopped. **'You know,'** he said, **'we were amused when that child told us what he was trying to do. Yet, here we are trying to do the same thing in our** discussion about God.

'It is as impossible for us to fully understand God as it is for that child to pour the entire sea into the little pit he has dug in the sand. The mystery of God is even greater than the ocean. Vast beyond compare. Our minds are too small to ever hope to contain it.'

> **REMEMBER!**
> **A mystery** is something so vast and so complex that it is beyond our capacity to ever completely figure out and solve.

When Christians call God **a mystery**, they mean that:

- Our language is of limited use when talking about God. Our words can only give us a vague idea of God's greatness.
- It is beyond the capacity of our minds to ever fully understand who God is.
- The best we can hope for is to gain some **insight** into the greatness of God. This can only be achieved through prayer, studying sacred texts and living a good life.

The Meaning of Worship

Christians respond to the mystery of God through acts of **worship**.

> **REMEMBER!**
> **Worship** is any action that shows:
> - You have faith in God.
> - You recognise that there is no one greater than God.
> - You want to give thanks and praise to God.

You can worship God in two ways:

- **In private**, i.e. on your own.
- **In public**, i.e. with others.

A Personal God

Like Jews and Muslims, Christians too worship **a personal God**.

> **REMEMBER!**
> **A personal God** is one who loves you and cares about what happens to you.

All three religions agree that only God is worthy of worship. As a result, Jews, Christians and Muslims reject **idolatry**.

> **REMEMBER!**
> **Idolatry** is the worship of anyone or anything other than God.

LIGHT THE WAY

However, if you read both Judaism's **Tenakh** and Islam's **Qur'an**, you soon notice that they present God as someone who is separated from human beings by an unbridgeable distance.

Both religions agree that God is great and good beyond compare. However, Judaism and Islam present God as a distant, awe-inspiring figure. Whenever God appeared on Earth in times past, it was only to speak to prophets, and then only from inside a burning bush, or through his messengers called 'angels'.

In contrast to Jews and Muslims, Christians take a very different approach to God. They reject the idea that God is in any way distant or remote from human affairs. On the contrary, through the Incarnation:

> 'The Word became flesh and dwelled among us.'
> John 1:14

The Gospels tell the story of how Jesus of Nazareth bridged the vast distance between God and human beings. God loves us so much that, in Jesus, God became human and lived among us, sharing all the joys and hardships of life on Earth, even going so far as to suffer and die on a cross.

The Sense of the Sacred

Christians put their faith in a God who lived and died as one of us. Such a God is anything but remote. Indeed, as the poet Patrick Kavanagh once commented, this God is intimately present in our lives and communicates with us through '**the bits and pieces of Everyday**'. How?

If you pause and reflect on all the people, places and events that affect your life, you can see how each one points **beyond** itself. Think of all those little acts of human kindness you have experienced. Think of any encounters you have had where you were struck by the beauty of the natural world. Each of these can be understood as **a symbol**. Why? Because each, in its own way, reveals something of the goodness and greatness of the God who created you and the world you share with others.

This awareness of the invisible presence of God in our lives is called **the sense of the sacred**.

> **REMEMBER!**
> **Sacred** means someone or something worthy of your total respect.

This sense of the sacred is expressed in **symbol** and celebrated in **ritual**.

The Meaning of Ritual

In everyday speech, the word '**ritual**' refers to some routine situation where we regularly do any of the following:

- **Perform a certain action**, e.g. stand up when the national anthem is played.
- **Say a particular thing**, e.g. wish someone a 'happy birthday'.
- **Wear distinctive clothing**, e.g. put on the colours of your favourite team when attending a football match.

For the world's religions, the word '**ritual**' has a somewhat similar meaning.

> **REMEMBER!**
> **A religious ritual** is where all the members of a religion say and do the same things every time they come together to worship God.

Example: Gestures performed by Christians during their religious rituals

Christians are expected to think about the **meaning** of certain gestures and keep this in mind when taking part in a religious ritual. For example:

- **Kneeling:** This means that you worship only God.
- **Standing:** This shows that you believe in the resurrection.
- **Blessing:** By tracing the cross with your right hand you identify yourself as a Christian.
- **Shaking hands:** This shows that you want to be a peacemaker in daily life.

> **REMEMBER!**
> **Gestures** are symbols that we perform.

Kneeling means you worship only God.

Places of Worship:

Every religion sets aside special places where its members can gather to worship through rituals. For example:

Jews worship in **a synagogue**.

Hindus worship in **a mandir**.

317

LIGHT THE WAY

 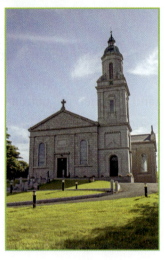 

Buddhists worship in **a vihara**.   Christians worship in **a church**.   Muslims worship in **a mosque**.

The Role of Ritual in Religion

Ritual plays an important role in every religion. Think about this:

- Rituals help you to put aside your day-to-day concerns and focus your attention on God.
- Though God is invisible, rituals make God seem less distant and more accessible to you.
- Rituals help to create and sustain a sense of community between the members of a religion. This is because they all come together to worship God in the same place, at the same time and in the same way.
- Rituals create a sense of continuity between believers today and their ancestors who also took part in the same rituals long ago.

Did You Know?

Anyone taking part in a ritual should do so with **respect**. Why? Because it helps to create the right atmosphere for worship.

Genuflecting in a Catholic church.

For example: Upon entering a church, Catholics are expected to trace the symbol of the cross with the right hand. Then they should **genuflect** (i.e. bend the right knee) toward **the Blessed Sacrament** (i.e. the Eucharist stored in the tabernacle) before sitting down.

They do these things to remind themselves that they have entered a sacred place and must now concentrate on God alone.

The Celebration of Faith SECTION E

Christian Worship

Depending on which tradition they belong to, Christians worship in either of two ways:

(a) **liturgical**; or (b) **non-liturgical**.

Liturgical worship

This is practised by Catholics, Anglicans and the Orthodox.

It consists of colourful and elaborate rituals. These rituals follow a fixed pattern of words and actions.

Liturgical worship is **altar-centred**. Here the main emphasis is on the celebration of the Sacrament of the Eucharist.

Non-liturgical worship

This is practised by Presbyterians, Methodists, Baptists and the Salvation Army.

It consists of plain and simple rituals which do not follow a fixed pattern of words and actions.

Non-liturgical worship is **pulpit-centred**. Here the main emphasis is on reading the Bible and listening to a sermon that interprets its meaning.

Both types of Christian worship are based on the promise that Jesus made at his Ascension. He said that he would always be with his followers. Christians believe that Jesus fulfilled his promise by sending the Holy Spirit at Pentecost.

Ever since Pentecost, Christian worship has been **a two-way process**. It involves Christians offering praise and thanks **to** God and receiving grace **from** God.

The Christian understanding of **grace** is rooted in the fact that we are imperfect creatures.

Each of us has to struggle every day to live a good life. Christians believe that it is only with God's grace that we can cope with all the challenges, problems and opportunities life presents. We receive God's grace through **the sacraments**.

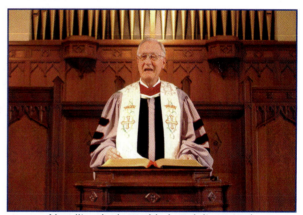
Non-liturgical worship is pulpit-centred.

Did You Know?

Grace is the love and strength that God gives to those who have faith in him.

A Catholic Explains the Sacraments

Christians believe that, after his resurrection, Jesus was no longer limited by the physical laws of the universe that restrict our human freedom of action. The Gospels tell us that:

- Jesus could appear suddenly in a locked room (see: **John 20:19**).
- Jesus could vanish at will (see: **Luke 24:31**).
- Jesus could be in two places at the same time (see: **Luke 24:34**).

Jesus showed that he was free to be present at any time and in any place as he chose to be. This is a profound **mystery**.

Before his ascension, Jesus promised his disciples, '**I will be with you, always.**' **(Matthew 28:30)**. Our Church teaches that Jesus has kept this promise. Jesus is present **today** whenever his followers come together in his name to celebrate **the sacraments**.

LIGHT THE WAY

> **REMEMBER!**
> The word **sacrament** means '**a holy mystery**'.
> **A sacrament** is a communal ritual. In it, Catholics recall and re-enact the life, death and resurrection of Jesus Christ and receive God's grace.

The Catholic Church teaches that there are **seven** sacraments. All seven were established by Jesus himself while he was here on Earth.

We divide the sacraments into three groups:

1. The sacraments of initiation

These are **Baptism**, **Confirmation** and **Eucharist**.

In these sacraments:
- ☐ You are accepted as a full member of the Catholic Church.
- ☐ You are given the grace needed to grow in goodness by following the example set by Jesus Christ.

The sacrament of Baptism.

2. The sacraments of vocation

These are **Holy Orders** and **Matrimony**.

In these sacraments, you are called to serve God and others by playing a specific role or performing a particular ministry in your community.

The sacrament of Matrimony.

3. The sacraments of healing

These are **Reconciliation** and **Anointing of the Sick**.

In these sacraments:
- ☐ Your sins are forgiven once you are genuinely sorry.
- ☐ You receive the grace you need to cope with suffering.
- ☐ You are prepared for the end of your earthly life before you begin your final journey into eternal life.

Did You Know?
The sacraments of Baptism, Confirmation and Holy Orders can be received **only once**. Holy Orders means to be ordained a deacon / priest / bishop.

In each of the seven sacraments we celebrate the presence of Jesus Christ in the key moments of our lives. For example:

Key moment in life	The sacrament that marks it
1. When you are born.	Baptism
2. When you pass from childhood into adulthood.	Confirmation
3. When you share with others and contribute to your community.	Eucharist
4. When you are ordained a priest/bishop.	Holy Orders
5. When you choose to get married and have a family.	Matrimony
6. When you admit your sins and ask to be forgiven.	Reconciliation
7. When you experience suffering or healing, or are preparing for death.	Anointing of the Sick

The Celebration of Faith SECTION E

In each sacrament, Jesus touches our lives through the words, gestures and material objects used such as bread and wine, oil and water.

Did You Know?

When Catholics participate in the seven sacraments, they give a commitment to make the presence of Jesus known to others by the way they live their lives.

However, you must be prepared to receive the sacraments. God's grace may be blocked from working if you are not open to receiving it. For a sacrament to be effective, you must have faith in it.

SPOTLIGHT ON: THE MASS – A CATHOLIC EXPLAINS

The sacrament of the Eucharist.

1. Meaning

The Sacrament of the Eucharist is the most important ritual of the Catholic Church. It should be the focal point of every Catholic's life.

> **REMEMBER!**
> The word '**eucharist**' means '**thanksgiving**'. In the Sacrament of the Eucharist, Catholics unite as a community to give thanks to God.

When Catholics talk about the Sacrament of the Eucharist, they usually refer to it as **the Mass**.

Did You Know?

Until quite recently, the Mass was celebrated in Latin only. The final words of the priest were '**Ite, missa est**', meaning: '**Go, the Eucharist is ended**'. In time, the entire ritual became known as '**the Missa**'. It is from this that we get the English name '**the Mass**'.

2. Origins

The Mass has its origins in the words and actions of Jesus Christ at **the Last Supper**.

Did You Know?

The Last Supper was the meal Jesus shared with his disciples on Holy Thursday evening.

It was during the Last Supper that the following happened:

> The Lord Jesus took some bread and thanked God for it and broke it, and he said, **'This is my body, which is for you, do this as a memorial of me.'**
>
> In the same way he took the cup after supper and said, **'This cup is the new covenant in my blood. Whenever you drink it, do this as a memorial of me.'**
>
> **First Letter to the Corinthians 11:24–25**

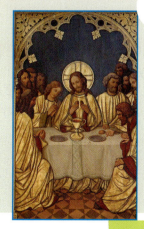

321

LIGHT THE WAY

Ever since, Christians have regularly gathered together just as Jesus asked them. They have repeated the words and actions of Jesus on that first Holy Thursday evening as they share bread and wine. In time, this gathering became known as **the Eucharist**.

The Eucharist is called **a memorial meal** because:

- It recalls and makes present **now** the actions of Jesus at the Last Supper 2,000 years ago.
- It reminds Catholics that Jesus is still with them as they face new challenges today.

3. The structure of the Mass

Since the 2nd century CE, the Mass has had four parts. We shall examine each in turn:

A. The Introductory rites

These prepare you for worship. They include:
1. The Entrance Procession.
2. The Greeting.
3. The Penitential Rite (i.e. The Confession of Sins).
4. The Gloria (i.e. The Glory be to the Father…).
5. The Opening Prayer.

In the Penitential Rite, you ask God and your fellow Catholics for forgiveness. If you have committed a mortal sin (i.e. a very serious and harmful act) you may attend Mass but you may not receive Holy Communion. You must receive the Sacrament of Reconciliation first.

B. The Liturgy of the Word

This includes:
1. The First Reading (Taken from **the Old Testament**).
2. The Responsorial Psalm
3. The Second Reading (Taken from **the New Testament**).
4. The Gospel Acclamation.
5. The Reading of **the Gospel**.
6. The Homily (i.e. the Sermon).
7. The Nicene Creed.
8. The Prayers of the Faithful.

God speaks to you when verses from the Bible are read aloud during the Mass. The priest's homily should explain these readings and say how the message they contain can be applied to your life.

C. The Liturgy of the Eucharist

This includes:
1. The Presentation of the Gifts.
2. The Eucharistic Prayer
3. The Our Father.
4. The Rite of Peace.
5. Holy Communion.

322

The Celebration of Faith **SECTION E**

Catholics believe that, during the Eucharistic Prayer, a miracle occurs. At a moment called **the Consecration**, the priest calls the Holy Spirit to come down upon the gifts of bread and wine. Then he says the very words Jesus used at the Last Supper over the bread and wine. At this point the following happens:

- The bread ceases to be bread and becomes **the body of Jesus**.
- The wine ceases to be wine and becomes **the blood of Jesus**.

Catholics call this the doctrine of **transubstantiation**.

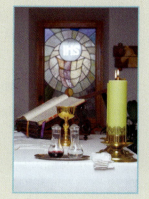

> **REMEMBER!**
> **Transubstantiation** means that the body and blood, soul and divinity of Jesus are really and truly present under the appearance of bread and wine.

This is the essential difference between the Eucharist and the other six sacraments. The other six sacraments communicate **the grace** (i.e. strengthening love) of Christ. However, **the Eucharist contains Jesus himself**.

This means that, when Catholics receive **the Holy Communion** (i.e. the consecrated bread) during the Mass, they receive the gift of the risen Jesus himself.

D. The Concluding Rites

These include:
1. The Final Blessing in the name of the Trinity.
2. The Dismissal (i.e. sending out) in the peace of Christ to love one another.

When you receive Holy Communion, you make a commitment to go out from the Mass and show how much difference your faith in Jesus really makes in your life.

4. The role of the bishop and the priest

Only a bishop or a priest (i.e. an ordained person) can **preside** at the Mass.

Why? Because bishops and priests have received **the Sacrament of Holy Orders**.

> **REMEMBER!**
> **To preside** means to lead the community in worship.

Did You Know?

Through **the Sacrament of Holy Orders**, the bishop/priest is given power by the Holy Spirit to act **'in persona Christi'** (i.e. to fulfil the role of Jesus Christ himself in the sacraments).

This is why only a bishop or a priest can consecrate the bread and wine during the Mass.

LIGHT THE WAY

However, the Mass is a **communal** act of worship. This means that when Catholics gather in the name of Jesus Christ, **all** of them (clergy and laity) share in the celebration of the Eucharist.

5. The participation of the laity

Many forms of contemporary popular entertainment, such as cinema and television, simply ask us to sit back, relax and enjoy the experience. They make no demands on us. They ask us to be **passive**.

> **REMEMBER!**
> **To participate** in worship means to play an active role in it.

All members of **the laity** (i.e. non-ordained Catholics) are called to **participate** in the Mass. We can do this in the following ways:

A. By preparing

You are expected **to fast** (i.e. not consume any food or liquid save water) for one hour before Mass. Also, you should arrive in time **before** the Mass is due to begin. You should read the missalette to become familiar with the theme of the Mass.

B. By listening

If you respect someone, you show this by paying attention when he/she is talking to you. This kind of **active** listening is an essential part of any relationship between people who care for one another. As Catholics, we are expected to pay attention to the readings at Mass. Not only out of courtesy to the person speaking, but because we have respect for the source of these readings, namely **God**.

We are asked to use our imaginations to bring Bible stories to life. For example, we try to picture what it would have been like to witness some important event in the life of Jesus. We can reflect on the meaning of a reading and think about how we can apply its message to our own lives today.

C. By reciting

At various moments in the Mass, we are asked **to recite** (i.e. say aloud) certain prayers, such as the Our Father, or **to respond to** others, as in the Prayers of the Faithful. We are also expected to think about what the prayer means.

D. By performing a ministry

We can perform any of the following kinds of **ministry** (i.e. roles):
- Prepare the altar with linen, candles and flowers before the Mass begins.
- Play a musical instrument.
- Sing in the choir.
- Act as a Minister of the Word, i.e. read a passage from the Bible.
- Act as a Minister of the Eucharist, i.e. distribute Holy Communion.
- Collect the money needed to run the parish.

The Celebration of Faith — SECTION E

E. By receiving Holy Communion

Full participation in the Mass means that you must **receive Holy Communion**. This means consuming the body of Jesus under the appearance of bread and, sometimes, the blood of Jesus under the appearance of wine.

As Catholics, we believe that Jesus is **really present** in the Eucharist. When we receive the Eucharist, we believe that we are receiving spiritual nourishment. This strengthens our faith in God.

ACTIVITIES

1. Wordsearch

Find the following words:

God
Supreme
Mystery
Insight
Worship
Private
Public
Personal
Sacred
Ritual
Symbol
Gesture
Mandir
Synagogue
Vihara
Church
Mosque
Respect
Grace
Sacrament
Initiation
Vocation
Healing

```
R H U T W R B N I P U B L I C
Y B L C C R I O N R I D N A M
V S Y E Y I Q I I G O T J Z H
D C K P U T B T T O R J I C W
K M O S Q U E A I I E I R K Q
I T N E M A R C A S E U J S E
G N I R L L G O T X H Z Y M W
S O S X L N D V I C O N E S O
D A L I I A P D O G A R Y A R
G N C L G R N K N G P M G R S
F R A R I H F O O U B B O A H
O E A V E U T G S O R I D H I
H Y A C F D U W L R S G A I P
L T G H E E M Y S T E R Y V K
E R U T S E G E P S W P W O C
```

325

LIGHT THE WAY

2. Say what it means!

(a) God is _____

_____ .

(b) Worship is _____

_____

_____ .

(c) A religious ritual is _____

_____ .

(d) Grace is _____

_____

(e) A sacrament is _____

_____ .

(f) Transubstantiation means _____

_____

_____ .

3. Match them!

Match each place of worship listed in column **B** with the correct religion in column **A**. Fill in your answers in the spaces provided.

A. Religion	B. Place of Worship
Hinduism	A mosque
Judaism	A vihara
Buddhism	A church
Christianity	A synagogue
Islam	A mandir

A. Religion	B. Place of Worship
Hinduism	
Judaism	
Buddhism	
Christianity	
Islam	

The Celebration of Faith   SECTION E

4. Crossword

Across
1. This word means 'a holy mystery'.
3. This word means 'thanksgiving'.
4. To say aloud.
6. When a Catholic enters a church and bends the right knee toward the Blessed Sacrament before sitting down.
8. This type of Christian worship is altar-centred.
9. The worship of anyone or anything other than God.
10. To lead the community in worship.
11. Something so vast and complex that it is beyond our capacity to ever fully figure out and solve.
12. Worshipping God with others.
15. To play an active role in worship.

Down
2. At this moment during the Eucharistic prayer, the priest calls the Holy Spirit to come down upon the gifts of bread and wine to transform them into the body and blood of Jesus Christ.
5. Worshipping God on your own.
6. Christians believe that it is only when God gives this to us that we can cope with all the challenges, problems and opportunities life presents.
7. To call God this means that no one is as great as or greater than God (2 words: 7, 6).
13. Someone or something worthy of your total respect.
14. If you are a Catholic, by taking part in the seven sacraments, you give a commitment to make his presence known to others by the way you live your life.

LIGHT THE WAY

5. Match them!

Match each explanation in column **B** with the correct gesture listed in column **A.** Fill in your answers in the spaces provided.

A. Christian gesture	B. Meaning
Kneeling	You want to be a peacemaker.
Standing	You recognise God's greatness and worship only God.
Blessing	You believe that Jesus rose from the dead.
Shaking hands	By tracing the symbol of the cross you identify yourself as a Christian.

A. Christian gesture	B. Meaning
Kneeling	
Standing	
Blessing	
Shaking hands	

6. Decide where they belong!

Unscramble each of the following names. Then match each one to the type of sacrament to which it belongs.

	SACRAMENT
I N M O R C I N T A O F	
T I N G A O N I N F O H E T K I S C	
C I O T A I I R C L N E O N	
I R Y M A M N O T	
S T H U E I R A C	
M P A T S I B	
Y H O L D R O R S E	

(a) The sacraments of initiation are: _____

(b) The sacraments of vocation are: _____

(c) The sacraments of healing are: _____

The Celebration of Faith SECTION E

7. Match them!

Match each life event in column **B** with the correct sacrament listed in column **A**. Fill in your answers in the spaces provided.

A. SACRAMENT	B. MOMENT IN LIFE IT MARKS
Baptism	When you choose to get married and have a family.
Confirmation	When you experience suffering or healing, or are preparing for death.
Eucharist	When you are born.
Holy Orders	When you admit your sins and ask to be forgiven.
Matrimony	When you share with others and contribute to your community.
Reconciliation	When you pass from childhood into adulthood.
Anointing of the Sick	When you are ordained a priest/bishop.

A. SACRAMENT	B. MOMENT IN LIFE IT MARKS
Baptism	
Confirmation	
Eucharist	
Holy Orders	
Matrimony	
Reconciliation	
Anointing of the Sick	

8. Think about it!

(a) Which of the seven sacraments can be received only once?
(b) How is a Catholic expected to prepare for the Mass?
(c) Why may only a Catholic bishop or priest preside at the Mass?
(d) What does it mean to say that '**the mass is a communal act of worship**'?
(e) Identify four kinds of ministry by which a member of the Catholic laity can play an active role in the Mass.
(f) For a Catholic, what does **full participation** in the Mass involve?

LIGHT THE WAY

CHAPTER 4   THE LITURGICAL YEAR

Times of Significance

Minute follows minute, hour follows hour as time flows steadily forward. As far as we can tell, we are the only creatures on Earth that are aware of the passage of time. Only human beings can remember what has happened in the past and imagine what might happen in the future.

We do not fully understand what time is. We know that we cannot change time, but we can **measure** it.

Our ancient ancestors learned how to measure time: first by dividing it into day and night, then into months by observing the phases of the moon and later into years by tracking the cycles of the seasons. In this way, they invented **the calendar**.

> **REMEMBER!**
> **The calendar** is our way of organising the year. We divide it up into days, weeks and months.

The first calendars were drawn up around 2,400 BCE by the Babylonians and the Egyptians. They helped them decide when to plant seeds and when to harvest their crops. The current, internationally recognised calendar is known as **the Gregorian calendar**. It was drawn up by **Pope Gregory XIII** and first introduced in 1582.

We are so used to the idea of the calendar that we can easily overlook its importance. For example, **the school calendar** allows you to plan for and structure the year ahead. It lets you know:

- When each term begins and ends.
- When parent-teacher meetings will be held.
- When the annual sports day will take place.
- When you will sit your examinations.

The calendar can also be used to serve another function. It allows us to mark **times of significance** in our lives.

> **REMEMBER!**
> **Times of significance** are days where we celebrate or recall important events in our lives.

For example, we use the calendar to remind ourselves to celebrate a happy occasion such as **a birthday** or **an anniversary**, and to recall a sad occasion such as **bereavement** (i.e. the loss of a loved one).

Similarly, nations use the calendar to remember important moments in their history. For example:

- Americans celebrate the birth of their nation on **Independence Day**, 4 July, each year.
- French citizens celebrate the birth of their modern state on **Bastille Day**, every 14 July.

330

The Celebration of Faith SECTION E

SPOTLIGHT ON: THE NATIONAL DAY OF COMMEMORATION

Our **National Day of Commemoration** takes place on the Sunday nearest to 11 July. It is attended by all the key political figures in the Republic of Ireland – the President, Taoiseach, members of the cabinet and the Oireachtas. The venue for it is the Royal Hospital in Kilmainham, Dublin.

The purpose of this event is to recall the sacrifice of all those Irish men and women who lost their lives in past conflicts. This includes all those who gave their lives in the cause of national liberation, those who died fighting in either of the two world wars, and those who were killed while serving overseas on United Nations' peacekeeping missions.

President Michael D. Higgins at the National Day of Commemoration, 2014.

The proceedings begin with a multi-faith service. This is led by representatives of the different religions – Christian, Jewish and Muslim. Each one takes a turn to offer a prayer, give a reading or lead in the singing of a hymn. Then wreaths are laid as a mark of respect and there is a fly-past salute by the Air Corps.

Times of Religious Significance

Just like individuals and nations, so too the world's religions use a calendar to mark out particular times each year that are important to them.

> REMEMBER!
> **Times of religious significance** can be either:
> - **Religious festivals** – when you celebrate important events in the story of your religion, e.g. Passover for Jews or Easter for Christians.
> - **Periods of preparation** – when you fast and pray before a festival begins, e.g. Lent for Christians or Ramadan for Muslims.

Times of religious significance play an important role in the life of every community of faith. How?

- They reinforce your sense of belonging to a particular religious tradition that is united by shared beliefs, e.g. being a Catholic in Christianity or being a Sunni in Islam.
- They recall the example of the founder. This can inspire you to put your beliefs into practice in your daily life.
- They concentrate your mind on the greatness of God. This encourages you to look to the future with hope.

331

LIGHT THE WAY

The Meaning of the Liturgical Year

Every religion has its own calendar. The Christian calendar is known as **the Liturgical Year**.

> **REMEMBER!**
> **The Liturgical Year** (also called **the Church Year**) is the way in which Christians recall and celebrate the key events in the life of Jesus Christ at different times during the year.
>
> The Liturgical Year does three things:
> - It commemorates the important events in the life of Jesus Christ **in the past**.
> - It celebrates the mystery of Jesus Christ living in his Church **in the present**.
> - It prepares Christians for the return of Jesus Christ **in the future**.

> **Did You Know?**
> All through the Liturgical Year, special place is given to **Sunday**. Sunday is the first day of the Christian week. It is also called **the Lord's Day**.

The Structure of the Liturgical Year

The Liturgical Year is divided into **seasons**.

The seasons of the Liturgical Year followed by Catholics, Orthodox and Anglicans are:

> **REMEMBER!**
> **A season** is a specific length of time. Each season contains times of religious significance.

- **Advent** – A time of preparation for Christmas.
- **Christmas** – The celebration of the birth of Jesus Christ.
- **Ordinary Time** – A time to reflect on Jesus's message about the Kingdom of God.
- **Lent** – A time of preparation for Easter.
- **Easter** – The celebration of the resurrection of Jesus Christ.

The secular calendar begins on 1 January. However, the Liturgical Year begins on the fourth Sunday before Christmas with the season of **Advent**.

> **Did You Know?**
> The Orthodox tradition celebrates the festivals of Christmas and Easter about thirteen days **after** other Christians. This is because the Orthodox tradition uses the older **Julian calendar**, whereas the rest of Christianity follows **the Gregorian calendar**.

The Celebration of Faith   SECTION E

SPOTLIGHT ON: THE SEASONS OF THE LITURGICAL YEAR

1. Advent

During Advent, Christians are called to prepare for the celebration of Jesus's birth. They can do this by:
- Thinking about the direction their lives are taking.
- Asking for God's forgiveness.
- Forgiving one another.

One of the customs associated with Advent is making an **Advent Wreath**. Each part of it has a specific meaning.

An Advent Wreath.

- **The Advent wreath** is circular and made of **flat, evergreen branches** to represent Christian belief in an everlasting God and everlasting life.
- **The holly with thorns and red berries** recalls the suffering that Jesus had to endure.
- **There are five candles.** Four are red or purple with a central white candle, which represents purity. The other four candles represent hope, peace, love and joy.
- **The candle flame** is a symbol of Jesus. Christians believe Jesus is 'the Light of the World'.
- **The ribbons** are purple to remind Christians that Advent is a time of preparation.

One candle is lit on each of the four Sundays in Advent. The fifth and final candle is lit during Midnight Mass on Christmas Eve to mark the coming of Jesus Christ.

2. Christmas

For Christians, Christmas is second in importance only to the annual celebration of Easter. The name '**Christmas**' is a contraction of '**Christ's Mass**', i.e. the Mass held to celebrate this event.

Did You Know?

The actual date for Jesus's birth is not known. Our current date for celebrating Christmas was not fixed until 350 CE, when Pope Julius I proclaimed 25 December as Jesus's birthday. Until then, this date had been used to mark the birth of Rome's sun god.

The main feasts within the Christmas season are:

A. Christmas Day – This begins with a Vigil Mass held after 6pm on Christmas Eve. On this feast day, Christians celebrate the mystery of **the Incarnation** (i.e. the belief that God became a human being in Jesus Christ).

333

LIGHT THE WAY

B. The Epiphany – This is celebrated on 6 January. It recalls the visit of **the Magi** (i.e. the Wise Men) to the infant Jesus.

C. The Baptism of the Lord – This feast day draws the Christmas season to a close. It is celebrated on the Sunday after the Epiphany.

Actions of Religious Significance at Christmas

Exchanging gifts
This could have its origin in any of three sources:
(a) The Magi's gifts to the infant Jesus.
(b) The practice of giving food and clothing to the poor begun by **St Nicholas of Myra** to honour the birth of Jesus.
(c) Early Christians who adopted the Roman custom of exchanging gifts at the beginning of each New Year.

Placing a lighted candle in a window on Christmas Eve
Lighting a candle decorated with holly and putting it in your window is an old custom in Ireland. It is intended to remind Christians that, on the very first Christmas, Mary and Joseph could not find a room to stay in Bethlehem. The lighted candle shows that today's Christians want to welcome Jesus Christ into their lives.

Did You Know?

The practice of displaying **a crib** containing the infant Jesus in a manger surrounded by Mary, Joseph and other figures was begun by St Francis of Assisi in 1223.
The practice of cutting down small trees, putting them in your home and decorating them with candles and fruit began in Germany during the 15th century. However, the practice of putting up a **Christmas tree** in your home did not spread to Ireland until the 19th century.

3. Ordinary Time

Ordinary Time refers to anytime during the Liturgical Year that is **outside** the seasons of Advent, Christmas, Lent and Easter.
Ordinary Time covers about 60 per cent of the Liturgical Year. It is divided into two periods:
- The first between the seasons of Christmas and Lent.
- The second between the seasons of Easter and the next Advent.

During Ordinary Time, the Gospel readings during the Mass focus on Jesus's teaching about the Kingdom of God – through the parables he told and the miracles he worked.

4. Lent

The name **Lent** comes from an Old English word meaning '**lengthen**'. This may have been because Lent takes place in the spring, when the hours of daylight grow longer.
Lent begins on **Ash Wednesday**. On this day, Catholics mark their foreheads with ashes in the shape of the cross. This is done to remind them that, without God's sustaining power, we would all be nothing more than ashes. Lent ends on **Holy Thursday** morning in Holy Week.

During Lent, Christians prepare for the celebration of Easter. Lent lasts for forty days, not including the six Sundays that fall within it. The number **forty** has a religious significance because **Jesus** spent forty days and nights fasting and praying before starting his public ministry.

In many countries, the day before Lent begins is called **'Shrove Tuesday'**. Traditionally, this was the day when Christians confessed their sins and asked to be forgiven before Lent began.

Lent is a time of preparation for the celebration of Easter. During it, Christians should:

- **Fast** – Give up certain luxury items such as chocolate.
- **Pray** – Set aside time each day to pray and become more aware of the presence of God in their lives.
- **Do good works** – Do something positive and creative to help other people, e.g. do **the Trócaire Lenten Fast** to raise funds for overseas development projects.

SPOTLIGHT ON: THE WORK OF TRÓCAIRE

- **Trócaire** is an Irish word meaning **'compassion'**.
- Trócaire is a charitable organisation. It is the official overseas development agency of the Catholic Church in Ireland.
- Trócaire has two aims:
  1. **Abroad**: To give whatever help that is within its resources to areas of the greatest need among the developing nations.
  2. **At home**: In Ireland, Trócaire works with schools and communities to raise awareness of problems affecting people in countries around the world.
- Trócaire's largest fundraising event is the annual Lenten fast.
- Trócaire works in countries in Africa, Asia, Latin America and the Middle East.
- Trócaire's programmes focus on:
  1. Supporting people in developing nations to build a reliable and sustainable way of life.
  2. Responding to refugee crises and natural disasters.
  3. Supporting human rights.
  4. Addressing the HIV/AIDS crisis.
  5. Supporting gender equality.
  6. Improving literacy levels.
- Trócaire works with people in need, regardless of their gender, nationality, race or religion.

5. Easter

Easter is the oldest Christian festival. It was celebrated as early as the 2nd century CE.

The origin of the name '**Easter**' is uncertain. **Bede the Venerable** said that the name comes from **Eastre**. She was an ancient pre-Christian goddess. Her festival was held each year at the spring equinox.

Easter is the most important Christian festival. It is the foundation of the whole Church Year. Why? Because all the other events in Jesus's life, from his Conception to his Ascension are important only because he rose from the dead on Easter Sunday morning.

Did You Know?

Unlike Christmas, which has a set date, Easter is **a moveable feast**. This means that Easter is not always held on the same date each year.
Easter is celebrated on a Sunday between 22 March and 25 April. This was decided by **the Council of Nicaea** in 325 CE. It said that:

> 'Easter must be celebrated on the first Sunday after the first full moon following the spring equinox.'

Since the moon circles the Earth in a 28-day cycle, the date of Easter changes from year to year.

Easter is divided into two parts:

1. **The Easter Triduum**

    This begins on Holy Thursday evening and ends on Easter Sunday evening.

2. **The Easter Season**

    This begins on Easter Sunday evening and lasts for fifty days. It includes two major feasts:

    (a) **The Ascension** on the seventh Sunday after Easter.

    (b) **Pentecost** on the fiftieth day after Easter Sunday. This is the last day of the Easter Season.

Did You Know?

Though not as commercialised as Christmas, Easter is closely linked in the minds of most children with chocolate eggs. **The egg** has long been associated with festivals held at this time of year. Even before Christianity, the egg was regarded as a symbol of new life associated with spring.
However, in medieval times, the egg took on a new meaning as it represented Jesus's rising from the hard shell of his stone tomb to a new and glorified life. Also, eggs were especially enjoyed during Easter because Christians were forbidden to eat them during the Lenten fast.

The Celebration of Faith   SECTION E

ACTIVITIES

1. Say what it means!

(a) Times of significance are _____

_____ .

(b) Times of religious significance can be either (i) _____

_____

or (ii) _____

_____ .

(c) The Liturgical Year is _____

_____

_____ .

2. Crossword!

Across

3. This is the name of the current, internationally recognised calendar.
5. A period of preparation for Muslims.
6. An Irish word meaning 'compassion'.
10. The loss of a loved one.
14. A specific length of time. Each one contains times of religious significance.
16. Celebrated on the fiftieth day after Easter Sunday. This is the last day of the Easter Season.
17. Unlike Christmas, this festival is a moveable feast.

Down

1. Our way of organising the year, by dividing it up into days, weeks and months.
2. The belief that God became a human being in Jesus Christ.
4. A time to reflect on Jesus's message about the Kingdom of God.
7. A time of preparation for Christmas.
8. A time of preparation for Easter.
9. The first day of the Christian week.
11. The name of an ancient pre-Christian goddess whose festival was held each year at the Spring Equinox.
12. In medieval times, this food item took on a new meaning, as it represented Jesus's resurrection from the hard shell of his stone tomb.
13. To give up certain luxury items such as chocolate.
15. This is celebrated on 6 January. It recalls the visit of the Magi (i.e. the Wise Men) to the infant Jesus.

LIGHT THE WAY

3. Fill in the missing words!

1. **The Advent wreath**

   (a) The ring of _____ symbolises the Christian belief in _____

   _____.

   (b) The holly with _____ and red berries recalls the _____ that Jesus had to endure.

   (c) The white candle in the centre represents _____.

   (d) The other four candles represent _____ .

   (e) The candle flame is a symbol of _____.

   (f) The ribbons are _____ to remind Christians that Advent is a time of _____.

2. **The exchange of gifts**

   This traditional practice could have its origin in any of three sources:

   (a) The gifts given by the _____to the infant _____.

   (b) The practice of giving food and clothing to the _____ begun by St _____ to honour the birth of Jesus.

   (c) Early Christians who adapted the _____ custom of exchanging gifts at the beginning of each _____.

4. Tick the box!

In each of the following, say whether it is **true** or **false**.

	True	False
1. We fully understand what time is.		
2. The first calendars were drawn up around 2,400 BCE by the Babylonians and the Egyptians.		
3. French citizens celebrate the birth of their nation on Independence Day, 14 July, each year.		
4. Ireland's National Day of Commemoration is held on the Sunday nearest to 11 July.		
5. Religious festivals celebrate important events in the story of a religion.		
6. The Christian calendar is known as the Liturgical Year.		
7. The Liturgical Year prepares Christians for the return of Jesus Christ in the future.		
8. Sunday is the last day of the Christian week.		
9. The Liturgical Year begins on the fourth Sunday before Christmas with the season of Advent.		
10. The Orthodox tradition celebrates the festivals of Christmas and Easter about thirteen days after other Christians.		
11. The Orthodox tradition uses the Gregorian calendar.		
12. Catholics and Anglicans use the Julian calendar.		
13. The name 'Christmas' is a contraction of 'Christ's Mass'.		
14. The date for celebrating Christmas was not fixed until 350 CE, when Pope Francis proclaimed 25 December as Jesus's birthday.		

The Celebration of Faith   SECTION E

	True	False
15. Christmas begins with a Vigil Mass held after six o'clock on Christmas Day.		
16. The Baptism of the Lord is the feast that draws the Christmas season to a close.		
17. The practice of displaying a crib with the infant Jesus in a manger was begun by St Francis of Assisi in 1223.		
18. Ordinary Time covers about 50 per cent of the Church Year.		
19. Lent begins on Holy Thursday morning.		
20. On the day Lent begins, Catholics mark their foreheads with ashes in the shape of the cross.		
21. Jesus spent forty days and nights fasting and praying before starting his public ministry.		
22. The day before Lent begins is called 'Shrove Tuesday'.		
23. Trócaire is the official overseas development agency of the Catholic Church in Ireland.		
24. Trócaire's largest fundraising event is the annual Advent fast.		
25. Easter must be celebrated on the first Sunday after the first full moon following the autumn equinox.		
26. The Easter Triduum begins on Holy Thursday evening and ends on Easter Sunday evening.		

5. Think about it!

(a) What do Catholics remind themselves of when they mark their foreheads with ashes in the shape of the cross on Ash Wednesday?

(b) Why is Easter the most important Christian festival?

LIGHT THE WAY

CHAPTER 5   PILGRIMAGE

Places of Religious Significance

Think about the following places:

- **Ajodhya, India** – Hindus believe that this is the birthplace of the god Rama.
- **The Western Wall, Jerusalem, Israel** – This is the only remaining part of the great Temple complex where the ancient Jews worshipped God.
- **The Temple of the Tooth, Kandy, Sri Lanka** – This contains a relic of Buddhism's founder, Siddhartha Gautama.
- **The Church of the Holy Sepulchre, Jerusalem, Israel** – This is built on the site of the crucifixion, burial and resurrection of Jesus Christ.
- **The Mosque at Madinah, Saudi Arabia** – This contains the tomb of the prophet Muhammad.

The Western Wall, Jerusalem.

The Temple of the Tooth, Sri Lanka

Each of these is **a place of religious significance**.

> REMEMBER!
> **A place of religious significance** is somewhere important to the members of a particular religion.

> REMEMBER!
> **A sacred site** is a place where people feel especially close to God.

A place of religious significance is also called **a sacred site**.

This does **not** mean that God is only present at sacred sites. On the contrary, God is **everywhere**.

The purpose of calling a particular place **'sacred'** is to remind us that:

- The whole world is God's gift to us.
- We should **not** take this gift for granted.
- We have a duty to treat this world with respect.

Sacred sites can be found dotted across the globe. Many of these have become places of **pilgrimage**.

The Celebration of Faith SECTION E

The Meaning of Pilgrimage

> **REMEMBER!**
> **A pilgrimage** is a spiritual journey made to a place of religious significance.
> **A pilgrim** is someone who goes on a pilgrimage.

A pilgrimage can be undertaken either by a pilgrim travelling alone or as a member of a guided group.

Why Go on Pilgrimage?

Joanie Hess is a retired nurse and a lifelong Catholic. She has unfinished business. Fifty years ago, her 14-year-old brother, Anthony, disappeared one Saturday afternoon. She will never forget the date: 15 October. He had just finished deliveries on his newspaper route in Tacony, Philadelphia. He stopped by home briefly, before going out again on his bike at 3:30 p.m. to meet his best friend. However, he never arrived. Neither he nor his belongings were ever found. Local police simply listed him as a runaway.

His sister is convinced that this is something he would not have done – he would never have run out on either his family or his best friend. She is convinced that he was abducted.

As Anthony's body was never found, no funeral Mass was ever said for him. Anthony's disappearance has haunted her and her family all these years. She accepts that he is dead, but she dreads **how** he died. Going on **pilgrimage** is Joan's way of saying goodbye to him.

Did You Know?

Christians go on pilgrimage for many reasons:
- To thank God for all the good things in their lives.
- To ask God for guidance before making an important decision.
- To ask God for the strength needed to face a major crisis or loss in their lives.
- To ask God's forgiveness for their sins.
- To revitalise their religious faith.
- To celebrate a major religious festival associated with a sacred site.
- To build bonds of friendship with other pilgrims.

However, if you want to reap the spiritual benefits of completing a pilgrimage, you must prepare before setting out on it.

If you are a Catholic, you should receive **the Sacrament of Reconciliation** (i.e. confess your sins to a priest). This shows that you want to put your sins behind you and to renew your relationship with God and other people.

This is necessary because:
- It helps you to focus your mind on the meaning and importance of what you are about to do.
- It reminds you to treat everyone you meet during your pilgrimage with respect.

341

LIGHT THE WAY

Did You Know?

In most religions, going on pilgrimage is a matter of personal choice. Islam is the only world religion that makes it **compulsory** for its members to go on **the Hajj** (i.e. the pilgrimage to Makkah). Muslims must complete the Hajj at least once in their lives.

Becoming a Place of Christian Pilgrimage

A place may become a Christian pilgrimage site for any of the following reasons:

- It may be somewhere associated with the life of **Jesus**, such as Bethlehem.
- It may be where **an apparition** (i.e. appearance) of **Mary** the Mother of Jesus is said to have occurred, such as Knock in County Mayo.
- It may be where people have been miraculously cured from serious illness, such as the grotto in Lourdes, France.
- It may be where **a saint** (i.e. holy man or holy woman) is buried, such as the tomb of St Thomas á Becket at Canterbury, England.
- It may be connected with some important event in the life of a saint, such as Croagh Patrick in County Mayo, where St Patrick fasted and prayed.

Croagh Patrick, Co. Mayo.

Usually, these places of pilgrimage contain **a shrine**.

> **REMEMBER!**
> **A shrine** is a monument that commemorates an important religious person or event.

Places of Christian Pilgrimage

There are many Christian pilgrimage sites dotted across the world. Here we will look at only a few of them.

SPOTLIGHT ON: THE HOLY LAND

For Christians, the holiest places on Earth are those in the Middle East that are closely associated with the story of their founder, **Jesus Christ**. Together, these places make up the area known as **the Holy Land**. Since the earliest days of Christianity, pilgrims have been attracted here by the opportunity to retrace Jesus's footsteps from his birth in Bethlehem to his death and resurrection in Jerusalem.

342

The Celebration of Faith   SECTION E

> **Did You Know?**
> Christians say they are '**pilgrims**' in two senses of the word:
> **Firstly** – As people who choose to go on a journey to a sacred site.
> **Secondly** – As people who must remember that life itself is a great journey. How this journey ends in the afterlife is decided by how well they have followed the example Jesus set.

The three most important pilgrimage sites in the Holy Land are:

1. Bethlehem

This is where **the Church of the Nativity** stands at the end of Manger Square. This church was built over what is believed to be the birthplace of Jesus Christ. Pilgrims follow a flight of steps which leads them down to a grotto below ground level. Here is an altar with a silver star set into the floor in front of it. This is said to mark the place where Jesus was born.

2. Nazareth

Here we find **the Basilica of the Annunciation**. It commemorates the Archangel Gabriel's message to Mary that she had been chosen by God to be the mother of the messiah.

The Basilica of the Annunciation, Nazareth.

3. Jerusalem

The most important site here is **the Via Dolorosa** ('the Street of Sorrows'). This is the route Jesus took as he was forced to carry his cross from Pontius Pilate's residence to his place of execution at Golgotha, just outside the old city walls.

Since medieval times, pilgrims have stopped at fourteen points along the Via Dolorosa for readings, prayers and meditation. Eventually, this pilgrim ritual formed the basis for what is now called **the Stations of the Cross**.

At the end of the Via Dolorosa is **the Church of the Holy Sepulchre**. This contains both the site of Jesus's crucifixion and the tomb in which he was buried. **St Helena**, the mother of the Emperor Constantine, had a church built here after her first pilgrimage to the Holy Land in 326 CE. The present building is usually crammed to capacity on Easter Sunday morning when Christians celebrate the resurrection of Jesus.

The third station on Via Dolorosa, Jerusalem.

Jerusalem is unlike other pilgrimage sites in the Holy Land because it is a sacred place for **three** religions. For Jews and Christians, Jerusalem is the holiest place on earth. For Muslims, Jerusalem is the third holiest place on earth (after Makkah and Madinah).

> **Did You Know?**
> The name '**Jerusalem**' comes from the Hebrew words *ir shalom*, which mean '**City of Peace**'.

343

LIGHT THE WAY

SPOTLIGHT ON: THE CITY OF ROME

This was where **St Peter** and **St Paul** were martyred. Peter was the first leader of the Christian community. His successors were given the title **'pope'**. The popes have lived in Rome ever since, except for a few brief periods in exile. The current Pope is named **Francis**. He is the first South American cardinal to be elected to the papacy.

The headquarters of the Catholic Church are located in **the Vatican**. This is an independent city-state near the centre of Rome. The Vatican covers an area slightly less than a hundred acres. It is the smallest country on Earth. It has a population of only one thousand people. Huge crowds of Catholics flock to the Vatican each week to attend one of the pope's public audiences and to receive his blessing.

Three particular locations draw the largest numbers of pilgrims throughout the year:

1. St Peter's Basilica

Dominating Vatican Square, this massive church stands on the site of St Peter's crucifixion and burial. It is the largest church in the world and covers more than 163,000 square feet. Designed by some of the greatest architects of the Renaissance, it took 176 years to complete (from 1450 to 1626).

St Peter's Basilica, Rome.

2. The Catacombs

Rome has many **catacombs** (i.e. underground tombs). These tombs were carved out of rock to provide burial places for the inhabitants of ancient Rome. Christians buried their dead here too. Some of the Christian tombs, especially those of martyrs and popes, contain paintings and inscriptions. Today, pilgrims visit them to honour the memory of the Christian martyrs who are buried there.

3. The Sistine Chapel

In 1473, **Giovanni de Dolci** was commissioned by **Pope Sixtus IV** to build the Sistine Chapel. He completed it in 1481. Today, visitors can marvel at the magnificent frescos that cover its walls and ceiling. These famous artworks within the Sistine Chapel were commissioned by **Pope Julius II** and painted by **Michelangelo Buonarotti**.

It is said that Michelangelo painted standing up on a huge scaffold, a small paint brush held above his head, for hours on end, limbs straining in concentration and effort. Other times, he painted lying on his back in a tight space, shoulders and arms wracked with severe cramp from long hours spent in the one position. Often, paint dripped onto his face and irritated his eyes.

Sistine Chapel ceiling painting.

Through freezing winters and scorching summers, Michelangelo kept at this work. For a month at a time, he slept in his clothes, often not leaving the chapel. In the long hot days of summer, he often painted non-stop for up to seventeen hours a day, pausing only to take a sip of wine and a mouthful of food to

The Celebration of Faith SECTION E

sustain him. Finally, after four exhausting years, the work was completed. The result was one of the greatest artistic masterpieces of all time.

No photograph does justice to the finished product. Michelangelo painted nine scenes taken from **the Old Testament**. Each painting was inspired by an important Bible story. He painted scenes inspired by **the Old Testament Book of Genesis**. These include: *The Creation of Light*, *The Creation of Stars and Planets* and *The Creation of Adam*. In all, Michelangelo covered the ceiling with over 300 separate, detailed portraits of men and women, as well as every kind of animal.

Twenty-five years after painting its ceiling, Michelangelo returned to the Sistine Chapel to paint another masterpiece: *The Last Judgment*. This fresco, painted on the wall behind the altar, took four years to complete. It depicts the Second Coming of Jesus Christ and the final judgement of humanity on the Last Day. It contains 390 figures surrounding the risen Christ, who dominates this stunning work of art.

Those who have been fortunate enough to stand in the Sistine Chapel and gaze at its paintings for themselves often claim that the people and creatures Michelangelo painted look so real that they seem to breathe.

SPOTLIGHT ON: THE CAMINO DE SANTIAGO

In recent years, **the tomb of St James at the Catholic cathedral of Santiago de Compostela** has become one of Europe's most popular shrines. Every year, about a quarter of a million people follow the medieval pilgrim route, known as **the Camino de Santiago**.

During the busiest pilgrimage years, in the 11th and 12th centuries, over a million people per year walked the Camino de Santiago. This was at a time when the entire population of Europe numbered no more than 50 million people.

Some of the trails for the Camino route date from as early as the 9th century CE.

Santiago de Compostela Cathedral.

There is no such thing as an 'official' start of the Camino. There are many possible routes to choose from. However, most people prefer to hike **the Camino Frances**. This route begins in St Jean Pied-de-Port or Roncesvalles at the foot of the Pyrenees Mountains in Southern France. It is the most heavily travelled and the most thoroughly networked with hostels, cafés and churches.

Did You Know?

The Camino de Santiago means 'the way of St James'. Usually, pilgrims just refer to it simply as 'the Camino'. It is a system of walking trails established, from the 9th century onwards, from points all over Europe. All of them converge on the tomb of St James the Apostle in the cathedral at Santiago de Compostela in western Spain.

LIGHT THE WAY

From St Jean, it is 800 kilometres (500 miles) to Santiago de Compostela. In other words, about two and a half million footsteps. You begin by making the passage through the mountains into northern Spain.

Usually, to complete the entire Camino you need a month. You need to walk an average of 25km (15 miles) per day to cover the distance.

There is no set way to walk the Camino. Everyone is free to do it as they see fit. There is no authority in charge of the Camino. You're on your own. You can start it and leave it at any point you wish. Since there are many options for stopovers along the route, you make your own choice, depending on your health and fitness. Some people choose to complete the Camino in stages: a section each year, starting the succeeding year at whatever point they left off the year before. You have to think things through, listen to your body and reach out to other people if and when you need to. Also, be sure to take account of the weather conditions and the distances you must travel.

The Camino could never be described as easy. The terrain is varied, both mountainous and flat, rocky and smooth. You pass through vineyards, meadows, towns, cities, forests and parks. You walk along highways, farm roads and canal towpaths.

Everyone walks at their own pace. Distance is often determined by injuries, particularly blisters, tendinitis and falls. Some pilgrims may need to stopover at a hotel for several days while they heal.

Clearly, long before you set out on the Camino, you need to prepare. This is an experience to be enjoyed, not endured. So, train to build your endurance. An average day on the Camino is 15 miles. Many people in reasonable shape can walk for 15 miles. But you must walk 15 miles every day for a month. Proper preparation avoids much unnecessary pain and disappointment.

Days on the Camino soon acquire a rhythm. You walk from early morning into the afternoon.

Also, it is advisable to learn some Spanish. In major cities, most people employed in services speak English, but there are far fewer English speakers in rural parts of Spain.

Veterans of the Camino recommend that you travel as lightly as possible. Only carry essentials, limiting your total belongings, including the backpack itself, to about 10 per cent of your bodyweight. Pack only two sets of clothes (shorts and shirts) because you can wash and dry one set of clothes each night and put on the other set. Rotating your clothes minimizes the weight in your pack.

Days on the Camino soon acquire a rhythm. You walk from early morning into the afternoon. Upon arriving in whatever town you choose to stay for the night, you must find a place to stay.

Accommodation varies widely in size and quality. In many smaller towns, there is **an albergue** (i.e. hostel), usually run by either the local council or the local parish. They differ in quality. Pilgrims are early risers, so hostels close their doors at 10 p.m. You must leave before 8 a.m. the following morning so that the building can be prepared for the next set of pilgrims. In larger towns, there are privately owned hostels and hotels.

Your basic packing list should include: clothes, toiletries, a journal, first-aid kit and survival goods (needle and thread, matches, etc.), a rain poncho, torch, compass, a towel and a sleep sack.

In the summertime, a full sleeping bag is not necessary. You can travel with just a silk sleep sack. They're light to carry and help protect you against bedbugs. However, it's always best to check a mattress thoroughly before putting your belongings on it.

The Celebration of Faith   SECTION E

Many pilgrims choose to switch their mobile phones off. Otherwise, they'd miss the experience of getting away from all the noise and bustle of everyday life, which is supposed to be a key part of the whole experience of going on pilgrimage. However, many use places with Wi-Fi access to periodically post messages on Facebook to let loved ones know that they are still alive and well.

All those following the Camino are expected to develop an attitude of charity and service towards one another. Perhaps this is helped by the fact that everyone is in the same boat: away from computers, telephones, work and other distractions. Also, because you travel light, you are stripped of your pretensions and worldly status. You may meet and befriend people from very different backgrounds than your own. Furthermore, almost everyone encounters similar hardships on route. You may help one another overcome difficulties you encounter. As a result, pilgrims become close in a way that's hard to put into words.

Some pilgrims have remarked that, as they walk along the same paths trodden by millions of pilgrims before them, they have a strong sense of being carried along.

Some people prefer to walk the whole way in the company of others. Some opt to walk the route alone. They may want to spend time alone with God and rejoice in the beauty of the landscape because they so rarely have any time to do so in their daily life back home. Most choose to alternate, spending some time alone and some time with others. The Camino is both a personal and a shared experience.

Water is available from fountains all along the Camino. The water in the hostels is generally safe for refilling bottles. However, this trek can be a challenge for vegetarians. Most traditional Spanish foods involve meat, such as: *pulpo* (octopus sautéed in olive oil and paprika) or *morcilla* (a spicy, dark blood sausage).

Although it is by no means exclusive to people of faith, the Camino is essentially a Catholic spiritual activity. Pilgrims are encouraged to perform **actions of religious significance** as they journey towards the tomb of St James at Santiago de Compostela.

> **REMEMBER!**
> **An action of religious significance** is something you do to show that:
> - You have faith in God.
> - You know that you are at a sacred site.

These actions include stopping at churches along the route either to participate in the Mass or just to say a prayer before continuing on. Some pilgrims have remarked that, as they walk the same paths trodden by millions of pilgrims before them, they have a strong sense of being carried along. It is as if they are journeying along a river of deep, ancient faith and tradition.

The landscape of northern Spain is quite spectacular. Much of the Camino passes through less industrialised areas, so that this pilgrimage becomes your entry point into a quieter, slower and more peaceful way of life.

Pilgrims who return home afterwards often experience culture shock. Once more you are surrounded by the sound and fury of our modern technological society. However, the great value of the Camino is that it gives you an opportunity to think about who you are, why you do what you do and where your life is going.

As one person who completed this pilgrimage put it, **'The Camino is pure medicine. It heals many hurts of the heart and the soul. Contact with nature does much good. When we are in harmony with nature and others, we feel better.'**

Did You Know?

Anyone interested can join **the Camino Facebook page**, which has thousands of members. Most of them are seasoned veterans, and some have written books about their experiences of it. You can ask questions and get answers from people who know what they're talking about.

LIGHT THE WAY

SPOTLIGHT ON: THE MARIAN SHRINE AT LOURDES

The grotto at Lourdes

Each year huge numbers of Catholic pilgrims flock to one or other of the many **Marian shrines** around the world.

> **REMEMBER!**
> **A Marian shrine** is a place that celebrates the role played by **Mary**, the mother of Jesus Christ, in the story of Christianity.

In terms of specifically Catholic places of pilgrimage, about 80 per cent of them are dedicated to '**Our Lady**' (as Catholics have traditionally called Mary). Many of these places have become centres of pilgrimage, because it is believed that Mary herself actually appeared there.

Did You Know?

Despite the respect shown for Mary at these shrines, pilgrims do not pray to Mary. Instead, they pray to Jesus Christ. The purpose of a pilgrimage to a Marian shrine is, first and foremost, to help the pilgrim develop a closer relationship with Jesus.
Further, Catholics are not expected to believe in any of the apparitions of Mary. They are free to accept them or not.

Lourdes, a town situated near the Pyrenees in southern France, is one of the most famous Marian shrines. However, it only became a place of pilgrimage in the mid-19th century. It is claimed that on 11 February 1858, a 14-year-old girl named **Bernadette Soubirous** witnessed the first in a series of eighteen **apparitions** (i.e. appearances) of Mary. These apparitions are said to have taken place over a six-month period in a little grotto, just outside Lourdes.

During the ninth apparition, Mary is said to have told Bernadette to dig at a certain place in the grotto. From that spot a previously unknown spring of water began to flow. Ever since, there have been stories of miraculous healings associated with this spring.

The local Catholic bishop investigated Bernadette's story and the reports of miraculous healings at Lourdes. After examining all the evidence, he concluded that the reports of apparitions were genuine. As a result, Lourdes was officially approved as a pilgrimage site for Catholics in 1862. Bernadette Soubirous was later **canonised** by **Pope Pius XI** in 1933.

> **REMEMBER!**
> **To be canonised** means to be officially declared **a saint** by the Catholic Church.
> **A saint** is a holy man or holy woman who has lived a life of exemplary goodness.

Today, large numbers of pilgrims visit Lourdes each year. Some of them are terminally ill and come in hope of being miraculously cured.

Each evening during the pilgrimage season, thousands of pilgrims take part in a torch-lit procession through the streets of Lourdes. Most walk, but those who cannot are guided through the streets in wheelchairs by volunteer helpers.

Although a huge basilica was built at Lourdes in the late 19th century, the number of pilgrims grew so large that it was decided to build a new, underground church. This was consecrated

The Celebration of Faith   SECTION E

on the one hundredth anniversary of the apparitions in 1958. It can hold up to 20,000 pilgrims at a time.

The highlight of the pilgrimage is a visit to **the grotto**, where those who are ill can bathe in its spring waters. There have been many stories of miraculous healings at Lourdes. However, out of the reported 5,000 cures, only **2 per cent** have actually been declared miracles by the Catholic Church. Perhaps the most famous of these is the story of **Gabriel Gargam**.

Basilica Lourdes

The Miraculous Healing of Gabriel Gargam

In December 1899, the train on which Gabriel Gargam was a passenger collided with another train. The force of this impact led Gargam to be thrown 52 feet from his carriage. He was left severely injured and paralysed from the waist down.

After eight months Gargam had wasted away to little more than a skeleton. He weighed only 78 pounds. His feet became gangrenous. He could take no solid food and had to take nourishment through a tube. He was brought to Lourdes in this terribly feeble condition.

Gargam was carried to the grotto and placed in its waters. However, all this exertion proved too much for him. It caused him to lose consciousness. It seemed that Gargam had died. So a sheet was placed over his body, and a Catholic priest said a blessing over him.

However, soon afterwards, there was movement from under the sheet. To the amazement of bystanders, Gargam raised himself up into a sitting position. While his family were looking on dumbfounded and spectators gazed in amazement, Gargam said, in a full, strong voice, that he wanted to get up.

The onlookers assumed that he was in a state of delirium before death. They tried to soothe him, but Gargam could not be restrained. He got up and stood straight. He walked a few paces and said that he was cured. On 20 August 1901, sixty prominent doctors examined Gabriel Gargam and said that he was entirely healed.

Adapted from: Body and Spirit, by Patrick Collins (Columba Press).

Like Gabriel Gargam, anyone who claims to have been healed after visiting Lourdes is asked to undergo a series of medical examinations. These are carried out by independent medical experts. Only when these experts are satisfied will a cure be declared **miraculous**.

However, many ill people have **not** been physically cured after making a pilgrimage to Lourdes. Despite this, most of them still say that the whole experience of going on pilgrimage was worthwhile. They say that, through God's grace, they received the courage and strength needed to cope with their illness. This brought them closer to God and helped them find a peace that had eluded them before.

Did You Know?

For a healing to be declared **miraculous** by the Catholic Church, seven conditions must be met:
- The illness suffered was serious.
- There was undeniable evidence that the person had really suffered from it.
- All other treatments of this illness had been tried and failed.
- The cure was complete.
- The cure was rapid.
- The cure was lasting.
- There is no known scientific explanation for this cure.

LIGHT THE WAY

ACTIVITIES

1. Wordsearch
Find the following words:

Sacred
Pilgrimage
Shrine
Holy Land
Bethlehem
Nazareth
Jerusalem
Via Dolorosa
Holy Sepulchre
Vatican
Catacombs
Sistine Chapel
Camino
St James
Lourdes
Mary
Bernadette
Canonised
Saint
Grotto
Miracle

M	V	F	N	M	G	S	P	D	W	B	V	E	S	S
M	X	I	A	A	T	R	E	L	E	N	R	V	B	A
P	E	R	A	J	Z	S	O	R	V	H	I	A	M	I
E	Y	L	A	D	I	A	N	T	C	H	P	T	O	N
E	L	M	A	N	O	A	R	L	T	E	I	I	C	T
P	E	C	O	S	D	L	U	E	N	O	L	C	A	D
S	U	N	A	E	U	P	O	I	T	X	G	A	T	E
P	A	Z	T	R	E	R	R	R	A	H	R	N	A	R
C	D	T	N	S	I	H	E	T	O	N	I	S	C	C
S	E	K	Y	B	S	M	Q	J	N	S	M	T	A	A
H	O	L	Y	L	A	N	D	F	S	F	A	O	D	S
R	O	M	E	H	E	L	H	T	E	B	G	R	P	Z
H	M	M	Q	S	E	D	R	U	O	L	E	P	S	T
S	I	S	T	I	N	E	C	H	A	P	E	L	Z	J
G	V	E	Y	F	Z	C	A	M	I	N	O	S	C	K

2. Say what it means!

(a) A place of religious significance is _____

_____ .

(b) A sacred site is _____

_____ .

(c) A pilgrimage is _____

_____

(d) An action of religious significance is _____

_____

_____

_____

350

3. Crossword

Across
3. The town where the Basilica of the Annunciation stands.
4. The mother of Emperor Constantine and saint who had the first Church of the Holy Sepulchre built in the 4th century.
7. It means 'an appearance'.
11. Hindus believe that this is the birthplace of the god Rama.
13. A monument that commemorates an important religious person or event.
14. The name given to the route Jesus took through Jerusalem as he was forced to carry his cross from Pilate's residence to his place of execution (2 words: 3, 8).

Down
1. The town where the Church of the Nativity stands.
2. Its name means 'city of peace'.
4. The name of the church in Jerusalem built on the site of Jesus's crucifixion, burial and resurrection (2 words: 4, 9).
5. The name of the prophet who is buried at the mosque in Madinah, Saudi Arabia.
6. Name given by Christians to the area in the Middle East containing places closely associated with events in the life of Jesus Christ (2 words: 4, 4).
8. The relic of Siddhartha Gautama that is contained in the temple at Kandy in Sri Lanka.
9. Someone who goes on a pilgrimage.
10. The only remaining wall of the Jewish Temple complex that once stood in Jerusalem.
12. The pilgrimage to Makkah that is compulsory for Muslims at least once in their lives.

LIGHT THE WAY

4. True or False!

In each of the following, say whether it is **true** or **false**.

		True	False
1.	A pilgrimage is a journey you must make on your own.		
2.	The name Via Dolorosa means 'Street of Sorrows'.		
3.	The Church of the Holy Sepulchre contains the site of Jesus's birth.		
4.	Jerusalem is a sacred site to two religions: Hinduism and Buddhism.		
5.	The headquarters of the Catholic Church is located in Lourdes.		
6.	Saint Peter was appointed by Jesus to be the first leader of the Christian community.		
7.	The title given to the leader of the Catholic Church is 'Pope'.		
8.	The Vatican is the smallest country on Earth.		
9.	The Catacombs are underground tombs in Jerusalem.		
10.	Pope Sixtus IV commissioned Michelangelo to paint the ceiling of the Sistine Chapel.		
11.	The fresco painted behind the altar of the Sistine Chapel is called The Last Judgment.		
12.	The Camino de Santiago translates as 'the Way of St John'.		
13.	The Catholic sacrament in which you confess your sins to a priest is called reconciliation.		
14.	A Marian shrine is one that celebrates the role played by Mary Magdalene in the story of Christianity.		
15.	Lourdes is a town situated near the Pyrenees in southern France.		
16.	The person to whom Mary is said to have appeared to in Lourdes was named Gabriel Gargam.		
17.	A holy man or holy woman who has lived a life of exemplary goodness is called a saint.		
18.	To be canonised means to be officially declared a pope by the Catholic Church.		
19.	Pilgrims who are ill visit the grotto in Lourdes to bathe in its waters.		
20.	All of the reported 5,000 cures at Lourdes have been declared a miracle by the Catholic Church.		

352

The Celebration of Faith   SECTION E

5. Fill in the missing words!

A.   Reasons why a site becomes a place of Christian pilgrimage
A place may become a Christian pilgrimage site for any of the following reasons:
1.   It may be associated with the life of _____.
2.   It may be where an apparition of _____ is said to have occurred.
3.   It may be where people have been miraculously _____ from serious _____.
4.   It may be where a saint is _____.

B.   Reasons why Christians go on pilgrimage
1.   To thank _____ for all the _____ things in their lives.
2.   To ask God for _____ before making an important _____.
3.   To ask God for the _____ needed to face a major _____.
4.   To ask God's _____ for their sins.
5.   To _____ their religious faith.
6.   To celebrate a major religious _____ associated with a sacred site.
7.   To build bonds of _____ with other pilgrims.

C.   The seven conditions that must be met before a healing can be declared miraculous by the Catholic Church
1.   The illness was _____.
2.   There was undeniable _____ that the person had really _____ from this illness.
3.   All other treatments of this illness had been tried and _____.
4.   The cure was _____.
5.   The cure was _____.
6.   The cure was _____.
7.   There is no known _____ for this cure.

6. Think about it!

(a) What is the purpose of calling a particular place 'sacred'?
(b) Why have Christians been attracted to going on pilgrimage to the Holy Land?
(c) Why has the Sistine Chapel become a popular site for pilgrims to Rome?
(d) What are the challenges that pilgrims who walk the Camino de Santiago must face?
(e) What is the attraction for pilgrims of walking the Camino?
(f) Why has Lourdes become a popular place of pilgrimage?
(g) What do some pilgrims, who have not been physically healed, say about the benefits of going on pilgrimage to Lourdes?

353

LIGHT THE WAY

Section F
The Moral Challenge

Chapter 1: Introduction to Morality 356
Chapter 2: Making Moral Decisions 369
Chapter 3: Sin and Forgiveness 384
Chapter 4: Stewardship 394
Chapter 5: The Afterlife 404

CHAPTER 1   INTRODUCTION TO MORALITY

A Father and Daughter Make a Stand

Today, millions of children around the world have no access to education, no chance to learn how to read and write. This situation is particularly serious in Pakistan, where it is estimated that fewer than half of the country's children complete primary level education.

Difficult as things are for boys, it is even worse for girls. Most girls are prevented from getting an education, partly due to poverty but largely due to prevailing social attitudes. Many men fear that women will become empowered and too independent if they receive an education. So, many parents prefer to marry their daughters off early. Almost a quarter of all girls in rural Pakistan are married before the age of eighteen. Even where parents allow their daughters to attend school, most only permit them to do so at primary level.

Ziauddin Yousafzai saw what was happening in his homeland. One-fifth of the population was living below the poverty line. This situation could not improve unless people were educated. So, he made **a choice**.

Malala Yousafzai with her father Ziauddin on the day she won the Nobel Peace Prize, 10 October 2014.

> **REMEMBER!**
> **A choice** is a decision either to do or not to do something.

Yousafzai chose to set up a school to give both boys and girls a chance to receive an education to equip them for life in the 21st century. He opened this school in Mingora, a town in the green and mountainous area of Swat in northern Pakistan. Within a few years one of the school's star pupils was Ziauddin Yousafzai's own daughter, **Malala**.

Malala Yousafzai was born in Mingora on 12 July 1997. From the outset her father and mother, Thorpekai, encouraged her to think for herself.

Mingora was a popular tourist destination, known for its colourful summer festivals. However, all that changed when **the Taliban** tried to take control of the region.

> **REMEMBER!**
> **The Taliban** is an ultra-conservative political and religious movement that first emerged among Muslims in central and southern Afghanistan in the early 1990s.

After years of fighting in Afghanistan, the Taliban decided to extend their power into the heartland of neighbouring Pakistan. By 2005, they had begun terrorising the people of the Swat valley. Assassinations of opponents, the flogging or beheading of those the Taliban branded 'criminals' and suicide bomb attacks on crowded market places became grim everyday occurrences. To speak out against the Taliban was to sign your own death warrant. However, this is exactly what Ziauddin Yousafzai chose to do. He was one of only a handful of local activists who openly did so. He tirelessly tried to rally locals to oppose the Taliban's atrocities.

Although a determined effort by the Pakistani army in 2009 pushed the main Taliban forces back into the mountains of northwest Pakistan, some elements of the Taliban remained to wage a vicious guerrilla campaign in the Swat valley. In particular, they began attacking girls' schools.

In 2009, at the invitation of the BBC, Malala began writing a daily blog about being a young girl living under the Taliban's threat to deny her **human right** to an education.

The Moral Challenge SECTION F

> **REMEMBER!**
> **Human rights** are those things you are entitled to because you are a human being. You need them in order to live a free and full life.

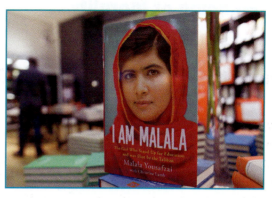

Malala Yousafzai's autobiography, *I am Malala*

In order to protect her identity, Malala used the name **Gul Makai** (a Pashto word meaning **cornflower**).

Malala's blog began to attract a lot of attention within Pakistan. Then she gained an international following when the BBC began to translate it into English for the global audience.

However, in 2011, Malala lost her anonymity. Her name was revealed to the world when she was nominated for the International Children's Peace Prize. That same year she was awarded Pakistan's National Youth Peace Prize.

At the age of 14, Malala learned that her outspokenness had not only won many admirers but many enemies too. Mullah Fazlullah, leader of the Pakistani Taliban, had issued a death threat against her. She had openly defied his organisation's ban on female education. Though worried for her own safety, Malala was more worried about her father's life. He had long been a vocal opponent of the Taliban. Also, she and her family did not think that the Taliban would actually try to murder a child. Events would prove otherwise.

On 9 October 2012, while Malala was travelling home from school, a gunman stopped and boarded the bus she was on and demanded to know which girl was Malala. When one of her friends looked at her on reflex, her identity was given away. The man opened fire, hitting her on the left side of her head. Two other girls were also wounded in the attack.

Malala survived the shooting but was left in a critical condition. She was flown to the military hospital in Peshawar, where a part of her skull was removed to relieve the swelling on her brain. When it became clear she needed further treatment unavailable locally, she was transferred by air ambulance to a hospital in Birmingham, England.

Malala underwent several operations, including one to repair a facial nerve that had paralysed the left side of her face. Thankfully, she had suffered no major brain damage. Within six months of the shooting, Malala resumed her studies at a school in Birmingham. However, the Taliban still considers her a target and the very real danger of assassination persists.

Since recovering from her injuries, Malala has continued to speak out on the importance of education and to oppose the Taliban. The European Parliament awarded her the Sakharov Prize for Freedom of Thought, and in 2014 she became the co-recipient of the Nobel Peace Prize.

In her autobiography *I am Malala* (published in 2013), she speaks of her love of books and her belief in their importance. She also speaks of her faith in Allah, whom she believes has chosen books as an important way to transmit his message to us. She is surer now than ever that education is the key to giving women a voice in the world. Education gives you the confidence to stand up for your rights. Malala believes that education provides us with the means to change this world for the better.

Like her father, Malala Yousafzai faced serious choices:

- How should she respond to what the Taliban was doing in her homeland?
- Should she keep her head down and only look after her own self-interest?
- How far should she be willing to go to stand up for what she believed in?

These are the kinds of questions that are dealt with by **morality**.

LIGHT THE WAY

The Meaning of Morality

> **REMEMBER!**
> **Morality** is the set of standards you use to judge whether an action is right or wrong.

Your **morality** guides your choices. Your choices reveal the kind of person you are – whether you are honest or dishonest, selfish or unselfish, trustworthy or untrustworthy.

Actions and Consequences

Morality is concerned with the following kinds of actions:

- Actions that are **free**: Where you are not forced to do one thing or the other.
- Actions that are **deliberate**: Where you are in control of what you are doing.
- Actions that are **informed**: Where you know and understand what it is you are doing.

Think about this example:

> A trained swimmer hears the cries of someone drowning in a river. He chooses to respond to these calls for help. He enters the water and rescues the person in distress.

This action has all three of the characteristics listed above:

- It is **free**: The rescuer chose to do it. No one made him do it.
- It is **deliberate**: The rescuer did not accidentally fall into the river. He chose to enter the water in order to rescue someone in danger of drowning.
- It is **informed**: The rescuer is a trained swimmer. He knew the risks involved in what he was doing.

This action is **good** (i.e. the right thing to do in this situation) because the rescuer saves a human life. Whenever our actions are free, deliberate and informed, we are said to be **responsible** for them.

> **REMEMBER!**
> **Responsible** means that you must answer for what you say or do.

This means that you can be praised or rewarded if you say or do the **right** thing. However, you can also be blamed or punished if you say or do the **wrong** thing.

Different Views of Morality

Morality is important to people everywhere. Sooner or later we all have to face situations that force us to ask '**What should I do?**' However, people often sharply disagree on matters of morality. Think about how people hold opposing views on moral issues such

358

as abortion and war. Some say they can be justified in some circumstances, while others say that they can never be.

One reason for these differences is that we do **not** agree about the standards we should apply when deciding whether an action is right or wrong.

Think about **how** we decide things. We tend to make a choice based on the one or more of the following:

- **Emotion:** how we feel about doing it.
- **Common practice:** if everyone else is doing it.
- **Authority:** if we are ordered or forced to do it.
- **The situation:** if the circumstances seem to demand that we should do it.
- **The consequences:** what we think may happen if we do or do not do it.
- **The law of the state:** whether it is legal or illegal.
- **Our religion:** whether we are faithful to its teachings or not.

It is because morality can be such a complex and confusing area that many people have traditionally turned to one or other of the world's religions for guidance.

Each religion offers advice about how to live a good life. This is why they all agree on **the Golden Rule**.

The Golden Rule

'In everything, do unto others as you would have them do to you'
(Matthew 7:12).

The Golden Rule means three things:
1. We should avoid selfishness.
2. We should respect one another.
3. We should treat one another with compassion.

However, the world's religions do **not** agree on precisely **how** the Golden Rule should be applied. They differ among themselves on issues such as abortion, capital punishment, euthanasia and war. This is why each one has its own **religious moral vision**.

> **REMEMBER!**
> **A religious moral vision** is the particular understanding of right and wrong that each religion has.

The members of a religion are expected to put its religious moral vision into practice through the things they say and do.

LIGHT THE WAY

The Christian Moral Vision

Christians are called to follow the example Jesus set. As a Jew, Jesus based his teachings on **the Ten Commandments** God gave to Moses.

> REMEMBER!
> **The Ten Commandments** are a set of ten short, clear rules about how we should live.

They are as follows:

1. You shall worship the Lord your God, and Him only shall you serve.
2. You shall not take the name of the Lord your God in vain.
3. Remember to keep holy the Sabbath day.
4. Honour your father and your mother.
5. You shall not commit murder.
6. You shall not commit adultery.
7. You shall not steal.
8. You shall not bear false witness against your neighbour.
9. You shall not covet your neighbour's spouse.
10. You shall not covet anything that belongs to your neighbour.

In his preaching, Jesus used the Ten Commandments as **a foundation** on which to build what he called '**the Kingdom of God**'. Jesus called on his followers to adopt a whole new way of relating to people.

When asked to summarise his message, Jesus responded by saying:

Did You Know?

Commandments **1 to 3** say what it means to love God.
Commandments **4 to 10** deal with how we should love and respect one another.

> '**First, you must love the Lord your God with all your heart, with all your soul, with all your mind and with all your strength. Second, you must love your neighbour as yourself.**'
>
> **Mark 12: 29-30.**

Through his example Jesus showed that this meant:
- Loving your enemies
- Caring for the poor
- Welcoming strangers
- Insisting on justice for all.

To follow Jesus's example, you must live a life of **virtue** and avoid **hypocrisy**.

1. Virtue

> **REMEMBER!**
> **Virtue** is a consistent tendency in your character to choose and then do what is good.

If you are **a virtuous person**, you are:

- **Loving**: you only want to help others by what you say and do.
- **Wise**: you have a clear understanding as to how you should live.
- **Prudent**: you always think before speaking and acting. You never knowingly promise more than you can deliver or intend to deliver.
- **Determined**: you resist temptation and have the courage to do what you think is right.
- **Unselfish**: you do the right thing without expectation of reward, even though it may cost you time, money or popularity.

For example:

- A virtuous person would not copy from someone else's homework, no matter how tempting it would be to do so.
- If given too much change in a shop, a virtuous person would return it without hesitation.

A virtuous person is someone who has worked hard to achieve **moral maturity**.

Did You Know?

Catholics believe that you can only become a virtuous person through (a) hard, persistent effort; (b) regular prayer; and (c) receiving the grace God imparts when you participate in the sacraments.

> **REMEMBER!**
> **Moral maturity** is where you accept your responsibilities as a member of your community. You show this by doing the right thing for its own sake.

2. Hypocrisy

The opposite of virtue is **hypocrisy**.

A hypocrite is always ready to deceive others and willing to manipulate them for narrow, personal advantage. Here you only do something good in order to gain popularity and reward, or to avoid punishment.

A hypocrite is someone who wallows in **moral immaturity**.

> **REMEMBER!**
> **Hypocrisy** means pretending to be good in order to get something you want.

> **REMEMBER!**
> **Moral immaturity** is where you not only refuse to accept your responsibilities as a member of your community but also, through your selfishness, cause harm to those around you.

LIGHT THE WAY

The Meaning of Moral Growth

Although physical maturity happens automatically as you grow older, moral maturity **does not**.

Think about how newborn babies have so much growing to do, both **physically** (in body) and **intellectually** (in mind), before they can look after themselves. Until then, they are totally dependent on the kindness of others.

Only gradually do babies learn how to focus their eyes to see. It takes time for their limbs to grow and muscles to harden, for them to learn to sit up and then crawl, before they can finally walk.

As the months pass, babies start to remember things and to recognise people. They learn to make sounds and then to speak. At first, they can say only a word at a time, but later they begin to put words together to make sentences.

> **REMEMBER!**
> **Moral growth** is the way in which you grow into someone who knows right from wrong.

Just as significant as this physical and intellectual growth is your **moral growth**.

The Stages of Moral Growth

Moral growth is **a life-long process**. It happens in a series of stages. Each one represents a step towards achieving **moral maturity**.

Stage 1

Only gradually does a child develop an understanding of right and wrong. At this stage, you begin to realise that your actions have consequences, not only for yourself but for others too. However, you often make the choices you do only because you want to get a reward (e.g. a new toy) or to avoid being punished (e.g. being sent to bed early).

Stage 2

As a child you do not yet make a particular choice solely because you realise that it is the right thing to do in a given set of circumstances. Rather, at this stage, you obey a rule because some **authority figure** (e.g. parent or teacher) says that you must. You obey a rule because you want to get the approval of some authority figure or to avoid their disapproval.

Stage 3

As an adolescent, you should be growing in self-confidence. At this stage, you should start to trust your own judgement more and rely less on that of other people. You should be beginning to see the whole purpose of having rules and obeying them.

Take, for example, a rule that says you should respect other people's property. You ought to realise that this rule should be followed, not simply because it is a rule or because someone in authority says so. Rather, you should follow this rule because:

- You realise it is wrong to steal in the first place.
- You understand the reason for this rule. The peace and harmony needed for community life would be impossible if we did not respect one another's property.

Achieving moral maturity is a life-long struggle. However, it is worth the effort. It makes it possible for us to enjoy loving, lasting and worthwhile **relationships** with others.

The Importance of Relationships

John Donne was the Anglican dean of St Paul's Cathedral in London. One day he heard a church bell tolling for a funeral. Out of curiosity, Donne decided to ask one of the mourners who was being buried that day. Then a thought struck him, and inspired him to write one of the most memorable passages in the English language:

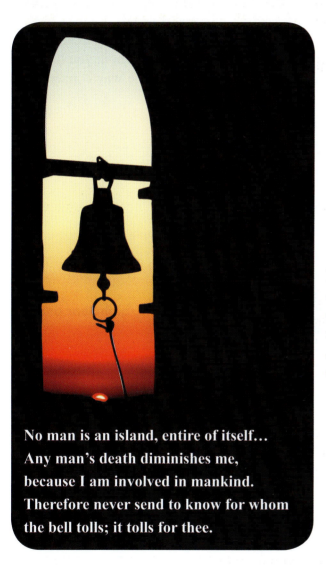

No man is an island, entire of itself… Any man's death diminishes me, because I am involved in mankind. Therefore never send to know for whom the bell tolls; it tolls for thee.

Donne had been powerfully reminded that we are **social** creatures. We cannot live a truly human life on our own. We need to build **relationships** with others.

> REMEMBER!
> **Relationships** are the different ways in which we are connected to one another and involved in each other's lives.

Relationships can exist between one individual and another, between an individual and a group, or between one group and another. Our lives consist of a whole network of relationships that we often take for granted. Just think about how many people you interact with each day and all the different reasons you have for doing so.

The Different Kinds of Relationships

We can identify three different levels at which we connect with one another:

- The interpersonal level.
- The communal level.
- The global level.

Let us look at each one in turn.

LIGHT THE WAY

1. Interpersonal relationships

These are one-to-one relationships. Sometimes they are with people you are close to and know well, such as family and friends. Other times they are with people you know less well. Perhaps you only meet them now and again, such as a neighbour, another student or a bus driver on your route home.

2. Communal relationships

These are relationships you have with groups you belong to. For example:

- A school
- A sports club
- A choir
- A drama society.

3. Global relationships

These are the relationships you have with people in other parts of the world, many of whom you have not met and may never meet. However, although you do not know them, you are in some way connected to them. For example:

- The people who grow and process the food you eat.
- The people who extract and refine the gas or oil you need for fuel.

SPOTLIGHT ON: DRUG ABUSE AND ITS IMPACT ON OUR RELATIONSHIPS

It is easy for us to underestimate the consequences our actions can have on others, both near and far away. This is especially true regarding the use of **illegal drugs**.

> **REMEMBER!**
> **A drug** is any chemical agent that changes how your body works or affects how you feel, think or act.
> **Illegal** means something prohibited by the law of the state.

People from all walks of life use illegal drugs. The most commonly taken are:

- Cannabis
- Cocaine
- Ecstasy
- Hallucinogens
- Heroin.

> **REMEMBER!**
> **Addiction** is when you become dependent on a particular drug.

Sometimes people develop an **addiction** without fully realising what they are getting involved in. However, more often than not, people become addicted **in spite** of knowing how dangerous it is.

The Moral Challenge   SECTION F

The consequences of drug abuse and addiction for your relationships are **serious**. Think about the following:

1. At the personal level

Depending on the particular drug, long-term abuse can cause you serious physical harm (e.g. HIV/AIDS or hepatitis) and/or trigger mental illness (e.g. schizophrenia).

2. At the interpersonal level

As drug abuse causes your life to fall apart, your relationships with family and friends begin to disintegrate too.

Since maintaining a drug habit is very expensive, it often leads an addict into crime. Eventually, you may use violence against anyone – even a family member or friend – in order to get the price of your next fix.

3. At the communal level

Usually, an addict becomes totally self-absorbed. In time, you will be prepared to deal drugs to anyone in any age group to fund your addiction. This spreads the misery of drug abuse throughout your community, affecting the lives of many others for the worse.

As your inhibitions break down, you find it more and more acceptable to commit acts of robbery. A large amount of violent crime is drug-related. So, the circle of suffering now expands and the number of victims of drug abuse increases.

Further, you can put other people's lives at risk if you use illegal drugs while employed in a position of trust, such as a doctor or a nurse, an airline pilot or an air-traffic controller, a bus driver or a train driver.

4. At the global level

The demand for illegal drugs creates a huge, lucrative market. Ruthless criminals compete with one another to control it in order to become rich.

These 'drug barons' form alliances with criminals overseas in places where the drugs are grown and processed for selling. Criminals, both here and overseas, share the vast profits and use their wealth to extend their influence over more and more people.

What starts out with one person's choice to abuse illegal drugs ripples outward to create a vast network of misery at the personal, interpersonal, communal and global levels. Clearly, the choices we make really do matter, often far more than we realise.

LIGHT THE WAY

ACTIVITIES

1. Wordsearch

Find the following words:

Malala
Choice
Taliban
Rights
Morality
Actions
Free
Deliberate
Informed
Responsible
Golden Rule
Commandments
Virtue
Hypocrisy
Maturity
Relationships

F	C	D	X	J	M	A	N	E	D	D	E	T	R	W
K	N	O	G	Y	C	A	M	H	E	J	C	A	E	Q
O	F	K	M	T	S	B	T	L	M	O	I	L	S	C
E	C	R	I	M	G	I	I	U	R	W	O	I	P	Y
C	C	O	E	R	A	B	R	O	R	I	H	B	O	Y
O	N	H	Z	E	E	N	O	C	N	I	C	A	N	T
S	E	L	U	R	N	E	D	L	O	G	T	N	S	I
R	I	J	A	V	N	N	T	M	G	P	Y	Y	I	L
L	S	T	V	I	R	T	U	E	E	D	Y	D	B	A
J	E	N	J	W	H	U	O	M	A	N	S	H	L	R
I	N	F	O	R	M	E	D	C	O	T	T	X	E	O
R	E	L	A	T	I	O	N	S	H	I	P	S	Z	M
U	A	G	V	U	P	D	V	G	A	L	A	L	A	M
C	V	Z	U	F	Y	Q	I	A	V	F	L	V	A	F
E	Y	H	U	K	K	R	H	R	L	T	M	B	W	B

2. Say what it means!

(a) Human rights are _____

_____ .

(b) Morality is _____

_____ .

(c) A religious moral vision is _____

_____

_____ .

(d) Moral maturity is _____

_____ .

(e) Moral immaturity is _____

_____ .

(f) Moral growth is _____

_____ .

(g) Relationships are _____

_____ .

3. Crossword

Across
1. A consistent tendency in your character to choose and do what is good.
3. A type of action where you are in control of what you are doing.
5. A type of action where you are not forced to do one thing or another.
6. A decision either to do or not to do something.
9. This means that you must answer for what you say or do.
10. These are relationships you have with people in other parts of the world, whom you have not met and may never meet.
11. These are relationships you have with groups you belong to.
13. A Pashto word meaning 'cornflower' (2 words: 3, 5).
14. First name of Ziauddin Yousafzai's daughter.
16. When you become dependent on a particular drug.
18. A type of action where you know what it is you are doing.

Down
2. These are one-to-one relationships.
4. An ultraconservative political and religious movement that first emerged among Muslims in Afghanistan in the early 1990s.
7. It means pretending to be good in order to get something you want.
8. It means something prohibited by the law of the state.
12. Fewer than half this country's children complete primary level education.
15. An action that is the right thing to do in a particular situation.
17. Any chemical agent that changes how your body works or affects how you feel, think or act.

LIGHT THE WAY

4. Fill in the missing words!

The Ten Commandments

1. You shall _____ the Lord your God, and Him only shall you _____.
2. You shall not take the _____ of the Lord your God in _____.
3. Remember to keep _____ the _____ day.
4. Honour your _____ and your _____.
5. You shall not commit _____.
6. You shall not commit _____.
7. You shall not _____.
8. You shall not bear _____ _____ against your neighbour.
9. You shall not _____ your neighbour's _____.
10. You shall not _____ anything that _____ to your neighbour.

5. Think about it!

(a) 1. Identify the two most important relationships in your life.
    2. What is it that makes these people so important for your life?
    3. Identify two practical ways you could show your appreciation for them.
(b) Give one reason why a morally mature person would follow the rules of the road.
(c) Read the following statement:
    '**A good person loves people and uses things, while a bad person loves things and uses people.**' What do you think this means? Explain your answer.
(d) Read the following extract:

> ### ONLY ONE LETTER MISSING
>
> Xvxn though this computxr is an old modxl, it works vxry wxll, xxcxpt for only onx kxy. You'd think that with all the othxr kxys working, onx kxy would hardly bx noticxd. But just onx kxy sxxms to ruin thx wholx xffort.
>
> Havx you xvxr said to yoursxlf, 'I'm only onx pxrson. No onx will noticx if I don't do my bxst.' But it doxs makx a diffxrxncx, bxcausx to bx xffxctive, a family, an organisation or a businxss nxxds complxtx participation by xvxryonx to thx bxst of his or hxr ability.
>
> So if you'rx having onx of thosx days whxn you think you just arxn't vxry important and you'rx txmptxd to slack off, rxmxmbxr this old computxr. You arx a kxy pxrson, and whxn you don't do your bxst, nothing xlsx around you works out thx way it's supposxd to.
>
> Adapted from: *Communicating at Work*
> by Ronald Adler, Fourth Edition, © McGraw-Hill,
> New York, 1992.

What point does this writer make about the impact our actions can have on others?
(e) Describe the consequences of **drug abuse** and **addiction** for people's lives at each of the following levels: (i) the personal level; (ii) the interpersonal level; (iii) the communal level; and (iv) the global level.

The Moral Challenge   SECTION F

CHAPTER 2   MAKING MORAL DECISIONS

The Importance of Moral Decisions

Have you ever thought about how many decisions you make in the course of each day? Even answering this question involves making **a decision**.

> **REMEMBER!**
> **A decision** is a choice either to do or not to do something.

Some decisions are important and should involve a great deal of thought, such as: **'Which subjects should I choose to study at third level in order to get a good job?'**

Other decisions are comparatively trivial and require little thought, such as: **'Which television programme will I watch?'**

The most important decisions we have to make are **moral decisions**.

> **REMEMBER!**
> **A moral decision** involves making a choice about what is the right or the wrong thing to do in a particular situation.

The moral decisions we make are based on **the values** we hold.

The Meaning of Values

In September 2013, a 62-year-old Brazilian businessman named **Chiquinho Scarpa** announced on his Facebook page that he had decided to bury his most prized possession – his £310,000 Bentley Continental Flying Spur convertible – in the backyard of his mansion in the wealthy Jardins neighbourhood of São Paulo. He said that he had been inspired to do so by a documentary he had seen on the pharaohs of ancient Egypt. Like them, he would bury his wealth in order to enjoy it in the afterlife. Scarpa scheduled his car's funeral for 20 September 2013 and, to great publicity, had a digger excavate a hole large enough to bury the car.

Scarpa drew severe criticism for what most people saw as a selfish act. People asked why he would not raffle the car and then donate the proceeds to some worthwhile cause. Surely he could put such wealth to a more constructive use?

However, things were not as they seemed. On the day he was supposed to lower his Bentley to its final resting place, Scarpa held a press conference and made this announcement:

'I have not buried my car, but everyone thought it was absurd when I said I'd do it. What is absurd is to bury your body, which can save many lives. Nothing is more valuable. Be a donor, tell your family.'

So, as it turns out, Scarpa had pulled off an ingenious publicity stunt to promote **organ donation**.

> **REMEMBER!**
> **Organ donation** involves giving doctors permission to have some of your healthy vital organs removed after you have died and given to those in need of transplants.

LIGHT THE WAY

Scarpa wanted to get people thinking about how they could do something to help others, even after death. He believed that only something as bizarre as threatening to bury an expensive car could get many people to stop and think about the **values** they hold.

Sometimes, when you hear someone ask, '**What is its value?**' you know that they are talking about **the price** of some item. For example, the '**value**' of a house refers to the actual sum of money it would fetch if put up for sale on the open market.

However, when we talk about '**value**' in the context of morality, we mean something different.

> **REMEMBER!**
> **A value** is anyone or anything that you think is good, desirable, important or worthwhile.

Your values and your actions are closely intertwined. Think about it:

- Your values influence the choices you make.
- The actions that flow from these choices reveal the values you hold.

Now read the following story:

SPOTLIGHT ON: LEONA HELMSLEY

By the 1980s, Leona Helmsley and her husband Harry had built up a fortune estimated at its peak to be around $5 billion. They owned the landmark Empire State Building in New York, as well as a huge chain of hotels. They flew everywhere in their own 100-seat private jet. When her husband became ill, Leona took over the day-to-day running of their empire. For this she was praised on the covers of glossy magazines as an unparalleled businesswoman.

Leona Helmsley getting into her car after leaving Federal Court, where she was tried for tax evasion in 1989.

However, those who worked for Leona Helmsley had a very different view of her. They called her '**the Queen of Mean**'. Why? Because of her casual cruelty towards her employees and for how she took every opportunity to mock those she called 'little people'. Also, despite her fabulous wealth, she was notoriously penny-pinching, always looking for a way to squeeze a bigger profit out of even the most trivial thing. For instance, she would frequently charge shoes she had bought herself to the company's accounts, wear them, then take them back to the shop where she had bought them and demand a refund.

It was her desire to save every possible expense on rebuilding her fabulous mansion that led to her downfall. *The New York Post* revealed that she had falsely tried to pass off the refurbishment of her private dwelling as a tax-exempt business cost.

Leona Helmsley was arrested and charged with tax evasion. At her trial in 1989, her own words came back to haunt her. The jury heard how she had told her housekeeper that:

'We don't pay taxes. Only the little people pay taxes.'

Leona Helmsley was found guilty and sentenced to eighteen months in jail.

When the judge came to hand out her sentence he said that her conduct had been **'the product of naked greed. You persisted in the arrogant belief that you were above the law.'**

> **REMEMBER!**
> **A law** is a rule set out by state authorities that all its citizens are obliged to obey.

Through what she said and did, Leona Helmsley revealed to the world the kind of person she was. The same is true for each one of us. The values we hold say a great deal about the kind of people we are, whether we are:

- Honest or dishonest
- Generous or selfish
- Compassionate or hard-hearted
- Courageous or cowardly.

Think about the following examples:

- If you are a doctor who values her patients' lives, you will do your utmost to care for their health.
- If you are a clergyman who values his parishioners, you will set a good example for them to follow.
- If you are an athlete who values his fitness, you will eat properly, abstain from alcohol, avoid illegal drugs and train hard to maintain your fitness.
- If you are a singer who values her voice, you will follow a lifestyle that protects it from harm.

The Sources of our Values

Values are **learned** through a process called **socialisation**.

> **REMEMBER!**
> **To learn** means to gain the knowledge and skills you need to function as a member of society.
> **Socialisation** is the way in which you learn what is meant by right and wrong, and develop the ability to tell one from the other.

Socialisation usually happens in the following ways:

- You follow the example of people you respect and trust.
- You learn '**the hard way**', i.e. from the consequences of your **own** actions.
- You learn from the consequences of **other** people's actions.
- You accept the rules laid down by those in authority over you, e.g. parents/guardians, teachers and so on.

Through socialisation, you develop your **own** set of values.

However, you also need to be aware of the ways in which many different **sources** can and do continue to influence your values.

> **REMEMBER!**
> **The sources of your values** are those things that influence your standards of right and wrong.

It is always important to ask yourself whether or not each of these sources acts as a force for good in your life.

371

LIGHT THE WAY

At certain times in your life, some of these sources can have a greater influence on you than others. Think about the following:

1. Your family

This is the first community you belong to. Here you begin learning how to treat others. For example, you should learn that it is good to share, to tell the truth and treat people with compassion and respect.

2. Your friends

Genuine friendships, particularly those with your **peers** (i.e. those of the same age as yourself), can help you to grow in self-confidence. They can encourage you to become a good listener, able to give as well as to receive and someone who is a trustworthy friend.

3. Your school

School authorities set rules to provide a safe environment in which you can develop your own particular talents. The aim here is to help you enter adult life as a mature, responsible individual.

4. Your religion

This offers you insights into life's great mysteries. It can have a big impact on your whole outlook on life. It offers you a set of values to guide you when faced with difficult moral choices.

5. The mass media

Here we are talking about the cinema, internet, radio, television and so on. What you see, hear and read can influence your worldview, your thoughts and actions – for better or for worse. So you need to think hard about the ideas that some in the mass media might want you to accept and act upon.

6. The state

Through its laws the state sets limits on your behaviour. If something is **legal** it is allowed, but if something is **illegal** it is not allowed.

All too often, people decide whether an action is right or wrong purely on the basis of whether it is legal or illegal. However, it does **not** automatically follow that if something is legal it is right, or that if it is illegal it is wrong.

The test of every law is whether it seeks to defend **the common good**.

> **REMEMBER!**
> **The common good** is whatever is in the best interest of the community as a whole.

The Moral Challenge   SECTION F

Making a Moral Decision

The only real test of your values – that is, what you really believe is right and wrong – comes when you are faced with a moral decision.

SP🔆TLIGHT ON: THE UNABOMBER

In 1995, **David Kaczynski** was the assistant director of the Equinox shelter for runaway and homeless youths in Albany, New York. The 20th of September that year is a date seared into his memory. That was the day his wife Linda asked him to read a pamphlet that had been published the previous day by *The New York Times*. It was a lengthy manifesto setting out the beliefs of **the Unabomber**.

> **Did You Know?**
>
> **The Unabomber** was the name given by US Federal agents to an elusive domestic terrorist. Over a period of 17 years, he used sophisticated home-made explosive devices to wage a postal bomb campaign against people working in America's airlines and universities. Unabomber was an acronym for **university**, **airline** and **bomber**.

By 1995 the Unabomber had killed three people and had horribly injured two dozen more. *The New York Times* had agreed to print his 35,000-word manifesto only because the Unabomber promised to halt his attacks if it did so.

As David Kaczynski read down through the Unabomber's lengthy rant against the modern world, he noticed certain phrases and forms of expression that seemed all too familiar. He could not shake off the sinking feeling that the author of this hate-filled document was none other than his older brother **Ted**.

David had not seen his brother in person for several years. Ted had a genius-level IQ. He had a brilliant grasp of mathematics and engineering. However, Ted had always found it difficult to fit in anywhere and had become more and more withdrawn. Finally, he had decided to become a hermit, living alone in a cabin he had built in the wilderness near Lincoln, Montana. He only communicated with David by letter.

David re-read his brother's letters to him. Like the Unabomber's manifesto, these letters were full of anger and bitterness about the advance of technology into every crevice of modern life. His brother had professed to him the very same extreme ideas that had driven the Unabomber to kill and maim the innocent.

David Kaczynski, right, brother of the Unabomber, and Gary Wright, a Unabomber victim, speak to students in a school in New York.

Yet, this was his brother. The same person who had always looked out for him when they were growing up. The person with whom he had shared a love of wildlife and the outdoors. David hoped he was wrong. But what if he wasn't?

David realised that he could not just sit back and do nothing. Too many people had already suffered. What if the Unabomber broke his word and struck again? How could he live with himself, knowing that he could have done something to prevent another death? And yet, if he did turn his brother in, Ted could receive the death penalty for his crimes. How could he turn upon his own brother and, perhaps, bring about his death?

After spending weeks agonising over what to do, David contacted the FBI. He was assured that they would not seek the death penalty if he helped them capture the Unabomber. So, in return, David gave the FBI his brother's name and location. When federal agents arrested Ted on 3 April 1996 at his cabin in Montana, they found a live bomb, ready to be dispatched to the

373

LIGHT THE WAY

Unabomber's next unwitting target.

At his trial in January 1998, Ted Kaczynski pleaded guilty and was spared the death penalty. However, he showed no remorse for his crimes and was sentenced to four life sentences plus thirty years.

The US government awarded David $1 million for helping them bring the Unabomber to justice. David used most of this money to help the families of his brother's victims and the rest to cover his legal costs.

As David Kaczynski discovered, the first step in making a moral decision is to try to put aside how you feel. Then you must calmly and carefully look at all the factors involved. This can be very difficult to do, but it is necessary.

What follows is **a checklist** of questions you should ask yourself **before** making a moral decision:

Situation:	What exactly is the problem facing me?
Information:	Do I have all the relevant facts?
Guidance:	Where can I get reliable advice?
Aim:	What do I want to achieve?
Motive:	Why am I doing this?
Method:	What is the best way to achieve this?
Impact:	How will my actions affect other people?

Only **after** going through this process should you follow your **conscience**.

The Meaning of Conscience

> **REMEMBER!**
> **Conscience** is your capacity to apply your knowledge and values to a particular situation and decide what the right thing to do is.

Whenever you stop to think about your actions and decide what you should do, you are using your conscience. However, as you have free will, you can choose either to follow your conscience or to ignore it.

Did You Know?
To follow your conscience means choosing to do what you believe is **right**.
To ignore your conscience means choosing to do what you believe is **wrong**.

Conscience in Action

Let us take a step-by-step look at how conscience works:

- **Your situation:** You walk into a shop. The counter is unattended. There is no security camera. You are tempted to take something without paying for it.
- **Your values**: You know that it is wrong to steal. If you take this item without paying for it, you will be doing something wrong.
- **Your decision**: If you are a morally mature person, you will stay true to your values. You will say **'If I steal this item I'll harm someone else. I'll deprive the shopkeeper of the money he/she is entitled to. So, I won't steal it. If I really want it, then I'll buy it when I can afford it.'**

The Development of Conscience

Sometimes, when you learn the details of some terrible atrocity, it may seem that not everyone has a conscience. Some people do dreadful things and do not seem to feel any **guilt**.

> REMEMBER!
> **Guilt** is the awareness that you have done something wrong and that you should be held accountable for it.

Every one of us is born with **a capacity** for conscience. This means that your conscience does **not** develop automatically. Like any other human capacity (e.g. your imagination), your conscience needs to be educated and nurtured as you grow up, so that it too develops properly.

Your family and other people who influence you have an important role to play here. You need to grow up in a loving environment and have the benefit of good moral example if your conscience is to develop properly.

However, you also have a role to play in the development of your own conscience. You need to develop the habit of listening to your conscience, so that it can have a greater effect on your behaviour. Also, you can strengthen your conscience by doing things such as:

- Learning about moral issues.
- Helping other people whenever you can.
- Praying to God, if you have religious faith.

The Kinds of Conscience

We can distinguish between three different kinds of conscience:

1. An informed conscience

Here you try to gather all the information you can about a moral issue.
You study this information carefully **before** making any decision.
The decision you make is consistent with your personal **worldview** (i.e. your beliefs and values). Your decision is motivated neither by a desire for reward nor by a blind obedience to rules. You do what you

LIGHT THE WAY

do because you honestly believe that it is the right thing to do in the circumstances.

2. A legalistic conscience

Here you obey rules **without** question. This can seem quite attractive because it gives you a false sense of security. However, that kind of thinking only encourages moral immaturity. The reasons for this are:

(a) Your thinking becomes dominated by a cold, rigid and closed-minded attitude.

(b) You are only motivated by a desire for reward or a fear of punishment.

If you have a legalistic conscience, you will **not** stop to ask if a particular rule is just or unjust, or whether it might be wrong to obey it.

3. A lax conscience

Here you consistently act in morally immature and selfish ways. This has the effect of distorting your whole understanding of right and wrong. You become increasingly **desensitised**. This means that any actions you once believed were wrong begin to seem less and less wrong, until they no longer seem wrong at all.

In time, you may become **indifferent** (i.e. immune to guilt). If you develop a lax conscience you may be willing to harm others and **not** care about it.

Did You Know?

You need to develop an **informed** conscience if you want to achieve moral maturity.

Difficulties We Face When Making Moral Decisions

We are not robots. We cannot be programmed to follow a checklist of questions every time we're faced with a moral choice. However, a checklist can be useful if it helps us to be on our guard against things that can interfere with our decision-making.

There are five areas where **difficulties** can arise when we are faced with a moral decision:

1. **Knowledge**: Do I really understand the problem? Do I have all the advice or information I need to make the right choice?
2. **Values:** What do I believe is important in life? Do I only care about other people when it suits me?
3. **Emotions**: Do I allow my feelings to have too great an influence on my decisions? Do I only help people I like?
4. **Peer pressure**: Do I only do certain things to win the approval of others?
5. **Reasoning:** Do I really try my best to figure out what is the right thing to do?

These difficulties often lead people to look for **guidance** when faced with a moral decision.

376

Sources of Guidance

> **REMEMBER!**
> **Guidance** is advice about what you should do.

Think about the following examples:

- If you were concerned about your health, you would visit **a doctor**.
- If you were worried about money, you would talk to **an accountant**.
- If you wanted to improve your diet, you would seek advice from **a nutritionist**.

Each of these is **an authority** in his/her particular field.

> **REMEMBER!**
> **An authority** is a trusted source of guidance on a particular area of life.

Authority plays an important role in religion. To illustrate this, just think about the difficulties raised by the following situations:

- How should a young, unmarried woman respond to a crisis pregnancy?
- How should a lone parent best care for a child who is severely disabled?
- How should you respond to a friend who suffers from an addiction?

Those who accept a particular religious moral vision often turn for advice to the sources of authority in their religion when looking for answers to such questions. This is what **Alfred Delp** did.

SPOTLIGHT ON: ALFRED DELP AND OPERATION VALKYRIE

Alfred Delp was a quiet, scholarly man. In his youth he converted to Catholicism and became a Jesuit priest. In 1939 he was sent to work in the parish of St Georg in his native Germany.

Delp was a thoroughly **honest** man.

> **REMEMBER!**
> **Honest** means being fair and forthright in your dealings. You keep your word and tell the truth.

Unlike most of those around him, Delp never let himself be fooled by the warped version of reality presented by Nazi propaganda. He had no illusions about Hitler. Delp knew that his nation's leader was a ruthless thug who delighted in destruction. Hitler showed no hesitation in imprisoning and killing anyone who stood up to him.

377

LIGHT THE WAY

Despite the great danger involved, Delp decided that he would do all he could to oppose Hitler. He began by helping to smuggle Jewish refugees to safety in Switzerland. Then he became an advisor to key members among the German army officers who were involved in **Operation Valkyrie**.

Did You Know?

Operation Valkyrie was a secret plot by the German resistance movement to kill Hitler and end Nazi rule over German-occupied Europe.

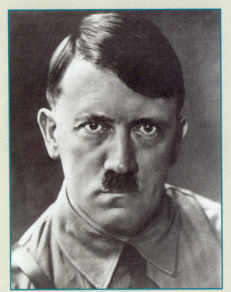

Alfred Delp was charged with having knowledge of an attempt to assassinate Hitler.

In July 1944, Delp was arrested by **the Gestapo** (i.e. the Nazi secret police). He was charged with having knowledge of the failed attempt to assassinate Hitler with a bomb hidden in a briefcase. At his trial it was shown that Delp had met with **Klaus von Stauffenberg**, the officer who had led the plot to kill Hitler.

There was no evidence to show that Delp had known the exact details of the assassination attempt. However, he was a well-known opponent of the Nazis. So, the court found Delp guilty of treason and sentenced him to death.

Both before and after his trial, Delp was brutally tortured. Then he was put in solitary confinement. The order to execute him was not carried out straight away. The Nazis offered him a deal: the torture would stop, his death sentence would be lifted and he would be released if he publicly rejected the Christian faith and left the Jesuit order.

To someone who was alone, injured and exhausted, it must have seemed a tempting way out. Delp thought hard about this offer before making his decision. As a Catholic, Delp **informed his conscience**. This means that:

- He prayed to God for guidance.
- He drew inspiration from the example Jesus set for him.
- He reflected on the teachings of **the Magisterium** of Catholic Church.

Delp followed his conscience. He rejected the Gestapo's offer. Despite their best efforts, Delp had remained true to his most deeply held beliefs and values. As a result, the death sentence was carried out and Delp was hanged on 2 February 1945.

People like Alfred Delp are said to possess **integrity**. He was prepared to follow his **conscience**, despite the high personal cost of doing so.

Did You Know?

Catholics believe that God continues to speak through the teachings of their Church. So, Catholics are obliged to listen carefully to the guidance offered by **the Magisterium** before they make a moral decision.

The Magisterium consists of the Pope and the college of bishops under his leadership. Their role is to guide the belief and practice of Catholics.

> **REMEMBER!**
> **Integrity** means staying true to your values, following your conscience and doing what you believe is right.

SPOTLIGHT ON: THE ABORTION ISSUE

> **REMEMBER!**
> **Abortion** is any procedure whose deliberate purpose is to end a pregnancy and cause the death of an unborn child.

Demonstrators in Dublin march from Dublin's Garden of Remembrance to the Dáil.

Various methods are used to carry out an abortion. These methods may involve the use of either drugs or surgery, or a combination of both, depending on how far a pregnancy has developed.

> **Did You Know?**
> An abortion must be distinguished from **a miscarriage**.
>
> **A miscarriage** is where an unborn child is spontaneously expelled from a woman's womb without any outside intervention.

Although abortion is now legal in most countries, the Catholic, Orthodox and most Protestant churches have traditionally taught that abortion is wrong under **all** circumstances.

Why?

They offer the following reasons:

- Every new human life starts at **conception** (i.e. when a man's sperm and a woman's ovum unite after sexual intercourse to form the first stage of human life).
- Though microscopic in size at first, this new life is human at **all** stages of his/her development.
- Abortion denies this new human being the most basic of all human rights – **the right to life**.
- All human life is **sacred**, from conception to natural death. If you deliberately harm an unborn child, you break the fifth commandment.

They say that when there is a medical crisis/crises, doctors should do everything possible to sustain a pregnancy as long as there is a reasonable prospect of saving the lives of **both** the mother and her unborn child.

> **REMEMBER!**
> **Sacred** means worthy of your total respect.

> **Did You Know?**
> The belief that abortion is unjustified pre-dates Christianity. The Hippocratic Oath, first sworn by Greek doctors in the 6th century BCE, stated: '**I will not give a woman an abortive remedy.**'

LIGHT THE WAY

A Summary of the Main Arguments

For Abortion	Against Abortion
1. A woman's decision to end her pregnancy is a purely private matter. It is her body. She should have the right to choose whether or not to have the baby.	**1.** There are two human beings involved here – the mother and the child. Abortion deprives another human being of the fundamental right to life.
2. Abortion is more a woman's issue than a man's. It is the woman who becomes pregnant, perhaps against her will.	**2.** The responsibility for defending human life rests equally on all people – both male and female.
3. A woman facing a crisis pregnancy should be treated with compassion. She should be given an abortion if she asks for it.	**3.** Sometimes an abortion is wanted for serious reasons. However, compassion for the woman's distress does not justify ending an unborn child's life.
4. A child might be conceived as a result of rape or incest. Such events are traumatic enough in themselves. There is no need to add an unwanted pregnancy to the situation.	**4.** Rape and incest are horrific crimes. Their victims need to be cared for. However, one wrong action does not justify another wrong action.
5. A severely disabled child may have a poor quality of life. This child may also impose great strain upon his/her carers. A woman should be offered the choice of an abortion if tests detect a severe disability while the child is still in the womb.	**5.** A disabled child is a human being. He/she deserves the same equality of respect and protection given to all other members of our society. Those who care for the disabled are entitled to all the support the state can provide. The 'quality of life' argument is open to abuse. It could be extended to cover not only the disabled but other groups too, such as the elderly.

ACTIVITIES

1. Say what it means!

(a) A moral decision involves _____ .

(b) A value is _____ .

(c) To learn means _____ .

(d) Socialisation is _____ .

(e) Conscience is _____ .

(f) To follow your conscience means _____ .

(g) Integrity means _____ .

2. Crossword

Across
4. Advice about what you should do.
6. It means being fair and forthright in your dealings. You keep your word and tell the truth.
7. The kind of conscience you need to develop if you want to achieve moral maturity.
8. Those people of the same age group as yourself.
10. It involves giving doctors permission to have some of your healthy vital organs removed after you have died and given to those in need of transplants (2 words: 5, 8).
12. A place where the authorities set down rules so that you have a safe environment in which to develop your particular talents.
14. This offers you insights into life's great mysteries.
17. It means that you have become immune to guilt.
20. The kind of conscience where you obey rules without question and never ask if something is just or unjust.

Down
1. Here we are talking about the cinema, internet, radio and television. It influences your worldview (2 words: 4, 5).
2. The kind of conscience where you are willing to harm others and not care about it.
3. A choice either to do or not do something.
5. Whatever is in the best interest of the community as a whole (2 words: 6, 4).
9. The name given by US federal agents to an elusive domestic terrorist who waged a postal bomb campaign in the US for over 17 years.
11. You learn them through a process called socialisation.
12. Through its laws it sets limits on your behaviour.
13. A rule set out by state authorities that all its citizens are expected to obey.
15. The awareness that you have done something wrong and should be held accountable for it.
16. A trusted source of guidance about a particular area of life.
18. This is the first community you belong to. Here you begin learning how to treat others.
19. This consists of the Pope and the bishops under his leadership. Their role is to guide the belief and practice of Catholics.

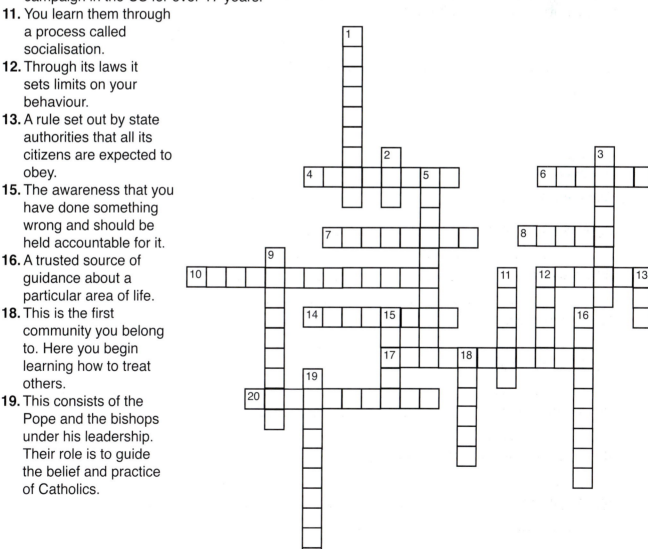

LIGHT THE WAY

3. Wordsearch

Find the following words:

Decision
Values
Organ donation
Law
Learn
Socialisation
Sources
Common Good
Unabomber
Conscience
Guilt
Informed
Legalistic
Lax
Indifferent
Guidance
Authority
Magisterium
Integrity

N	M	N	L	C	E	G	V	M	N	I	T	E	L	C
O	Y	M	O	B	O	A	U	O	J	N	D	E	R	O
I	T	T	L	I	L	M	I	I	E	M	G	F	S	N
T	I	I	I	U	T	S	M	R	D	A	B	W	O	S
A	R	G	E	R	I	A	E	O	L	A	I	A	U	C
S	G	S	T	C	O	F	N	I	N	D	N	L	R	I
I	E	V	E	L	F	H	S	O	R	G	X	C	C	E
L	T	D	V	I	I	T	T	O	D	H	O	D	E	N
A	N	K	D	X	I	U	K	U	G	N	X	O	S	C
I	I	N	A	C	J	W	G	A	A	K	A	N	D	E
C	I	L	I	N	F	O	R	M	E	D	R	G	C	U
O	M	A	G	I	S	T	E	R	I	U	M	S	R	H
S	R	E	B	M	O	B	A	N	U	Z	D	B	K	O
N	R	A	E	L	L	P	I	T	C	Y	Q	E	D	E
E	A	I	O	N	T	G	U	X	O	Z	K	Z	S	P

4. Fill in the missing words!

This is a **checklist** of questions you should ask yourself **before** making a moral decision:

1. **Situation:** What exactly is the _____ facing me?
2. **Information:** Do I have all the relevant _____?
3. **Guidance:** Where can I get reliable _____?
4. **Aim:** What do I want to _____?
5. **Motive:** _____ am I doing this?
6. **Method:** What is the _____ way to achieve this?
7. **Impact:** How will my actions _____ other people?

5. Think about it!

(a) Say what each of the following actions tells you about the values of the person doing it:
1. Refusing to gossip behind someone's back.
2. Borrowing something without first asking permission from its owner to do so.
3. Recycling waste material.
4. Telling lies to get out of trouble.
5. Neglecting to feed a pet animal.
6. Studying hard for an upcoming examination.
7. Drinking alcohol above the legal limit and then driving a vehicle.
8. Keeping a sum of money you have found without making any attempt to find its owner.
9. Paying your fair share in taxes.
10. Stopping a disagreement between two friends developing into a serious row.
11. Volunteering to work for a charitable cause.

(b) What point was Chiquinho Scarpa trying to make when announced that he was going to bury his luxury car?

The Moral Challenge   SECTION F

(c) Why do you think Leona Helmsley refused to pay her fair share in taxes?

(d) 1. Why did David Kaczynski decide to tell the FBI that he suspected his older brother Ted was the Unabomber?

2. Do you agree/disagree with his decision to do so? Why?

6. Examine the arguments **for** and **against** abortion. Which of them do you find the **most** convincing? Give reasons for your answer.

7. Read the following:

> An ocean liner sails from port with 2,000 people on board. However, there are not enough lifeboats on board to carry all the passengers to safety if the ship is threatened with sinking. This is because the owner of the ocean liner is only concerned with fulfilling the minimum safety requirements. A vessel of this size is only required by law to carry lifeboats for 1,000 passengers.

(a) Which of the three types of conscience is this an example of?
(b) Give a reason for your choice.

8. Read the following:

> A drug dealer is interviewed by a reporter. He is asked if he ever thinks about the impact of the drugs he sells on the lives of those who buy them. He responds by saying that he is not the slightest bit concerned about how it affects them. He is just 'providing a service'. He does not force anyone to buy these drugs. If anyone gets hurt because they have taken these drugs, it has nothing to do with him.

(a) Which of the three types of conscience is this an example of?
(b) Give a reason for your choice.

9. Do you think Alfred Delp had **integrity**? Support your answer with evidence taken from his life story.

10. Read the following statement:

> 'As far as knowledge about ourselves and the way we should treat one another, we humans still have a lot to learn.'

(a) Can you think of two examples taken from today's news headlines that would support this statement?
(b) What does this tell you about the need to seek **guidance** from reliable sources when faced with a moral decision?

383

LIGHT THE WAY

CHAPTER 3   SIN AND FORGIVENESS

The Human Condition

Human beings can achieve great things. We can put space stations into orbit around the Earth and land astronauts safely on the surface of the Moon. We can cure diseases that once killed millions of people. In the field of technology, we have made tremendous progress when compared to our Stone Age ancestors.

Yet, when it comes to living together in peace and caring for one another, we still have a long way to go. In this regard, we are no different from those people who used stone tools rather than precision lasers. Just think about our repeated tendency to go to **war** with one another.

> **REMEMBER!**
> **War** is an armed conflict between rival groups. Each side puts people forward to fight and to kill one another.

People tend to justify going to war for the following reasons:

- To overthrow an unjust government.
- To expel a foreign occupier.
- To gain control over natural resources and trade routes.
- To gain revenge for a past defeat.

However, most wars are terribly destructive, in both lives and property. For example, during the 20th century alone, more than 150 million people may have died in the various wars fought. The vast majority of these casualties were civilians, not soldiers. So, for most nations, the disadvantages of going to war generally seem to outweigh any advantages.

After spending many years studying the most costly wars fought down through the ages, statistician Matthew White sadly concluded that the real reasons most people have gone to war are:

- Because they could.
- Because they wanted to.
- Because everybody else around them was doing it.

As a quick internet search of conflicts being waged around the world today shows, there is little evidence to support the claim that we are all that different from our ancestors.

Perhaps it is because we drive down motorways in automobiles, while our Stone Age ancestors paddled down rivers in dugout canoes, that we think that human beings have changed. But it is not so. We are only divided from these people by a few thousand years. There has not been enough time for us to change.

We are just as likely to do the right thing or the wrong thing as they were. We are just as likely to commit **an actual sin** as they were.

The Meaning of Actual Sin

When **Leonardo da Vinci** was painting his masterpiece, ***The Last Supper***, he looked for someone to model for the figure of Jesus Christ. Finally, da Vinci found who he was looking for – a handsome young chorister named Pietro Bandinelli.

Several years went by but da Vinci had not yet finished his masterwork. All the apostles had been painted except one – Judas Iscariot. So da Vinci went looking for a suitable model. He wanted to find someone whose face had been hardened and distorted by a wicked life.

Leonardo da Vinci (1452–1519)

Finally da Vinci found a street beggar whose face was so villainous that the artist shuddered inwardly whenever he had to look at him. So, he hired this beggar to sit for him as he painted the face of Judas on the canvas.

It was only when he had finished painting him that da Vinci thought to ask the beggar his name. The man's answer shocked the great artist. **'Don't you recognise me?'** the beggar asked. **'I am Pietro Bandinelli. I also sat for you as your model for Christ.'**

This story serves as a warning. If we allow **actual sin** to take over our lives, it will corrupt and destroy all that is good in us, just as it did to Pietro Bandinelli.

> **REMEMBER!**
> **Actual sin** is any free and deliberate action where you choose to do what you know is wrong or refuse to do what you know is right.

There are two kinds of actual sin:

- **Sin by commission**: This happens when you **choose** to do something you know you should not do.
- **Sin by omission**: This happens when you **neglect** to do something you know you should do.

Usually, actual sin comes from our pride and selfishness. Actual sin damages our relationship with God, other people and the natural world. The degree of damage done depends on how serious the sin is. This is why the Catholic Church makes a further distinction between **two** kinds of actual sin. These are **mortal sin** and **venial sin**.

Venial sin should not be taken lightly. It can cause you to gradually move away from God. Eventually, it can bring about the complete breakdown of your relationship with God and other people.

All of this raises an important question: Why are we prone to committing actual sin?

Christians say that this is due to **original sin**.

Did You Know?

Christians believe that we are **all** sinners to a greater or lesser extent. No one has the right to feel superior. **You may condemn the act but not the person**. No one has the right to condemn another.

Did You Know?

Mortal sin: This is the most serious kind of sin. It **destroys** your relationship with God, other people and the natural world.

Venial sin: This covers less serious kinds of sin. It **damages** your relationship with God, other people and the natural world.

LIGHT THE WAY

The Meaning of Original Sin

Few people in history have ever exerted as much control over the day-to-day lives of their fellow human beings as **Joseph Stalin**. From 1926 until his death in 1953, he was the undisputed ruler of the Soviet Union. By then, Stalin had transformed his country into a military superpower that rivalled the United States of America. However, all this was achieved at a terrible cost in human life. Stalin's policies may have caused the deaths of more than 20 million of his own people. Many died as prisoners in his slave labour camps, others died of starvation due to his economic policies, while those who spoke out against this were executed by his ever-watchful secret police.

Joseph Stalin (1878–1953)

Three years after Stalin's death, his successor **Nikita Khrushchev** made a speech to a large gathering of the Soviet Union's ruling Communist Party. To the total amazement of all present, Khrushchev condemned all the terrible things Stalin had done. When Khrushchev ended his speech, there was no applause. No one had dared to speak like that for longer than anyone could remember. Everyone present was unsure how to react, so great was their fear that this was some kind of trick.

However, one person could not resist this opportunity. He had a note passed up to Khrushchev just before the new leader was about to leave the speaker's rostrum. This piece of paper did not bear the questioner's name and only asked one question: **'If Stalin was as bad as you say, why did you not do something about it?'**

Khrushchev was angered and embarrassed by this question. He had been a loyal and long-serving minister in Stalin's government. Yet, as the note implied, he had done nothing whatsoever to challenge Stalin during those terrible years.

So, Khrushchev decided to take on his questioner directly. He went back to the microphone, waved the piece of paper and asked: **'Who wrote this note? Who wants me to answer this question?'**

Again, there was complete silence in the crowded hall. Khrushchev waited a minute or so to see if anyone would meet his challenge. No one did. There was only silence from the audience. Then Khrushchev spoke into the microphone again: **'There now, you have your answer!'**

It is all very well to criticise the behaviour of others and ask why they failed to do the right thing. However, we are not usually so quick to face up to our own moral failures. In truth, every single human being experiences the same challenge in life: it is hard to live up to your responsibilities. When confronted with a moral decision, it is often far from easy to do what you believe is right. Usually, it is much easier to take the path of least resistance, even though this may not be the right one to follow.

Just think back over certain events in your own life so far. You will recall times when, against your own better judgement, you said or did something you knew was harmful, especially to someone you claimed to love.

St Paul thought deeply about this common human experience. He wrote that:

> 'I cannot understand my own behaviour. I fail to carry out the things I want to do and I find myself doing the very thing I hate.'
>
> Romans 7: 16

The Moral Challenge SECTION F

Even though we may each know the difference between right and wrong, we so often choose to say or do the **wrong** thing. We all find it a great challenge to do the **right** thing. However, moral maturity demands that we must each be ready to stand up for certain values when making a moral decision.

Why is it so difficult for us to do the right thing? Christians say the answer can be found in what they call '**original sin**'. They ask people to stop and reflect on the story of **the Fall**, as told in **Genesis 3:1-11**.

Did You Know?

For Christians in contemporary society, taking a stand on moral issues is becoming more and more of a challenge. This is because it takes courage to believe what people around you may dismiss as nonsense, and to live by values that put justice and integrity before popularity and financial reward.

The Story of the Fall

We are told that God created the first human beings. In this story they are given the names **Adam** and **Eve**. These first people lived in a place called '**the Garden**'. Here God provided them with everything they needed to enjoy happy and fulfilled lives. However, when tempted by Satan, the first people betrayed God's trust. They acted out of pride and selfishness. They deliberately disobeyed God. When they did this, they committed the **first** sin. This first sin by our earliest ancestors is known as '**the original sin**'. Because of it, God punished the first humans by banishing them from the Garden.

The story of **the Fall** was **not** written to offer us a literal, historical account. Instead, it was written to help us grasp some very important religious ideas.

What the story of the Fall means

1. The first humans let their pride get the better of them. In their arrogance, they aimed to raise themselves up to the same level as God.
2. When they tried to do this, they chose to do something they knew was wrong.
3. This caused them to fall away from the state of innocent goodness in which God had created them and in which God had wanted them to live.
4. So, it was the selfish actions of these first humans that brought **moral evil** and the suffering it causes into the world.

REMEMBER!
Moral evil is the harm caused when we freely and deliberately choose to do something that we know is wrong.

LIGHT THE WAY

The Catholic Church teaches that the original sin committed by the first people has had far-reaching consequences for every person born since. Why?

This original sin broke the proper relationship that should always have existed between human beings and the God who created them. As a result, the first humans were not the only ones affected by it. The effects of that original sin have been passed on to every human being born since, weakening our resolve to do what is good and avoid what is evil. This is why, today, each of us has to struggle within ourselves to do the right thing and avoid doing the wrong thing.

Did You Know?

Christians believe that, because of original sin, we cannot live truly good lives by relying purely on our own efforts. However, God did not create us and then simply abandon us. God offers each of us **the grace** (i.e. the strengthening love) we need to find the courage to make good moral decisions.

The Meaning of Forgiveness

Christianity takes actual sin very seriously. This is because of its **harmful effects** on our lives. Think about this:

1. Sin separates you from God and from other people.
2. Sin makes you self-centred and destructive.
3. Sin destroys your self-respect, leaving you isolated and in despair.

However, Christianity does **not** only focus on sin. It also offers you a way to overcome it and make a fresh start. This begins with **forgiveness**.

Sometimes, when someone offends or harms you, you may be told to just '**forgive and forget**'. However, such advice completely misses the whole point of **forgiveness**. Think about the following story:

Shortly before Christmas 1983, in a bare, white-walled cell in Rome's Rebibbia prison, the then pope, St John Paul II, came face to face with a prisoner named Mehmet Ali Agca. This was an extraordinary meeting. Only two and a half years earlier, Agca had shot the pope, leaving him critically wounded. Agca was serving a life sentence for that attempted assassination.

For twenty-one minutes the two men sat and talked. After this they parted with a handshake. What they said to one another remains a secret. However, we do know that the pope forgave the man who had tried to kill him.

Pope John Paul II meets Ali Agca in prison in Rome, December 1983.

Forgiving someone who has done you great harm can be far from easy. St John Paul II never fully recovered from the injuries he experienced on 13 May 1981. Forgiving someone who had caused him so much suffering was far from easy. It demanded great courage, humility and a deep faith in God.

Not to forgive is to remain trapped in your past. You become focused only on getting revenge. It poisons all your relationships, whether they are with God or with other people.

Forgiving allows you to rebuild your life and begin moving forward.

REMEMBER!
Forgiveness means to let go of the anger and hate you feel towards one who has harmed you or someone you love.

However, the story of St John Paul II and Mehmet Ali Agca illustrates important points about the relationship between forgiveness and **justice**.

> **REMEMBER!**
> **Justice** means getting what you are entitled to and giving others what they are entitled to.

As a devout Christian, John Paul II believed that:

- Forgiveness does **not** mean forgetting what has happened.
- Forgiveness does **not** mean allowing others to walk all over you.
- Forgiveness does **not** mean letting someone escape from an appropriate punishment for their actions.

Though Christians are expected to forgive those who have harmed them, they are still entitled to justice. Not even forgiveness should be allowed to override justice. Those who have done wrong should always be held **responsible** for their actions.

> **REMEMBER!**
> **Responsible** means that you are held accountable for what you have done.

In Mehmet Ali Agca's case, justice demanded that he serve a long prison sentence for what he had done.

The pope bore no ill will towards Agca. However, Agca had to be held accountable for his actions. The punishment he had received, a lengthy prison sentence, was appropriate for what he had done – namely, attempting to murder a fellow human being.

St John Paul II believed that we each have the power within us **to change**. This decision to change is what brings God's forgiveness for our sins. He hoped that, one day, Mehmet Ali Agca would come to realise this too.

This was a message that Jesus never tired of preaching during his public ministry. Jesus taught that there is no human answer to sin. The answer to sin can be found only in the gift of God's forgiveness.

Jesus said that he had come into this world to free us from the oppressive power that sin has over our lives:

- Through his **miracles**, Jesus demonstrated his power over all the harmful effects of sin in our world, such as disease, loneliness and starvation.
- In his **parables**, Jesus taught that God has unlimited love, even for the worst of us, and that God will forgive our sins if we really want to reform our lives.

A Catholic Explains the Sacrament of Reconciliation

We believe that the Sacrament of Reconciliation does three things:

1. It celebrates the love and forgiveness of God.
2. It expresses the belief that, through the power of God and the actions of the priest, your sins are forgiven.
3. It offers you the chance to repair the damage done to your relationship with God.

The Sacrament of Reconciliation follows this format:

- **The welcome:** The priest, representing the risen Jesus, welcomes you.
- **The blessing:** You trace the symbol of the cross and say how long it has been since you last received this sacrament.

LIGHT THE WAY

- **The confession:** You say you are sorry for any sins you have committed and admit your responsibility to the priest.
- **The penance:** You must be prepared to make up for what you have done. A penance to fit your sins is given, e.g. you must say a prayer or help another person. You complete this penance to show that you really want to change your life.
- **The act of contrition:** Here you should express your genuine sorrow for your sins. You also promise not to repeat these sins in future.
- **The absolution:** Only God has the power to forgive sins. Here, the priest is authorised to act in God's place. The priest says a short prayer and **absolves** you (i.e. forgives your sins).
- **The aftermath:** You show your thanks to God by living a better life from this point onwards.

Did You Know?

The seal of the confession means that a Catholic priest is forbidden from revealing to anyone else what you said to him during the sacrament of reconciliation.

However, a priest has the right to **refuse** absolution, and is required by the Catholic Church to do so, if he has good reason to believe that the person asking for forgiveness is not genuinely sorry for their sins.

ACTIVITIES

1. Wordsearch
Find the following words:

War
Venial
Grace
Casualties
Actual sin
Da Vinci
Last Supper
Commission
Omission
Mortal
Stalin
Khrushchev
Paul
The Fall
Adam
Eve
Moral evil
Forgiveness
Justice
Sacrament
Reconciliation
Penance
Contrition
Absolution

K	T	S	J	L	A	D	L	M	A	E	P	T	C	S
I	H	Z	S	D	I	A	A	B	M	T	A	J	O	E
P	E	R	A	E	I	V	S	V	N	S	U	O	N	I
L	F	M	U	N	N	O	E	E	I	S	L	R	T	T
A	A	Y	E	S	L	E	M	L	T	N	E	C	R	L
T	L	V	E	U	H	A	V	I	A	P	C	A	I	A
R	L	L	T	V	R	C	C	I	P	R	J	I	T	U
O	W	I	O	C	E	E	H	U	G	G	O	J	I	S
M	O	B	A	N	P	M	S	E	H	R	R	M	O	A
N	I	S	L	A	U	T	C	A	V	P	O	A	N	C
C	O	M	M	I	S	S	I	O	N	P	E	F	C	G
N	O	I	T	A	I	L	I	C	N	O	C	E	R	E
Q	V	O	L	O	M	I	S	S	I	O	N	J	U	C
E	C	N	A	N	E	P	S	T	A	L	I	N	T	S
R	A	W	E	C	W	Q	X	J	U	W	I	D	S	O

2. Crossword

Across
5. We can land astronauts safely on its surface.
9. The surname of the undisputed ruler of the Soviet Union between 1926 and 1953.
10. This sin is explained by the Story of the Fall in Genesis 3: 1-11.
14. These people make up the vast majority of casualties in war, not soldiers.
17. It means that you are held accountable for your actions.
18. Not to forgive is to remain trapped in your past. You become focused only on getting this.

Down
1. Through them, Jesus demonstrated his power over all the harmful effects of sin in our world, such as disease, loneliness and starvation.
2. The surname of the artist who painted *The Last Supper*.
3. We can now cure these things that once killed millions of people.
4. The name of pope who forgave the man who had tried to assassinate him (2 words: 4, 4).
6. The sin you commit when you neglect to do something you know you should do.
7. In them, Jesus taught that God has unlimited love, and that He will forgive our sins if we really want to reform our lives.
8. The sin you commit when you choose to do something you know you should not do.
11. The seal of the confession means that this person is forbidden to reveal to anyone else what you said to him during the sacrament of reconciliation.
12. It means armed conflict between two rival groups.
13. The decision to do this is what brings God's forgiveness for our sins.
15. The strengthening love God offers each of us to find the courage to make good moral decisions.
16. This is the most serious kind of sin. It destroys your relationship with God, other people and the natural world.
18. This sacrament celebrates the love and forgiveness of God, expresses the belief that, through the power of God and the actions of the priest, your sins are forgiven and offers you the chance to repair the damage done to your relationship with God.
19. This is a less serious kind of sin. It damages your relationship with God, other people and the natural world.

LIGHT THE WAY

3. Fill in the missing words!

The Sacrament of Reconciliation

(a) **The welcome:** The _____, representing the risen _____, welcomes you.

(b) **The blessing:** You trace the symbol of the _____ and say how long it has been since you _____ received this _____.

(c) **The confession:** You say you are _____ for any sins you have committed and admit your _____ to the priest.

(d) **The penance:** You must be prepared to _____ for what you have done. A penance to _____ your sins is given. You _____ this penance to show that you really want to _____ your life.

(e) **The act of contrition:** Here you should express your genuine _____ for your sins. You also promise not to _____ these sins in future.

(f) **The absolution:** Only _____ has the power to _____ sins. Here, the priest is authorised to act in _____ place. The priest says a short prayer and _____ you.

(g) **Thanksgiving:** You should show your _____ to God by living a _____ life from this point onwards.

4. Think about it!

(a) Read the following story:

> On the morning of 27 September 1854, the American passenger steamship *SS Arctic* was off the Grand Banks, an area of the North Atlantic where warm air from the Gulf Stream hits cold air from the north, creating heavy fog.
>
> The captain, James Luce, ordered his lookouts to keep a close watch out for other ships.
>
> Shortly after noon, one of the lookouts sounded the alarm. Another ship had suddenly emerged from a thick fog bank, and the two vessels were on a collision course.
>
> The other ship was a French steamer, the *Vesta*. The propeller-driven *Vesta* had been built with a steel hull. The *Arctic*, though the larger of the two vessels, had a wooden hull.
>
> The *Vesta* rammed the bow of the *Arctic*, and in the collision the steel bow of the *Vesta* acted like a battering ram, tearing open the *Arctic's* lighter hull. The damage to the *Arctic's* hull allowed seawater to pour into the ship. The vessel began to sink into the icy ocean.
>
> The *Arctic* carried only six lifeboats. Had they been carefully filled, they could have held 180 people, or almost all the passengers, including all the women and children on board.
>
> The ship's captain tried to save as many lives as possible. He instructed the crew to ensure that when the lifeboats were being loaded, it was '**women and children first**'. However, most of the crew disobeyed his command.
>
> Instead of keeping their cool, most crew members panicked, commandeered the lifeboats and saved only themselves. The passengers, abandoned and terrified, tried to make rafts or to cling on to pieces of wreckage. However, the freezing waters of the North Atlantic made survival almost impossible.
>
> The most reliable estimate is that about 350 people died in the sinking of the *SS Arctic*. Not one of the 80 women and children on board survived. However, 60 crew members did.

1. What is your reaction to this story?
2. Could this large loss of life have been prevented even after the collision had occurred? Explain your answer.
3. Why do you think most of the crew of the *Arctic* responded to this disaster in the way that they did?
4. Would you describe the behaviour of the *Arctic's* crew members who seized the lifeboats for themselves a sin of commission **or** a sin of omission? Explain your answer.

The Moral Challenge   SECTION F

(b) Read the following story:

> On 20 September 2004, the on-board CCTV camera of a bus travelling along a busy road in England recorded a woman lying unconscious on the road. She was found to be bleeding heavily from a wound to her head.
>
> The bus's CCTV camera recorded several other motorists swerving to avoid striking the woman. However, not one of these drivers stopped to help her. None of them telephoned the emergency services. They all ignored her plight and drove on.
>
> Only the driver of the bus stopped to help her. He protected her from oncoming traffic and called police and paramedics to the scene.

1. How would you describe the behaviour of the bus driver towards the injured woman? Why do you think he treated her this way?
2. How would you describe the behaviour of the other motorists who ignored the injured woman? Why do you think they acted in this way?
3. What is **your** reaction to this story?
4. Have you come across a similar story? If so, what happened?
5. What does this incident tell you about the impact of **sins of omission** on our lives?

(c) 1. Identify any two situations where people might find it difficult to forgive someone who had harmed or offended them or someone they loved.
2. What, do you think, is the difference between **getting revenge** and **receiving justice**?
3. Do you think it is ever possible to resolve the conflicts between either individuals or nations without both sides being willing to forgive? Explain your answer.

5. Say what it means!

(a) Actual sin is _____

_____ .

(b) Moral evil is _____

_____ .

(c) Forgiveness is _____

_____ .

(d) Justice is _____

_____ .

393

LIGHT THE WAY

CHAPTER 4   STEWARDSHIP

To the Edge of Extinction

Asian elephants are on the World Wildlife Fund critically endangered list.

It is often said that we only appreciate the importance of something when it's gone. In the late 19th century, the passenger pigeon was a familiar sight to people all along the east coast of the USA. These birds were so numerous that their flocks would stretch for miles across the skies as they migrated each year to their breeding grounds in New England. However, excessive levels of hunting soon changed that. By 1914, a species that, only forty years previously had numbered more than five billion birds, had become **extinct**.

> **REMEMBER!**
> **Extinct** means that a particular form of life has completely died out.

The passenger pigeon is only one of about 130 species of bird that have become extinct due to human action within the last six centuries.

But why should we worry if some creatures become extinct? Perhaps the following story will make the importance of preserving the different plant and animal species clear.

SPOTLIGHT ON: THE EXTINCTION OF THE DODO

The destruction of the dodo of Mauritius remains one of the best known cases of animal extinctions.

A full-grown adult **dodo** was a large bird, weighing around 50 lbs. It stood about 3 feet tall on two stout yellow legs. It had a large black beak and greyish blue feathers that covered its body except for a white plume on its tail. Its wings were very small, making it flightless.

Did You Know?

Mauritius is a large island in the Indian Ocean. It is far from any other land mass.

The dodo lived undisturbed on Mauritius for so long that it lost both its need and its ability to fly. There were no mammals on the island. So, the dodo could safely live and nest on the ground. It had an abundant food source in all the ripe fruit that fell from trees that covered the island.

394

The Moral Challenge   SECTION F

However, in 1598, Portuguese sailors discovered Mauritius on their route east to the Spice Islands. The dodo was unlike anything they had ever seen, and, having lived in solitude on the island with no natural predators, it had no fear of humans. This made it easy prey.

The dodo was a welcome source of fresh meat for the hungry sailors. Huge numbers were killed for food. But worse was to follow. The ships that came to Mauritius had rats aboard, some of which escaped onto the island. In time, settlers brought monkeys and pigs with them. These killed the dodos' chicks and ate their vulnerable eggs in their easily accessible nesting grounds. Within 100 years of the arrival of humans on Mauritius, the once abundant dodo had become extinct.

No one paid much heed to the disappearance of the last dodo in 1681. This is because it would take years before people began to notice its harmful impact on the islands' trees.

By the mid-20th century it was becoming obvious that the beautiful Mauritian **calvaria** (a hardwood tree) was dying out. There were only thirteen left on the island. Scientists reckoned that all of these remaining trees were about 300 years old. No new trees had germinated since the late 1600s.

Since the average lifespan of this tree was about 300 years, the last members of the calvaria would soon die, and the species would be extinct. It was no coincidence that these trees had stopped reproducing three centuries earlier. Why?

Because the dodo played an essential part in the life-cycle of the calvaria tree. The dodo ate the fruit of this tree. Their seeds had such thick hulls that they could only sprout and grow after they had been eaten and run through the dodo's digestive tract.

Fortunately, ornithologist Dr Stanley Temple discovered that turkeys could mimic the action of the dodo's digestive system. This has allowed the calvaria tree to be saved from extinction.

The tragedy of the dodo highlights the harmful effects we can have upon the environment. It is all too easy to disrupt the delicate balance of nature by destroying whole species. People not only wiped out the dodo, but disrupted nature in unforeseen ways.

This story serves to highlight the dangerous implications of driving any life form to extinction. This point is particularly important today. Due to human activity, more and more species are now threatened with extinction.

Waking up to Reality

The disappearance of both the passenger pigeon and the dodo could soon be repeated by many other species. Some fear that if current trends continue, the following animals may also become extinct by the middle of this century: the albatross, the elephant, the penguin, the polar bear, the tiger, the turtle and the whale.

Sadly, for most of our history, people have behaved as if the Earth has an unlimited capacity to absorb whatever abuse we may heap upon it and still continue to support human life. However, an overwhelming amount of scientific evidence shows that this idea is completely mistaken.

Just think about those things that are essential to us:

- Air
- Water

Australia's little penguins (or fairy penguins as they are also called) – another endangered species.

395

LIGHT THE WAY

- Food
- Shelter
- Clothing
- Medicines.

Without these six things we could not survive on the Earth.

We get all of these things from our planet's natural resources. However, it now seems that most of us are so busy pursuing our own individual needs and desires that we have grown indifferent to the consequences of our actions on **the environment**.

> **REMEMBER!**
> **The environment** is the world and everything in it: the air, the soil, the water, the plants, the animals and … **us**.

SP☀TLIGHT ON: THE CHALLENGES TO THE ENVIRONMENT

1. Pollution

Pollution occurs mainly when we carelessly dispose of waste products, either household or industrial. For example:

- **Land pollution** – Landfill sites containing harmful chemicals can poison the soil and pollute the water table.
- **Air pollution** – The burning of fossil fuels (e.g. coal and oil) produces sulphur oxides which cause rainwater to become acidic, killing trees and poisoning aquatic life.

An Asian boy wearing a mask to protect against air pollution in Beijing.

2. Deforestation

Deforestation means the cutting down of the Earth's rainforests. Driven by a huge increase in demand for hardwoods, tropical forests covering an area as great as the USA were cut down during the last century. If the destruction of the rainforests continues at this pace, then they may disappear altogether by the middle of **this** century. This would be a catastrophe for four reasons:

- The rainforests provide the oxygen that allows us to breathe.
- Chopping down trees sterilises the Earth. Soil quality is badly affected in places where the ground is severely exposed to erosion by the weather.
- Deforestation interferes with the natural process of **transpiration**, i.e. the process whereby water contained in liquid form in plants is converted to vapour and released into the atmosphere. As a result, rainfall patterns are disrupted, causing severe drought.
- Half of all our medicines come from plants and trees that will only grow in tropical rainforests.

396

The Moral Challenge SECTION F

3. Climate change

Approximately 90 million barrels of oil are consumed per day worldwide. As a consequence of burning all this fossil fuel, there has been an increase in the levels of carbon dioxide in the atmosphere. This has contributed to a rise in the Earth's average temperature.

Most scientists fear that, if nothing is done soon, this rising temperature will trigger dramatic changes in our planet's climate. Consider the likely effects of the following two events:

- **The shrinking of major glaciers** – This would cause rivers to run dry and trigger conflicts in many places over control of scarce water resources.
- **The melting of the ice sheets** – This would lead to a rise in sea levels that would cause extensive flooding in coastal areas and trigger a massive refugee crisis.

Climate change and melting ice sheets threaten the survival of many species of wildlife.

The Need for Action

According to the World Conservation Union's list of threatened species, up to half of all major living species are now in jeopardy. We can no longer afford to ignore how our actions affect the environment. After all, we have only one Earth and we cannot replace it. If the human race is to have a future, we need to change the way in which we relate to the fragile environment of our home world.

This is what led **Wangari Maathai** to take action.

SPOTLIGHT ON: WANGARI MAATHAI

Kenyan environmentalist, human rights campaigner and Nobel Prize winner, Wangari Maathai.

Wangari Maathai (1940–2011) was born in Kenya, eastern Africa. Throughout her life she demonstrated a deep love for her homeland and its people. In her autobiography *Unbowed*, Maathai recalled her early childhood in the shadow of Mount Kenya.

'At the time of my birth, the land around my home was still lush, green and fertile. The seasons were so regular that you could almost predict that the long, monsoon rains would start falling in mid-March. In July you knew it would be so foggy you would not be able to see ten feet in front of you, and so cold in the morning that the grass would be silvery-white with frost.'

As a child, Maathai was fascinated by the rich and diverse plant and animal life of her native Kenya. So, when she won a scholarship to study at the University of Pittsburgh in America, she chose to study veterinary anatomy.

Maathai returned to Kenya in 1965 and attended the University of Nairobi. She became the first Kenyan woman to earn a PhD. She began teaching in the university and later became a professor. She was the first woman to hold such a post at that university.

By this time, Maathai had become increasingly worried about the changes she was seeing in Kenya's environment. She noticed that the seasons were becoming less dependable and that

LIGHT THE WAY

the country's vegetation was fast disappearing. Indeed, by the 1970s, the majority of Kenya's forests had been cut down but not replaced. The poor needed wood for cooking, while the wealthy cleared land for agriculture and commercial development.

Her deep concern about Kenya's alarming rate of deforestation led Maathai to quit her job in the university and devote all her energies to saving the environment. In 1977, she set up **the Green Belt Movement (GBM)**.

Since its foundation, the GBM has been responsible for planting over thirty million trees in Kenya. Its members are mostly rural-based African women. The 6,000 nurseries they now run across Kenya serve two functions:

- They reforest the countryside.
- They give work to over 100,000 people.

Until recently, the Kenyan government refused to support the GBM. They thought it challenged the old social order. For the first time, the GBM gave many women independence from men.

It was only a matter of time before Maathai's work led her into direct confrontation with Kenya's president, **Daniel Arap Moi**. He had ruled Kenya with an iron fist since 1978 and intimidated his political opponents.

One particular business venture was very dear to President Moi's heart. It was a plan to build a huge skyscraper at Uhuru Park, one of the few remaining open spaces left in the capitol city of Nairobi. The whole project would cost about $200 million and feature a huge statue of the president himself at the site.

Maathai pointed out the need to preserve such green spaces. She led the opposition campaign against building in Uhuru Park. Few people thought that she had any chance of stopping the plans of the country's most powerful man. However, thanks to her successful appeals to public opinion in the local media, and her gaining the support of the United Nations and major donor agencies, she forced President Moi to abandon the scheme.

President Moi and his supporters were furious at their very public defeat. They had completely underestimated Maathai until now. They would not make the same mistake again.

Throughout the 1990s, Maathai was punished for her outspokenness. President Moi and his supporters tried everything they could to intimidate her and force her out of public life. She was repeatedly arrested and then released. Her home was broken into and she was followed and harassed by the police. However, she refused to give up.

Maathai launched a campaign to save the **Karura** forest. After she had prevented its destruction, she was attacked by hired thugs and hospitalised because of her injuries. Some believe that only her high profile in the Western news media stopped Maathai's opponents from murdering her.

In 2002, Maathai was elected to Kenya's national assembly (i.e. parliament). That same year, President Moi was forced to retire under the country's constitution. His successor, **Mwai Kibaki**, appointed Maathai as the Assistant Minister of the Environment, Natural Resources and Wildlife. This allowed her to support and expand the work of the GBM.

In recognition of her great work, Maathai was awarded the Nobel Peace Prize in 2004. She was the first environmentalist to win this important award.

Wangari Maathai was a great example of what it means to be **a steward** of the environment. She showed how it is possible to build a successful, collective and long-term approach to the environment in a community.

Being a Steward

> **REMEMBER!**
> **A steward** is someone who is appointed by God to care for the Earth.

In **the Old Testament** it is written about the very first humans that:

> 'God blessed them, and God said to them; Be fruitful and multiply and fill the earth and subdue it; and have dominion over the fish of the sea and over the birds of the air and over every living thing that moves upon the earth.'
> **Genesis 1:28**

However, God made it clear that:

> 'The land belongs to me and you are only strangers and guests.'
> **Leviticus 25:23**

According to these sacred texts, we need to begin by accepting three truths:
1. God created the Earth.
2. We do not own this planet. It belongs to **God**.
3. The Earth is **a gift** given to us by God. We have been entrusted with its care.

How should we show our gratitude to God for this gift? By taking seriously our **responsibilities** as stewards, namely:

- Showing due respect for all the different forms of life that co-exist upon the Earth.
- Sharing our planet's resources fairly and wisely.
- Handing on the environment in a living and fertile state to future generations.
- Putting right any harm that has been done to the environment in the past.

There is no better example of Christian stewardship in action than that offered by the life and work of **Sister Dorothy Stang**.

399

LIGHT THE WAY

SPOTLIGHT ON: SISTER DOROTHY STANG

Dorothy Stang was outspoken in her efforts on behalf of the poor and the environment.

Dorothy Stang was an American Catholic nun and environmentalist who worked for the **CPT** in Brazil's **Amazon rainforest**.

Did You Know?

The **Amazon rainforest** is one of the largest remaining forests on Earth. It covers 1.6 million square miles. Its trees and vegetation make up 40 per cent of all the tropical rainforests on Earth. This forest hosts 50 per cent of the world's plant species.

The CPT was set up by the Brazilian Catholic bishops in 1975. Its purpose was to teach sustainable farming methods to poor settlers who wanted to build a future for their families. This meant showing them how to extract natural forest products to earn a living, but without having to resort to cutting down the trees.

However, in time, the CPT's work became more and more dangerous. Powerful businessmen had discovered the rich natural resources of the rainforest. They decided to exploit these resources without any concern for the impact this would have. They made it clear that they would not let anyone get in their way.

Sister Dorothy referred to the rainforest as '**the Earth's lungs**'. She became more and more worried by the destruction caused by illegal logging operations and the willingness of politicians to let this destruction continue.

She became a leading figure in the campaign to protect the rainforest. She sought to educate and empower the peasants. She encouraged them to use only **sustainable** (i.e. environmentally friendly) farming techniques.

As a result, both big agribusinesses and illegal loggers saw her as a threat. They wanted to force the peasants off their land in order to steal its resources. She was doing everything in her power to stop them. It didn't surprise her to learn in the late 1990s that she had been put on a 'death list' by these powerful vested interests. Already, hired gunmen had shown no hesitation in murdering hundreds of human rights advocates, environmentalists and farmers who had stood up to them.

Although she knew she was putting her life in even greater danger, Sister Dorothy went to the capital, Brasilia, to give evidence before a parliamentary investigation into deforestation. She named the businesses responsible. These businessmen responded by claiming that the 73-year-old nun was a terrorist. They falsely accused her of supplying peasant farmers with weapons. She received direct death threats, but she refused to be intimidated and continued her work. Then, on Saturday, 12 February 2005, two hired gunmen killed Sister Dorothy as she was walking to a meeting in a little village. Many people consider her **a martyr**.

REMEMBER!
A martyr is someone who is willing to die for what he/she believes.

400

The Moral Challenge SECTION F

Following Sister Dorothy's brutal murder, Brazil's president ordered 20,000 square miles of the Amazon to be placed under environmental protection. This action has given some hope to human rights defenders and environmentalists that, if more people cared, the destruction of the Amazon rainforest might yet be prevented. For as Sister Dorothy frequently warned:

'The death of the rainforest is the end of our life.'

Sister Dorothy Stang referred to the rainforest as 'the Earth's lungs'.

ACTIVITIES

1. Wordsearch

Find the following words:

Extinct
Dodo
Calvaria tree
Air
Water
Food
Clothing
Shelter
Medicines
Environment
Pollution
Landfill
Deforestation
Drought
Flooding
Maathai
Steward
Earth
Gift
Stang
Amazon
Rainforest
Oxygen
Destruction
Martyr

N	I	T	S	E	R	O	F	N	I	A	R	K	E	E
O	A	F	B	S	L	A	N	D	F	I	L	L	D	N
I	H	C	L	K	E	M	O	G	H	D	W	E	L	V
T	T	C	D	O	A	N	N	X	R	T	S	F	C	I
U	A	B	A	R	O	I	I	A	Y	T	R	O	I	R
L	A	F	T	L	H	D	W	C	R	G	S	A	A	O
L	M	Y	O	T	V	E	I	U	I	H	E	V	E	N
O	R	T	O	O	T	A	C	N	E	D	G	N	X	M
P	H	L	M	S	D	T	R	L	G	N	E	P	T	E
G	C	I	I	K	I	U	T	I	A	Z	A	M	I	N
I	D	E	F	O	R	E	S	T	A	T	I	O	N	T
F	Q	I	N	Y	R	K	S	R	E	T	A	W	C	S
T	U	S	T	H	G	U	O	R	D	C	R	A	T	G
A	M	A	Z	O	N	D	O	D	O	T	I	E	M	Y
F	L	R	T	W	R	Z	H	K	X	R	Y	N	E	K

2. Say what it means!

(a) Extinct means _____.

(b) The environment is _____.

(c) A martyr is _____.

401

LIGHT THE WAY

3. Crossword

Across
2. Half of all of them come from plants and trees that will only grow in tropical rainforests.
3. The name of a large island in the Indian Ocean where the dodo lived.
4. It means environmentally friendly farming methods.
7. The Green Belt Movement has been responsible for planting over 36 million of them in Kenya.
8. If the major ones shrink, it would cause rivers to run dry and trigger conflict in many places over control of scare water resources.
9. Approximately 90 million barrels of this fuel are consumed per day worldwide.
10. This mainly occurs when we carelessly dispose of waste products.
11. If the sheets made of this were to melt, it would lead to a rise in sea levels that would cause extensive flooding in coastal areas and trigger a massive refugee crisis.
12. The name of the hardwood tree that began to die out because the dodo had become extinct.
13. The surname of the American Catholic nun and environmentalist who worked to save Brazil's Amazon rainforest.
15. A type of fuel that includes coal and oil. When burned it produces sulphur oxides. These cause rainwater to become acidic, killing trees and poisoning aquatic life.
17. This means the cutting down of the Earth's rainforests.

Down
1. This word is used by stewards to remind us that the Earth belongs to God and that we have been entrusted with its care.
2. The surname of the woman who set up the Green Belt Movement in Kenya.

402

The Moral Challenge   SECTION F

5. The Amazonian rainforest has been described as playing the same role for the Earth as these parts of the human body. Without them you cannot breathe.
6. The process whereby water contained in liquid form in plants is converted into vapour and released into the atmosphere.
7. After she named them before a parliamentary inquiry, the businessmen who were destroying the rainforest claimed that Sister Dorothy was really one of these.
12. The initials of the organisation set up by the Brazilian Catholic bishops to teach sustainable farming methods to poor settlers.
14. Sister Dorothy believed that the death of the rainforest would mean the end of this on Earth.
16. The nationality of the sailors who first discovered the dodo on their way east to the Spice Islands.

4. Think about it!

(a) Read the following statement:

> All things are connected like the blood which unites one family. All things are connected. Whatever befalls the Earth befalls the sons of the Earth. Man did not weave the web of life; he is merely one strand in it. Whatever he does to the web he does to himself.
>
> Attributed to **Chief Seattle** of the Duwamish tribe.

1. What does this statement mean?
2. How did Wangari Maathai come to understand the importance of its message when she returned to Kenya after studying abroad for several years?
3. How successful were her efforts to put this important insight into action?
4. Why did Wangari Maathai believe it is in the best interests of **everyone** to care for the environment?

(b) Read the following statement:

> So what if 99.9 per cent of the world's plant and animal species become extinct. The important one – us – will still be here. There's no need to worry!

1. What does this statement mean?
2. Why do some people have this opinion about the environment?
3. Give one example of how people who think like this treat the environment.
4. How would Sister Dorothy Stang have responded to such a statement?

403

LIGHT THE WAY

CHAPTER 5   THE AFTERLIFE

Belief in the Afterlife

Looking back over the course of human history, we can see that most people in most civilisations have believed in some kind of **afterlife**.

> **REMEMBER!**
> **The afterlife** means a life after death.

Ancient terracotta warriors found in the tomb of Emperor Shih Huang T of China.

Think about the following examples:
- During excavations of the floor of the Skhul and Qafzeh caves in Israel, archaeologists discovered human remains that had been buried there about 100,000 years ago. In each grave the person was buried with a few simple possessions (e.g. tools). This would suggest that they thought they would need these things in the afterlife.
- In ancient Egypt, the **Pharaoh Tutankhamen** was buried with all his treasure. It was believed that he would be able to enjoy his great wealth in the afterlife.
- In ancient China, the tomb of **Emperor Shih Huang T** was surrounded by six thousand terracotta warriors, horses and chariots. These figures were supposed to protect him on his journey into the afterlife.

Each of the major world religions offers its own ideas about what happens to us after death. However, before we go any further, we need to explain what we mean by **death**.

The Meaning of Death

According to the World Health Organisation, **death** occurs when:
- Your brain no longer controls your vital bodily functions.
- You cannot breathe without the aid of a life-support machine.

> **REMEMBER!**
> **Death** is the permanent ending of all the bodily functions that keep you alive.
> **Dying** refers to the way in which your life comes to an end.

The Meaning of The Soul

Humans are **unique**. We are the **only** creatures who know that we will eventually die. Why is this so?

Because of all the creatures on this planet, only humans have complex **minds**.

> **REMEMBER!**
> In humans, **the mind** refers to your capacity to choose, imagine, reason, remember and understand.

404

The Moral Challenge   SECTION F

Think about it:

- We are the only creatures capable of using language, planning for the future, thinking about the past, producing works of art and inventing technology.
- Only we are capable of loving, appreciating beauty and treating one another with compassion and respect.

The source of our human capacity to do all these things is called **the soul**.

> **REMEMBER!**
> **The soul** is the invisible life force that animates your body.
> Your soul is **spiritual** and **immortal**.
> **Spiritual** means your soul is not a physical thing.
> **Immortal** means your soul survives the death of your body.

Your soul was created directly by God and infused into your body at the very moment of your conception.

However, you are very much a part of the physical world. You need a body to interact with others, to learn and to express yourself. So, the body and the soul belong **together**. Neither by itself is a human being. Therefore, each person is a **unity** of body and soul.

It is important to keep this in mind when exploring Christian beliefs about life after death.

Possible Evidence for the Afterlife

In recent years, there has been much interest in what are known as **near-death experiences**.

> **REMEMBER!**
> **Near-death experiences** (**NDEs**) are what people who have been declared **clinically dead** but then restored to life claim to have happened to them.
> **Clinically dead** means that your heart stops beating and your brain is unable to sustain any of its usual thought processes.

Stories of NDEs come from all over the globe. People of different ages, occupations and religious persuasions (even atheists) claim to have had them. It is estimated that about one in five people who have been revived after a heart attack claim to have had a near-death experience.

Did You Know?

What about cases where people who were clinically dead do not recall having an NDE? This inability to recall an NDE may be similar to the situation where some people can vividly remember their dreams while others have no memory of them.

405

LIGHT THE WAY

Think about the following true story:

In the early hours of the morning of 2 February 1973, **Vicky Noratuk** was a passenger in a vehicle that was involved in an automobile accident. She was taken by ambulance to Harbor View Hospital in Seattle, Washington, USA. The doctors in the accident and emergency department declared her clinically dead. However, drawing on all their experience and skill, the medical team saved her life and managed to revive her.

Afterwards, Vicky told her doctors about her near-death experience. The first thing she could remember after the car accident was becoming aware that she was somehow outside her physical body. She could recall looking down on her own body, with her hair shaved off as the doctors and nurses tried to deal with her head injuries.

After this Vicky found herself moving away. She felt herself being drawn into a tunnel that led her towards a beautiful bright light. When she reached the end of this tunnel she found herself in a place of such beauty that no words could do it justice. There she was greeted by deceased family and friends.

Then she found herself in the presence of a being whom she identified as Jesus Christ. He led her through a review of her entire life. He asked her what she had learned from her life and asked her to be more willing to forgive. He also told her that the life she would be returning to would be hard, but to remember what she had learned in the days ahead.

Then, suddenly, Vicky felt wracked with pain. She woke up in a hospital bed to find that she had suffered a skull fracture, a concussion and injuries to her neck, back and legs.

Fascinating as the doctors found this, it was what Vicky said next that mystified them. She was able to describe her hospital surroundings in detail, as well as the exact sequence of events in the accident and emergency department on the night she was admitted.

How could she do so? Vicky Noratuk had been **blind since birth**. Her senses could not have provided her brain with the visual information she now possessed, as she had no memories of any of these things to draw on.

Christian Teaching on the Afterlife

Each of the world's religions offers its own explanation of what happens to the soul after the death of the body. Here we will concentrate on what Christianity has to say.

The New Testament offers important insights into the Christian understanding of the afterlife. These are:

- Your soul will survive the death of your body. Then your soul will be united with a new and glorified body like that of the risen Jesus.
- You will enjoy a whole new kind of life because death will no longer have any power over you.
- Just as the risen Jesus was still recognisably the **same** person the apostles had known before his death, so too you will survive death with your own individual identity intact.

For Christians, death is **not** the end. Death is a moment of **transition**, i.e. when the soul separates from the body and crosses over from this life to the next.

A Christian Explains Judgement

Christians believe that, immediately after you cross over into the afterlife, you will experience **judgement**.

A fresco in the Duomo in Florence, Italy, depicting the last judgement.

> **REMEMBER!**
> **Judgement** is when you are held accountable by God for your actions in this life.

We believe that you are judged by the standard of behaviour Jesus set during his public ministry.

Read and reflect upon the following Gospel passage:

The Parable of the Sheep and the Goats

When the Son of Man comes in glory, all the nations will be assembled before him and he will separate people one from another as the shepherd separates sheep from goats. He will place the sheep on his right hand and the goats on his left.

Then the Lord will say to those on his right hand, 'Come, you whom my father has blessed, take for your heritage the kingdom prepared for you since the foundation of the world. For I was hungry and you gave me food; I was thirsty and you gave me drink; I was a stranger and you made me welcome; naked and you clothed me, sick and you visited me, in prison and you came to see me.'

Then the virtuous will say to him in reply, 'Lord, when did we see you hungry and feed you; or thirsty and give you drink? When did we see you a stranger and make you welcome; naked and clothe you; sick or in prison and go to see you?'

And the Lord will answer, 'I tell you solemnly, in so far as you did this to one of the least of these brothers and sisters of mine, you did it to me.'

Next he will say to those on his left hand, 'Go away from me. For I was hungry and you never gave me food; I was thirsty and you never gave me anything to drink; I was a stranger and you never made me welcome, naked and you never clothed me, sick and in prison and you never visited me.'

Then it will be their turn to ask, 'Lord, when did we see you hungry or thirsty, a stranger or naked, sick or in prison, and did not come to your help?'

Then he will answer, 'I tell you solemnly, in so far as you neglected to do this to one of the least of these, you neglected to do it to me.'

And they will go away to eternal punishment, and the virtuous to eternal life.

Matthew 25:31–46

Jesus set a very high standard. He said that you must recognise God's presence in the people you meet in **this** life if you want to spend the afterlife with God.

LIGHT THE WAY

Who Judges Us? A Christian Explains

Jesus taught that, in this life, it is never too late **to repent** (i.e. say you are sorry) and ask for God's forgiveness. Think about the story of the repentant thief who was crucified alongside Jesus.

> ### The Story of the Repentant Thief
>
> One of the criminals hanging there mocked him. 'Are you not the Christ?' he said. 'Save yourself and us as well.' But the other spoke up and rebuked him. 'Have you no fear of God at all?' he said. 'We got the same sentence as he did, but in our case we deserved it: we are paying for what we did. But this man has done nothing wrong.' 'Jesus,' he said, 'remember me when you come into your kingdom.' 'Indeed, I promise you,' Jesus replied, 'today you will be with me in paradise.'
>
> Luke 23:39–43

The message here is clear. God is always willing to forgive you if you are genuinely sorry for your sins. Indeed, Paul wrote:

> 'God wants everyone to be saved.'
> 1 Timothy 2:4.

REMEMBER!
Saved means freed from the power of sin and welcomed to share eternal life with God.

Yet, we are told that not everyone is saved. Why?

The answer is this: you are free to choose your own path in life.

As a human being, you are born with the capacity to make your own moral decisions. God will not take this freedom away from you, because you could not be human without it. God will not interfere with your right to choose how you should live your life. That's **your** call.

So, it is **not** God who passes judgement on you; rather **you pass judgement on yourself**. You do this by the choices you make in this life. These choices decide your destiny in the afterlife. **God cannot save you if you do not want to be saved**.

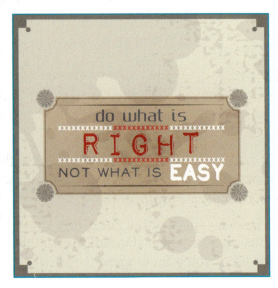

408

Trying to Describe the Afterlife

Think about the following:

> **Did You Know?**
> Human language is designed to describe life in **this** world. It has a very limited value when we are talking about the afterlife.

The motion picture **The Mask** tells the story of Rocky, a teenager afflicted with a severe facial deformity. Kind and gentle by nature, Rocky volunteers to help out at a summer camp for blind teens. He hopes that if they can't see his face, then they may judge him on who he is, rather than what he looks like.

Over the course of the summer, Rocky becomes romantically involved with one of the blind teenage girls. Blind since birth, she doesn't know what he means when he talks about colours or clouds. So, he tries to think of a way to communicate these things to her. Finally, after much thought, he finds a way.

Rocky leads his girlfriend into the camp's kitchen and brings her over to the refrigerator. He takes out a stone he put in there earlier and places it in her hands. '**That's the colour blue**,' he says.

He then takes her to the oven and takes out a rock which has been warmed. As he carefully allows her to slightly touch it, she comments on how hot it is. '**That's red**,' he says.

Then Rocky takes some cotton wool and places it in her hands. '**That's what clouds are like**.' For the first time, this young blind girl feels like she understands what colours and clouds are.

Of course, she never sees colours and clouds as they really are. However, by comparing them to something she already knows she is able to get a sense of what they're really like.

This is why, over the centuries, Christian artists and poets have used images from this life to help us gain some understanding of what the afterlife is like.

A Christian Explains the Afterlife

As Christians, we believe that everyone is offered three choices in the afterlife. These are:

1. Heaven

In everyday usage, the adjective 'heavenly' refers to some highly pleasurable experience. For Christians, **heaven** means this and much, much more.

To achieve heaven immediately after death, you must have done your utmost to love God and other people during this life.

In heaven you enjoy **the beatific vision**.

> **REMEMBER!**
> **Heaven** is not a physical place. It is an everlasting state of being, reached only by those who are **pure**, i.e. free from all sin.

> **REMEMBER!**
> **The beatific vision** is the perfect happiness and peace enjoyed by those who directly experience the goodness and glory of God.

409

LIGHT THE WAY

Heaven is the complete answer to all the deepest longings of the human heart. If you attain heaven, all your needs will be met and all your hopes fulfilled. You will be reunited with all your loved ones who have gone before you. You will become a member of a community of perfect love and harmony where you will see God as God truly is.

This is very difficult for us to grasp here and now. This is why St Paul wrote:

> 'No eye has seen, nor ear has heard, nor the heart of man nor woman conceived what God has prepared for those who love Him.'
>
> 1 Corinthians 2:9

2. Purgatory

After death, you may find that you are neither destined for hell nor yet ready for heaven. This is why God created **purgatory**.

REMEMBER!
Purgatory is not a physical place. It is a state of being where you undergo a process of purification to prepare you for heaven.

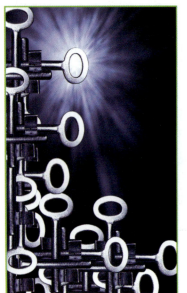

Purgatory is unlike both heaven and hell in that it is **temporary** (i.e. not permanent).

Purgatory is necessary, not because God wants you to suffer but because your sins prevent you from being the kind of person God always intended you to be. You must purge yourself of these sins in order to be capable of fully loving God and other people. Only then can you attain heaven.

There is no way to know how long you must remain in purgatory before you are ready to enter heaven. The afterlife does not measure time in the same way as this life.

3. Hell

The New Testament contains a number of references to **hell**. It is usually described as a place of '**unquenchable fire**' and '**total darkness**'. However, these images were only intended to act as a warning and to emphasise the need to avoid hell.

REMEMBER!
Hell is not a physical place. It is a state of being for those who die in **mortal sin**, i.e. those who have chosen to completely reject God's love and to totally separate themselves from God and from other people.

Hell is **self-imposed** (i.e. you make it for yourself by the way you live your life).

Unlike purgatory, hell lasts forever. It is an utterly empty and frustrating existence. Yet, how can hell be anything else, if you have freely chosen to devote all your talents to a completely destructive and selfish way of life?

410

The Moral Challenge   SECTION F

ACTIVITIES

1. Wordsearch

Find the following words:

Afterlife
Burial
Tutankhamen
Death
Unique
Mind
Soul
Spiritual
Immortal
Transition
Judgement
Repent
Heaven
Pure
Permanent
Beatific vision
Purgatory
Temporary
Hell
Saved

T	T	C	E	A	L	Z	T	R	J	O	L	T	Y	R
N	M	L	N	U	Y	D	N	U	Z	A	D	I	R	E
O	P	U	O	H	K	R	D	O	T	X	N	S	A	P
I	H	S	X	G	E	G	O	R	K	E	I	P	R	E
S	H	T	M	L	E	L	O	T	M	Z	M	I	O	N
I	H	D	D	M	O	M	L	A	A	G	T	R	P	T
V	D	B	E	H	M	A	H	A	C	G	A	I	M	A
C	E	N	Y	I	Z	K	F	W	S	P	R	T	E	L
I	T	T	R	A	N	S	I	T	I	O	N	U	T	K
F	N	A	Y	A	D	C	U	G	E	L	C	A	P	H
I	B	H	T	A	E	D	C	N	D	R	B	L	E	B
T	W	U	P	W	W	Z	D	D	I	E	L	A	X	X
A	T	N	E	N	A	M	R	E	P	Q	V	I	O	N
E	P	U	R	E	A	X	R	Y	P	E	U	A	F	S
B	U	R	I	A	L	Y	K	V	N	M	K	E	S	E

2. Say what it means!

(a) The afterlife means _____ .

(b) The soul is _____

_____ .

(c) Near-death experiences are _____

_____

_____ .

(d) Judgement is _____

_____ .

(e) The beatific vision is _____

_____

_____ .

411

LIGHT THE WAY

3. Crossword

Across

6. It means that you make it for yourself by the way you live your life.
9. A word used to describe the moment when the soul separates from the body and crosses over from this life to the next.
10. The name of the Chinese emperor who was buried surrounded by 6,000 terracotta figures (3 words: 4, 5, 1).
12. It means you are freed from the power of sin and welcomed to share eternal life with God.
13. It is not a physical place. It is an everlasting state of being reached only by those who are pure, i.e. free from all sin.
15. Your body and soul belong in this way.
17. When you are held accountable by God for your actions in this life.
19. The permanent ending of all the bodily functions that keep you alive.
20. It is not a physical place. It is an everlasting state of being for those who die in mortal sin, i.e. those who have chosen to completely reject God's love and to totally separate themselves from God and other people.

The Moral Challenge   **SECTION F**

Down

1. It means that your soul survives the death of your body.
2. It is not a physical place. It is a state of being where you undergo a process of purification to prepare you for heaven.
3. It means to say that you are sorry for your sins.
4. He set the standard of behaviour by which Christians are judged.
5. The name of a blind American woman who claims that she had a near death experience (2 words: 5, 7).
7. When you are declared clinically dead, this part of you is unable to sustain any of its usual thought processes.
8. Your soul was created directly by God and infused into your body at this particular moment.
9. It means 'not permanent'.
10. It means that your soul is not a physical thing.
11. The number of choices everyone is offered in the afterlife.
14. Refers to the way in which your life comes to an end.
16. The name of an Egyptian pharaoh who was buried with all his treasure.
18. In humans it refers to your capacity to choose, imagine, reason, remember and understand.

4. Think about it!

(a) Explain this statement: '**Christians believe that death is a moment of transition**.'
(b) What does it mean to say that '**we pass judgement on ourselves**'?
(c) Read the following story:

> A man spoke with God about Heaven and Hell. '**I will show you Hell**,' said God. And they went into a room which had a large pot of stew in the middle. The smell was delicious and around the pot sat people who were famished and desperate. All were holding spoons with very long handles which reached to the pot, but because the handles of the spoons were longer than their arms, it was impossible to get the stew into their mouths. They were angry, frustrated and starving. Their suffering was terrible.
>
> '**Now I will show you Heaven**,' said God.
>
> So they went into an identical room. There was a similar pot of stew and the people had the same identical spoons, but they were well nourished, happy and talking to one another.
>
> At first the man did not understand.
>
> '**It is simple**,' said God. '**You see, they have learned to feed one another**.'

How does this story help to explain **the difference** between heaven and hell?

NOTES

NOTES

LIGHT THE WAY

NOTES